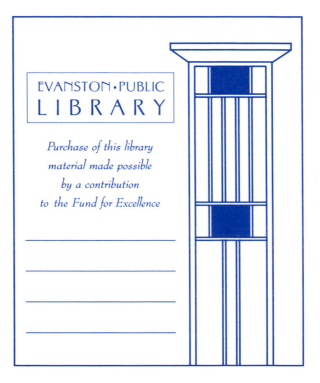

THE HISTORY OF ITALIAN CINEMA

GIAN PIERO BRUNETTA

TRANSLATED BY JEREMY PARZEN

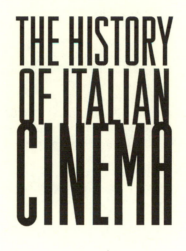

THE HISTORY OF ITALIAN CINEMA

A GUIDE TO ITALIAN FILM FROM ITS ORIGINS
TO TH E TWENTY - FIRST CENTURY

PRINCETON UNIVERSITY PRESS   PRINCETON AND OXFORD

Published by Princeton University Press, 41 William Street,
Princeton, New Jersey 08540
In the United Kingdom: Princeton University Press, 6 Oxford Street,
Woodstock, Oxfordshire OX20 1TW

Library of Congress Cataloging-in-Publication Data

Brunetta, Gian Piero.
[Guida alla storia del cinema italiano, 1905–2003. English]
The history of Italian cinema : a guide to Italian film from its origins
to the twenty-first century / Gian Piero Brunetta ; translated by Jeremy Parzen.
p.   cm.
Includes bibliographical references and index.
ISBN 978-0-691-11988-5 (hardcover : alk. paper)
1. Motion pictures—Italy—History. I. Title.
PN1993.5.I88B69313 2003
791.430945—dc22   2008043733

British Library Cataloging-in-Publication Data is available

The translation of this book has been funded by SEPS—
Segretariato Europeo per le Pubblicazioni Scientifiche, www.seps.it

This book has been composed in Goudy

Printed on acid-free paper. ∞

press.princeton.edu

Printed in the United States of America

1   3   5   7   9   10   8   6   4   2

.‿ CONTENTS ‿.

ꞏ‿PREFACE‿ꞏ

In thanking Princeton University Press, translator Jeremy Parzen, and editor Hanne Winarsky, I cannot conceal my satisfaction in finally reaching a North American readership. The publication of this book follows a number of aborted attempts to have my oversized works translated in the 1980s and 1990s. This time around, the tale is not nearly as long-winded and it was conceived for an international audience as a bona fide guide to Italian cinema for film buffs and students who are approaching the subject for the first time. I guide them through one hundred years of history in which Italian cinema interweaves its own history with that of a just decades-old nation. Italian cinema would later become a privileged depository of the national identity and its poet.

I would like to thank the many archives, institutions, private and public American libraries, and scholars whose contribution was instrumental in completing the research I began more than thirty-five years ago. Without their help, this book would have been wholly different and undoubtedly not nearly as rich with information. I began working on my *History of Italian Cinema* project in the mid-1970s and Editori Riuniti published the first volume in 1979. I made my first research trips to the United States beginning in 1977. Thirty years ago, materials on Italian silent film, Italian films from the 1920s, and even Italian film during fascism were extremely difficult to find. Back then, researching 1920s and 1930s Italian cinema was like a sheer-face, solo grade-6 (Alaskan scale) climb or trying to sail around the world by yourself. Most filmic materials were believed to have been lost and printed records were scattered over myriad locations and were mostly inaccessible.

Over the course of my numerous expeditions to the United States, I made many emotional, wondrous discoveries of silent films and 1930s-era films that I would have never found in Italian film collections. I was also able to consult records that allowed me to study Italian cinema's impact outside of Italy and the American subsidies that led to Hollywood's triumphant return to Italian screens at the end of World War II. The George Klein archive at the Library of Congress was a true gold mine in this respect and had never before been explored. Besides the Library of Congress, I also worked in the National Archives in Washington, the Museum of Modern Art in New York, the Eastman House in Rochester, the Pacific Film Archives in Berkeley, and the archives of the University of California at Los Angeles. I also had access to a number of collections held by private individuals who allowed me to consult their treasures. At the same time, my trips to North America gave me the opportunity to discuss my research with scholars like Jay Leyda (the father of American film history), William Everson, Annette Michelson, Robert Sklar, Dudley Andrew, P. Adams Sitney, Seymour Chatman, Rick Altman, Gaetana Marrone-Puglia, and other important contributors to the study of film history and theory in the United States. Much of their advice and many of their methodological suggestions proved highly useful in my work.

Thirty years ago, Italian cinema—from neorealism to Fellini and Antonioni, and even Italian mythological films—were loved and admired by American audiences and intellectuals. But very little study had been devoted to Italian film in the United States. At the many conferences I have attended at American universities, Italian Cultural Institutes, and countless American institutions, I have always been greeted by packed houses of curious students and generous and passionate persons who considered the masterpieces of postwar Italian film an important medium for learning about Italy.

Italian cinema as a whole has made a vital mark on the works of young directors like Coppola, Scorsese, Lucas, and Spielberg. Like Tarantino after them, they immediately recognized the influence of Italian genre films and art-house films on their works. My interest in the Italian influence on American cinema led me to create a seven-episode program for Italian television directed by Gianfranco Mingozzi with the title *Storie di cinema e di emigranti* (*Stories of Cinema and Immigrants*, 1986). The series examined the exchanges and reciprocal influence between Italy and its cinema and American cinema up to the generation of Coppola and Scorsese.

Thanks to Peter Bondanella's pioneering 1983 survey of Italian film (*Italian Cinema: From Neorealism to the Present*) and to the development of Italian film studies programs at American universities (and not only in their Italian Departments), a new spring of Italian film studies has dawned in the United States. Original, firsthand archival research in the United States (often carried out with sophisticated interpretative instruments) has helped to create new ways of looking at general aspects of Italian cinema and even specific periods and individual directors. Besides Bondanella, who has published important works on Fellini and Rossellini, there are a number of American scholars who have helped to raise awareness of Italian cinema and its top directors over the past few decades: Mira Liehm, Marcia Landy, Elaine Mancini, Milicent Marcus, James Hay, P. Adams Sitney, Angela dalle Vacche, Giuliana Bruno, Gavriel Moses, Manuela Gieri, Seymour Chatman, Tag Gallagher (with an excellent book on Rossellini), Jean Dillon, Maria Wyke, Anna Maria Torriglia, Rebecca West, Barth David Schwartz, Maurizio Viano, Patrick Rumble (in the study of Pasolini), Steve Ricci (for his work on fascist-era film), and Giorgio Bertellini (for his work on the popularity of Italian silent film in Italian American communities).

In recent years, the growth of Italian film studies in the United States is such that even the omnivorous reader has trouble keeping up-to-date with every publication. Where once only the great films of the postwar era or art-house films interested new generations of scholars, today Italian film studies in the United include Italian genre films; the economic and cultural history of the Italian film industry; specific groups of Italian filmmakers or phenomena; the relationship between Italian cinema and literature; psychoanalytic readings of Italian cinema; philosophical and semiotic interpretations; and Italian cinema as a source for historic, micro-historic, and even mythological studies. It is with great satisfaction, admiration, and often with a touch of envy (for the facility with they can consult once-inaccessible sources) that I have watched recent generations of American scholars employ ever more sophisticated historiographic tools in the study of Italian cinema. It is my hope that continued comparative historiographic research conducted by the international scientific community will also be able to reach wider audiences.

I am convinced that twentieth-century Italian cinema—during the 1910s, at the height of neorealism's popularity, and again in the 1960s—represents a "guiding" art form for Italy, a depository of its memory, history, and national identity. In the most difficult moments in Italian history, the country's cinema has served as an ambassador of its culture and creativity.

From its beginnings, Italian cinema has been appreciated, adored, and celebrated in the United States for its artistic and cultural quality and ambition and for its ability to compete with lyric opera in transmitting the iconographic values and models of European history. The reciprocal influences between American and Italian cinema began as early as 1912, when a forward-looking film distributor from Chicago, George Kleine, decided to purchase the distribution rights—and not just for the U.S. market—to a spectacular film made in Rome by Cines, *Quo vadis?*, based on the novel by Henryk Sienkiewicz. In the years that followed, a series of colossal films invaded American theaters and helped to transform the small nickelodeons into gigantic cathedrals in every major urban center of the United States. These films portrayed Homeric battles and Napoleonic campaigns, and featured masses of extras, set designs, and special effects that brought volcanic eruptions, earthquakes, and storms at sea to the screen. Films like *Cajus Julius Caesar*, *Gli ultimi giorni di Pompei* (*The Last Days of Pompei*),[1] *Spartacus*, and *Cabiria* and tens of other historical-mythological films would become models for directors like Griffith and De Mille and would establish the narrative forms, style, prosody, and syntax for the production of these films in America. With the advent of World War I, the troops of Julius Caesar and Augustus made room for the great stars of early Italian cinema, led by Francesca Bertini, Lyda Borelli, and Menichelli. This rapid transformation of the Italian film industry laid the groundwork for the birth of the Hollywood star system.

Neorealism represents a second defining moment in the relationship between the American and Italian film industries. Beginning with *Roma città aperta* (*Rome, Open City*) and *Paisà* (*Paisan*), American distributors played an important role in bringing the films of Rossellini, De Sica, De Santis, and Visconti to the U.S. market. These works immediately influenced American filmmakers: from the acting to the cinematography, from the social and political themes to the use of realistic sets and locations and Italian directors' efforts to protect their authorial and artistic integrity.

At the height of the 1960s, beyond the influential role played by Fellini and Antonioni, Italian genre films also had an impact, from mythological and horror films to police thrillers. Their influence was widespread and enduring and would affect American directors' approach to genre and art-house films even in recent decades.

I

The history that you are about to read is the fruit of research conducted over the past thirty-five years. During this period, I published my first *Storia del cinema italiano* (*History of Italian Cinema*) between 1979 and 1982, in two volumes (it was expanded in 1993 with a four-volume edition). Published in 1991, my *Cent'anni di cinema italiano* was an attempt to blend together the history of Italian cinema with the history of Italy and the transformation of Italians' dreams, needs, and behaviors.

This present work, *The History of Italian Cinema*, offers easier, more agile consultation. Conceived as a study tool for university students who are approaching the subject for the first time, it was created using the best of the two previous books. Its purpose is that of giving readers an analysis of Italy's national history in the context—implicit and explicit—of the dynamics of international cinema.

I have attempted to focus on the moments in the history of Italian cinema that made it a model for not only European and American filmmakers but for South American, Asian, and African filmmakers as well.

Although I have included data and tools that will prove useful for future research, this work represents my attempt to synthesize a highly complex topic into a navigable "history as narrative" and "history as problem solving." I have avoided excessive simplification while attempting to capture the richness and many facets of the subject matter and its field of forces in each chapter.

The connecting thread of this book is "global history" and it is based on a reworking of chapters I wrote for *Storia del cinema mondiale* (*History of International Cinema*), published by Einaudi in seven volumes between 1999 and 2002.

On one hand, I have examined the glorious moments in which Italian cinema and its directors, actors, and films have affected the modes, rhythms, and forms of storytelling and the language of international film. On the other hand, I point out that recent Italian cinema no longer plays that starring role. Its health is bad and these are desperate times. Nonetheless, its heart continues to beat. The stethoscope reveals it is the heart of an organism in the process of renewal and it receives its lifeblood in young veins from all of its creative parts.

The current renewal is probably the most legitimate reason for consolation and hope. Box-office returns from the spring of 2007 seem to suggest that cautious optimism is merited.

One of the more positive signs of 2007 was the international triumph of Gabriele Muccino's *The Pursuit of Happiness*. Produced in the United States, the film showed Italian cinema's commercial potential in international markets and revealed new possibilities for future productions. At the same time, Hollywood's tribute to Ennio Morricone with an Honorary Oscar award gives Italians reason to be proud.

Early 2007 saw the release of *Centochiodi* (*One Hundred Nails*), an *opera mondo* (or "modern epic," as the expression has been translated), by Ermanno Olmi who has stated publicly that he wanted to end his career with a fictional film. He has created a small cosmogony in this film and a "definitive" work. It is hard to imagine that he could make a better film than this. In it, he again squeezes and undresses a message that he has always held close to his heart: a film made of sounds, colors, aromas, smells, and flavors that have become ever more difficult to taste, recognize, and discern.

It is my hope that his cinema—free and constantly capable of renewing itself and dealing with themes able to touch the hearts of an international audience—can serve as a model for the directors who animate the new landscape of Italian cinema, from Matteo Garrone to Paolo Sorrentino, from Ferzan Ozpetek to Emanuale Crialese and Saverio Costanzo. Despite the difficulties the future holds, I believe that his example can help them to continue to remain faithful to themselves and to the lessons of their fathers. The road ahead is filled with great challenges created by the new era of twenty-first-century digital cinema.

Gian Piero Brunetta
Padua, September 2007

THE HISTORY
OF ITALIAN
CINEMA

INTRODUCTION

.⌣ The *Epic* History of Italian Cinema ⌣.

The history of Italian film is an *epic* that has guided and shaped the course of international cinema. It can be examined in terms of its uniqueness, but it should also be studied as part of the field of forces with which it has been compared since its beginnings.

It has developed in a process that is at times slow, defensive, and regressive, at times rapid and expansive. It encompasses many different histories that have influenced, affected, changed, and interacted within its fabric and shaped the context in which it has evolved.

Today, Italian cinema can be studied in an entirely new way thanks to recent and effective developments in the field of cinema studies. It can be broken down and analyzed on a microcellular level, but it can also be observed from a panoramic viewpoint that makes it possible to focus on its many different dimensions at the same time. Such perspective can put its history into a wider context thanks to the accessibility of information and images that was unimaginable a few decades ago. It is thus possible to follow its development parallel to and in view of its contacts with cinema from other countries. Until recently, silent films and early talkies were literally impossible to find after their initial commercial run. Now they are available in videocassette and DVD formats, and they can also be taped from public and private television channel broadcasts. Many have been restored, and even when the original cut of these films has not been maintained intact, their primitive charm has at the least been brought back to life.

Private video libraries have made in-depth comparative film study possible. Thanks to these collections, thousands of titles once destined to be lost are now part of a shared heritage that can be studied by cinema historians, social historians, sociologists, and linguists alike.

Videocassettes have taken the place of screenings and have deprived us of the added emotional value of viewing a film with an audience. But video has also made a fundamental contribution to cinema studies: it has given scholars the ability to view older films the same way that twentieth-century photographic reproduction made it possible to view ancient paintings. The distorted optics created by video have given rise to a new microcellular analysis of works that had little or no theatrical value or other worth in their original context. Such research has produced important results.

Today, properly restored silent films projected at the right speed with the correct aspect ratio and accompanied by an appropriate soundtrack can recreate a part of the historic and cultural atmosphere in which even the oldest films were originally screened. These films have begun to enjoy a second life, and whether considered alone or in the plurality of the other films of their era, we can more easily understand them and contextualize them in a wider perspective. To the critical eye that searches for something other than aesthetic value and true cinematic gems, every film—no matter how insignificant—contains information and important elements for the understanding of all of the histories and complex systems of signification in cinema.

The history of cinema has slowly become a legitimate discipline endowed with unique characteristics. It has also obtained legitimacy as a privileged topological space that appeals to different types of researchers. It is a new discipline with undefined borders that tend to expand and combine adjoining but distinct territories.

The field of cinema study has grown thanks to theaters that have launched ambitious, long-term research and heritage projects, retrospectives, and film series—each and every one of them a worthy cause. It has also expanded thanks to scholars from different fields who have conducted systematic film surveys and compiled statistics on cinema history, thus opening new inroads in research and redefining the landscape of film studies in view of its monuments and its ruins.

The most surprising results have come from the United States, France, Spain, and Britain and even from research conducted by young scholars in Belgium, Austria, and Holland. As public and private archives have become more accessible to researchers, they have responded by heeding the call emanating from collections previously unexplored. Cultural foundations have archived myriad resources relating to cinema: from governments, religious organizations and institutions, and production houses, as well as from archives from directors, screenwriters, critics, set photographers, and designers. As these materials have become part of the public domain, the research has become more consistent and less reliant on the critics' moods, ephemeral judgments, moral prejudices, and dogma.

The reshaping of the field has brought about significant contributions to film studies: retrospectives, specialized festivals, and the informed restoration of old films conducted in accordance with strict standards established over the past few years. But there have also been important essays and other contributions made by isolated researchers working outside the academy. I watched enthusiastically as the approach to cinema studies changed during the 1980s, and with a good sprinkling of polemical irony, I have called this the "Copernican revolution" of film studies.

Until a few decades ago, any work devoted to Italian cinema history, even the least ambitious, was up against a series of insurmountable obstacles: the inaccessibility of older films; the nonexistence of production house archives or any other type of archive; the difficulty of transforming the critic—even the intelligent and cultured critic—into a historian capable of developing an organic research project; and problems in tracking down original sources in order to compare and study them with the proper tools.

The film critics of the 1930s and even those of the generations following World War II never felt a natural calling to write about cinema history. The historian's verve and mindset could be found in only a handful of texts. Few studies (mostly articles and essays) were based on rigorous and systematic research using firsthand sources. Most of the research was drawn from the shelves of private libraries and true advances in the field were far and few between as were new directions in research. As a result, there were scarcely any clear milestones by which the reliability of data or the newness of information could be measured.

From the 1960s on, structuralists and semioticians (first) and then psychoanalytic theorists set the standards for the development of historical research in Italian film studies. But their approach turned out to be less gratifying than hoped. They never found support and legitimacy among their highly ideologized contemporary historians, who were prejudiced against iconographic sources in general and cinematic ones in particular.

Today, the balance of forces has changed greatly and film history has awoken. At the least, there has been a reawakening of those who see Italian film history as a privileged depository of memory that contains a variety of tools ranging from social history to socio-linguistics, from iconology to aesthetic iconography, and from economic history to the history of intellect and imagery. It makes use of traditional sources and mixes them with others assembled in a wholly new way depending on the researcher's creativity and intelligence. Thanks to the expanded presence of university film studies, there is also a new awareness that prompts younger researches to roll up their sleeves, dust off public and private archives, and consult film libraries and periodical collections. As a result, an enormous amount of new materials has surfaced. As these are examined and interpreted, they allow scholars to redefine the entire cinematic landscape and to contextualize its phenomena more precisely by studying relationships between lights and shadows, between high, low, and full reliefs, and by trying to fill in the voids and gaps with informed conjecture.

While critics tend to separate, to distinguish, to condemn, and to create hierarchical values (often with ephemeral longevity), the historian's primary task is to shed light on the relationships between different elements. This must be achieved within a framework where superficial data do not hinder the perspective or depth of the historian's vision. This work should be associative by nature and its primary aim should be an integrated vision of the various elements and sources available and the subjects addressed in a given redaction of history.

I

What are the most useful sources available to the film historians today? Films have a privileged role, of course, and they represent the heart and the focal point of the historian's research. But they are not the only important sources.

In *Apologie pour l'histoire* (*The Historian's Craft*), twentieth-century French historian Marc Bloch wrote of the infinite variety of historical sources: "Everything that man says or writes, everything that he makes, everything he touches can and ought to teach us about him."[1] Today, every document that offers information on even minor aspects of civilization or *Homo cinematographicus* has the right to be recognized as a worthy source: whether it is celluloid or a piece of paper, a manuscript, an administrative memorandum, or any material that is part of film production; whether it is a producer's letter, or an early version of a script, or a sketch for costumes and sets; whether it is material indirectly related to the life of a film, from set photos to advertisements, posters, merchandise, and promotional campaigns, from censorship and reviews to everything that plays a role in forming the cult following of a film and the social effects that a film may have.

Oral histories must not be forgotten either. Significant contributions have been made in this field by Jean Gili, Aldo Tassone, Lorenzo Codelli, and especially Francesco Savio, whose book *Ma l'amore no . . .* (*But Not Love . . .*), published in 1975, was the first major opus devoted to Italian cinema during the age of the talkies, from the 1930s through World War II, and it paved the path for subsequent filmographic studies.

During this phase and beginning with the origins of film in which the entire field is being systematically redefined, it is not just a matter of establishing what sources exist but rather hypothesizing new ways that all areas for research can be reassessed and reassembled. Researchers must look beyond the immediate horizon of current sources and embrace the breadth and variety of sources that have been neglected until now. Thanks to Aldo Bernardini and Vittorio Martinelli, the *terrae incognitae* of silent films are now familiar to us— at least as far as the data and information for each film is concerned. It is now possible to study this grand history, its identities, its unity, and its multiplicity. Access and control now overlap, and newly possible comparative studies can lead to discoveries that revise longstanding mythologies. The true task ahead is that of revisiting all filmic materials and redefining the overall picture as texts reemerge.

Italian movies of years past have sprouted up in the most disparate and distant corners of the world. They represent an irreplaceable patrimony of twentieth-century history and Italian culture. Our task is to reconsider them today and to overcome the syndrome of the collector who handles inert material. We must rediscover the aroma of its blood and the energy of its passions and feel the breath of its poetry and the landscape of its artistic spirit.

II

Anyone planning a new work on Italian cinema, whether individual or collective, can now review film sources from a global perspective, gauging the sources' breadth in an entirely new way with respect to scholars of the past. The new researcher will feel the same enthusiastic assuredness experienced by Persian King Cyrus at the sight of his troops on the eve of their battle with Croesus, just as it is described in Xenophon's *Cyropaedia*.

The cinematic patrimony of silent film, once thought to be lost, has progressively reemerged in remarkably different and improbable places, however foreseeable they may seem today. A literally gigantic quantity of filmic and extra-filmic materials has now been cataloged, partially restored, and preserved in film libraries, archives, and private collections all over the world. Many film libraries have opened their catalogs to the public. These collections are well organized and ordered in coherent groups, thus making them analyzable individually and as a whole, and in terms of their interrelationships and their dynamic with respect to the entire system. Today we can view silent Italian films preserved in FIAF (International Federation of Film Archives) film libraries, and many of the missing titles, once considered forever lost, have also been recovered.

With these newly recovered materials, a new philology of film has been born and it has found its international capital in Italy and Bologna. It consists of a more systematic and detached working method whereby all available sources are reexamined and compared with materials from other counties. This methodology is formulated according to long- and mid-term goals, and it is properly subsidized. It allows scholars to redraw all the maps and relationships between text, context, and peritext and to compare the shared elements of cinematic figures and works. Such an approach is taking the place of historiography of memory and film criticism, disciplines that have often been too shortsighted and ill-equipped to accept the new. Such work has been carried out by researchers, scattered all over Italy, backed by the academy and other institutions. The historiographic bricolage created by these scholars is commendable and their passion has made up for the long-term lack of economic support and coherent media projects.

As we look down on them from above and rotate our gaze 360 degrees, we can see the entire panorama of film archives that have become available over the past thirty years.

To the left, we see the group of short- to mid-length films salvaged by Davide Turconi in the early 1970s. First screened at the unforgettable film festival in the city of Grado, Friuli, this collection became a centerpiece of the film library built by the Associazione italiana per le ricerche di storia del cinema (AIRSC [Italian Association for Cinema History Research]). It also became a fundamental launching point for scholars who were to brave the uncharted waters of Italian silent and talking films.

Right next to the Turconi films, we see the historical and mythological silent films preserved in the impressive George Kleine Collection of Early Motion Pictures (*Quo Vadis?*, *Spartacus*, *Marc Anthony and Cleopatra*, *Scuola d'Eroi* [*School for Heroes*], *Gli ultimi giorni di Pompei* [*The Last Days of Pompei*]) or the small groups of works gathered in archives in North America—from the John Allen Collection to the Pacific Film Archive—where there is a splendid color print of *Cenere* (*Ashes*) starring Eleonora Duse at the George Eastman House International Museum of Photography and Film in Rochester, New York.

Over the past several years, a number of archives have been opened in Central and South America, including the Mexico City film archives, and many titles from the 1920s have been unearthed.

In Japan, thanks to the donation of the Tomijro Komiya collection (in late 1988) to the National Film Center of the Museum of Modern Art in Tokyo, many Arturo Ambrosio films from the 1910s have been saved and restored.

In yet another answer to the call, there is also the legion of feature-length films and documentaries in the Collection Desmet in Amsterdam, where it is possible to focus in on the films of the great divas and to see the fire of their fatal passions reignite on the screen, not to mention the impressive Film d'arte italiana (Italian Art Film) collection in Paris.

In the center of the panorama, as we move toward the Italian archives, there is the small but important Pastrone collection at the Museo nazionale (National Museum) in Turin. Its most prestigious title is *Cabiria*, which has been the subject of a milestone restoration project. And there is the collection of Emilio Ghione serialized films; the bodybuilder films at the Cineteca italiana (Italian Film Library) in Milan; and the Luca Comerio archive, which was salvaged by two independent Milanese filmmakers, Yervant Gianikian and Angela Ricci Lucchi, who made the collection an integral part of their creative repertoire. Unfortunately, they did not love it enough to rescue it and they neglected to hand it over to film librarians who could have philologically restored the films.

With these sets of films ideally taking the lead, there are silent films that have been restored in the laboratories of the Cineteca di Bologna (Bologna Film Library), not to mention the invaluable collections of Titanus, Lux, and Vides recently purchased by the library. In Bologna today, there are restored prints of *Assunta Spina* (*Assunta Spina* or *The Last Diva*), *Rapsodia Satanica* (*Satan's Rhapsody*), *Carnevalesca*, *Kiff Tebbi*, and *Maciste all'inferno* (*Maciste in Hell*), and there are also pre-censorship, restored prints of *Totò e Carolina* (*Totò and Carolina*) by Monicelli, *Il bidone* (*The Swindle* or *The Swindlers*) by Fellini, and *Spiaggia* (*Riviera*) by Lattuada.

Films of the past have often been doomed to destruction because of a variety of factors, including time itself. But they have also proven to be extraordinarily resilient in some cases, better than once thought, and able to survive the limitations of preservation efforts. Silent film was long considered a lost continent that had been practically forgotten. But in the past twenty years, many of these films have enjoyed greater archival, philological, and historiographic attention. Little by little, they have reemerged in all their glory from the mysterious, inaccessible caverns of public and private archives throughout the world.

In terms of percentages, only a modest number of silent films have been restored and recovered (literally thousands of titles are listed in Bernardini and Martinelli's filmographies). As for talkies, the number of titles lost is much more modest and thus their comprehensive study is relatively reliable. Almost all of the documentaries produced by the Luce Institute have been salvaged and can be viewed on the Internet. Of the over 600 films that were produced between 1930 and World War II, more than 450 titles are available today at the Cineteca nazionale (National Film Library) in Rome. The library also has a good number of films produced after the war because in 1948 it became mandatory by law to deposit a copy of any film made with the Cineteca.

Only in recent years, as plans for reprinting, cleaning, and salvaging films have expanded, problems in the philological restoration of the films have arisen and so have questions of how to shape film library policies in order to reflect the prestige and historical significance enjoyed by the Italian film industry. Many important advances have been made in the restoration of silent films: most recently, the recovery and restoration of a film by Lucio d'Ambra, *Le mogli e le arance* (*Wives and Oranges*), made in 1917. But the current approach is not yet suitably developed to meet the real challenges. Projects for the restoration of the Italian cinematic heritage have not yet reached a level of coherent coordination among the various libraries for mid- and long-term strategies. But the processes for recovery and salvage have been set in motion and their effects have been evident in recent articles on the subject.

Hopefully, a new historiographic spirit will continue to ascend—like a Pentecostal light—among university scholars in Italy and abroad. Using tools borrowed from other disciplines, it is up to researchers to redefine the territory and to reexamine the internal relationships and breadth of Italian film studies. The need to do so is even more urgent in the light of the fact that Italian cinematography has played a fundamental role in influencing world cinema at various moments of its history. It has shaped the course of international film with its rich authorial and stylistic modes and its extraordinary ability to interpret and retell the real stories and imagery of society.

III

Even in a simple comparison of Italian cinema with that of other European countries, the final analysis shows Italian film history to be relatively unified despite its complex, multisided structure, irregular development, and discontinuities. Its processes of invention and expression have long been guided and determined by a spirit that uniformly links them to the same matrices, modes, forms, myths, and souls. This perception grows even stronger as we move deeper into the past fifty years of Italian cinema. At first glance of the whole, continuity seems to prevail over discontinuity, and the periods where Italian cinema was more or less in crisis—except for the case of neorealism—did not completely erase the referential paradigms and models. Nor did its underlying texture disintegrate, at least not until the 1970s, and an extraordinary level of interaction between independent and commercial production was maintained. Italian cinema has always shown a strong sense of independence and intolerance for any type of external meddling. From its very beginnings, it laid claim to high culture and to artistic and literary genius, and it has always sought to establish bridges to literary, theatrical, and pictorial traditions.

From its earliest decades, Italian cinema has breathed in and digested the surrounding cultural atmosphere and that which preceded it. It then fed on contemporary political humors without forgetting to set its sights beyond its borders, even in times of autarchic culture. Ethical-pedagogical trends have played a much greater role in shaping Italian cinema than ideological currents have, even in moments of greater political pressure and less creativity. And even when Italian cinema was its most restricted, when it followed a progressivist flag and found its identity in the catchphrases of the day, it always maintained its autonomy and was traversed by winds and currents that blew and flowed in more than one direction.

To begin with, Italian cinema has never followed a given model for production, nor has it ever metabolized or developed an industrial culture. You could call it—and particularly in its past seventy years—"industry without industrialists." You could also say that it has long resided in the middle of the road, suspended between craftsmanship and industry. The early Turin entrepreneurs, with their "film factories," were much closer to an industrial mentality than the great film tycoons who emerged in the period immediately after World War II.

The second important element is the artisanal tradition of the Italian Renaissance workshop. As Italian filmmakers have tried to revive a film industry that has remained paralyzed for nearly three decades, it has become clear that the Renaissance workshop is the ideal creative model—the foundry, if you will—for Italian film production.

It's one thing to examine the history of Italian cinema in the light of aesthetic theories that evaluate the results of a given work or in the light of critics whose judgments are often conditioned by extra-filmic factors. If, on the other hand, we consider the entire creative process and the entire field of competing forces that accompany its history, the terrain begins to appear much more articulated, inhabited, and traveled by creative forces that have yet to be recognized for their specific contributions. Just think of the fundamental role played by Cinecittà as a foundry for Italian cinema from the day it opened its doors. It was a world where the legacy of the Renaissance workshop was celebrated and yet it always looked to the future and repeatedly played an avant-garde role in adapting itself to new technologies. During the period between the two world wars, many dreams found their costumes and sets in its laboratories. Mussolini's dreams of world conquest were outfitted there as well but more than any others, the dreams—small and large—of the bourgeoisie for a better life were dressed with clothes churned out by Cinecittà's tailors and costume designers.

In fact, from the first decade of the twentieth century until the present, there has been no other film studio where you could find so many anonymous cooks working together confusedly in a boiler-room kitchen of creativity where dialogues and situations were crafted: screenwriters, painters, architects, sculptors, critics, and poets, all of them top caliber. Beginning in the 1930s— thanks to architects, costume makers, and set designers like Antonio Valente, Gino Sensani, Gastone Medin, Maria de Matteis, and Virgilio Marchi—the theory and practice were set in motion by artists who created period sets and costumes suited to a given film's characters.

An "Italian style" developed and came to set the standard for the postwar period, handed down to filmmakers like Visconti, Lattuada, Soldati, Castellani, Bolognini, Rosi, Scola, the Taviani brothers, Cavani, Bertolucci, and Pasolini. In the decades that followed, it would help to shape international cinema, influencing directors like Scorsese, Coppola, Ivory, and Campion. Costume and set designers Danilo Donati, Piero Tosi, Dante Ferretti, Gabriella Pescussi, and Milena Canonero are just some of the Italians who have shaped international cinema with their work. Ferretti, for example, was recently honored by the Academy of Motion Picture Arts and Sciences in Los Angeles with a retrospective. But together with the architects, inventors of cinematic space, and tailors of dreams, we also need to remember the "masters of light" like Ubaldo Arata, Aldo Tonti, Otello Martelli, Massimo Terzano, Giuseppe Rotunno, G. R. Aldo (Aldo Graziati), and others who got their start in the 1960s, like Vittorio Storaro, Carlo di Palma, Luciano Tovoli, and Dante Spinotti. We should also devote study to the Italian musicians, like Renzo Rossellini, Nino Rota, Giovanni Fusco, Ennio Morricone, and Pino Donaggio, who have made notable "authorial" contributions to filmmaking. And editors like Eraldo da Roma, Ruggero Mastroianni, Kim Arcalli, and Roberto Perpignani. And special-effects inventors, like the father of E.T., Carlo Rambaldi.

These artists and others have made an impressive mark on international cin-ema and they have often helped to shape its linguistic and expressive ele-ments. Nor should we forget the great screenwriters like Cesare Zavattini, Tonino Guerra, Sergio Amidei, Ennio Flaiano, Suso Cecchi d'Amico, Piero Tellini, Age e Scarpelli, Leo Benvenuti, Piero de Bernardi, Bernardino Zap-poni, Stefano Rulli, and Sandro Petrarglia: film after film, they helped to cre-ate models of the Italian language and its usage, preserving Italian dialectics even during the reign of fascist linguistic purism.

Until just a few years ago, cinema critics and scholars have always kept these artists in the background. Now, more than ever, they deserve our atten-tion and recognition for their contributions. Not only is such recognition merited, but it is part of a correct historiographic approach to film studies, a working method that can multiply our points of view and focus in on the processes and different dimensions of Italian film production. These chapters need to be written and anyone writing a new history of Italian cinema needs, for all intents and purposes, to write these chapters from scratch. The same holds for the history of Italian documentary filmmaking because it is a history that is anything but independent and detached from the history of Italian fiction films. In many cases, documentary filmmaking served as a laboratory for the formation of Italian filmmakers and their experiments.

The third important point is that, however imperceptible this phenome-non may be in other countries, in Italy myriad external forces have also shaped the natural topology of cinema and the conception, development, modifica-tion, and survival of its defining traits: critics, magazines, cultural organiza-tions, institutions, government subsidies, religious and secular associations, festivals, and film series.

More so than in any other country, Italian film critics have never limited themselves to simply doing their job. As often as possible, Italian film critics have tried be part of the directorial body by guiding it, revealing its errors, and showing it which path to take. They have attempted to play a mothering, pedagogic, and managerial role, acting as its wet nurse and its Jiminy Cricket. Many magazines played this role in the 1950s, first and foremost *Cinema Nuovo* and its editor-in-chief Guido Aristarco. For at least a decade, he was promoted to the role of opinion leader as he battled for neorealism, the transformation from neorealism to realism, and the separation of militant criticism and politi-cally driven governmental control.

The history of Italian film criticism should be viewed in a positive light for its role and influence in the cultural debate and in the battle of ideas in postwar Italy. At the same time, its negative effects should be studied as well.

Italian critics were often obtuse and unwilling to accept the new. They often valued ideology over intelligence, and their immovability often impeded their ability to question and perceive the texts they examined. The history of Italian film criticism also needs to be rewritten in terms of the many directors and films that were enthusiastically received abroad but sent to the firing squad at home by Italian reviewers.

IV

Now we come to the elements that define the traits and identity of Italian cinematography.

As we attempt to link what I've written up to now with an overview of Italian cinema, we get the impression that we are standing before a giant topological space dominated by the laws of chance and chaos. Then, as we observe its foundations, beyond reaffirming and recognizing the highly artisanal skills of its workers, we appreciate all the more the need to celebrate it as a privileged depository of twentieth-century historical memory—micro- and macro-history, material and lived history, the desired and dreamed-of history of the Italian people. The silver screen became an extraordinary opportunity to rewrite the geography and history of a nation that recaptured political and geographical unity only a few decades earlier. From the outset, film offered itself as a powerful medium for the creation of symbols and mythologies of an artificial national identity. No other cultural or education means could produce equal results.

As we continue to consider its structural elements, we recognize—beyond its undeniable visual greatness—an iconosphere fed by the tradition of Italian painting. In certain moments, Italian cinema was in perfect step with twentieth-century artistic experimentation. It also becomes clear that, throughout its history, Italian cinema drew heavily from literature. The legacy of Italian theater revealed itself in dramatic celluloid as well, but at the same time it sought and found its own specificity in the "seventh art." Save for rare exceptions, it was language and not the action that unfolded around the story that determined the prosody, syntax, rhythm, and scansion of narrative in Italian silent film.

Italian cinema was a self-declared inheritor and son of literature and the figurative arts. It constructed its foundation using literary and artistic structures and it drew confidently from the wider patrimony of international literature and art. At a certain point, Italian cinema learned how to use the screen as a magic helper for small, collective dreams, as a mirror and an accurate diary of daily life in Italy, an anamorphic lens through which directors could celebrate the vices that form the backbone of the Italian national character.

One of its strongest characteristics was given by its capacity to draw from the *commedia dell'arte* and to construct a morphology and typology of the Italian that slowly moved away from farm life toward industrial life and modernity. It did so by hyperbolically multiplying the network of masks in the *commedia dell'arte*. The lessons of Pirandello and sixteenth-century improvised comedy gave life to the "thousand and one" masks of Italians as they moved between the old and the modern worlds.

Then, between 1945 and 1948, the works of Rossellini, De Sica, De Santis, and Visconti unleashed an energy so powerful that it changed—in the short and long terms—the cultural coordinates, systems, and paradigms and poetics of international cinema. In the case of *Roma città aperta* (*Rome, Open City*) and *Paisà* (*Paisan*), we must take into account the fact that these were not just films but "events." These films not only absorbed the tradition of films that came before them, but they also created a new benchmark for Italian and international cinema.

Beyond any monumentalization of its defining elements, neorealism marked a complete reappropriation of visual power, not so much in the sense of the pure documentation of the existing world but rather in the sense that it captured shared feelings and experiences. It embodied Italians' will to become masters of their own history and destiny and it became a new way of seeing life for its anonymous, everyday stars. Italian cinema publicly made use of the history of a country that had been materially and morally destroyed by a senseless war it had not wanted. Italian cinema assumed the natural role as ambassador of a country animated by a strong will to be reborn.

In certain ways, even the prevalence of an authorial logic seemed to leave room for a body of work that celebrated its own birth as the fruit of collective will and strength.

In the early 1950s, before the advent of television, the movie theater became a crossroads in the metamorphosis of the Italian people's way of seeing the world. The small screen would only accelerate that transformation in the years that followed. The decline of neorealism did not come at the expense of the entire film industry, which actually began to expand and to welcome international co-productions. During this period, Italian cinema launched increasingly ambitious projects that aimed to circulate its products—commercial and artistic—beyond its borders in Europe and in other continents. But the true strength came from Italian cinema's ability to metabolize certain elements of neorealism. Italian filmmakers applied the lessons of neorealism even to the melodramatic and the comedic and as a result, even in its lower registers, Italian film reveals significant elements of social history and of the transformation of collective life and popular iconography in Italy.

V

This vast set of patterns, cultural models, and contradictory structures finds its point of confluence, congruence, perfect balance, and greatest success in the 1960s.

This was the phase in which Fellini and Antonioni created their *opera mondo*, as Franco Moretti put it, literally their "world works" or "modern epics," as the expression has been translated into English. During this period, continuity and renewal increased the creative potential of Italian cinema. All the dynamics and forces that we have discussed began to fuel one another and the entire Italian film industry grew as a result. The crisis of 1968 together with the "years of lead" that followed, the progressive crisis created by private television, and its wild utilization of cinema were just some of the causes of a gradual dispersion of strength and of the loss of polycentric creativity and shared standards of quality.

In many respects, Italian cinema is still interesting, even though it has been completely transformed and is now illuminated by small flames and flashes of creativity scattered across the entire country. But it is no longer supported by the same distinctive will and ability to create.

Despite all the forces that have been working against it for some time now, I would like to hope that Italian cinema still has a reserve of life-giving energy. Perhaps it is waiting for a new series of favorable factors before it will entrust a new generation of filmmakers with the task of facing the technological and artistic challenges of the new millennium.

1

.⏝ THE SILENT ERA ⏝.

In the Beginning, There Was *La presa di Roma* . . .

Suddenly, as if by some unknown collective impulse, there was a ghostly silence and it became pitch black. The electrical light switch had functioned properly. In the large frame, on the wide surface of the calico canvas, the following words were vividly illuminated in large red letters by the projector from the booth: *La presa di Roma* [*The Capture of Rome*] . . . Then the words disappeared. In their place, the martial figure of General Carchidio, the Count of Malavolta, emerged. It was crisp, very lifelike, and realistic. The image trembled just slightly, if at all. On September 18, 1870, General Cadorna had sent Carchidio to the farthest outposts [of the Italian Wars of Independence]. Standing next to him was Carlo Bartolini, the highest-ranking Vatican official, and lieutenant Cesare Visconti of the Dragoons . . . At that point, Carchidio was blindfolded, as his predecessor Caccialupi had been . . . This was the first frame. It disappeared when the lights came back on, and then was followed again by darkness.[1]

With this account by Gualtiero Fabbri, it is possible to reconstruct the first Italian film, *La presa di Roma* by Filoteo Alberini, including the text of the captions, the toning, and the content and order of the six action sequences: the attempt to obtain a bloodless surrender and the refusal of General Herman Kanzler, head of the Papal Army; the attack of the *bersaglieri*, or so-called sharpshooters; the hopeless defense; the breaching of Porta Pia; the surrender ordered by Pope Pius IX; and the last sequence with the symbolic finale.

Even though today it is conceivable that there were other cinematic experiments in the decade between the Lumière brothers' invention and *La presa di Roma*, one must consider the legend of the prototype and the starting point for the entire history in order to understand the building blocks of Italian cinema.

Today, we possess a remarkable amount of information regarding this film:[2] the location where it was first screened publicly in Rome (at the beginning of Via Nomentana, where Porta Pia was breached);[3] the date of its official christening (September 20, 1905, the twenty-fifth anniversary of the victorious attack by the Modena Brigade of the Twelfth Battalion of Bersaglieri); the length of the film (250 meters); the Ministry of War's contribution to the production; the correspondence between the film's sequences and the scenes of *La gran battaglia e presa di Magenta* (*The Great Battle and Capture of Magenta*, another important turning point in the Italian Wars of Independence), staged at the Circo Olimpico Africano in Reggio Emilia, March 11, 1860;[4] the iconographic and photographic sources (the paintings of Michele Cammarano and the photographs of Fuminello, a contemporary of Alberini); the author of the script (Professor Cicognani); and even accounts of the standing ovation the film received from the audience. In this initial event of Italian cinema, we can recognize some of its early characteristics and the rapid, powerful development that would follow. "Italian cinema seems to have been born under the sign of the Risorgimento," as Giorgio Cincotti has observed.[5]

These praiseworthy efforts in exploring the origins of Italian cinema have revealed the remarkably secular, unified spirit that inspired this film. It was an event that led—after centuries of division and foreign domination—to the birth of the Italian nation. This is clear especially in the final sequence of the film, in which a brilliant beam of light shines down on a female figure who personifies Italy. She clasps the tri-colored flag in her hand, with Cavour, Victor Emmanuel II, Garibaldi, and Mazzini beside her—a perfect rendering of traditional Risorgimento iconography.

In the process of challenging French cinematic dominance, Alberini produced a spectacular film that was at once accurate in historical detail, celebratory, and educational. The screening itself made the story seem all the more real and lifelike—a page seemingly taken straight from Manzoni's teachings on the historical novel. As it set out to conquer a city-dwelling audience, this film effectively put an end to touring cinema.

The Epic Story of Traveling Cinema

In just a few short years, the advent of cinema led to the disappearance of a slew of optical tricks that had fed the imagination of millions in the squares and fairgrounds of Europe for two centuries. As a result, a shared visual vocabulary and the establishment of a shared market of images began to take shape.[6]

The traveling bioscopes preceded the advent of cinematic civilization and marked the public's first contact with the wonders of film. These projectors created a continuously growing form of hybridization and integration among social classes, a shared visual vocabulary, and the earliest elementary manifestations of the new universal language.

Traveling bioscopes invaded Italy during the first decade of the twentieth century and can be considered the first messengers of the Lumières' new invention. In Italy, these itinerant preachers functioned as they did elsewhere in Europe, and in many cases they often worked in more than one country. Thanks to research conducted in recent years (for example, Bernardini's detailed census of early Italian cinema),[7] we know precisely where these impresarios traveled, how much they earned, the size of their carriages, the type of organs they used (Gavioli, Marenghi, and Limonaire), and even details regarding the impresarios themselves. We know that this type of entertainment grafted itself to a deeply rooted tradition of traveling carnivals and that it helped weave a fabric of shared emotions, expectations, and desires, and the rituals and phenomena of quasi-religious cults that brought together the Low Countries and the Ukraine, England, and Spain. Robert Musil once observed that "over the course of millennia, neither churches nor cults have been able to cover the world with such a seamless network as that created by cinema in thirty years."[8]

Although there was some variation, Italian owners of traveling bioscopes faced roughly the same problems as in other European countries. Authorities posed identical restrictions. Spectators were lured by similar tactics that affected the senses but also their imagination and subconscious. The posters used the same typeface. The barkers spouted the same patter. Family elders and religious institutions use the same methods to block screenings in Catholic and Protestant countries alike.

In any case, the travels, the exploits, and the signs left behind by these shows have a touch of the epic about them. The shows became a sight but were also a visual translation of oral poetry: the light that was emitted by the Lumières' device was none other than the voice of the Muse and the projector took the place of the bard's lyre by exponentially expanding its communicative powers.

We could wander aimlessly through the forest of sources in the municipal archives and libraries of small Italian towns in order to understand these impresarios' epic story. But, first and foremost, it is important to clarify that their common denominator was the courage with which they, like their predecessors, challenged their audiences' laws and moral currents before, during, and after the projections. The suggestive double-entendres were just one method: "A Flea in the Bedroom," "The Bath," "A Case of Flagrant Adultery," "The Committee Member," "Yvette's Bedroom," "The Two Models," and "The Uncle Pays a Visit to a Sculptor's Studio," among others.

The micro-stories in these films are significant inasmuch as they represent the entire system by metonym, thanks to the interchangeability of the events: by reconstructing just one of these plots, we can understand a piece of the collective adventure, which seemed to reproduce through cloning. The impresarios that traveled through Italy with their bioscope shows were very similar on the surface. They had names like Teobaldo Baroli, Luigi Alessandro, Domenico and Almerico Roatto, Alessandro Buchovich, Johann Bläser, Karl Böcher, Antonio and Giovanni Cini, Gino Protti, Salvatore Spina, and Giovanni Zamperla, among others. They used the same types of organs and the voluptuous girls in the caryatids of their carriages were generally nude from the waist up. They used the same multicolored typeface for their advertisements. They wore the same style of clothes. Their barkers used the same patter and were often given citations by local authorities (in Treviso, at least one cinema was charged with disturbing the peace with the "noise of yelling").[9] After briefly consulting with a few Italian scholars, André Gaudreault, who has studied the art of carnival barking in various countries, hastily concluded that Italy was different from other countries because, he claimed, the figure of the Italian barker has not been documented.[10] His notions would have been a bit less generic had he carefully read Sergio Raffaelli's seminal work on traveling cinema, in which he mentions film-barkers like Gennaro Attanasio and Giovanni Sardini, "el Coco," or Fureghin al Ponte della Piavola, who cries: "Oh, how wonderful! What a wonderful drama! Oh, a magnificent drama! . . . Eight hundred twenty-five meters of pure drama! Nearly one thousand meters of drama!"[11] Because the tradition of traveling shows had its roots in the commedia dell'arte, early Italian cinema was able to adapt itself seamlessly to the standards of other European countries. In 1901, in an important city square like Porta Genova in Milan, wrote Raffaelli, of the fifty-six "booths," two were cinemas. But by 1902, there were five, and by 1907 there were twelve (there was even a sign that read "Cinema and Sharp Shooting"). Giovanni Zamperla's cinema was among the more noted cinemas present in Porta Genova, as was Arnaldo dell'Acqua's "Cinema and Rink." Five years later, of the fifty-three booths on the piazza, only Thaddeus Kühlmann's cinema remained.

In the first decade of the twentieth century, fairs and other types of gatherings began to occupy the piazza. Nonetheless, within the panorama of popular entertainment, cinema had quickly garnered its place in the collective imagination. Thanks to the traveling cinemas, an early and consistent horizon of expectations had been shaped: *vedute*, scenes, and visits to different places in the world, from the Tuileries Gardens in Paris and the source of the Zambezi River to more intimate scenes like a Parisian bath and the snake dance, from street scenes in Porto, Portugal, and the catastrophic earthquake of Messina to the *Viaggio dalla terra alla luna* (*Le Voyage dans la lune*, G. Méliès, 1902) shown by the Gentili Cinema in 1904.

Signs of crisis for traveling cinemas became apparent as the first decade of the twentieth century came to an end. Many impresarios opened theaters in the cities (a Sala Splendor [Splendor Theater], a name that would become very popular, was born in 1910 in the city of Ivrea, thanks to Giuseppe Boaro).[12] A handful chose to continue, but their stories are now lost in the shadows and their calls and clamoring are the residual traces of a vanished civilization that we study today, as though we were archeologists.

A Bandwagon with Room for Everyone

Once Italian cinema jumped the technological hurdle, it began to take its first steps toward something bigger. With no inferiority complex whatsoever, it aimed to conquer the international market.

The birth of Italian cinema coincided with the end of a fundamental phase in the film industry: once traveling cinema had fallen by the wayside, theaters began to spread throughout Italian cities like an epidemic. The following is a 1907 journalist's account of the proliferation:

> Cinema . . . Cinema! Is there any place where this magical word has not been printed? We cannot take a step, take a turn down a crowded artery of our city or even a dark alley in some outlying neighborhood without seeing this word: printed and reproduced in every manner imaginable, in every size, with every typeface, in every shape. On posters, on government bulletin boards, on the shutters of closed stores, on walls, on street signs, on rooftops, in capital letters, in boldface letters, up high and down low, everywhere.[13]

Before people could forget the traveling cinema carriages and the added entertainment they offered (like "Museum and Cinema" or "Seesaw, Photography, and Cinema"), movie theaters had already found their way to the heart of the cities. Movie theaters quickly integrated into the urban environment and became a defining element of the cityscape. The early city theaters on record had names like Iride (Rainbow), Lux (Light), Radium (Beam), Cristallo (Crystal), Smeraldo (Emerald), Astra (Stars), and Cinematografico Solar (Solar Cinema). The first Cinematografico Splendor was opened by Michele Sala on Via Roma in Turin in 1898. The names were a lure; the beams they emitted were a magnet and galvanic fluid, attracting proletarian and bourgeois audiences alike.

Beyond their radiance and integration into the urban fabric like small constellations, these theaters were similar to what the late nineteenth-century author Edmondo de Amicis would have called "a carriage for everyone" (after the title of his novel *La carrozza di tutti*). Whether in the orchestra seats or the balcony, representatives of all social classes and all ages sat together side by side. Except for the so-called black evenings—when titillating movies were shown—most evenings, women, young people, and children made up the greater part of the audience.

The proliferation of movie theaters in urban centers (by 1907, there were already fifteen permanent movie theaters in Livorno; seventy in Milan by 1908) and in small towns was so rapid and overwhelming that in 1913, then ex-Prime Minister Luigi Luzzati published an article in the daily newspaper *Il Corriere della sera*, in which he hypothesized a grandiose scenario on the basis of available data and reasonable forecasts for development:

> In small and big cities, cinema has become an honest pastime for all social classes. It has even reached small towns and villages . . . It is not farfetched to hypothesize that of 80,000 townships, no less than one half have a cinema. Nor would it be excessive to assume that there is an average of 3 cinemas for every 2,000 townships, basing this figure on a conservative estimate for those townships where applicable. This means that there are roughly 6,000 cinemas. Nor would it be inappropriate to surmise that, on average, 200 people visit each cinema every day. This means that there are 1,200,000 viewers per day. With 300 days in the year [when the cinemas can be open for business], this means that the total is nearly 360,000,000.

In just a few short years, cinema had effectively become the most popular form of entertainment, a necessary amenity, a space for secular culture where an increasingly mixed audience found itself seated in hardy pews made from poplar trees:

> In the audience at the cinema, there are many types of people who are very different from the ordinary. They are so fresh and amusing that they are often more entertaining than the show itself. Aside from the lovers, who often do not

watch the film and who do not understand anything, there is an elderly soldier
. . . There is the regular who knows all the stars and their studios. There is the
mechanic who loudly offers advice to the projectionist . . . There is the young
noblewoman who takes notes on style and salon etiquette . . . Lastly, there
are the photographer, the painter, the architect, the seamstress, the fashion
designer—every social station.[14]

Thanks to studies conducted by Bernardini,[15] today we can reconstruct
the journey that brought the *Cinématographe* to Italy: on March 13, there was
a screening in Rome at the La Lieure studio on Mortaro Street; on March 29,
the Lumières' apparatus arrived in Milan; on March 30, it was in Naples, and
so on and so on, in Genoa, Venice, and Turin. The lights of the Lumières and
Edison spread along routes that within a few months covered all of Italy.

Called the "most recent masterpiece in the field of the amazing," the
Lumières' invention was immediately received with a mixture of wonder, curiosity, attraction, and admiration: "We used the word amazement not because
of the despicable abuse of this word, but rather, because it is truly the word
that expresses the sentiment felt while watching the animated reproduction
of scenes from life."[16]

In the beginning, even mixed in with the many scientific and pseudo-
scientific inventions that seemed ceaselessly to replace one another and blend
in together at traveling carnivals or amusement park houses of wonders, cinema began to draw crowds of curious onlookers—thanks to its ability to reproduce life. But it was also an unprecedented opportunity to immortalize the
memory and the *petite histoire* of persons who had no story and had always
been ignored by history. On one hand, the era's chroniclers offered detailed
accounts of the films' content, but they also documented the ever-growing
lines of viewers first waiting outside the traveling cinemas and then at the
urban movie theaters. Lured by the voices of barkers,[17] audiences flowed together en masse, in Turin as in Trieste, in Milan as in Venice, in Rimini as in
Este, and in Messina as in Livorno.[18]

A rich series of works based on local micro-histories and articles based
on analytical research conducted in archives and periodical collections allow
us to draw a detailed, reliable map of the arrival and circulation of early cinema
entertainment in Italy. With few exceptions, these contributions have developed thanks to a group of common individuals who often seem to have
been cloned. A healthy bulimic disposition, local pride, and elementary post-
positivistic methodology are shared by researchers from north to south: from
Trieste to Catania, from Bressanone to Rimini. These histories are interesting
in their morphogenetic qualities, which allow nearly invisible local discoveries

to find shared bonds and dimensions in a much vaster framework that extends even beyond Italy.

Thanks to this series of erudite contributions, the ability to reconstruct the history of the movie theaters, the audiences, and the ways and the range with which cinematic culture formed in a given location has also allowed us to obtain fragmented socio-cultural data about a wide range of sectors, from farming to heavy industry, from capital cities to small towns. Nearly all of these works find their strength in the remarkable amount of newly discovered data and long-neglected information that make it possible to bring lost memories to the light and once-forgotten territories to the forefront. On the other hand, the weakness in almost every case is the lack of a historiographic mentality or approach that would have otherwise allowed the researchers to analyze the materials and bring them back to life in a wider context. But this is the limitation of a type of historical field that has been defined and conditioned—despite its inherent merit and the value added by the researchers' passion—by the works published in the past few years.

From Turin to Sicily: Phases of Development and Crisis

From 1905 to 1912, Italian film production went through an initial period of rapid development, then a period of crisis—partly due to the slump in the international economy—and, finally, a mature, innovative, and competitive phase that helped it open European and American markets. Filoteo Alberini proved to be a stimulus: production companies sprung up everywhere, first with little funding, then with more substantial backing from noblemen, industrialists, bankers, stockbrokers, and landowners who were attracted by the new type of investment. Production fever flooded Turin, which was in the process of industrialization; Naples, with its back-streets economy; and Rome, with its noblemen and bankers. In many respects, it was like the Klondike Gold Rush. According to a filmography compiled by Bernardini, there were seven titles in circulation.[19] A year later, there were ten times as many. Even though the industry had yet to reach the levels of exponential growth that it would achieve in the years preceding World War I, the number of films produced and the rise in exports made it a notable sector in Italy's industrial development. The pure spirit of capitalism never descended upon the heads of the early producers. But that changed with Stefano Pittaluga's arrival on the scene. Comparable to an American tycoon, he was the first modern, forward-thinking entrepreneur among them, and he was the only one capable of devising a plan for vertical concentration.[20] Pittaluga was the first producer who managed to obtain substantive support for the industry from the Italian government.

The history of early Italian cinema's evolution was inconsistent. Certain areas were defined by pre-industrialist and pre-capitalist traits; in other areas it was more in line with the automobile industry, which was undergoing a period of industrialization and modernization. Turin, the laboratory for the new Italy, for example, became the "pacesetter for the expansion of cinema, taking part in an endeavor—like that of the automobile—that would shape the twentieth century."[21]

After a few years, it would become possible to identify certain common significant denominators: polycentrism, patronage, the love of risk and adventure, and oscillation between family-run companies and the business models borrowed from the mechanical engineering and automobile industries, from which the film industry adapted certain structural and developmental characteristics.

In the beginning there were four capitals of Italian cinema: Turin, Rome, Milan, and Naples. Other cities—Genoa, Palermo, Catania, and Venice—would join this list, although they played a subordinate role because production operations often lasted only as long as it took to shoot a given film. Italy started producing films about ten years later than did other countries, partly because in the years that followed the Lumières' invention, it was necessary to explore means of distribution and operation, market potential, and the nature of demand.

Polycentric production expanded effortlessly in an Italy still divided by linguistic and cultural barriers and by socio-economic development. The early production houses were linked to the economy of the territory in which they operated, and their future depended on circumstance, a love of risk and adventure, luck, and entrepreneurial intelligence. Even though little research has been conducted on the relationship between the economics of cinema and the regions where films were produced, a small offering of data helps in understanding the different levels of development and concentration during the silent film era in Italy: between 1905 and 1930, there were 245 production houses in Rome; in Turin, there were 103; in Milan and Naples there were just more than half that number; 24 in Genoa; 9 in Florence; and in no particular order, there were production houses that lasted the length of a film in Treviso, Foligno, Viareggio, Montecatini, and Cefalù, among others. As was the case for companies like Alpina, Ars, Biblia, Fenix, and Elium in Turin, many production houses could not manage to finish or release their first film.

During the first decade of the twentieth century, production growth was balanced around Italy, but the world war proved a watershed in the industry and led to the concentration of operations in Rome. The many cinema capitals gave life to productions that were at times very different, at others very similar. In Turin, producers intended their films to compete with the French; consequently, they adapted international literary and theatrical works to the screen. In Rome, they set their sights on the celebration of their imperial glory. On the other hand, the Neapolitans hoped to achieve an almost hegemonic control of the entire country, but they also drew from literature and naturalist theater.[22] No one would be accused of excessive nationalist pride for contending that Turin, the "city of imagination" as Cesare Pavese called it in *Mestiere di vivere* (*The Burning Brand*), assumed the role of international cinema capital with its hundreds of films, thousands of persons employed in the industry, and the constant flow of investment by Turin's industrialist aristocracy.[23] In 1914, there was even a moment when Giovanni Agnelli became a partner in Cenisio Film. But that project was put on hold due to the outbreak of war.

In 1905, the first film production company, Alberini and Santoni, was born in Rome. By April 1906, it had become the Società Anonima per Azioni Cines (Cines Inc.), with 250,000 lire in capital stock.[24] The birth of Cines brought with it a member of a powerful family of industrialists, Adolfo Pouchain, who was appointed to its board of directors. The company did not hide its ambition to conquer the international market and was aided in this respect by capital from the Banco di Roma (Bank of Rome). By 1907, Cines had opened a sales office in New York. A few years later, thanks to George Kleine, it invaded the U.S. market with its now historical giants. That same year, nine new production houses were operating in Italy: three in Turin (Ambrosio, Carlo Rossi, and Aquila), two in Rome (Cines and Fratelli Pineschi), two in Milan (Luca Comerio and Baratti), and two in Naples (Manifatture cinematografiche riunite [United Cinematic Manufacturers] and Fratelli Troncone).

The story of these production houses makes it clear that film production in Italy was not a truly advanced industry, even though the working method, the marketing strategies, and the sales were typical of the sweeping industrial transformation that was taking place in Italy at the turn of the century. In any case, because of the coexistence of production houses so different from one another and with varying amounts of capital, it is important that scholars not limit their studies to the major companies. Attention should also be given to filmmakers who operated on a purely local level and to isolated individuals who managed to make only one film. These producers were scattered across Italy like spots on a leopard, nearly invisible in some parts of the country.

Over the past three decades, scholars have begun to work on systematic studies of the earliest production houses (here again, Bernardini has initiated surveys of early cinema production throughout Italy). In certain areas, the advancement of knowledge has come about thanks to theses authored by students who have sifted through national archives, chambers of commerce, and the archives of regional business bureaus.[25]

A few years ago, the Cineteca and University of Bologna launched a project to restore and study the films produced by Film d'Arte Italiana (Italian Art Films), a production house founded in 1909 as a branch of the French Film d'Art. Over the past decade, tens of its films have been restored and the project has revealed the thematic, stylistic, and narrative range of a production house that was conceived with the goal of adapting theatrical and literary masterworks to the screen. The concept was to use—whenever possible—the *plein air* and the very places where the stories were set. In 1912, Film d'Arte Italiana decided to focus on contemporary stories, the dramas of economic and emotional catastrophes, the ruination of families, adulterers, and destructive passions. These included Ugo Falena's *Dall'amore al disonore* (*From Love to Dishonor*, 1912) and *Usuraio e padre* (*Usurer and Father*, 1914) and *Effetti di luce* (*Lighting Effects*, 1916), directed by Ercole Luigi Morselli and Ugo Falena.[26] His films were shaped by his nineteenth-century moralistic view of the world. But, as a whole, his films were important inasmuch as they showed the many forces disintegrating the institution of family.

During the first decade of the twentieth century, Turin clearly led Rome and Milan in terms of production: in 1907, 107 films were made in Turin, while 40 were produced in Rome and 6 in Milan. The following year, the numbers were, respectively, 289, 107, and 81. But by 1909, the industry was in crisis, due in part to strategic changes made by foreign production houses—American ones in particular. Producers in other parts of the world had begun to react to the imperial reign of Pathé et Gaumont. But there were also other factors, like pressure from lobbying groups and municipal and religious authorities who believed this new form of entertainment to be dangerous for the masses. Once producers achieved a certain level of success and were able to identify their audiences and the general facets of the demand, they began almost automatically to repeat the same winning formulas. The race to imitate had begun and producers began to compete with one another using the same stories and types of film. This phenomenon clearly emerged in Turin and Milan, where, in multiple instances, producers used the same stories at the same time, trying, by any possible means, to beat their competitors by borrowing their ideas and crew and by creating products very similar to one another. The problem also existed on an international level, as evidenced by documents in American archives in which the Cines producers of *Quo vadis?*, directed by Guazzone, claimed that the film did not copy American products, and where it is clear that at least two production houses sought to compete for the American market with *Gli ultimi giorni di Pompei* (*The Last Days of Pompeii*). This internal tension between the major production houses had a positive effect over the short term, and it played a fundamental role in the linguistic and expressive development of filmmaking and in the development of production value. The length of films began to change in Italy in 1909, and when producers started work on *L'Inferno* (*Dante's Inferno*), they claimed it would be less than 1,000 meters in length, despite the fact that the average length was still set around 250 to 300 meters.

During this period of restructuring and expansion, a large number of aristocrats made investments by transferring funds from their real estate investments and land assets. These esteemed Italian nobles included the Pacelli, Fassini, Visconti di Modrone, Colonna, and Capece Minutolo families. Milanese company Luca Comerio quickly became Saffi-Comerio before Airoldi di Robbiate bought into it. In just a few months, he turned it into Milano Film after removing its founder. Besides the constant inflow of capital, the presence of aristocrats also greatly influenced efforts to increase the cultural and artistic value of film. Count Giuseppe de Liguoro's relationship with Milano Film was a good example of this phenomenon. In 1911, the company's executive board consisted of president Count Pier Carlo Venino and advisors Count Giovanni Visconti di Modrone, Count Carlo Porro, Prince Urbano del Drago, and Count Mario Miniscalchi Erizzo.

During the period of expansion, the nascent industry lived a life of adventure in which the love of risk and the prospects of enormous profits did not hide producers' inability to forecast ticket sales, the precarious nature of the business itself, and the lack of investment security. The hope to make gold from the fruit of ephemeral shadows led a varied crowd of individuals to tempt fate at the betting table of this new industry. Arturo Ambrosio was the owner of a photography studio in Turin before he founded his production house Ambrosio, Ernesto Maria Pasquali was a journalist before Pasquali, Giuseppe Tempo was a pharmacist before Tempo, and Carlo Sciamengo was an engineer before he became president of Itala. Later, actors and agents joined in, as did stockbrokers, businessmen, and painters. The following passage provides an idea of the modest means of the earliest production houses in Turin and helps us understand how hard it was to grow and establish a footing in the market: "Pasquali and Tempo's first studio, remembers lawyer Mario Donn, had only

three or four offices and a shed where they kept the scenery, tools, and costumes and where the set designer worked. The soundstage was a simple, exposed stage. About four or five meters from the ground, ropes were used to
run a white canvas overhead."[27]

The year 1912 marked the greatest expansion in terms of the number of
films produced: 569 in Turin, 420 in Rome, and 120 in Milan, of which Milano
Film made 88.

By this time, the major production houses' catalogs had established
the basic features of their films, which were divided by genre and length.
They also had begun to advertise their products according to their different
types. During this period, between the cinema's first real crisis and World War
I, there was an initial boom in the development of the industry, its expressive range, its ability to play on multiple levels by refining select genres, and
its expansion of certain working methods and the length of the stories. The
focus on the first real strategies for production, distribution, and sales increased
cinema's narrative and stylistic range—and bolstered producers' awareness of
the medium's spectacular potential. All of these elements were influenced
by the ascendancy and expansion of the filmmaker's approach to time-space
relationships.

The three decades before the war marked the greatest expansion and
consolidation of the industry: Italian filmmakers enjoyed their greatest success
and glory in the United States during this period.[28] But, with its female stars,
its Mark Antony and Caesar, and its comedies, it also conquered markets in
Russia, Argentina, France, Spain, and Great Britain.[29]

Here again, Bernardini's research has helped illuminate this series of in-
terrelated stories. But there is still a need for an authoritative, compelling
work that reflects on the overall picture and is able to focus on the relationship
between the economy of cinema, its features, and its ties to Italy's economic
development. Thanks to Alberto Friedemann's systematic, detailed research
on the actual sites used for filmmaking in Turin during the silent era, and his
detailed history of the different companies, today we know those companies'
exact locations, the equipment they used, their executive projects, the dimensions and locations of the soundstages, and even their marketing and press
offices.[30] The simple distribution of these companies throughout the city shows
that their location was arbitrary and that they never reached any level of
concentration comparable to that of other industries that sprung up, for example, near the Dora Riparia River and became concentrated in the same section
of the city. This lack of concentration and the isolation of each company were
perhaps the first elements to mark the extreme fragility of their business, their

inability to create a working system, and the difficulty in reaching markets without using teamwork and sharing technology. Even a superficial glance reveals the structural weakness of the Italian film industry, despite the fact that there are no company records that scholars can use to paint a broader picture of fragments of events now erased or buried.

During this phase of expansion and conquest of the international market, contracts with foreign distributors—first and foremost with American distributors—included massive acquisitions of films besides historical-mythological and fantasy titles. After the success of *Quo Vadis?*, Rome-based Cines and George Kleine's company in Chicago signed an agreement whereby the American distributor acquired exclusive American rights (including the Philippines, Canada, and Alaska) to sell, screen, rent, print, reprint, publish, and otherwise utilize all of Cines's films. The Italian company was to submit every film to Kleine, who would pay 75 cents per meter of celluloid. For many years, Italian films had been purchased without being screened. This contract clarified the terms and added others whereby Kleine was to pay substantial advances for more sophisticated productions like *Quo Vadis?*[31] For a number of years, Italian films overwhelmed the competition.

The first signs of crisis appeared during the vigil leading up to the war. From that moment on, international markets began to close, one after another. Following the outbreak of war and the advent of the longer, multiple-reel films, the number of titles dropped: 268 in Turin, 184 in Rome, and 64 in Milan. By 1917, the balance of power had tipped and Rome became the capital of production with 159 films, 59 in Turin, and 40 in Milan. By 1923, the crisis was in full-swing: 26 films produced in Turin, 74 in Rome, and 8 in Milan. In Naples, where 4 production houses had produced 30 films in 1912, the numbers remained roughly unchanged. Neapolitan filmmakers were able to withstand the crisis of the 1920s and managed to make 57 films between 1923 and 1925, while 47 were produced in Turin during the same period (although in 1925, Turin produced barely 4 films).

Besides the more noted production companies (Cines, Milano Film Aquila, Itala, Caesar, Ambrosio, and Pasquali), there were also others that have never been analyzed because of their fragility, their meteoric rise and fall, and the difficulty in making sense of a jungle of names so similar to another—if not identical. Between 1913 and 1914, for example, there were three companies called Superfilm: one in Naples, one in Genoa, and one in Turin. During the silent era in Turin, over 120 production houses went into business. Among these, one of the most memorable (if only for its unusual name) was Photo-Emporium, a company worth 60,000 lire. Its mission was "manufacturing and sales in every branch of photography, lenses, cinema, and all related fields of production and applications." Born in 1908, the Società Italiana Films was converted to Unitas, a company whose mission was to make Catholic films. There were others like De Giglio, which started as a rental company, and Giano Film, which produced four films in 1914. In Turin, between 1907 and 1910, other companies appeared with names like Films Italia, which became Navone Films, and Roma Films. In the years that followed, the attempts to launch film production companies would expand exponentially.

The Great Migration:
From the Library to the Universal *Cinémathèque*

The common denominator that united the earliest producers and "artistic directors" (individuals with limited powers) was their sense of omnipotence and the titanic syndrome that shaped their first moves. The history of the world, the tradition of fine art, universal literature, and a timeless repertoire of theatrical works represented an inexhaustible easy-to-access resource and a gift of nature within everyone's reach.

Cinema wanted to slice the bread of science, art, and culture and serve it to the masses and upwardly mobile bourgeoisie. It wanted to transform this bread, as if by transubstantiation, into a living being made of bodies and blood for a new type of periodic ritual. And it also wanted to light fuses of patriotic spirit with works like *Garibaldi* (1907), *Pietro Micca* (1908, the story of an Italian patriot and a hero in the Spanish War of Succession), and *Il piccolo garibaldino* (*The Garibaldi Boy* or *The Garibaldian Boy*, 1909). These films planted visible symbols and powerful elements that would help shape Italy's national conscience in their viewers' minds. More than in other countries, cinema in Italy was not only a gateway to modernity but also a useful tool in cultural restoration, a magical means of locomotion for all kinds of trips into the country's history and its artistic and literary past.

The cinematographic iconosphere became a hyper-system or hyper-language that had room for concentrations of literature, history, theater, sculpture, opera, and music. The artistic directors of Cines, Ambrosio, Pasquali, and Film d'Arte produced roughly ten *tableaux vivants* in which they managed to squeeze the juices from Homeric poems and Shakespeare's masterworks. They animated figures from medieval and Renaissance paintings. And they did so without excluding adaptations of comparable images from portraiture and popular illustration.

In 1906, Cines produced *Otello* (*Othello*) and in 1907, *Giuditta e Oloferne* (*Judith and Holophernes*). The same year, Rossi in Turin released a *Napoleone I*

(*Napoleon I*) while Ambrosio offered viewers a *Pagliacci*. In the years that followed, a river of famous historical and literary figures appeared in illustrated books, neoclassical and pre-Raphaelite frescoes, lithographs, engravings, photographs, and monuments. These images shaped Italy's cinematographic iconosphere, forming an uninterrupted chain of characters on the screen who were capable of forging new relationships with viewers: *Amleto* (*Hamlet*), *Giordano Bruno*, *Romeo e Giulietta* (*Romeo and Juliet*), *Giuditta e Oloferne* (*Judith and Holophernes*), *Lorenzino de' Medici*, *Lucia di Lammermoor* (*Lucy of Lammermoor*), and *Pia de' Tolomei* were just some of the titles produced in 1908. Each of these films was an adaptation of popular iconography.

Even with their earliest catalogs, the major production houses accepted the subdivision of the market by genre, a move that empowered the most ambitious among them. In the beginning, cinema was enthusiastically embraced by positivist intellectuals and pedagogues as an ideal school for the masses. But Italian producers were more interested in winning over bourgeois audiences who were attracted neither by cinema's popularity nor by the excessive social promiscuity of the early metropolitan movie theaters.

Early Italian films were cinematic adaptations drawn from the newly forged (or emerging) Italian library, an ideal library in which poetic, narrative, and theatrical classics were mixed in with feuilletons, abridged libretti, and biographies of famous men. Homer, Dante, and Boccaccio lived together in good company together with Eugène Sue, Zévaco, Alexandre Dumas, Lucio d'Ambra, Pietro Cossa, Gabriele d'Annunzio, and Raffaello Giovagnoli. There were many forces and many different literary works competing to build up Italy's still uncertain national identity and this *cinémathèque* was ideal as an *opus caementicium*. Early Italian cinema was generally secular, although it was also sprinkled with a small percentage of religious themes that did not seem to weigh on Italy's overall identity. The selection of subjects and the abundance of titles were based on a preexisting series of key texts in the Italian library and on its circulation abroad. The 1908 film *Pietro Micca*, based on the life of one of Italy's most popular heroes, was probably inspired by a Bencivenni painting. *Il Fornaretto di Venezia* (*Venetian Baker*, 1907) was the first film exported to the United States by the Roman production house Cines: the original play, *Il Fornaretto di Venezia* by Dall'Ongaro, was one of the principal texts of popular literature (it was successful even as a puppet theater production).

This process of pre-narrative transcodification paralleled the attempt to reduce literary texts to their corresponding visual stereotypes using tested processes of serialization and thousand-year-old artisanal practices drawn from the tradition of the amanuensis. In their highest forms, these variants were

drawn from medieval summaries and compilations, from the techniques employed in medieval *abbreviatio* and all of its subsequent variations, and even
from the more recent but still-to-be-discovered production of portraits, theatrical set design, and *tableaux vivants*. The usage of the term *quadro* (painting)
to denote a filmic sequence in early Italian cinema is an indication of this
phenomenon. Shakespeare, in particular, was the author who served as the
leader in conquering international markets. In 1909, the production house
Saffi signed a contract with D'Annunzio for six films, and it released the first
version of Manzoni's *I promessi sposi* (*The Betrothed*). Comerio released *Sepolta
viva* (*Buried Alive*) in 1908, a film based on the novel by Francesco Mastriani.
The following year it was Xavier de Montépin's turn with the Ambrosio production of *Il ventriloquo* (*The Ventriloquist*), directed by Arrigo Frusta. All the
while, Cines continued to pillage works by popular authors. Among its other
titles, Film d'Arte Italiana in Rome released an *Otello* (*Othello*), a *La signora
dalle camelie* (*The Lady of the Camellias*), and a *Carmen*.

As they implemented their production and editorial policies, the production houses subdivided their releases according to a rigid hierarchy of levels
and styles. Their goal was to create standardized stereotypes and related models. The top level, which defined the style of the production house, included
adaptations of classics and historical films. Whether these classics were
adapted to the screen to expand Italian culture at home or for the export of
Italian culture abroad, the phenomenon was linked to the early organizational
phase of the modern culture of the masses (a topic explored by Fausto Colombo in his book *La cultura sottile* [*Thin Culture*]) and with the beginning of
the regular export of products connected with the mass emigration during
the same period.[32] The pedagogical-pedantic nature of these films (defined by
Colombo as the "cricket strategy") was often just a cover for a series of thematic choices in which exact transference of the ruling class could be dumped.
The Italian library-*cinémathèque* was not rich with titles, but it was well organized: certain variations, or the return of given adaptations, allow us to identify some emerging tendencies that led to the development of the historical-
mythological fantasy film, the opera film, and the films that launched the star
system into orbit.

No other European country rivaled Italy in the scope of its overflowing
inter-textual adaptations. For its iconographic measuring stick, the Italian system used "great manner," to borrow a phrase used by early twentieth-century
art historian Heinrich Wöllflin in regard to the Renaissance. There was a
disproportionate relationship between the modest investment and the range
and ambition of filmmakers' cultural objectives. But the choice of lofty models
played a decisive role, at least in the beginning, inasmuch as it launched the

entire system and made it visible to audiences around the world. Italian cinema was a crossroads and alchemic melting pot of the great currents of literature and the figurative arts. It grew and developed rapidly; its defining features quickly emerged, thanks to its faith in an ability to convert all preexisting and contiguous forms of artistic and literary writing to the screen. In the eyes of the early producers and artistic directors, literature and art became magical helpers in their quest for cinema's complete artistic legitimacy. In 1918, in the magazine *In Penombra*, Enrico Guazzoni wrote:

> I could see vast horizons for cinematography . . . You could have called me an utopist, a poet . . . In cinematography, I could see the fusion of all the arts, painting, sculpture, theater . . . I believed that cinematography, unlike theater, would make it possible to envision immensely vast fields . . . I believed it would have almost no limitation . . . that it could reproduce figures and the environment in which they moved. In a word, I believed it could reproduce the entire world.

Together with literature, literati also moved toward cinema. Writers played a variety of roles, quickly accepting—at times enthusiastically, at others guiltily—and helping erect the new edifice of entertainment using the same words, material, and means they had used to manufacture their novels and poems. This phenomenon was not limited to Italy. In the beginning, there were armies of Italian, German, and French intellectuals who offered their skills. They were followed by Spaniards, Brits, Austrians, Russians, Swedes, and Danes. Cinema was their "fatal attraction" and it became a larger and more lucrative market square where they could show off their wares as they sought to sell their writing. In 1908, the Société Cinématographique des Auteurs et Gens de Lettres was founded in France. Soon after, writers and poets could be seen at the doorstep of production companies across Europe. They were drawn there by flashing signs for earnings disproportionate to their craft. These included, in no particular order: Apollinaire and Artaud, Antoine and Colette, Karl Kraus, Hofmannsthal, Blasco Ibáñez, Jacinto Benavente, Arthur Schnitzler, and Mayakovsky. In Italy, Verga, Capuana, Bracco, Martoglio, Gozzano, Serao, Deledda, Di Giacomo, Pirandello, Nino Oxilia, Lucio d'Ambra, Yambo (Enrico Novelli), Federico de Roberto, Marco Praga, Giannino Antona Traversi, Enrico Buti, Domenico Tumiati, and Umberto Fracchia— they were all successful writers or dramatists. Beginning in 1909, when cinema was still just a baby, and for years to follow, writers were caught by surprise and embarrassed by their for-hire performances, at which they worked diligently to erase any trace. Sooner or later, they all gave in, offering their talents to the highest bidder. For all intents and purposes, they helped create works that were soon recognized for their quality—no less so than their literary works had been. Novelists, poets, and dramatists were all recruited by the film industry in its search for greater cultural dignity.

Historical Films Set Out to Conquer the World

By the end of the first decade of the twentieth century, the film industry had begun asking writers and intellectuals to condense classical poems or successful contemporary works while keeping their original spirit intact. This trend gave birth to a new type of writer, who was paid to synthesize and squeeze the juice out of an entire poem, novel, or opera sometimes using just a few captions or subtitles.

There were many films in which writers played with time: Maggi's *Nerone* (*Nero or the Fall of Rome* or *Nero or The Burning of Rome*), *Il granatiere Roland* (*Grenadier Roland*), and *Nozze d'oro* (*After Fifty Years* or *Golden Wedding*); Giuseppe de Liguoro's *Marin Faliero, Doge di Venezia* (*Marin Faliero, the Doge of Venice*); *Otello* (*Othello*), directed by Yambo in 1909 (produced by Pineschi); Bertolini and Padovan's *L'Inferno* (*Dante's Inferno*); De Liguoro's *L'Odissea* (*Homer's Odyssey*); and *Il piccolo garibaldino* (*The Garibaldi Boy* or *The Garibaldian Boy*), released by Cines. And there were the great historical films that followed during the golden age before World War I. Careful study of the iconographic sources for these films reveals the producers' will and desire to reach the same heights as the great schools of painting in history. They wanted to digest the lessons of the Renaissance painting, just like those of neoclassicism and symbolism, but they also incorporated the influences of contemporary commercial illustration.

Enrico Guazzone played an important role in creating a series of historical artistic films. He was the first Italian director truly capable of orchestrating large casts, composing images, organizing space, creating narrative syntax, and making the most of set design.

The discovery of the potential of open space in production design, which had slowly freed itself of papier-mâché backdrops, allowed thousands of extras to move and clash, to parade, and to decree the life and death of gladiators and Christians in Roman circuses and arenas. More than anything, the use of open space gave life to a policy of virtual power. It could transmit energy and convey vitality to a static, monumental, and repetitive conception of time. As the action space began to expand on the screen, so did the space in the theater and in audiences' imagination.

Now geared for historical films, production houses in Rome and Turin increasingly set their sights on winning over the international moviegoer. Before Hollywood became the world's cinema capital, Italian producers of historical films and the city of Turin tasted the short-lived, alluring, and inimitable sensation of dominating cinematic imperialism. The historical genre rapidly assumed a central role in production, imposing a style and a stamp of Italian identity on all the films produced. The genre had been born of educational and pedagogical intentions and was destined to become dead weight when compared to the dynamic motion of other genres. But for a short time, it was the guiding force and an unmistakable tipping point for the imperial ambitions of the national spirit typified by Giovanni Giolitti, who served as prime minister of monarchic Italy from 1898 to 1921. Historic films conveyed a winning image of Italian culture and history to the world. They also proved useful to supporters of nationalist ideology, pervaded as they were by political themes linked to an Italy preparing itself for war.

Thanks to the genre, Italian cinema embraced mythology and, in particular, it revived the mythology of Italy's origins as well as that of Western civilization, not to mention the mythology of centuries-old Roman domination. During this period, the Italian-Turkish War brought Italy into Libya. The conflict gave a decisive push to the confluence of cinematic production, nationalist ideology, and the ambitions of a small country that had been unified and liberated only a few decades earlier.

The five years between *Nerone* (*Nero or the Fall of Rome* or *Nero or The Burning of Rome*) and *Cabiria* marked an era of Italian cinema in which linguistic, syntactic, and expressive development combined with the rise of nationalist spirit. It also converged with a series of semantic displacements of the meaning of Roman history that reflected change in domestic and international politics in Italy. Before Mussolini had a chance to write, "May the spirit of Rome be reborn in fascism," in the pages of *Popolo d'Italia* (April 21, 1922), the images of triumphal Roman parades, Roman salutes, and lictor's fasces could be seen in films like *Quo Vadis?*, *Cajus Julius Caesar*, *Spartacus*, *Salambò* (*Salambo*), *Marcantonio e Cleopatra* (*Mark Antony and Cleopatra*), *Nerone e Agrippina* (*Nero and Agrippina*), *In hoc signo vinces*, and *Cabiria*. All of these films were made between 1912 and 1914, and they helped resuscitate a distant history that legitimized Italy's past and inspired its dreams.[33] A few years later, this compact set of historical films helped establish symbols that would guide the political rituals of fascism. These works delivered the spirit for conquest that seemed to arrive from the distant past, thanks—as was true in other cases—to its prime supporter and apostle, Gabriele d'Annunzio.[34]

Maggi's *Nerone* (*Nero*, 1909) can be considered the genre's archetype, the film that accelerated the entire system. Inspired by Pietro Cossa's comedy, this film drew from Bartolomeo's watercolors and neoclassical painting for its iconographic references and transformed them into *tableaux vivants*. It also borrowed from the Barnum Circus's grandiose spectacle, "Nero, or the Destruction of Rome," produced in 1889.[35] At any rate, even though the dominant codes were theatrical, the film's spectacular effects broke new ground in its use of large casts (the scenes of mass panic and the city aflame, for example), and the dramaturgy gave space to both the individual and group movements of the cast. After *Nerone*, the system's next milestones were *La caduta di Troia* (*The Fall of Troy*), *L'Odissea* (*Homer's Odyssey*), and *L'Inferno* (*Dante's Inferno*), works that were screened around the world. In these films, the richness and originality of the makeup worked well and were credible in scenes shot on location. The faith in the translatability and transcodification (*L'Inferno* was intended as a faithful visual adaptation of Doré's illustrations of Dante's *Commedia*) made these films the crossroads of many different codes, models, and tendencies toward limitless forms of entertainment.

The films made by the big studios in Rome, Milan, and Turin between 1912 and 1914 were afflicted by unprecedented egomaniacal set design. During this period, production designers favored an approach more akin to Antonelli's architecture than to circus shows or the grandiose sets used for theatrical and operatic productions at La Scala. Not an inch of the entire historical-geographic atlas was left unturned, and sooner or later every epoch and every style found itself within view of the movie camera. In the previous decade, camera operators sought out and captured the surface of the visible. But in the historical films produced during this period, the camera became a veritable counterclockwise time machine. Filmmakers fragmented, compressed, miniaturized, and expanded history. Using visible transformations, they gave life to an autonomous invention capable of re-creating real and imaginary places with complete liberty. The typical closed theatrical set was replaced to allow casts of thousands to irrupt in the foreground. In 1897, Pellizza da Volpedo depicted a compact column of proletarians marching toward the twentieth century in his celebrated oil painting *Il quarto stato* (*The Fourth Estate*); now that same column was marching in Napoleon's and Julius Caesar's armies and directors set it loose, letting it grow uninhibited in earthquakes, volcanic eruptions, and catastrophes of every type imaginable. In 1913, writer Giuseppe Prezzolini captured the spirit of such casting when he wrote, "Not an actor! An entire nation in each scene!"[36]

With its production of *Quo vadis?*, Cines had set in motion a marketing strategy that became a progressive model for international filmmaking. In earlier days, the stills from a film were reprinted in specially published editions of the novel with the following caption on the cover: "Illustrations from the film produced by Cines." This strategy was replaced by the publication of actual press releases that highlighted elements from the lavish productions: shooting took six months; 1,500 to 2,000 extras were used; 25 lions were rented; authentic locations were used for the principal scenes like Anzio, Lake Avernus; the ancient Greek city of Cumae near Naples; and the Apian Way for the apparition of Christ (from a letter sent to Kleine's French representatives, February 21, 1913).

From the use of Renaissance perspective in *La caduta di Troia* (*The Fall of Troy*) to the makeup in *L'Inferno* (*Dante's Inferno*), from the crowds of extras in the battle scenes of *Cajus Julius Caesar* to the eruptions in *Gli ultimi giorni di Pompei* (*The Last Days of Pompeii*) and the circus scenes in *Quo vadis?*, there seemed to be no limit to the camera operator's omnivorous gaze. Even though up through *Cabiria*, the analysis of these films reveals somewhat limited dynamics in cinematography and editing, there is no denying that the historical genre offered enormous expressive potential in terms of lighting, the use of large casts, and the discovery of the dramatic function of spatial relationships and the plurality of their meaning.

Figurative imagery and the conscious utilization of space as a subject and central part of a story were by no means easy or immediate. It was no simple matter for directors to free themselves from the chains of traditional theatrical and operatic set design. It was often the conventional nature and direct recognizability of the iconography that caused the screen to become that window onto infinity described by Baudelaire. These images inspired desire among audiences and left them wanting to further explore higher levels of culture and ideals.

As far as production value was concerned, the cinematographers' newly acquired skill allowed them to think about light as a chromatic palette. It revealed a progressive awareness of the possibility of passing beyond the typical two-dimensional space of medieval painting toward the distinctive, three-dimensional perspective of Renaissance painting. Thanks to the historical genre and the need to orchestrate the movements of large crowds in historical films, cinema began to use the laws of Renaissance perspective.

Director Giovanni Pastrone was a complex and complete figure, an entrepreneur and artist who could be compared to directors like Griffith, Ince, and Gance.[37] And although he created remarkable sets beginning with his earliest work, *La caduta di Troia*, Guazzoni was—as we have seen—the most erudite director in terms of the figurative arts and the one most aware of the challenges posed by cinematic set design and the rules of constructing space. A painter and set designer, he became the Cines artistic director in 1910.

By virtue of its many innovative elements, Guazzoni's film *Quo vadis?* allowed the entire narrative system and film industry to take a giant leap forward. His characters moved through space with unprecedented freedom as he championed the individual/crowd dialectic using models adopted and recycled without any substantial variations for decades by American cinema as well.

This type of film allowed popular imagery to project its desires for the future and to face its fears as it manipulated sentimental vicissitudes and political intrigue. These works borrowed from operatic models and showed that even the most famous figures in history had secrets, emotional weaknesses, and never-before-revealed episodes. Audiences were just as interested in these elements as they were in the feats recorded by history.

History was a backdrop, while passion, jealousy, hatred, and revenge clashed in the foreground. The law of the heart prevailed over that of the state. Muscular Ursus was the prototype of a battalion of heroes, descendant from Hercules, who continued to appear under the guise of Maciste until the end of the 1920s: in the end, he performed in a circus show, slaying a bull with his bare hands and revealing the potential of the dialectic between the strongman and the crowd.

Other successful themes were extreme upward social mobility and the reversal of class roles, that is, the slave who falls in love with the nobleman, the freedman who saves the day (as did Maciste in *Cabiria*).

This genre reached fully developed adulthood on an international level between 1913 and 1914. Thanks to the Kleine archive, today we know that *Quo vadis?* screened for 22 weeks at the Astor in New York, 14 at the Garrick in Philadelphia, 13 at the Tremont in Boston, 8 in Chicago at the McVickers, and 5 weeks in 3 other city theaters. This film's distribution in 1913 reveals that there was no major American or Canadian city that did not show it for fewer than 6 days, save for Butte, Montana, where it was in theaters for only 5 days.

By this point, the standard was very high—but the zenith was hit with *Cabiria*, directed by Piero Fosco (Giovanni Pastrone). In a brilliant marketing move, the screenplay was attributed to D'Annunzio.

Although he only wrote the captions, D'Annunzio received credit for the screenplay. As early as 1910, he had given up the French rights to his tragedy *La nave* (*The Ship*) and five other works, which were adapted for the screen by Ricciotto Canudo. After accepting credit for *Cabiria*, D'Annunzio "endorsed" the quality of this film from Italy for its international campaign. In doing so, he gave it a stamp of artistic and cultural legitimacy. This move fundamentally changed the balance in the relationship between cinema and literature in Italy and other countries.

Cabiria was the northern star in the history of early Italian cinema. This film introduced myriad innovations, which included but were not limited to its creative use of the dolly and close-ups (although these two aspects of the film have received more attention in the past). But it was also remarkable for the complexity of the plot, its content, and its significant ideological substance, Segundo de Chomón's makeup and his spectacular inventiveness, the flair of the costumes, the grandiosity of the set designs, the dramatic effect of the lighting, and the creative use of captions and their rhythmic, prosodic, and dramaturgical functions.

As "author" of the film, D'Annunzio wanted to give the written word a role analogous to that of an epic poem by using a high stylistic register. It had a sort of pseudo-Homeric function, like that which we see when the poet himself makes the implicit voice and the written word appear in the film as the author's voice—his signature line at the end of the film. Up until the very last caption, the literary text managed to create a world that exists parallel to Pastrone's iconosphere.

During World War I, producers were limited by the circumstances of the conflict and the changes in audiences' tastes. Many chose to pursue other careers. Pastrone never managed to make his *La Bibbia* (*The Bible*), a film for which he intended to use a cast of thousands. Giulio Antamoro's *Christus* (*Christ*, 1916) and Guazzoni's *La Gerusalemme liberata* (*Jerusalem Liberated*, 1918) were admirable for their attention to artistic detail and the spectacular results obtained with crowd scenes, but they did not seem to keep up with the pace of contemporary international production values.

In the decade that followed, there were films that evoked the grandeur of the past but ran against the current with respect to the expressive and narrative dynamic of contemporary cinema. They were prisoners of a monumental ideal of entertainment that no longer interested international audiences.

Cretinetti and Company in Grandma Speranza's Parlor

Even comedies enjoyed great success during the five years that led up to World War I, yet they never managed to become a strong, central dish in the Italian menu. They had been conceived as a dessert, a sweet counterpoint to dramatic passion. Unlike the Americans, the Italians never produced a star capable of elevating the genre to the point that it could assume a central role. Just as in literature, comedy occupied the lowest level of the cinematic hierarchy. It collected the leftovers from all the other genres and styles and it never seemed to want, at least in its early years, to assert an autonomous narrative and expressive identity.

In Chaplin's American films, on one hand, the metamorphosis of certain comedic elements and the genre's appropriation of dramatic and tragic components were irreversible. Italian comedians, on the other hand, maintained their ties and kinship with earlier forms of popular entertainment. The American comedian had utter freedom in terms of society. His habitat was the small town, the seaside, the center of Manhattan, and the Wild West. In Italian silent films, the comedian almost always found himself in one of the big cities. His character was drawn from the world of the bourgeoisie and the lower middle class. Thus, his acting parodied bourgeois rituals. Instead of parodying the imperfect mechanisms of industrialized civilization, Italian production houses parodied the irresistible social climb of the dandy. In these films, symbols of prestige manifested themselves and made viewers laugh with strictly logical and ideological consistency, as did the transformation of the urban setting and public transportation, taboos and the highly visible transformation of etiquette, new and old rituals, and new and old characters and institutions.

A micro-society of characters in uniforms, overalls, dress shirts, tuxedos, and tailcoats were slowly sucked into the action, and their dress became one of the central elements of transformation and character portrayal, even though some of the more significant elements of theater were still present. Besides flesh-and-blood characters with their dresses, fancy lady's hats, outfits, fashions, bowler hats, straw hats, and canes, there were also mannequins, statues, and portraits in artists' studios that became their alter-egos through the transference of the characters' desires. Comedic filmmakers visibly mixed parody with the entertaining observation of desire. Thanks to comedy and comedians, the silver screen became the favored outlet of desire. In the beginning, there was just a modest range in the characters' emotions. But characters in comedies soon had farther-reaching, more ambitious economic goals as they sought to climb the social ladder. In early films, lady's clothing and hat stores, with their French fashions, were the ideal backdrop for the stimulation of desire— to a lesser degree than in operetta but free of the antagonism between the characters. This setting was perfect for showing off female stars' bodies and it facilitated the process of identification between the characters' desire and that of the audience: a paradise that remained just out of the characters' reach. Beginning in the 1970s, the same thing would happen to the accountant Ugo

Fantozzi (played by Paolo Villaggio), the eponymous hero of a cinematic saga based on early Italian comedic cinema and elevated and enlightened by a clearly Kafkaesque spirit.

From the Cretinetti ("Foolshead") comedies to the gallery of monsters that would appear in the 1960s and 1970s, Italian comedies captured the meaning of a society undergoing rapid transformation. Italians were being subjected to new rules and attitudes, to new forms of urban dissemblance and unprecedented forms of dissimulation. In comedic films more than in any other genre, social dynamics were measured through the continuous collision of individuals who belonged to different social classes and categories. It did not matter that the hero had to cross his sword with the doorman's broom or that sizes of their clothes and shoes were overstated—in accordance with circus clown rules. The model for these characters was the dandy, and the films adapted a language of gestures to conform to the rhythms and parodies of the circus and cabaret. Comedic actor Leopoldo Fregoli represented the richest and most sophisticated union of theater and cinema: the first cinematic comedic actor in Italy.

When director Pastrone hired actor André Deed, Italian and French comedic cinema began to blend. Together, they showed the thin line between cinema and previous forms of popular entertainment as they drew from a tradition of town square entertainment mixed with other more recent forms, like cabaret and vaudeville.

In the catalogs of all the production houses, comedies quickly grew in numbers. Although few of the fifty or so comedic acts really stood out from the pack, there were some successful performers who can be considered the genre's stars: Marcel Fabre, better known as Robinet, who worked for Ambrosio; André Deed, who worked for Itala playing Cretinetti; Ernesto Vaser, Ambrosio's second-string comedian, who played Fricot; Lea Giunchi under contract at Cines; Pacifico Aquilanti; Emile Vardannes; and Giuseppe Gambardella.

For a few years, myriad comedies represented a strong point in many of the studios' catalogs. There were titles like *Cretinetti paga i debiti* (*How Foolshead Pays His Debts*), *Cretinetti cerca un duello* (*Foolshead Looks for a Duel*), *Cretinetti ha rubato un tappeto* (*Foolshead Steals a Rug*), *Come fu che l'ingordigia rovinò il Natale di Cretinetti* (*How Greed Ruined Foolshead's Christmas*), *Cretinetti al ballo* (*Foolshead at the Ball*), *Cretinetti al cinematografo* (*Foolshead Goes to the Movies*), *Cretinetti più del solito* (*Foolshead More Than Usual*), *La paura degli aeromobili nemici* (*Fear of Enemy Aircraft*), *Il duello di Flicot* (*Flicot's Duel*), *Kri Kri detective* (*Bloomer, Detective* or *Invincible Sleuth*), *Lea e il gomitolo* (*Leah and the Yarn*), *Kri Kri e la suocera* (*When a Man's Married*), *Kri Kri fuma l'oppio*

(*Bloomer Smokes Opium*), *Il calvario di Polidor* (*Polidor Gets His Way in the End*), *Polidor ha rubato l'oca* (*Polidor Steals a Goose*), *Polidor statua* (*Polidor a Statue*), *Il pranzo di Polidor* (*Polidor's Dinner*), *Polidor cambia sesso* (*Polidor Becomes a Woman*), *Robinet ama il ballo* (*Tweedledum Loves the Ball* [or *Dance*]), *L'abito bianco di Robinet* (*Tweedledum's White Suit*), *Robinet aviatore* (*Tweedledum as Aviator* or *Tweedledum, Aviator*), *La prima bicicletta di Robinet* (*Tweedledum on His First Bicycle*), *Robinet ha rubato cento lire* (*Tweedledum Has Stolen the Wrong Ticket*), *Tontolini cerca denaro* (*Tontolini Wants Money*), and *Tontolini a bagni di mare* (*Tontolini Goes to the Seaside*). As in literature, cinema placed comedy on a lower stylistic level. Comedies absorbed the odds and ends of other genres and, at least for a while, they never seemed to assert their narrative and expressive autonomy.

Of the most significant traits of the Italian comedy was its ability to offer an alternative to documentaries. Italian comic films documented the attitudes of lower- and upper-middle class society, which was still unable to cut its ties to nineteenth-century society, being traversed by social and modernist currents.

The Italian comedy was conceived as the equivalent of a humoristic rough draft. As in a circus clown act, the story was constructed around one action that was often catastrophic in nature. Italian comedies owed a good part of their success to their ability to parody and ridicule the imperfections of ritual and convention and the difficulties faced by the catechumen as he quickly learned the rules of bourgeois society.

Italian comedies tended to stop at the threshold of modernity as they tried to subvert the "bad taste" of Guido Gozzano's Nonna Speranza (Grandma Hope) and her parlor, although there were some notable exceptions: Anatmoro's *Pinocchio* (1911), with Ferdinand Guillaume; *Le avventure straordinarissime di Saturnino Farandola* (*The Extraordinary Adventures of Saturnino Farandola*, 1913), directed by and starring Marcel Fabre, a film that introduced Robida's graphic invention to the screen;[38] and *La paura degli aeromobili nemici* (*Fear of Enemy Aircraft*, 1915), *L'uomo meccanico* (*The Mechanical Man*, 1921), a post-futurist film directed by Andrè Reed. Unlike American comedies, Italian comic films offered precious and often enlightening insight into the attitudes of a society rising toward higher rungs in the social ladder while undergoing a visible transformation in its socio-anthropological behaviors. As a whole, Italian comic films were like a backward etiquette manual for the social climber in Liberty society. During a period of social turbulence in Italy, Fabre, Deed, Vaser, and Guillaume showed how it took more than merely buying a new hat or evening jacket or taking up a sport if you wanted to enter into a higher level of society. I have cited the four films above as exceptions for their fantastic inventions: a cross-contamination of genres and the freedom with which they adapted works of classic literature (for example, *Pinocchio*). They showed how the futurist spirit had descended upon the lowest of genres and how it sought to influence fantasy films and science fiction in terms of the modes and forms of human metamorphosis.

While Italian comedies showed the difficulty of climbing the social ladder, they never displayed a sense of social rebellion the way that Chaplin always did. Laughter and drama in Deed's films were the result of his inability to reach a level of competence that would guarantee his integration into the world that he parodied but greatly desired.

As World War I loomed on the horizon, comic films began to lose their direction and ability to understand social dynamics. Comic acting no longer met the needs of new potential situations. The war and then fascism all but restricted their access to such new situations. In the catastrophic crisis that followed, comedies were the first bodies to be sacrificed.

Femmes Fatales

In his famous painting of the *Woman in Three Stages* (1893–94), Edvard Munch depicted the woman in three phases by synthesizing and foreshadowing the phantasmal trinity of the woman dreamer, the lustful woman, and the monastic woman. This work was destined to dominate Italian cinematic imagery in the second decade of the twentieth century. It began with a small set of films with revealing titles: *Amore di Apache* (*An Adventurer's Love* [*The Love of an Apache*]), *Amore di madre* (*A Mother's Love*), *Amore di sirena* (*The Love of a Siren*), *Amore d'oltretomba* (*After Darkness, Light* [*Love in the Afterlife*]), *Amore e astuzia* (*Love and Craftiness*), and *Amore . . . voluttà . . . morte . . .* (*Love, Pleasure, and Death*). Made in 1912, these films offered a relatively broad phenomenology of the theme of love. In the years before the war, the power of armies and military might was rapidly replaced by the power of emotion and passion, due in great part to the support offered by the actresses' bodies. Sweet Ophelia and Melisande, Carmen and Salomè, Nanà and Lulú, Ibsen, Wedekind's creations, Zola and Barbey d'Aurevilly, and even D'Annunzio, Puccini, and Strindberg invented a new genre that was a child of opera, literature, and theater. It celebrated the absolute power of emotion and their primacy: "She loved him until death and even beyond!" was the final caption of *Ma l'amore mio non muore!* (*My Love Will Never Die!*). This film represented the coming together and cinematic metamorphosis of centripetal force derived from theater, opera, folktales, painting, poetry, and advertising design. Passion in all its forms—"fatal," savage, murky, gypsy, and Slavic; the "sins" of the mother, father, children, druggist, and others—found its ultimate condensation and embodiment in the silent song of the screen. Titles like *Amore e strategia* (*Love and Strategy*), *Amore e sacrificio* (*Love and Sacrifice*), and *Amore e raggiro* (*Love in a Tangle*) blended together with others like *Amore e libertà* (*For Love and Country* [*Love and Freedom*]), *Amore e patria* (*Love and Motherland*), and *Amore e guerra* (*Love and War*). Through the portrayal of the power of emotion, love as self-sacrifice, and their multiple morphology, these women were the *belles dames sans merci*, the merciless rulers of destinies for those unfortunate souls who happened to fall in love with them. They were demons who emerged from the collective fears of the European man's subconscious. They represented the female embodiment of the myth of Don Juan. They were exponents of modernity who, despite their humble means, ascended the social ladder, often paying a high price for their hybrid nature.

Sing, O Goddess . . .

These were the years when Cesare Lombroso published a book on delinquent women and another pseudo-scientific essay on the mental inferiority of women became an international bestseller. As Freud later observed, these were years when male libido substantially poured itself into the rituals of war. These were also the years when women became the quintessence of the forces of nature in Italian cinema and the new stars of the social and emotional scene. A woman who could not yet emancipate herself through hard work but who was determined to use her body as a commodity—and did, who chose her own sentimental destiny and the course of her entire life. A hyper-sexualized woman capable of wearing many masks as she journeyed toward redemption and beatification.

The star system found an ideal home in Italian cinema, where it cast its roots, developed, and received the genetic imprint of European culture.

It is a well-known fact that the star system has never received much attention from critics or Italian film historians. Not until the 1950s did scholars like Edgar Morin (and in Italy, Giulio Cesare Castello) offer the first trepid studies of the vast phenomenon and its specifics. Luckily, in recent years, this has changed and it is much easier to find interesting research conducted using firsthand sources. These studies have observed the system's complex network of connections and influences and have led to new interpretations.[39]

We have previously observed Italian cinema's dependence on and direct affiliation with nineteenth-century theater. But here we begin to sense an

emerging need to recognize the specifics and the ways in which the phenomenon had emancipated itself from the traditions of the stage and opera.

Our purpose here is to study the Italian star system as it quickly became
the guiding phenomenon for the rest of the world. In roughly five short years
leading up to World War I, Italian cinema saw the baptism and rapid, triumphant rise of the Italian star system—and then its catastrophic and irreversible
decline. At least in the beginning, it was like a proof ripped from the pages
of a manual on the theory of chance. No one foresaw the phenomenon, but
it expanded with great speed and played a decisive role in making cinema
the leading form of entertainment, a modifier of behavior, imagery, and the
collective consciousness. The early star system appeared suddenly in the cinematic firmament during the second decade of the twentieth century. Almost
all agree that the spark came from outside Italian cinema, with Asta Nielsen's
dance in the Danish film *Afrguden* (*The Abyss* or *The Woman Always Pays*,
1910). It ignited the phenomenon with the intensity and splendor of a super-
nova, quickly exploding into myriad fragments destined to reignite swiftly
over all of international cinema.

The Italian film star phenomenon was born and began to develop before
World War I. But it also benefited from a preliminary phase. Leopoldo Fregoli
represents the most conspicuous case of early Italian stardom. As early as 1897,
he recounts in his memoirs, he had the opportunity to meet Louis Lumière
and to explore the secrets of his laboratory.

The Lumières agreed to lend Fregoli their equipment and they gave him
a series of films. He decided to shoot (or rather, he decided to have a young
cameraman's apprentice, Luca Comerio, shoot) a few numbers from his
show ("Fregoli Pulls a Prank," "Fregoli Goes Out to Eat," "Fregoli's Dream").
But most important, he revealed the secrets of his transformation to the audience with his *Fregoli Behind the Scenes*, the first ever example of "backstage"
story. Cinema gave him the ability to officiate over the earliest case of ritual-
ized stardom: the camera invented by the Lumières became his publicity vehicle, a tool that helped him consolidate and expand his success, to build a
bridge between the widely popular cabaret genre and this newborn form
of entertainment.

But the true birth, explosion, triumphant rise, and irreversible decline of
the Italian star phenomenon took place between 1913 and 1920. It took its
first steps in Italy with *Ma l'amor mio non muore!* (*But My Love Will Never
Die!*), directed by Mario Caserini. As soon as it was released, this film created
a widespread secular cult by establishing visual archetypes, the morphology of
acting, and the vocabulary and syntax of emotions destined to become a point

of reference for many future sovereigns of Italian and international film. Lyda Borelli's influence on subsequent cinematic acting is comparable to that of Alamanno Morelli's nineteenth-century *Prontuario delle pose sceniche* (*Handbook of Theatrical Poses*). The added value was her stirring up the fires of romantic, melodramatic, decadent, and symbolist imagination all at once. Borelli entered the frame and invoked the viewer's gaze; with a single gesture, she sparked the collective desire: an immediate diva.

Today, the quality of restored versions is very good. Their relative resemblance to the original allows the viewer to redefine and measure the scope of the phenomenon's cultural influence and the radiant power of its international reach. They also make it possible to find analogies between opera, pictorial, and graphic movement and the songs and acting associated with superstardom. Thanks to close-ups and these superstars' style of acting, cinema became "a silent song": cinema seemed to fulfill Wagner's and Nietzsche's theory of the total work of art. The superstar phenomenon gave birth and legitimized the aesthetics of silence.

Using the "glorious bodies" of its stars, from Francesca Bertini to Lyda Borelli, from Pina Menichelli to Hesperia, from Leda Gys to Eleonora Duse, cinema constructed a monument to contemporary culture and transformed societal attitudes in films like *Ma l'amore mio non muore!* (*But My Love Will Never Die*), *Rapsodia satanica* (*Satan's Rhapsody*), *La memoria dell'altro* (*The Memory of the Other One*), *Tigre reale* (*The Royal Tigress*), *Odette*, *Maddalena Férat* (*Madeleine Férat*), *Il fuoco* (*The Fire*), *Thaïs*, *Perfido incanto* (*The Wicked Enchantment*), *La signora dalle camelie* (*The Lady of the Camellias*), *Malombra*, *Cenere* (*Ashes*), *Assunta Spina*, *La serpe* (*The Serpent*), *Storia di una donna* (*The Story of a Woman*), *La donna nuda* (*The Naked Woman*), *Il fauno* (*The Faun*), *Fior di male* (*Flower of Evil*), and dozens of other titles.

Italian divas radiated a light that transcended cinematic space. They resembled prismatic bodies, emitting light from a variety of sources. At times, they seemed priestesses of the liberty style, symbolism, and the culture of D'Annunzio and Puccini. At others, heiresses to the sovereigns of nineteenth-century theater, or daughters of the stars of pre-Raphaelite painting, or sisters to the women created by painters like Burne-Jones and Arthur Hacker, illustrators like Mucha, Dudovich, and Cappiello, and sculptors like Rutelli and Canonica.

The diva asserted her newfound rights. She overturned centuries-old values and models. She revealed new dimensions of the human spirit. She revitalized romantic imagery, which had been put on guard by positivist culture, and she reaffirmed its relevance in an era where the great models of virility were provided by war.

The crowds of viewers scattered across the world shared the emigrant's dream of the promised land. For them, the star phenomenon opened up new dreams of conquest and horizons of desire, and it allowed them to contemplate territories previously considered taboo. And it also made visible the dark zones of the subconscious.

As the direct inheritors of the theatrical prima donna, the divas set in motion a series of new phenomena: in the eyes of the masses and the collective imagination, these icons took the place of the men-symbols—now more distant and blurry.

Once again, D'Annunzio was the prophet of this transition. As one of the first European intellectuals to understand the mythopoetic power of the mass media, he was the inventor of a series of spectacular public events and of roles destined to become reproducible and imitable models of an "inimitable life," even in cinema. Beyond D'Annunzio, other leading figures of the theater decided to head toward the new promised land of entertainment, a medium that all but directly changed linguistic and theatrical modes. These included Giovanni Grasso, Ermete Novelli, Ermete Zacconi, Giacinta Pezzana, Eleonora Duse, and Lyda Borelli.

Besides D'Annunzio and other central characters like Andrea Sperelli and Elena Nuti, who starred in the film version of his novel *Il piacere* (*The Child of Pleasure*, written in 1889), other important figures included Alphonse Mucha (in *Ma l'amore mio non muore!*, *Il fuoco*, *La serpe*, etc.), Arnold Böcklin (*Rapsodia satanica*), Maurice Maeterlinck, Von Hofmannsthal, Whistler, Moreau, Alberto Martini, Augusto Majani, the fabric of Mariano Fortuny, the works of Fogazzaro and Dumas *fils*, the symbolist and crepuscular poetry of Fausto Maria Martini, the sculptures of Rodin, and the historic canvases of the pre-Raphaelites. The fragmented muscular bodies of dozens of artists and the fluttering atoms of mystic-erotic iconography all fed or formed the backdrop for the apparitions of these divas.

It was a cinematic Olympus inhabited solely by women for all intents and purposes. Men were blurry, secondary figures. The few exceptions were not sufficient to mount an opposing force (these included Bartolomeo Pagano as the Maciste who was catapulted from the third century BC to the present, to end wars and to cure the ills of society with his fists and a small band of slaves; there were also Emilio Ghione, André Deed, and a small group of comedians).

An army of Eves and Temptresses, Sirens, Ophelias, Circes, Dianas, and Salomès, graceful figures with prehensile lips like the petals of a flesh-eating flower, with an eye capable of killing or paralyzing like a Medusa, they arrived on horses made of light. They converged toward the screen and took possession of the hearts of filmmakers and viewers alike. From *Ma l'amor mio non muore!* to *Storia di una donna* and *Fior di male*, cinema distilled the humors and restored the aromas and spirit of one's own cultural artistic habitat—at both the core and the surface. Borelli's long locks seemed taken from Dante Gabriel Rossetti's *Beata Beatrix*. Bertini's close-ups seemed reproductions of paintings by Klimt (in *Salomè* especially). While Borelli's movements in *Rapsodia satanica* (1917) brought to mind jewels or compositions by Lalique and Tiffany, recurring images of the woman-tigress or the woman-leopardess were allusions to paintings by Fernand Khnopff, as in *La sfinge* (*The Sphinx*), for example. In films like *Carnevalesca* (*Carnivalesque*), Borelli's appearances brought to life the characters painted by Boldini and De Nittis. Francesca Bertini's death in *Odette*, Pina Menichelli's passion in *Il fuoco* and *Tigre reale*, Soava Gallone, Maria Jacobini, and the other divas reminded viewers of John Everett Millais's *Ophelia*, Beardsley's *Salomè*, John William Goodward's *The Toilette*, or posters by Chéret and Mucha, or the most important representatives of art nouveau, from Hoffmann to Guimard and Horta.

But the phenomenon must not be reduced to a pure overflowing of form or to the metamorphosis of an iconographic or poetical system. If it were, we would not understand its reach and international influence. The collective machine of desire was unleashed by a series of celebrations of the strength of the senses, of sex and the laws of nature that women were able to interpret as they became priestesses and willful victims of all the rites carried out in honor of Eros. These included the opportunity to imitate even the smallest elements of the female star: a gesture, fashion, toasting, hugging, kissing.

Among fundamental literary, artistic, and theatrical archetypes and grammar, the following can be identified. In part, they correspond to the four elements: earth, air, water, and fire.

1) The *belle dame sans merci*, the femme fatale parodied by Collette in some of her most memorable pages and later defined as female vampire ("Vamp," who found her ideal actress in Theda Bara), the cruel and merciless dominator of the destiny of men who entered into the radius of her gaze, a rapacious and merciless being (Pina Menichelli shined in these roles, as we clearly see in *Fuoco* and in *Tigre reale*, even though she also knew how to transform herself into a sweet, submissive lover like Turandot).

2) The *femme de nulle part*, the mysterious beauty, the woman without roots or certain identity (besides the characters played by Musidora, in my opinion, Lil Dagover is the actress who loved to play roles of this type, roles that Elena Makowska took on in Italian cinema).

3) The demonic woman; Mérimée's *Carmen* and Bizet as portrayed by Pola Negri; Verga's *La lupa* (the "She-Wolf"); Alba d'Almaviva in *Rapsodia satanica*;

Maria the deceiver in *Metropolis*; the serpent-woman played by Bertini in *Serpe*, a character who led her victims down the road of perdition in accordance with the principles of Catholic morality.

4) The woman who makes the most of her body and uses it as a factory or small business, like Wedekind's and Pabst's Lulú, Zola's Nanà, the lost woman, but also the deSadian fallen angels like the main characters of *Via senza gioia* (*Street without Joy*) and *Diario di una donna perduta* (*Diary of a Lost Girl*), and the character played by Lya de Putti in *Varieté*.

5) The mother, depositor and guarantor of family values and even the Fatherland; here, the gallery ranges from Duse in *Cenere* (*Ashes*) to Soava Gallone in *Maman Poupée* (*Mother Doll*), to Henny Porten in dozens of roles, and to the great Bernhardt in *Mères françaises* (*Mothers of France*).

6) The sweet descendants of Ophelia and Cinderella, the lovesick woman who suffers in the shadows and is ready to sacrifice her love on the altar of social laws and who in some cases can also be rewarded. In Italian cinema, *Addio giovinezza!* (*Goodbye to Youth!*) and *Scampolo* (*Street Urchin*) are examples of this.

7) The butterfly, the chaste woman free to express herself through the language of her body and through a body devoted to the religion of dance and art, a woman whose greatest representative would be Loie Fuller (her serpentine dance performances were immortalized by early twentieth-century cinema); she inspired the butterfly movements in dances by Lyda Borelli in *Rapsodia satanica* and by Mistinguett, Paulette Paulaire, and Josephine Baker in the 1920s.

By exploring close-ups and seeking out close contact, cinema was able to glimpse the "beyond" of which the camera-operator Serafino Gubbio speaks in Pirandello's 1916 *Quaderni di Serafino Gubbio* (*The Notebooks of Serafino Gubbio*). It was capable of perceiving meaningful elements of the internal landscape and it had the privilege, unique in the figurative arts, of capturing the *photogénie* of which Louis Delluc wrote in regard to Italian women stars following World War I.

The memory of Lyda Borelli's performance is tied to scenes and moments in which the moving image seemed to come to a stop, a moment when it became a painting, a sculpture, a song. But the memory is also linked to an internalization of acting and to the physicality of communication. In many cases, it is also bound to the power of eroticism as revealed by Gramsci as early as 1916. Today, we cannot help but admire the attempt to make visible the movements of the psyche, the dissociation of personality, and the storms of the soul through the language of the body. From her debut film, Borelli performed a series of movements using her arms and body that symphonically modulated an entire range of emotions, from falling in love, to love itself, to overwhelming passion. In *Rapsodia satanica*, her arms spread like a butterfly's as if to free her body from the veils, and she reached a new benchmark of stylization (reminiscent of Loie Fuller and Isadora Duncan) that surpassed that of the graphic arts, the applied arts, poetry, and dance. In the central part of the film, when the star feels "desire beating at the doors of her heart" and surrenders to the "delirium of youth," her acting and her body manage to produce a ritualistic communion with the audience in a most solemn manner. Borelli was the diva who best managed to guide her viewers into the labyrinths and darkest zones of emotion and desire. Adapted from the novel by Antonio Fogazzaro (published as *The Woman* in English), *Malombra* represents one of the few Italian Gothic films in this sense.[40] It responded to internal voices and its character risked everything—even life itself—for a fleeting moment of love. In most of her films, the heroine is a superwoman who could compete with the superman of D'Annunzio (or, for that matter, Nietzsche's, Lombroso's, Nordau's, or Wagner's). Even through existential lethargy and crises, she was affected by a bulimia that invigorated her. In *Rapsodia satanica*, Borelli, like Faust, was not afraid to make a pact with the devil in order to obtain eternal youth.

While Borelli was born as a Minerva, a diva from the moment she first appeared on the screen, Francesca Bertini needed time to evolve. Cinema embraced her micro-physiognomy, her extreme malleability, and her chameleon-like ability to play a socially diverse array of characters. She also possessed a wide emotional range and could change registers and styles, switching with extreme ease from comedy to realistic drama, from melodrama to tragedy.[41] Her portrayal of Assunta Spina, in the eponymous film by Gustavo Serena, is worthy of appearing in the anthology of history's greatest roles. The power of her interpretation touched every object surrounding her. While Borelli was the leading actor of symbolist and liberty culture, Bertini, above and beyond her stardom, was a versatile, modern actor: her example lived on and would be inherited by future stars like Greta Garbo and Anna Magnani.

The unstoppable effect of the Puccini syndrome would become one of the common denominators of star-driven filmography. The operatic tradition would ultimately become linked to the problems of modernity as it sought to breach evolutionary and psychoanalytic theories.[42]

The movie-going public nourished its imagination with heroines for whom "amor vincit omnia." For the most part, those characters were sisters of D'Annunzio's "admirable beasts" and Puccini's heroines of the "vie de Bohème." These characters seem to validate Remy de Gourmont's theories on the similarities between the sexual behaviors of the animal world and those of a human species whereby only the call to mate is of value. The same holds for Cesare Lombroso's theories, published in 1893, regarding "delinquent women" in which he equated feminine beauty with a pre-development, almost savage, state. Puccini's heroines were innocent and pure, but then became delirious in search of the "dérèglement de tous les sens." They were the sweetest of mothers denied of their motherhood, and then they became women capable of loving "up until death, and then beyond." One could even say they prevailed in a field of women who sought to fulfill primitive, destructive instincts. They refused to accept their destiny as victims and instead took the road toward madness.

Whether burial at sea or in a grave covered with flowers (as in Millais's *Ofelia*), whether in a hospital cot, in a straw bed, or underneath a canapé, it would take a hecatomb of female sex symbols and the world they represented to allow the birth of a new woman in the 1920s. With actors like Karenne, Jacobini, Vergani, Boni, and Gys, this "girl-next-door" lacked aura but would lead viewers down new paths, pointing them toward new horizons (however modest but accessible) of collective desire.

Men as Sex Symbols: Masks and Bodies

Emilio Ghione was one of the two male actors (the other is Bartolomeo Pagano as Maciste in *Cabiria*) who were able to rival the fame and success of the top divas during the war. At the same time, his films are even more striking today for the power of their settings and the distinctness of their landscapes. "There is more Italy," wrote Umberto Barbaro, "in Emilio Ghione and Kally Sambucini's *I topi grigi* [*The Gray Mice*] than in any other Italian film from that period."[43] But it is not just the realism of *I topi grigi* that strikes us today. The contemporary viewer will also be impressed with the surprisingly good directing and the original acting, rooted in a technique of stylization and understatement. Just as with its expressionist style of acting, the film's apparitions have a symbolic charge that prevails over its realism. Za-la-Mort's skeletal mask matches perfectly with the clothes and beret, but it also becomes camouflaged, changing into a stone or the bark of a tree, blending in with the landscape.

In 1913, Ghione directed his first film, *Idolo infranto* (*The Fallen Idol*), with Francesca Bertini. For all of 1914, he worked for the Caesar film studio in Rome, where he was able to display his preference for works based on the glory of nineteenth-century popular literature and feuilletons. His models were French detective films and dramas. In the years that followed, he worked for L'Aquila Film, where he offered audiences works like *Ciceruacchio* and

Oberdan, together with adventure films inspired by the success of French serials, and in particular the *Fantomas* and *Judex* series.

Beginning with films like *Nelly la gigolette ovvero La danzatrice della Taverna Nera* (*Nelly the Gigolette or The Dancer of the Black Tavern*), in which the character Za-la-Mort made his first appearance, *Anime buie* (*Dark Souls*, 1915), and *La banda delle cifre* (*The Numbers Gang*, a story told in three installments), Ghione's financial and popular success seemed to grow exponentially. Za-la-Mort would soon be joined by his inseparable companion, Za-la-Vie, played by Kally Sambucini, who had a remarkable ability to combine femininity and strength, gifts that certainly did not make her look bad compared to her American counterparts.

The most famous series of all, *I topi grigi* (*The Gray Mice*), placed Ghione in the Mount Olympus of early Italian film stardom. Produced by Tiber, the story was subdivided into eight episodes, inspired by characters Rocambole and Fantomas. Ghione remained faithful to the figure of the criminal who respected the code of honor and who could carry out his own personal justice. He did not do so in order to disrupt the peace, but rather, to remedy egregious injustices. Although they portray criminal acts of all sorts, Ghione's films always were centered in morality, loyalty, friendship, and love. His characters helped the weak and spurned the world of the rich. These elements were entirely missing in his contemporaries' films, which celebrated fatal passions, man-eating women, and femmes fatales. More often than not, in the moments of greatest dramatic tensions, his characters turned their thoughts to idyllic country life. "Silent, little white welcoming house," reads the caption in the second episode, *La tortura* (*Torture*), "piping-hot soup, ladled daily as you travel farther and farther away."

For their interior shots, most cameramen wrapped their characters in soft light and modulated the chiaroscuros. They made the air seemingly vibrate and cast the blond heads of the starlets in a halo of light, embracing the drama in warm light that kept their sensuality at a perfect temperature. Ghione, on the other hand, set his stories against the squalor of the outskirts of town, although he continuously changed the backdrop, able to pass seamlessly from the country and the pleasant outlines of the hills to the darkest depths of the metropolis and the demimonde of the interiors of aristocratic palazzos. Most important, he used the camera to create harsh light, violent and devoid of chiaroscuros, with crisp contrast. Such lighting accentuated the characters' angular features and made the misery of the backdrop all the more abrasive and painful.

Some have observed in *I topi grigi* an immediacy and objectivity missing in the romantically picturesque *Assunta Spina*. Today, the term *realism* seems less applicable to Ghione's work. At the same time, the category of fantastic imagination and its myriad perspectives help in understanding the counterpoint in Ghione, who has been banished from the world of nobility, and to fathom the backdrops he favored for his characters. In many instances, the setting became the character and took on a true narrative autonomy. The colors and elasticity of the settings were so marked that they left little space for social commentary. But such a miserable Italy cannot be found in any of his contemporaries' films, not even in those shot in Naples.

Success made Ghione a prisoner of his characters and he would remain bound to his Za-la-Mort like Christ to the cross, to borrow an expression used by the actor himself. "His," wrote Curzio Malaparte in 1937, "was a true Pirandellian drama."[44] Petrolini liked to say that his character Gastone had been ruined by war and women. To this Ghione responded that he had been ruined by Za-la-Mort.

The Realist Legacy

In the minds of Italian and foreign viewers alike, historical films created grandiose worlds that celebrated and reaffirmed Italy's powerful role as the beacon of civilization. Although it shed no light on the real Italy, the path paved by these films became a transitional point and fundamental framework for the creation of fascist practices and rituals. Such works offered fascism what would become its traditions and deepest ideological roots—on a silver platter.

During the phase of its full-fledged development, Italian cinema was marked by the shared presence of multiple directions and elements in its stylistic and narrative development. At this time, however, the realist component was marginal and weak and would only become substantial and truly visible in the far distance.

Although other movie genres did not play a leading role during this phase, they certainly merit the scholarly attention (studies by Antonio Costa illuminated these; see his work in I leoni di Schneider [Schneider's Lions]). Their rich variety helped to redraw the map of Italian film genre: from the fantastic to the Gothic, these films were best represented by Saturnino Farandola's adventure films and Gallone's Malombra.

Not until the second half of the 1930s (also due to the writings of Umberto Barbaro and other critics who published in the journal Cinema) would Nino Martoglio's Sperduti nel buio (Lost in the Dark) become a "mythical locus."[45] Based on the eponymous play by Roberto Bracco, this film became a mandatory destination in the critical, poetical, and theoretical pilgrimage. This film embraced Italy's literary and figurative heritage, providing a direction for the future of Italian cinema. The only known copy of *Sperduti nel buio* was lost in a train car after 1943, together with other films seized by the German army at the Centro Sperimentale in Rome.

Directed by Martoglio, the film was part of a trilogy of works produced by Morgan Film (the others, *Capitan Blanco* [*Captain Blanco*] and *Teresa Raquin*, based on Zola's *Thérèse Raquin*, also known as *The Adulteress* in English). The principal actors were Giovanni Grasso, Virginia Balistrieri, and Maria Carmi, while the star of *Teresa Raquin* was the great Giacinta Pezzana, who had played the part with immense success on the stage some forty years earlier. All three of these films were lost. But even without them, it is clear that they played a central role in the formation of geniuses destined for significant development in the future of Italian film.[46]

The only film from the naturalist genre to be saved in its entirety was *Assunta Spina*, with Bertini. A recently restored print allows us to admire its stylistic accomplishment, the excellent acting, and its ability to stand on its own even today. This film satisfied the camera's natural hunger for reality and showed that drama and tragic passion could also be found in the world of the proletariat.

Such works represent an anachronistic centrifugal subset when compared to the dominant tendencies of films that sprung from the works of D'Annunzio and from liberty and symbolist culture. Gauging from the attitudes of the producers, critics, and censors, it is clear that these films (together with less financial successful productions and those less in step with the times) were seen as suspect and were held back because of their social precariousness. Albeit for just the *éspace d'un matin*, it only took a handful of counterculture movies to tip the expressive scales of early Italian cinema.

Italian cinema had natural realist leanings and a tendency to work *en plein air* using the immediate surroundings and objects (although without relying on them or their potentially noble significance). These elements, and its need to use the movie camera to read the dramas written on the faces of common people, possessed a natural strength missing from more complex dramatic works with sophisticated sets and acting. On one hand, certain productions celebrated fatal passions and Roman glory, and in doing so, aspired to a higher level. On the other hand, realistic films descended toward the lowest levels of mimesis and could often be confused with comedies and documentaries. These films, however, revived the models of the bards and storytellers. Through their mixture of styles, these works rediscovered tragedy and pathos.

Despite the many adverse factors, the one film that survived, *Assunta Spina*, allows scholars to establish a bridge between these films and the Tuscan *macchiaioli* painters and a highly significant moment in the strongest tendencies in Italian cinema.

Deconstructing and Reconstructing
the Cinematic Universe: The Futurist Word

It may seem like a paradox: while futurism, the singer of modernity, was able to perceive and intuit the power of cinema on theoretical and poetical levels, it did not manage to use this new means of expression as a weapon—nor did it appropriate cinema as the art form of all art forms.[47] At the same time, as Giovanni Lista has shown, futurism was greatly influenced by its "multiple assimilations from cinema and its methods," by the use of close-ups, overlays, and editing within the frame, by the dynamization of movement, and by the unconventional cuts of images.[48]

Every study of the influences of cinema on twentieth-century literature and figurative arts begins with the futurist nucleus and its apparent inability to translate cinematic poetics in an immediately applicable and striking manner. The futurists themselves steadfastly affirmed cinema's artistic autonomy: "Cinema is an art unto itself. Therefore, cinema must never copy the stage. By virtue of its essentially visual nature, cinema must fulfill the evolution of painting: it must detach itself from reality and from photography."[49]

Thus, for entire groups of artists and intellectuals who wanted their works to reflect the rhythms and tempos of modernity, the silver screen became a form of Freudian transfer for collective desire. More than anything else, these artists wanted to launch themselves forward, to suppress the traditional time-space coordinates, and to inhabit the future. From the futurists to the surrealists and the constructionists, the discourse on cinema and its potential seemed to associate cinema with their desire to create a "total" work of art (*Gesamtkunstwerk*) and the power to create tactile, visual, aural, and olfactory sensations in ways that no other form of artistic expression had previously achieved. But futurism preceded all of this. In articles published in *La testa di Ferro* (December 26, 1920) and *L'Impero* (1926), Marinetti was partly correct when he claimed that futurist cinema had preceded avant-garde cinema and films like *Entr'acte* and *La roue*, among others:

> Marinetti's films and the *Manifesto* appeared in 1916: they preceded, by far, the theory and praxis of the French "discovery." Thus, it is clear that we were

the first to produce so-called bourgeois cinema, and we can rightly claim to also have been the first to produce avant-garde films. Those devils had invented certain effects that, at the time, were astonishing: the result was a comic absurdity that not even the Americans could have outdone . . . Despite its intemperance and contradictions, the *Manifesto* was nonetheless rich with insights so exact that these foreign theorists only restated them without adding anything new.[50]

In a commentary on the international debut of *Vita futurista* (*Futurist Life*) in Florence, published in *L'Italia futurista*, Emilio Settimelli had proclaimed exultantly: "Regardless of what might have been said or not, the performance that we gave at the Nicolini [theater] marks a turning-point for international art . . . Ours is no more than an attempt. And a modest attempt at that. But the credit for the first flight in this direction goes to and remains that of Futurism . . . Fortunately for us, the time has disappeared for those who only know how to create art using roses, 'white marble,' and glorious bronze."[51]

Now lost, *Vita futurista* was the only film produced in 1916 at the Cascine di Firenze hippodrome by a futurist group led by Emilio Settimelli. All that is left of this film are a few posters and frames and some detailed accounts of their evenings there. Thus, the first true cinematic act was the *Manifesto della cinematografia futurista* (*Manifesto of Futurist Cinema*), published the same year, even though the Ginanni-Corradini brothers (better known as Ginna and Corra) had begun to experiment with the "music of colors" and produced four abstract films in 1911 in which they tried to create chromatic harmonies and visual music: *Accordo di colore* (*Harmony of Color*), *Canto di primavera*, *Les Fleurs* (*The Flowers*), and *Studio di effetti tra quattro colori* (*Study of the Effects between Four Colors*). In 1912, Corra himself called cinema a "true chromatic symphony."[52] The year before, Anton Giulio Bragaglia coined the term *fotodinamismo* (photodynamism) as he was experimenting with photographic decomposition of movement.[53] Upon closer examination, the Corradini brothers had not yet completed a definitive move to futurism; their experiences seemed more infused with Wagnerian spirit than with the Marinettian word. Their experiments were aborted soon after birth, when they were quickly disavowed by Umberto Boccioni, who disparagingly accused them of "cerebrality." Later, similarities were observed between their films and Fabre's *Amor pedestre* (*Pedestrian Love*, 1914) and Marinetti's *Le basi* (*The Bases* or *The Feet*, 1915). The chronology of these films indicates that they inspired the futurists.

Aldo Molinari's 1914 film *Mondo baldoria* (*Revelry World*) was an "unauthorized" attempt to interpret the futurist spirit. It was immediately condemned by Marinetti, who, perhaps following this episode, was compelled to crystallize his vision of the relationship between cinema and futurism in an ad hoc *Manifesto*. Many scholars hold that the *Manifesto* is an early document of a poetics that would become a guide for all subsequent avant-garde cinema. In it, the author declares that cinema is a magic instrument capable of creating cosmogonies and opening perspectives that other art forms cannot: "It is necessary to liberate cinema so that it becomes the ideal instrument of a new and immeasurable art, vaster and more agile than any before it . . . In futurist film, the most disparate elements will be used as means of expression: from slices of real life to spots of color, from the line to words in freedom, from chromatic and plastic music to the music of objects . . . We will decompose and recompose the universe as our wondrous whims strike us."

In Italy, futurism found ideal players and directors like Luca Comerio, who went as early as 1911 to capture images from the war in Libya, or cameramen who installed their cameras in airplanes. As Paul Virilio has noted, these filmmakers poised themselves with their mechanical eye to redefine the world and discover its new tempos and rhythms.[54] There are clear aesthetic affinities between Marinetti's poems like "Monoplano del papa" ("The Pope's Monoplane" or "The Pope's Airplane," 1910) and "Il bombardamento di Adrianopoli" ("The Bombardment of Adrianopole") and Comerio's early films. Before they sang the lights and rhythms of the cities, filmmakers discovered the beauty of the nighttime lights of machine guns and cannon blasts. Marinetti took his first flight to the Libyan front in 1912: it is highly likely that his emotions and imagination were in perfect step with those of director Comerio, who put his hand-cranked camera into action from the heights of that very same sky.

The only Italian film that can be defined as futurist (albeit loosely) is *Thaïs* (1917), directed by Anton Giulio Bragaglia, who used Enrico Prampolini's abstract, geometric script for the work's final part. The rigor of straight and curved lines and the symbols and images used to create the main character's dreams were not, however, a bowing to futurist poetics. Bragaglia's film was a transitional work and its screenplay was nothing but a stylized variation based on contemporary films by Camillo Innocenti, Duilio Cambellotti, and Aristide Sartorio. With marked understatement, Bragaglia himself wrote of his experience: "My modest attempt, combined with the absolute lack of means, was by no means intended to be, nor could then have been, a notable film. Modern screenwriting is so multiform that it makes my first cinematic work look like a joke."[55]

The failure of the futurist project was due to both the lack of technical competence and the impossibility of reconciling the industry's production and distribution needs with the poetics of the group. The film *Vita futurista*

would become a seminal model not only for futurist poetics but also for independent filmmaking.

Although it appeared as one of the latter documents of the movement,
the cinematic manifesto represents a central moment of expansion and a focal
point for understanding the cinematic universe. The *Manifesto* ignited a process of atomic fission and although its effects were not comparable to those
achieved in other artistic fields, it helped shape the entire international cinematic landscape.

In examining and comparing the different programs and directorial practices of the avant-garde, it seems that everything had been previously declared
and predicted in the futurist text, a document capable of illuminating the
works of Hans Richter and Dziga Vertov, Man Ray and Viking Eggeling, Ger-
maine Dulac and Louis Delluc, René Clair and Luis Buñuel.

Cinema in the 1920s, between Imminent Catastrophe and the Fascist Transformation of Italy

On January 9, 1919, with the support of the Banca Italiana di Sconto (Italian
Discount Bank) and the Banca Commerciale Italiana (Italian Commercial
Bank), the charter of the first cinematic trust was signed, the Società Anonima
Unione Cinematografica Italiana (UCI [Italian Cinematic Union, Private
Corporation]), headquartered in Rome, with 30 million lire in capital stock,
a sum that would soon be doubled. The UCI united the most prestigious Italian brand names, and it enjoyed conspicuous financial resources, thanks to
the liquidity of the banks following World War I and support from the financial world.[56] Unfortunately, the new organization had no project other than
that of producing a warehouse of titles that would prove difficult to sell and
would never be seen.

Vittorio Martinelli's survey of Italian cinema in the postwar era shows
that, except for the comedies and colossal historical-mythological films, all
the genres appear to have surpassed the conflict's trial by fire.[57] Film production was in full swing, despite the signs of irreversible losses with foreign and
domestic audiences.

Relying on films featuring Italian divas, film production during the tenure
of the UCI borrowed heavily from popular literature, feuilleton, serialized stories, and theatrical repertoires. With an increasingly structural role, the theme
of slave labor came to the forefront in an attempt to plug the leaks in the
sinking ship.[58]

Among the many causes of this crisis (disorganization, unpredictability, increases in costs due to stars' ever-growing demands, an end to the development of new technology, the loss of foreign markets, and the inability to compete with foreign production),[59] one of the most significant was the lack of generational renewal. On both thematic and narrative levels, Italian cinema remained the prisoner of producers and directors who were overly conditioned by the word. The same men who just a few years earlier had dominated world markets now seemed no longer able to break new ground, incapable of conceiving products for an international market. In a memo to Guido Pedrazzini, the president of Cines, American distributor Kleine wrote that producers who wanted to conquer the American market needed to keep in mind that the Italian style of acting, just like the types of stories that appealed to "Latin" audiences, held no interest for American audiences.[60] In essence, Kleine was explaining to Pedrazzini that the international success of The Three Musketeers was due not to Alexandre Dumas but to Douglas Fairbanks.

At a certain point, it seemed that the many different players on the field—producers, directors, actors, critics, and audiences—were incapable of communication. Italian critics declared their disdain for the feuilleton, the serials, and the films based on popular literature, and they were quick to make merciless comparisons with foreign cinema. Such disorientation continued to grow because of the UCI's excessive policy of accumulating titles and the hemorrhaging of technicians and laborers who were attracted by and left for other European countries. The political situation, the imminent March on Rome, and fascist conquest of power were additional elements that stirred the already fragile cinematic organism, which had already been undermined by various ills.

The industry continued to cling steadfastly to literature and theater for inspiration. Save for a few exceptions, the last wave of female movie stars triumphed in the postwar era. This female-dominated cinema revealed a gallery of figures who lived on the margins of society. Instead of fighting for emancipation, as they did in American cinema, they battled endlessly to defend their personal virtue, more likely to invoke the aid of providence than that of society. It was a cinema of verbal and visual transgressions but with no change of roles, a cinema in which the Puccini syndrome triumphed: "Everything belongs to him, me included," says the star of Biondina (Blondie, 1923), based on the novel by Marco Praga and directed by Amleto Palermi. Such characters accepted a social game that had all but vanished from European society. Eugenio Perego's 1919 Storia di una donna (Story of a Woman) is a classic example. Although it employed a new narrative structure (the main character's diary is discovered after her death and reveals a series of chapters in her story constructed like the Stations of the Cross), it nonetheless mixed various storytelling models and once again proposed a nineteenth-century, melodramatic moralist tale.

After endless Calvaries in which the heroines were mistreated, beaten, tortured, raped, humiliated, wrongly accused, abandoned together with their newborns, or forced to abandon their illegitimate children, the prize for their misfortunes was either death (often by the hand of the abandoned child, as in Perego's film) or confinement to a convent. Their strength in enduring all types of spiritual and physical pain was rewarded at best with recognition of their roles as mother or wife. No protest or rebellion was allowed. Such reactionary (embodied by the overwhelmingly popular *Über den physiologischen Schwachsinn des Weibes* [*On the Psychological Deficiency of Women*] by Paul Möbius, published in 1900) was well-represented in these films. It complemented the Puccini-derived model in which the lead female characters were caught in the vortex of passion and were ready for just about anything—primarily, self-sacrifice for the sake of their beloved.

This immense crowd of women lacked the strength necessary to attract, galvanize, and seduce audiences with their performances and light of their faces. Above all, these characters did not have the power to subjugate their viewers. The exceptions were Leda Gys and the city of Naples as the backdrop, beginning with *Miracolo* (*Miracle*, 1920) and then *Vedi Napule e po' mori!* (*See Naples and Then Die*, 1924) and *Napule . . . e niente cchiú* (*Naples . . . and Nothing More*, 1928). As producer Gustavo Lombardo developed the tradition of Neapolitan filmmaking, he fostered her gifts for directness, freshness, and vital energy, and her sympathetic personality. Gys was the first lady of Neapolitan film and she stood apart from the models, by then abandoned, provided by star/starlets Bertini and Borelli.[61]

As if propelled by a strong sense of *cupio dissolvi*, the studios increased production just as the market was beginning to shrink. The number of films doubled and tripled; the stars' salaries grew exponentially.

The rivalry between the two men at the helm of the UCI, lawyers Giuseppe Mecheri and Giuseppe Barattolo, only accelerated its collapse. The early death of the former and the latter's illusions of grandeur, combined with inexperience and a poor understanding of the market, sped them down the road to catastrophe. The final blow came with the 1921 bankruptcy of the Banca Italiana di Sconto. As late as 1921, there were 350 films approved by the censors, but by 1924, this number had dropped to barely 60. By the time the first talkies appeared, the number of UCI films could be counted on one hand.

Just as the number of Italian titles was decreasing, American filmmaking underwent a period of Malthusian growth, as did the size of audiences and the cost of production. In 1924, figures provided by the Società Italiana Autori Editori (SIAE [Italian Association of Authors and Editors]) reveal that cinema, with 39 percent of overall spending, had become the most popular form of entertainment. Five years later, it represented 62 percent of spending in entertainment industry in Italy.

For all intents and purposes, even though there was no real plan or strategy, American cinema's march on Rome coincided almost perfectly with the rise of the Black Shirts. In the summer of 1923, United Artists opened an office in Rome and it did not take long for the other major studios to follow suit. The history of Italian cinema during this period can be viewed as a history of cinematic imagery, memory, and the outpouring and fostering of the desires, dreams, passions, and hopes of millions of moviegoers. And for a decade and a half, this history mirrored the popularity and consumption of American cinema in Italy.[62]

The only Italian tycoon who was up to the task of creating a de facto vertical monopoly was Stefano Pittalunga, who was able to do so through his business interests in production, distribution, and theater ownership. Pittaluga was a gargantuan figure of the 1920s and his foresight and lobbying would affect the relationship between Italian filmmakers and the government for decades to come. Another figure whose role must not be discounted was Gustavo Lombardo, who not only managed to survive the crisis but also to keep Neapolitan cinema alive. Drawing from theatrical, folkloric, and naturalist models, he continued to make films deeply rooted in the reality of life in Naples without interruption, all the while keenly aware of changes in viewers' tastes.

With each passing year, Italian cinema began to lose contact with audiences as the response to the films waned. This was true for colossal films, like Leopoldo Carlucci's *Teodora* (1922); Mario Corsi and Ugo Falena's *Frate Sole* (*Brother Sun*, 1918); *Nave*, directed by Gabriellino d'Annunzio and based on the novel by his father (*The Ship*, 1921); Georg Jacoby and Gabriellino d'Annunzio's *Quo Vadis?* (1924); and Carmine Gallone's *Gli ultimi giorni di Pompei* (*The Last Days of Pompeii*, 1926). This was also true of films based on dramas by Tolstoy, Daudet, Ibsen, and Pirandello, as well those drawn from popular literature like *Il ponte dei sospiri* by Domenico Gaido and films that borrowed from or were inspired by novels by Emilio Salgari, Eugène Sue, and Ponson du Terrail.

For the modern viewer, who is often predisposed to wonderment and unconditional acceptance of any film that has been saved and restored from the silent era, the most striking element in even the most spectacular films is the nearly absolute lack of linguistic and expressive evolution with respect to earlier films. The captions interrupt the rhythm and the casts of thousands seem unaware that in the meantime the world has seen D. W. Griffith's editing—and not just his.

With the many 1920s films that have been restored, which can now be viewed in nearly ideal conditions, and the many attempts to study them, it is important to keep in mind that this enormous group of Italian films—more than 1,500 titles—has almost vanished from the historical memory without a trace. Scholars must recognize that the well-intentioned movement to restore these films, however productive and worthy of encouragement, will not bring about a fundamental change in the evaluation of Italian cinema in relation to that of other countries.

Studies of the fascist transformation of Italian cinema have also revealed the lack of cultural and creative substance in films that attempted to emulate fascist ideology, to celebrate its achievements, or to find in it a nobility or genealogic tree. Many of these filmmakers seemed inspired by Garibaldian themes and in many ways foreshadowed the work of historiographer Gioacchino Volpe, who saw all of Italian history as teleologically oriented toward fascism. Mario Volpe's *Il grido dell'aquila* (*The Cry of the Eagle*, 1923) was an example of this movement, as were films inspired by Garibaldi and the Risorgimento, like Silvio Laurenti Rosa's *Garibaldi e i suoi tempi* (*Garibaldi and His Times*, 1923), and films inspired by Italy's colonialization, like Mario Camerini's *Kiff Tebbi* (Arabic for *As You Will*, 1928). *Il grido dell'aquila*, the first propaganda film, was a sort of instant film produced just after the March on Rome. It mixed together documentary footage and parts of unfinished film about World War I and the disillusion of war veterans. Although lacking in quality, Volpe's film was traversed by a strong Unitarian spirit and established a continuity between the Risorgimento, World War I, and fascism. This theme would be revived in the 1930s in Giovacchino Forzano's *Camicia nera* (*Black Shirt*, 1933) and Alessandro Blasetti's *Vecchia guardia* (*Old Guard*, 1935). Immediately following the March on Rome, many believed that Mussolini possessed a thaumaturgic ability to save Italian cinema ("Long live Mussolini!" the cry went. "Just as Italy has risen again, can the Italian film industry not do the same?"). The propagandistic and didactic potential of the cinematic medium quickly became clear. In 1924, the birth of L'Unione cinematografica educativa (Educational Cinematic Union), or Luce (meaning "light"), marked a significant political-cultural moment that would be felt across the world.[63] The fascist regime took total control of cinematic information and Mussolini proclaimed himself the father of the enterprise.

Traditional historiography has yet to consider Luce's cinematic archives and their relationship to fascist imagery and the portrayal of Mussolini. Scholars have never considered these materials to be deserving of primary interest. The fascist monument of images is, however, only a part—until now the most visible and well-known element—of its enormous collection. No less significant, the other part tells many stories about how Italy, the Italians, and the world were portrayed outside of Italy. For all intents and purposes, Luce had two souls during the first phase of its history: a "natural" soul, distinguished by the presence of education and didactic genes; and a soul that it acquired opportunistically, which went to work for the regime and its leader as a documenter and visual singer of its enterprises. In the beginning, the production component was called SIC (Latin for *thus*), or Sindacato istruzione cinematografica (Union for Cinematic Education). It was created to produce and distribute educational films. A small, privately owned company, it was launched in 1924 by Luciano de Feo, a lawyer and journalist with notable experience in international economic politics. In September of the same year, Mussolini, impressed by a documentary on government work titled *Dove si lavora per la grandezza d'Italia* (*Working for Italy's Greatness*), transformed Sic into an organization that received support from various governmental agencies; then he baptized it l'Unione cinematografica educativa, known by its acronym, Luce.

Although it would still take a few years for fascism to become seriously involved in the film industry and for legislation to foster its revival, Mussolini was convinced of the enormous propagandistic potential of this new medium after seeing only a few short documentaries. Not long after the founding of this organization, in an official letter dated July 14, 1925, he asked the Ministries of the Interior, Colonies, Treasury, and Public Education to recognize Luce officially and to use it for the purpose of "education, instruction, and propaganda." On November 5, Luce was transformed by official decree into a semipublic entity (called the Istituto Nazionale Luce [Luce National Institute]) to be overseen by the government.

Thanks to Luce, the fascist regime was the first government in the world that exercised direct control over newsreels. Mussolini was the first head of state who could create, almost daily, a gigantic arc of triumph for his achievements. Starting in 1926, the screen of newsreels was mandatory in all Italian theaters. Political propaganda was the primary purpose, but the filmmakers also experimented with new forms of communication and journalism linked to their narration of the Italians' daily lives as if they were making entries in a diary.

On January 24, 1929, Luce was officially declared the single cinematic entity in the service of the government and as soon as the Ministero di Cultura Popolare (Ministry of Popular Culture) was created, it took control of operations.

Landscape with Ruins and Figures

Hindered by a lack of expressive development, experimentation, and thematic renewal, the last silent films made in Italy were banished to the shadows and could not compete with contemporary cinema in other countries.

Although some interesting films were made during this period (in Naples, the "strong man" tradition continued with Mari, Palermi, Aldo de Benedetti, Brignone, and Roberto Roberti),[64] certain films stand apart as extraordinary anthropologic documents of living conditions in 1920s Italy: for example, Perego's films with Leda Gys, *Vedi Napule e po' mori!* (*See Naples and Then Die*), *Napoli è una canzone* (*Naples Is a Song*), and *Napule . . . e niente cchiú* (*Naples . . . and Nothing More*). The only directors who attempted to compete with American and French standards were Lucio d'Ambra, Augusto Genina, Carmine Gallone, and Mario Camerini.

A successful writer and journalist, D'Ambra has remained difficult to classify because all of his works had been lost until a few years ago. Besides having played an important role in developing stories for Genina, Righelli, Perego, and Palermi, he also created the first brilliant comedies. He came up with original storylines, and he focused on the narrative rhythm and cinema's potential in exploring nonrealistic territories. He wrote stories that were absurd and nonsensical, that borrowed from the rhythms of ballet and from his interest in formal elements closely linked to the language of cinema.[65]

D'Ambra vividly captured his memories of the pioneering phase of Italian cinema in three volumes and various other writings.[66] During the 1930s, when Italy attempted to claim that the pioneers of Italian cinema had invented all forms of narrative and had laid the groundwork for cinematic genres, D'Ambra was called the creator of the characters in silver screen bourgeois comedy. D'Ambra breathed into the atmosphere he found in the work the grotesque theater of Sicilian writer Rosso di San Secondo and mixed it with ballet and a few elements borrowed from futurism. Today, thanks to a series of important discoveries, the study of D'Ambra can finally be based on firsthand materials. He played a significant role in the legitimization of the treatment, but he should also be remembered as a director and a pioneer of theory.[67]

Before talkies prompted Camerini, first and foremost, to look for an Italian way of making movies with sound, 1920s Italian comedy was the only genre that tried to compete with films from other countries, like those of Ernst Lubitsch and Cecil B. De Mille.

The eclectic Genina was the most attuned to audiences, and he was able to move between genres with agility and professional security, effortlessly from adventure to melodrama to grotesque films. For example, he directed the recently restored *La maschera e il volto* (*The Mask and the Face*, 1919), based on the play by Chiarelli. Ever flexible, he also directed brilliant comedy like *Cyrano de Bergerac* (1922), which enjoyed enormous success with audiences.[68] Genina should be remembered for one of the most intense adaptations of the 1920s, *Addio giovinezza!* (*Goodbye to Youth!* 1927), as well as for his ability to make marketable films even during the years of greatest crisis. It was Genina, in any case, who became the pontifex of European cinema with his *Prix de beauté* (*Miss Europe*, 1930, shot in France), a film that combined elements from the silent and talkie eras with American and European star power. With this film, he interpreted new forms of star power as he blended melodrama with a realistic story, which he shot with the eye of a documentary filmmaker. Despite the success of many of his films, Italian cinema continued to sink deeper and deeper with each passing year. Nor would the strong men be able to save it, even though none of their films lost money at the box office: Galaor, Maciste, Sansone (Sampson), Saetta, and Astrea, as portrayed by the faces and bodies of Bartolomeno Pagano, Luciano Albertini, Giovanni Raicevich, Aurèle Sidney, Domenico Gambino, Bruto Castellani, and Carlo Aldini.[69]

Credit for the rich collection of films that featured Maciste can also be attributed to Stefano Pittaluga, whose company, Fert, managed to survive the crisis that followed the downfall of UCI. The most important Maciste films from that decade were L. R. Borgnetto's *Maciste in vacanza* (*Maciste Goes on Vacation*, 1921); Camerini's *Maciste contro lo sceicco* (*Maciste versus the Sheik*, 1926); and *Maciste all'inferno* (*Maciste in Hell*),[70] *Maciste nella gabbia dei leoni* (*Maciste in the Lion's Cage*), and *Il gigante delle dolomiti* (*The Giant of the Dolomites*), all three directed by Guido Brignone in 1926.

Camerini applied the lessons he learned from Genina's films—the sense of rhythm within the story, attention to detail, and the use of improvisational acting—to his own work. More so than Genina, Camerini was quick to discover his ability, and he refined his approach to filmmaking during the 1920s; in doing so, he became a leading director at just the right time, as technology changed and talkies arrived in Italy.

The Sun of the Rebirth

On the eve of the arrival of talkies in Italy, a group of Italian intellectuals headed by Alessandro Blasetti decided to cut away any link to the cinema of the past. They believed that farm life represented the most efficient subject matter to resolve the misfortunes of Italian cinema and to meet the expectations and objectives of the current regime. Although the magazine *Cinematografo* would not be an actual promoter of the film, it served as the group's moral compass. Despite its rallying cry—*"Ruralizzare l'Italia!"* ("Ruralize Italy!")—it would take more than a pair of boots for Blasetti to portray and interpret an undiscovered world on the silver screen.

The few surviving sequences of his film *Sole* (*Sun*, 1929) and the screenplay, which survived in its entirety, show the industry's efforts to renew cinematic iconography.[71] They also demonstrate how cinema attempted to document the fascist answer to the Soviets' five-year plans and to celebrate the "general line" of modernization. The epicenter of this program was the reclamation of swamp land that had been considered indomitable since Roman times.

Together with *Sole*, Camerini's *Rotaie* (*Rails*, 1929) should also be considered a starting point for the long-awaited revival of Italian cinema. Emblematically, *Rotaie* represents the threshold between two distinct moments in Italian cinema history. Inspired by Kammerspiel films, it is a perfect example of a barebones budget production that married brilliant comedy and realist, socially conscious filmmaking. Using his gift for observation, Camerini depicted individuals who had no history as well as the idiosyncrasies of the high and middle bourgeoisie. He knew how to give his actors direction and how to tell a story with a light touch as he mixed drama and comedy.

The results of *Rotaie* and *Sole* come nowhere close to those of contemporary productions in other countries. These two films were released just as Fritz Lang, on the eve of his departure for the United States, reached expressive maturity with *Metropolis* (1926) and *Frau im Mond* (*Woman in the Moon*, 1929). During that same period, Pudovkin, Eisenstein, and Vertov produced their masterworks and the avant-garde played its best hand. At any rate, Blasetti's and Camerini's films were indicative of the generational transformation that was taking shape. They represented a new cinematic culture that was closer to its audience. Although such culture was immersed in the political climate of the day and, in Blasetti's case, pervaded by the fascist spirit, here it seemed unaffected by the nationalistic and anti-cosmopolitan *strapaese* movement, uninterested in denouncing the limits of isolation and cultural autarchy. But the regime had yet to exploit it.

With the end of the 1920s, there was an emergence of the will to find new inroads for Italian cinema. Thanks to the invention of sound, all the players—whether in the midst of crisis or in excellent health—were forced to reinvent the rules of the game.

2

⌒ From Sound To Salò ⌒.

Rebirth, Characters, and Mythologies

On November 5, 1928, as the king of Italy looked on, Mussolini inaugurated the Istituto Internazionale del Cinema Educatore (International Institute for Cinema Education), an organ of the Society of Nations, whose administration had chosen Rome for the institute's home.[1] The dictator spoke of three fundamental discoveries in the history of humanity and the superiority of cinema with respect to the printed word and still photography: "Still in its first phase of development, cinema offers great advantages over newspapers and books: it speaks to the eyes; in doing so, it speaks a language comprehensible to all peoples of the earth. Herein lies its universal character. It offers innumerable possibilities for an educational collaboration of international breadth."

Until this moment, no one had gauged the true importance of the institute, which was to be led by Luciano de Feo, director of Luce from 1924 to 1928. But with the birth of this international institution and this public declaration by the head of the Italian government, the revival of Italian cinema received its first shot in the arm. In many instances, Luciano de Feo acted as deus ex machina, not least of which was his founding of the Venice Film Festival. His ability to understand the international nature of cinema, coupled with his influence over Mussolini, would ultimately lead to what was hailed as the "rebirth" of Italian cinema. Thanks to De Feo, the regime invested in the seventh art because it had become the most popular form of pop culture and entertainment. He also understood that the visibility and international attention were due to a privileged and magical helper.

A year later, a decisive and concrete sign of renewal came in the unveiling of the new Cines-Pittaluga facilities on Via Vejo in Rome, with a christening by minister Giuseppe Bottai. "*Commendator* Pittaluga," said the minister, "the film industry pertains to the artistic order, the economic order, and political order of a nation." The regime's formal commitment to the industry would ultimately result in legislation passed in 1931 (Law 918) whereby, for the first time, a European state invested non-recoverable capital in the entertainment industry.[2]

During the facility's first year of life, Pittaluga completed 10 of the 12 films made in Italy that year (compared with 350 foreign films distributed there) and he promised the government the delivery of 3 propaganda films in exchange for a sizable grant. With this support from the regime, which would become the largest producer and shareholder in Italian cinema, Pittaluga created the conditions and groundwork for renewal.[3]

Thanks to strong-willed personalities like Blasetti and Camerini and the push toward a theoretical dialogue, the directors of sound movies acquired new substance and legitimacy that would influence future production. The 1930s were an extraordinary period for the incubation, gestation, and first manifestations of those characters and identities in Italian cinema that would develop in the postwar era. The advent of sound was accompanied by a chaotic climate of enthusiasm, intelligence, passion, and hope. Today, scholars should recognize the significance of this cultural breeding ground, the founding fathers, and the series of contradictions—typical of the Italian reality—that made it possible for fascists and antifascists to live side by side and collaborate in a free ideological and creative trade zone.[4] To be sure, fascism was an imperfect dictatorship, but among all the areas where it exerted its influence, cinema was the most open to contamination and influence from outside agents from such antithetical realities as the Soviet Union and the United States. The 1930s were years marked by professional development and the challenge—of which filmmakers were acutely aware—to achieve the narrative and cinematic standards that prevailed in the rest of Europe and America. This period also saw the affirmation of the directorial "I" and a new attempt to give life to a modest but autarchic star system. The ties to the past had been broken once and for all and with the release of the earliest sound films, it was already possible to identify characters destined to endure in the mid and long terms.[5]

More than seven hundred films were made in Italy from 1930 to 1943.[6] While the number of films was relatively small in the beginning, there was constant growth, and by 1942 production levels had surpassed a hundred films per year. As late as 1934, Italian films accounted for 10 percent of the market. When the state became a cinematic entrepreneur and provided real capital, producers—old and new—began to feel that they were no longer bound by market rules. With the aid of the state, the minimum capital growth rate corresponded to a strong increase in the product growth rate. When Cinecittà opened in 1937, the era of budget-conscious production was over and the investment began to exceed even that of Hollywood. The privileges of the new producers derived from the fact that, thanks to state subsidies, the amount of funds invested was smaller than that for Hollywood films: the state absorbed losses and did not share in potential earnings.

In 1934, the Direzione Generale per la Cinematografia (Cinema Governing Board) was founded. Its director, Luigi Freddi, was a strong-willed man who had closely studied American production methods. His goal was to lead Italian cinema toward its glorious new destiny, but he was also determined that the objectives of the regime and the demands of the market not come into conflict with one another. The board's function was to oversee film production, but it allowed certain forces to model themselves after international production standards instead of autarchic criteria.

Until the very end, the regime's attitude was that it would not use cinema as its favored medium for propaganda. While the Luce newsreels played an important role in propaganda and were closely monitored (as we will see), fictional films enjoyed an extraterritorial status.[7] Even propaganda films were the fruit of careful production and directorial choices and generally were not influenced or affected by political pressure. The aesthetic ideals of Benedetto Croce seemed to guide the early public affirmations of militant intellectuals and institutional figures who declared themselves in favor of cinema. If cinema is art, they held, then cinema must not be a slave to power. In his remarks in favor of the 1931 law, minister Bottai, who had played a highly visible role in the March on Rome, said that he did not frequent the cinema, but noted, "audiences invariably become bored when cinema seeks to educate."[8]

Well aware of the fact that propaganda offered no financial reward, producers and directors embraced propagandistic themes only when new historical events engaged the entire country.[9] They realized early on that the regime did not like to be reminded of its previous thuggish tactics.[10] Instead, they chose to reorganize their depictions, beginning with the need to feature rural life in Italy and fascism's first efforts to modernize it following the initial phases of terror. By the end of the 1920s, *"Ruralizzare l'Italia"* ("Ruralize Italy") had become the motto of the group of young directors headed by Alessandro Blasetti as they set out to discover rural Italy and its otherwise unknown people, who had never appeared before on the silver screen.[11]

Of all of fascism's masks and metamorphoses, its ruralist element was the most effective in its self-portrait as revolutionary movement born from the hardship of life in the Italian countryside. Inspired by Soviet revolutionary cinema, fascism wanted to show that its origins lay in farming life during its early phase of self-portrayal. Fascism encouraged such representation for quite some time, as can be seen in two films by Blasetti, *Sole* (*Sun*, 1929) and *Terra madre* (*Mother Earth*, 1931), in Forzano's *Camicia nera* (*Black Shirt*, 1933), in Mario Baffico's *Terra di Nessuno* (*Nobody's Land*, 1937), and even in Marcello Albani's *Redenzione* (*Redemption*, 1942), a monument to early fascist thuggery and intimidation tactics, a film shrouded by an air of death.[12]

In lieu of a celebration of fascism, which had been born as if through parthenogenesis in the mind of its founder, fascist filmmakers preferred a collective portrait, animated by myriad subjects and articulated through multiple planes of perspective.[13] The campaign was an internal front where the flame of the combative spirit continued to be fueled. The choice to show Black Shirts intermingled in a family portrait of farmers was an excessively obvious way of continuing to exhibit the folksy origins of the regime. It was also a means of making fascist thugs seem more likeable, as if they were divine protectors of the sacred hearth, which had been desecrated by the so-called Reds. Violence, armed skirmishes, and retaliatory expeditions were shown once again, after years of being edited out.

The ruralist films of the 1930s mixed different registers: from the reclamation of swampland to revitalization of infertile arid areas, from the construction of brand-new cities for farmers and the so-called Battle for Wheat to the battles against subversives, socialists, and all those who did not take part in the world war. The *linea generale*, (general line) was fascism's answer to the Soviet five-year plan.

"With fascist will, this film must surpass the Soviet masterworks of Pudovkin and Eisenstein as well as those by German Walter Ruttman with their clearly flaccid literary forms." These lines introduced an unpublished treatment by Ezra Pound and Ferruccio Cerio, submitted to the Decennale film competition in 1932 (part of the celebration for the tenth anniversary of the rise of fascism).[14] The regime also had plans for a program inspired by the New Deal.[15] At the beginning of the 1930s, the farmers who had been left behind would be enlisted to revive the combative spirit and to redeem and colonize new lands to form the basis of the regime's imperialist project.

From Cines to Cinecittà

Until 1938, fascism did not oppose Hollywood's depiction of Italians and Italy. The regime believed that American filmmaking lacked the ability to foment social conflict. For directors like Freddi, Vittorio Mussolini, and Alessandrini, America was a model of youth, vitality, and adventure that they viewed fondly. On the other hand, as late as 1938 and the passage of protectionist legislation,

73 percent of all tickets sold in Italy were for American films. The regime still maintained that it was more useful to import films than to sustain a depressed industry that was unable to support itself by its own means.[16]

While no antibodies were activated to ward off the American invasion, the defense of film production in the early sound years was based in the citadel of Cines to the nearly exclusive advantage of Pittaluga, who would die in 1931 before he could sow the fruits of his labor.

During this period, Cines *was* Italian cinema and its sole representative. First, Ludovico Toeplitz, son of the delegate administrator from the Banca Commerciale Italiana, was called upon to act as chairman, and then intellectual Emilio Cecchi was made its artistic director.[17] The latter launched a production plan and sought to renew the marriage of literature and cinema (Pirandello and Alvaro were called upon as collaborators) and to reshape stereotypes of Italians and Italy. He pushed documentary filmmaking and encouraged his directors to vary the locations for their films.

As soon as the protectionist legislation was approved, new production houses began to flourish and in a few years important producers began to emerge. While Gustavo Lombardo consolidated Titanus without ever compromising its folksy physiognomy, the most ambitious productions, second only to Cines, were those of Giovacchino Forzano. Comedy writer, librettist to Mascagni and Puccini, successful director, friend of Mussolini (with whom he made the film *Campo di Maggio*, also known as *100 Days of Napoleon*, in 1935), Forzano represented the most culturally ambitious soul of fascist cinema.[18] He was able to unite his entrepreneurial spirit with a knack for commercial success and a good dose of creativity. His studios in Tirrenia, located halfway between Pisa and Livorno (hence the name of his production company, Pisorno), were an exemplary model of speculation, political cronyism, and entrepreneurial spirit. Tirrenia was the first city in Italian cinema capable of providing a complete cycle of film production, and the surrounding countryside could be used to reproduce nearly any geographic setting.[19]

Other production houses began to appear sporadically: in 1934 Lux was launched in Turin by Riccardo Gualino, one of the greatest and most enlightened Italian industrialists, who had been exiled to Lipari for political reasons.[20] For a number of years, the only film produced by Lux was *Don Bosco* in 1935, directed by Goffredo Alessandrini. Then, from 1939 to 1944, its production increased significantly, including important films like Blasetti's *La corona di ferro* (*The Iron Crown*, 1941), Camerini's *I promessi sposi* (*The Spirit and the Flesh*, from the novel *The Betrothed*, 1941), Castellani's *Un colpo di pistola* (*A Pistol Shot*) and *Zazà* (1942), Soldati's *Malombra* (1942), Vergano's *Quelli di montagna* (*Soldiers on the Mountain*, 1943), Matarazzo's *Il biricchino di papà*

(*Daddy's Little Devil*, 1943), and Castellani's *La donna della montagna* (*The Mountain Woman*, 1943). When he was allowed to return and became president of Lux, he favored films based on literary classics and would continue to produce similar films even after the war.

While Gualino was by far the most complex and rich personality to emerge during these years, other notable individuals included businessmen and contractors Michele and Salvatore Scalera, Carlo Roncoroni, and Giulio Manenti, president of the eponymous studio. The Scalera brothers had completed important projects in Libya before becoming filmmakers. Before he was called upon to develop the new Cines and oversee Cinecittà, Roncoroni had been the director of public works and development. And, in 1934, Angelo Rizzoli entered the scene, with his Novella Film. He entrusted a foreign director, Max Ophüls, to make *Signora di Tutti* (*Everybody's Woman*) with Isa Miranda. He hoped to use film to renew his previous success in magazine publishing. Finally, the state itself, through Freddi, decided to become involved in production, distribution, and theater operation.[21] The state invested heavily in services and capital goods and it became a low-interest lender to the industry. Ultimately, it decided to build a distribution company and chain of theaters called ENIC.

The decisive shot in the arm came with legislation passed on February 5, 1934, which created the so-called entertainment corporation. This entity was created to exert constant pressure on the government and to foster its power for decades to come. As far as the film industry was concerned, fascism hoped to become the guiding light for a series of initiatives intended to make cinema the shining gem of its economic and cultural policies, which were ever more vulnerable to foreign contamination and influence.

In 1935, the Centro Sperimentale (Experimental Center) opened its doors, headed by Luigi Chiarini. Thanks to Chiarini and Umberto Barbaro (a noted antifascist, who would help him to launch the Centro's cultural and educational initiatives), the Centro was destined to become an industry nucleus for cultural and professional preparation. It was an oasis where students could develop their character, personality, and moral fiber as the future filmmakers of Italy.[22] The Centro was also perhaps the best example of the contradictions of fascism's institutions and its policy of exile and "free zones" within its cultural centers. Unaware of the social dangers, fascism believed that it could control the free zones.

Shortly thereafter, Cinecittà opened its doors. Built on 16,000 square meters, it was the most modern and best-equipped studio in Europe and it marked a challenge to American dominance.[23] Cinecittà rose from the ashes of Cines, which had been destroyed mysteriously by fire in 1935. Roncoroni, who had spearheaded its conception and launch, died at the end of 1938. A year later, ownership of the entire complex was ceded to the state, and in January 1940, Freddi was nominated as its new chairman. In a few short years, the number of Italian films increased notably and the industry quickly reached a top slot in world cinema in terms of quality and production value. Italian filmmakers were now making technologically advanced films that allowed them to compete even with Hollywood.

The strength of Italian filmmaking derived from the fact that Italian filmmakers had adapted the Renaissance workshop model to suit the industry's needs. It was their foundry, the ideal environment for Italian creativity. Cinecittà was the most important example of the reincarnation of Italy's artisanal know-how, a species that had been endangered by the country's industrialization. This approach was initially conceived as a weapon—defensive and offensive—in the war against Hollywood's colonization. But it was actually an island where the Italian working method, handed down for generations but nearly forgotten, could now flourish. It was a self-sufficient, complete universe, similar to what the Arsenale (the famed arsenal of Venice) represented for the medieval world.

A world inhabited by an army of blacksmiths, cabinet makers, electricians, masons, plasterers, plumbers, draftsmen, tailors, painters, makeup artists, and hairstylists, it gave shape and an unmistakable quality to the dreams and imagination of hundreds of directors and screenwriters. Cinecittà was an essential element in the industry's becoming aware of its creative ability. Italian cinema wanted to reach audiences across the globe and compete on an international level. But it would take more than Cinecittà to achieve Italian cinema's true greatness and to fully develop its depth.

Thanks to the so-called Alfieri law of June 6, 1938, and subsequent legislation passed on September 20 of the same year, the foreign films that had dominated the market were barred at Italy's borders. Internally, the industry then witnessed what has often been dubbed a "production spree." In 1939, 50 films were made, 83 in 1940, and 119 in 1942. During this period, the box office for Italian films grew from 13 to 50 percent. This state of euphoria would last until 1943.

During the war years, moviegoers crowded theaters in greater numbers than ever before. In 1941, 258 new theaters opened their doors. This growth coincided with the proliferation of new production companies, which, for the most part, were unable to release more than one film (in 1941, 59 production companies made 89 titles).

Cinema's seemingly primary function during this period was that of helping audiences forget the horrors of the conflict. The general consensus among filmmakers was that documentaries and feature-length films should avoid triumphant overtones and instead celebrate the values of humankind. Despite its growth, film production continued to reveal its fragility: on average, films needed state subsidies just to break even. Fascism had set in motion a mechanism that was destined, like the phoenix, to rise again in the postwar period from the ashes of old cooperative entities.

Luce, a Cinematic Monument to Mussolini

The fact that fascism chose not to exercise control over the motion picture industry was due in part to the complete control, from its inception, of the education and journalistic activities of the Istituto Nazionale Luce. This institution received political and economic support that led to rapid growth and the emergence of some of its defining features. In exchange, it celebrated fascist pageantry and documented its outward transformation, its taste for conquest, the formation of its rituals and myths, and its efforts to make the outside world identify the nation with a dictator, who, from the outset, had wished to expand his visibility and international clout. Through their use of newsreels, fascism and its leader were able to construct—on a nearly daily basis—the equivalent of Augustus's *Monumentum Ancyranum*. This visual monument to the Duce and his peace- and wartime achievements marked the first time that a world leader and political regime made direct use of the cinematic medium.

The first newsreel was released in June 1927 and 44 were produced that year. Before sound was introduced in 1931, 900 newsreels were screened in Italy. From 1931 to 1943, 2 separated newsreel series were released: the first ended during January–March 1940 and included 1,693 newsreels; the second, 379. Every week, 4 newsreels were made, each roughly 250 meters in length. It was mandatory for all Italian theaters to screen the newsreels and at a certain point, for all theaters in the empire. In the 1930s, Luce produced special newsreels in foreign languages. But Luce also produced a great number of short-, mid-, and full-length feature documentaries and it later released fictional films.[24] Today, these titles, together with the newsreels, form an extraordinary and irreplaceable anthropological documentation of Italy. In these films, the impoverished and underdeveloped Italy is practically invisible and remains, as much as possible, beyond the camera's gaze. The filmmakers behind these newsreels and documentaries wanted to show Italy's march toward modernization without ever forgetting its traditional roots. This massive collection of materials can be considered a unique and seamless text based on repetitive models that were formalized early on and then slowly and subtly changed as to appear imperceptible. These films represent a coherent system in which a modern model of communication was shaped and transmitted as it simultaneously created the Mussolinian mythology and constructed a custom-made iconology of Mussolini's journey through domestic and international politics. Lastly, it provided a positive, contagiously euphoric portrayal of "Italia in cammino" ("Italy on the march"), to borrow a phrase from the title of the famous book by fascist-era historian Gioacchino Volpe.

From 1931 to 1940, there were four distinct periods in the evolution of Mussolini's politics. They began with the battles of the ruralist movement, followed by the bourgeois transformation of fascism. Next came the march toward imperial conquest, and lastly, the mobilization for global conquest. Each phase corresponds to a period in the development of the newsreels: changes in vocabulary and language, a new organization of news items, a growing number of news features, and the creation of repeating news features, including the overarching "Notizie dall'Impero" ("News from the Empire") created in 1936. These stages in the evolution of the newsreels help shed light on the ideological changes within the regime.

The violence and aggression of fascist thuggery and intimidation tactics were quickly sublimated and channeled through reports of great athletic achievement, like Italo Balbo's Atlantic crossing as told by Mario Craveri in Italy's first documentary with soundtrack, Lo stormo atlantico (Atlantic Flight, 1931).

Luigi Freddi had never placed great stock in Luce, in part because of its relatively unaligned spirit. In 1938, with his support, the Industria Documentari (Documentary Industry), or Incom, was created and charged with the dismantling of Luce's monopoly on documentary filmmaking and bringing it under the more stringent control of the Ministry of Popular Culture.

In tandem with the Centro Sperimentale di Cinematografia, Luce helped shape the careers of camera operators and directors who, in some cases, would go on to make fictional films. A cut above their peers, these directors were able to give voice to every element in their films, from objects and landscape to architecture, from the history of place to the characters themselves.

Many memorable documentaries were released by Luce during this period, including Pasinetti's Sulle orme di Giacomo Leopardi (In the Footsteps of Giacomo Leopardi, 1941), Città bianca (White City, 1942), I piccioni di Venezia (The Pigeons of Venice, 1942), and La gondola (The Gondola, 1942); Giorgio Ferroni's Vertigine bianca (White Vertigo, 1942), All'aria aperta (Field Trip, 1942), and Passo d'addio (Swan Song, 1942); Fernando Cerchio's Ali fasciste (Fascist Wings, 1941), Ritorno al Vittoriale (Return to [D'Annunzio's] Vittoriale, 1942), and *La scuola di cinema* (*Film School*, 1942); Giacomo Pozzi Bellini and Roberto Rossellini's *Fantasia sottomarina* (*Undersea Fantasy*, 1940); as well as works by Pietro Francisci, Romolo Marcellini, and Robert Omegna, among others. There were also many notable fictional films, including ambitious productions like the films made by Forzano for the ten-year anniversary of fascism, *Camicia Nera* (*Black Shirt*, 1933); D'Errico's *Il cammino degli eroi* (*The Path of Heroes*, 1936); Gallone's *Scipione l'Africano* (*Scipio the African* or *The Defeat of Hannibal*, 1937), a film that Luce produced, as the major partner, with ENIC; Marcellini's *Grano fra due battaglie* (*Between Two Battles, Wheat*, 1941); and Baffico's *I trecento della settima* (*The Three Hundred of the Seventh*, 1942), a film that told the dramatic story of the heroic resistance of an Alpine battalion in Albania, produced just before the fall of fascism. Giorgio Ferroni, Romolo Marcellini, Fernando Cerchio, Mario Baffico, Basilio Franchina, and Corrado d'Errico are just some of the names of cameramen and directors who were able to complete their apprenticeships thanks to the short- and feature-length films made at Luce before they launched their careers as directors of fictional films.

The war years revealed Luce's limited usefulness as a propaganda tool and its evolution failed to keep in step with that of the regime. A special department was created to make its war movies richer in terms of their visual power, editing, and screenwriting. But Luce continued to crank out propaganda, as if it had suddenly lost its ability to connect with Italian audiences.

The Mussolinian Journey and Its Mythology

Thanks to his previous professional experience, Mussolini was a capable journalist; his talent in exploiting the mass media was unmatched by that of other dictators and leaders on the European political stage. He was the first politician who would not stop at a generic appreciation of the power of cinema as a weapon of persuasion and manipulation of reality; he was the first to use it to control both documentary and fictional filmmaking.

For twenty years, he was the celebrity capable of capturing the imagination of the Italian people. He was the sovereign of Italian politics and entertainment. An omnipresent and omnipotent superstar, a personality who could step into every role, he played an endless solo that showed him in every light imaginable: in the trappings of the middle class, playing the tuba or wearing a tuxedo, in his bathing suit, in an aviator's jumpsuit or horseman's uniform, donning a motorcycle helmet or a tennis outfit, and, of course, every kind of military uniform.

During the 1920s and early 1930s, Il Duce was very careful to portray himself as a man who had come from the people, in whose service he had placed himself totally and without reservation. With time, this relationship would be reversed. On one hand, he made good use of his experience as a teacher and politician who had marched in socialist ranks, who had delivered speeches in the town square, and who knew how to connect with the masses. On the other hand, he took on the affectation of the futurists, borrowing from the rituals created by D'Annunzio at Fiume when he saw that they were perfectly suited to his needs.

In the beginning, he was clumsy and uncontrolled but ever narcissistic, smug, and determined to live out the fascist ideal of virility. Over time, Mussolini continued to reshape his image and began to control it more rigorously. As the silent era ended and sound arrived, he seemed to slow down with respect to the motorized exacerbation of the 1920s. His speeches were more neatly measured and targeted. His close-ups were immense and calculated and his cinematic iconography borrowed from the various figurative arts. Unlike Nazism, fascism did not have an office for propaganda, and Mussolini himself simultaneously played the roles of director, screenwriter, and cinematic sovereign.

The study of the evolutionary dynamic of Mussolinian imagery allows us to understand how the idea of sacred public ritual and the communion of the crowd with the body and voice of its leader developed. Its acceleration culminated in 1936 during the empire's spring, in the wake of Leni Riefenstahl's *Triumph des Willens* (*Triumph of the Will*, 1935), with its shots of oceanic gatherings at the Olympic games. After seeing Riefenstahl's work and the newsreels produced by the Nazis, the Italian film industry abandoned the Soviet model and opted instead for more sophisticated techniques that emphasized spectacular elements. Inspired also by the Nazis' rigid ritualism, the Italians abandoned their ruralist and thuggish ideology in favor of an Italy that had already undergone a complete fascist transformation, a compact Italy, like a man ready to devote his life to Mussolini's service.

Two distinct moments perhaps best marked the complete digestion of borrowed Nazi ritualism and the fulfillment of a communion, which had otherwise never fully succeeded. The first was the nighttime announcement of victory in the Ethiopian war, with searchlights that provided a halo for Il Duce. The second was Mussolini's return from Munich in 1938 when he was cheered by well-wishers along his route homeward. That evening, a crowd gathered in Piazza Venezia and lit votive candles to show their appreciation and their faith in their leader. In these two moments, the actor was physically assumed into heaven in a divine light. All that remained was the sound of his voice.

With the declaration of war, the fall from grace began. During the war, Mussolinian imagery and mythology began to show their first signs of wear. As if he had been sidelined, Il Duce seemed a mere extra when he appeared at the front or in public ceremonies. From the moment he was liberated by German soldiers at Campo Imperatore in 1943 and throughout the Republic of Salò period, he appeared in public less and less, an old and sick man, an unrecognizable ghost of his former self, weak and without the mass consensus that had accompanied him on his twenty-year journey.

The Fathers of the New Italian Cinema

The first Italian sound film was Gennaro Righelli's *La canzone dell'amore* (*The Song of Love*), based on a short story by Pirandello, which debuted in Rome on October 6, 1930.[25] The circumstances that allowed Righelli, a director with twenty years of experience, to beat Blasetti to the punch were purely arbitrary. The success of the film was due more to the melody of the song than to the prestige of Pirandello. Everything in this film felt the effects of a merely modest budget, from the acting to the screenwriting, from the directing to the sound quality. But the cinematography was excellent, especially in the location shots, and the story dealt with a theme dear to those members of the female audience who played new roles on the social scene and faced life with new ambitions. The film struck a deep chord in the hearts of moviegoers and was met with enthusiasm and the sense of marvel that always accompanies the birth of a new technological miracle.

Despite Righell's success, Pittaluga chose to bet on the clearly more aggressive and volcanic Blasetti, to whom he entrusted three films from 1930 to 1931: *Nerone* (*Nero*) with Ettore Petrolini; *Resurrectio*, which had been slated to be the first talkie in Italy; and *Terra Madre* (*Mother Earth*). In doing so, he consecrated Blasetti as Cines's top director. Italian cinema began to rise up in the name of its directors, and Blasetti received a field promotion to the rank of commander of the entire industry.[26]

Blasetti was a self-taught director and his contagious passion helped him leap over any type of obstacle that he faced. He had edited magazines and written articles that called for the "rebirth" of Italian cinema. But then, suddenly, he found himself behind a camera and it was as if he had spent a lifetime directing films.[27] With only his second film, he was declared a master. Throughout the 1930s, he worked tirelessly, making a wide range of films: dramas, comedies, historical films, and works that celebrated the fascist epic.

Although some of the films were better than others, he showed remarkable flexibility, a mastery of all aspects of film production, narrative ability, a keen sense of rhythm, and a capacity to direct his actors, whether they were professional or recruited from the street. He was acutely aware of the signifying power of light and the composition of the image and his creativity was clearly inspired by Soviet cinema (even though it is probable that he had not seen Soviet films himself, he had absorbed the lessons of Soviet filmmaking through his friends and collaborators). He was also well versed in the Italian traditions of painting and figurative arts.

Early talking cinema in Italy was a free-trade zone where filmmakers could exchange ideas, cultural models, art forms, and trends that came from the most disparate and distant sources. Thanks to cinema, autocratic Italy was not isolated from contemporary international cinematic culture and was receptive, however indirectly, to its trends.[28]

The films made during this period thoroughly absorbed and assimilated the remaining bits and pieces of the avant-garde, from futurism to surrealism, movements that had been crushed and marginalized by calls for a return to order. This is evident in Blasetti's films, in particular, in those in which he collaborated with Ettore Petrolini and, later, in genre films like Carlo Ludovico Bragaglia's *O la borsa o la vita* (*Your Money or Your Life*, 1933), in *Camicia nera* (*Black Shirt*, 1933), in Ruttman's *Acciaio* (*Steel*, also released in 1933), and in Barbaro's *L'ultima nemica* (*The Last Enemy*) and the early films of Totò and Macario. The interaction and relationship between Italian cinema and the avant-garde during this period merit the attention of contemporary scholars. In particular, Italian film studies could benefit from research on the avant-garde lexicon and the presence of nonsense and the fragmentation of the logical chain of events in 1930s Italian cinema, and on its visual syntax and the presence of centrifugal formalist tendencies within the language of cinema, which usually leaned toward normalization and direct comprehensibility. The presence of the avant-garde can be felt throughout the 1930s. This aspect has never been fully studied and such research would allow scholars to connect more than one dot between Italy's autarchic cinematic culture and the culture of international cinema. Blasetti possessed immense charisma and a natural ability to lead. With remarkable humility, he knew how to learn from persons whom he admired—from Petrolini to Barbaro and Zavattini—without ever worrying about their political orthodoxy. His personal fascism was the child of a socialist soul and it nourished itself with egalitarian utopias and respect for intelligence and professionalism.

From the outset, Blasetti's journey was anything but linear and coherent. The subject of *Resurrectio* is the feeling of social panic caused by a storm during a concert at the Conservatorio di Santa Cecilia. The conductor takes it upon himself to restore order. Thanks to his determination, the audience returns to its seats. The film ends with a view of the chimneystack of a factory from inside a small café, a frame reminiscent of Sironi's painting from the same period. With this film, Blasetti revealed different pieces of his talent as he paid homage to the avant-garde, to Ruttmann, and to contemporary Italian painting.

Blasetti's early mastery of cinematic forms, syntax, and language continues to amaze viewers today. With the advent of sound, new roads were opened to Italian cinema. With his ability as an experimenter, Blasetti was able to explore the new medium's expressive and linguistic possibilities. Based on a drama by Raffaele Viviani, who also starred in the film, *La tavola dei poveri* (*A Feast for the Needy*, 1932) offers a clear idea of Blasetti's capability and potential. His directorial presence can be felt in his challenging camera moves and in his Soviet-influenced editing style, which also brings the camera into direct contact with the locations. Cecchi collaborated on the screenplay and it would be because of him that Blasetti would find the inspiration for his film *1860* (1933) in Giuseppe Cesare Abba's *Noterelle da Quarto al Volturno* (*The Diary of One of Garibaldi's Thousand* [Abba's diary as a soldier in Garibaldi's army, *From Quarto to Volturno*]). This commercial yet erudite film was marked by a strong spirit of unity, a courageous use of dialects, and constant references to Italian painting. Blasetti had decided to tell a Garibaldian epic from the point of view of the Sicilian shepherds who witnessed Garibaldi's "expedition" firsthand. Throughout the film, he maintained this anti-rhetorical and anti-celebratory choice. Especially in the first part of the film, the images tell the story of the powerful Sicilian countryside and how its primitive beauty was seemingly reflected in the beauty of its people. While this stylistic theme was already present in previous works, in this film, Blasetti clearly wanted to show the stories of individuals; the collective story of the film's characters melts into the landscape.

In Blasetti's early films, Sicily, the Pontine marshes, Naples and Siena, the Tuscan countryside, Rome, Civitavecchia and Genoa become the backdrop for a cinematic vision intended to embrace, as widely and as inclusively as possible, all of Italy. Blasetti wanted to capture its new spirit, to push beyond its surface and record the people and the nation's palingenetic will. But his gaze was never direct. Instead, he used pictorial and literary filters to shape the frame and the dialogue. The influence of nineteenth-century painting—in particular, the Tuscan *macchiaioli* (from Fattori and Borrani to Abbati and

Sernesi)—has been documented by an accurate comparative study.[29] In Blasetti, even the Veneto—today a region rife with tension and separatist sentiment—was an idealized cradle for the message of unity: "By golly," says one of his characters in a thick Veneto accent. "Come on! It's time to celebrate, friends! It is time for the unification of Italy."

In 1935, Blasetti directed *Vecchia guardia* (*Old Guard*), one of the few works in which he celebrated nascent fascism. Upper-echelon fascists did not like the film, perhaps because its epic spirit was immersed in a dark, morbid atmosphere, perhaps because fascism had already donned new clothes and new masks.[30]

From *Aldebaran* (1935) to *Ettore Fieramosca* (1938), from *Un'avventura di Salvator Rosa* (*An Adventure of Salvator Rosa*, 1940) to *La cena delle beffe* (*The Jester's Supper*, 1941), from *La corona di ferro* (*The Iron Crown*, 1941) to *Quattro passi tra le nuvole* (*Four Steps in the Clouds*, 1942), the films that followed showed Blasetti's extraordinary ability to adapt combined with a growing passion for storytelling and his progressive detachment from the regime. In film after film, Blasetti revealed a talent that allowed him to express himself on a wide variety of levels as he tackled all the cinematic models of contemporary international filmmaking. He was a great director who knew how to use his actors as he revived the Italian star system. Capable of adapting the camera to any dramatic or stylistic challenge, he showed that he knew how to make his camera moves with absolute confidence, whether in period films, in adaptations of theatrical works, or in films set in the present day. The best example of his ability is perhaps *La corona di ferro*, a collection of folklore and imaginary tales, a successful blend of the Mediterranean epic with the Nordic saga. Bolstered by Virgilio Marchi's set design (whereby Kandahar seems a would-be counterpoint to Fritz Lang's *Metropolis*), the film offered a countercurrent and centrifugal pacifist message as Italy found itself on the verge of war.[31]

Blasetti's collaboration with Zavattini on *Quattro passi tra le nuvole* allowed him to take part in the active revival of the industry by the new generation of directors and he was able to make felt his sense of insufficiency and need to break away—a call for profound renewal, both moral and ideological.

The points of contact between Blasetti and Camerini were few and far between. But thanks to their parallel careers, Italian cinema found a new path toward the discovery of its identity, its vocabulary, and its dominant and fertile themes.

The title that brought success to Mario Camerini was *Gli uomini che mascalzoni . . .* (*What Scoundrels Men Are!*), a film in which he showed the lightness of his touch, a talented level of style and narrative that would long accompany him in becoming the father of future Italian comedy.[32]

The novelty of the story was in part due to the fact that it was a high narrative about everyday people. The camera seamlessly captured the events in their lives as it had seemingly inserted itself into the flow of the existence of anonymous, proletarian characters. In a period that was dominated by triumphal marches, parades, and pennants unfurled, Camerini was able to carve himself a space for the observation and portrayal of the everyday, non-antagonistic Italian, antithetical in every way to the Italian that Mussolini envisioned. Released in 1932, this film heralded what would become known as Camerini's petit-bourgeois pentalogy: *Darò un milione* (*I'll Give a Million*, 1935), *Ma non è una cosa seria* (*But It's Nothing Serious*, 1936), *Il signor Max* (*Mister Max*, 1937), and *Grandi magazzini* (*Department Store*, 1939). In the last two films of the series, De Sica, together with Assia Noris, reached the apex of his success as a film star.

The sanguine Blasetti used the camera as a weapon, as means of discovery, decomposition, and recomposition of reality. For him, it was an educational, edifying, social and political medium with which he always made his authorial presence felt. Camerini, on the other hand, tended lightly toward self-erasure. He used the camera in a constant and coherent manner, as if it were an added but entirely natural organ of his body, a sort of sight-enhancing prosthesis that helped him see the world through the eyes of anyone. Camerini had no pre-constituted messages to communicate to his audience, nor did he want to convince his viewers of the superiority of a given idea. He adapted his gaze to the stories of his characters. It followed them at a respectful but short distance and it revealed the strong emotional involvement, the sympathy, and the attention with which he followed the lovers' quarrels of his characters as he shared their daily dramas and problems.

Blasetti liked to show off his knowledge and compare himself to the masters. While Camerini had indeed fully absorbed the cinematic lessons of the past, he applied them almost invisibly. When he started out, Camerini had no need to declare his lineage because he had began working in cinema as early as 1913. Today he has every right to be compared to Frank Capra and Ernst Lubitsch: he had a remarkable ability to create narrative mechanisms that were perfect in their internal balance and he had a true knack for recounting the emotional and professional vicissitudes of characters plucked from the proletarian and petit-bourgeois crowd. However distinct their approaches, no one can deny that Camerini and Blasetti played important guiding roles, albeit parallel to and distinct from one another, in the development of Italian cinema during the 1930s. Perhaps thanks to the magic presence of Zavattini, the two were destined to meet in the early 1940s.

During the 1930s, Camerini enriched his filmography with more titles that showed his notable interest in dramatic storytelling. These included *Giallo* (*Mystery*, 1933); *T'amerò sempre* (*I Will Always Love You*, 1933); *Come le foglie* (*Like the Leaves*, 1934); and his colonial adventure film, *Il grande appello* (*The Last Roll-Call*, 1935), the only film in which the director seemed to breathe in the euphoria and climate that preceded the empire's period of conquest (although he based the work on French colonial cinema).

Camerini's work during 1940 was proof of his undeniable gift and his ability to dominate all forms of storytelling. These films ranged from *Una romantica avventura* (*A Romantic Adventure*, 1940) to *I promessi sposi* (*The Spirit and the Flesh*, from the novel *The Betrothed*) and his remake of *T'amerò sempre* (1943). But as far as Italian comedy is concerned, these works also marked his passing of the torch to his natural heir, Vittorio de Sica. Camerini's body of work represents the fundamental bridge between pre- and postwar comedy and is an essential model for rigorously crafted simplicity through the elimination of elements.

Jack-of-all-trades director Gennaro Righelli, who should be remembered for his *L'aria del continente* (*Continental Atmosphere*, 1935) and *Pensaci, Giacomino!* (*Think It Over Jack*, 1936), among other films, liked to pluck his characters from the petit bourgeoisie and middle classes. With good-natured moralism, he attacked the survival tactics employed by members of aristocratic society who, for the most part, had been uprooted and remained outside the processes of production. By the 1930s, the political situation had become more stable; the bourgeoisie, which had been infused with elements plucked from the lower classes, now returned to its status as a positive model and the protagonist of a society undergoing modernization. For the modest moral born of comedies by Camerini, Righelli, Mario Mattoli, and then Camillo Mastrocinque, Max Neufeld, and in part those by De Sica himself, directors chose a road divergent from the ambitions of fascism and Mussolini's portrayal of the Italian. On one hand, these films drew from storytelling models used in American cinema; on the other hand, from Italian dialectal comedies and Hungarian comedies.

More so than postwar Republican Italy and the years of democratic government, the 1930s showed how Cinecittà and Italian cinema in general were able to create a free zone, an open city that gave refuge, protected, and valued the work of Italian Jewish directors and intellectuals and émigrés from Germany and Austria following the advent of Nazism. Rudolph Arnheim, Max Ophüls, Max Neufeld, and Hans Hinrich intravenously infused the blood of

autarchic invention with Central European culture and atmosphere. To borrow a phrase from Manzoni's notes on his Florentine revision of *I Promessi
Sposi*, they rinsed the clothes of the Italian Cinderellas in the waters of the
Rhine and the Danube. They favored not laughter, but rather, a means for
smiling and creating small parallel worlds in a dramatic moment. In return,
they received protection, opportunity, and support for their work and talent.
In any case, in the years that followed the advent of the Freddi era, numerous
foreign directors and actors were invited to work in Italy with directors known
for their avant-garde works, like Walter Ruttman to directors like Jean Renoir,
who, on the eve of the war, was asked to collaborate on a version of *Tosca*
(*The Story of Tosca*, 1941) in Rome, thanks to Visconti.

Among those who arrived in Italy, there were many notable directors:
Abel Gance, Gustav Machaty, Jean Epstein, Jean-Paul Paulin (who replaced
Dreyer in 1936 as the director of *L'esclave blanc*, released as *Jungla nera* [*Black
Jungle*] in Italy), Pierre Chenal, Luis Trenker, Marcel l'Herbier, Jean Choux,
Edgar Neville, Ernst Marischka, Ladislao Vajda, Akos Rathonÿ, Wladimir
Striževskij, and Christian-Jaque. There were also actresses like Edwige
Feuillère, Martha Eggerth, Gaby Morlay, Anneliese Uhlig, Carola Höhn,
and Clara Tabody, and screenwriters like Boris Bilinskij and Liuv Christoff,
among others. The margin for tolerance was possible thanks to the nature of
the industry, which sought to reconcile its contradictions by recognizing and
supporting professionalism and technical ability. This was no small achievement and Italian cinema can be proud of this fact: such tolerance did not
diminish the quality of the final product, but it helped make it possible for
the industry to have the same tolerant stance when the balance of powers was
completely reversed.

Vittorio de Sica made his debut as a director in 1940 with *Rose scarlatte*
(*Red Roses* or *Twenty-Four Red Roses*), followed by two comedies, *Un garibaldino al convento* (*A Garibaldian in the Convent*) and *Maddalena . . . zero in
condotta* (*Maddalena, Zero for Conduct*). In 1941, he directed *Teresa Venerdì*
(*Do You Like Women* or *Doctor Beware*). With his early works, he seemed to
have fully absorbed the Camerinian model and successfully reproduced its
settings, situations, dialogues, and style. De Sica was no Camerini clone, but
rather, his student, capable of subtly differentiating himself from his teacher.
In the process, he managed with equal effectiveness to play the dual roles of
subject of the action and subject of the emission of the message.[33]

With *I bambini ci guardano* (*The Children Are Watching Us* or *The Little
Martyr*), De Sica was no longer concerned with demonstrating that he had
learned his trade well. For this film, he abandoned Camerini's magical atmosphere; the whole experience of the real is lived through the eyes of a child.

The strong emotional charge and the ability to operate the camera at a child's height for the first time (thus taking on the child's point of view) marked the first true signs of De Sica's directorial personality and the genesis of his poetics, which had begun to take shape thanks to his relationship with Zavattini.

The lowest common denominator shared by all of these artists began to be the screenwriter. One in particular, Cesare Zavattini, was destined to play the role of father and guardian angel of Italian cinema as it headed toward new horizons.[34] Working with him at a Tayloristic speed, Aldo de Benedetti and Alessandro de Stefani packaged the plots and dialogues of at least one-quarter of the Italian films produced during this period, from historical and adventure films to comedies and the so-called *telefoni bianchi* (white telephone) films with their upper-class settings, from propaganda films to musicals. De Benedetti wrote the screenplays for early comedies by Camerini and De Sica while at the same time he worked for Neufeld and Bragaglia. In some instances, he was not credited because the 1938 racial laws had come into effect.

From the outset, the various writers who began working in the Italian film industry in the 1930s were keenly aware of the variety of Italian dialects and regional accents and vocabularies. They were also conscious of the influence that foreign words had on the national language as it was taking shape. Such terms made it possible for dialogue to breathe in the air of modernity and cosmopolitan culture. Upon closer examination, it becomes clear that, despite the lack of any propagandistic intentions, commercial film production and the language of cinema became the focal point of tensions in the search for a true national linguistic identity.

The screenwriters who began working in the industry in the early 1930s— from Ivo Perilli to Alessandro de Stefani, from the comedy writer Aldo de Benedetti to the erudite Giacomo Debenedetti, from Aldo Vergano to Eduardo de Filippo to Zavattini and Amidei, from Metz to Marchesi—managed to reach a level of communicative stabilization in a purely organic manner as they created a language for daily communication that soon would become a model for a society in which interpersonal and professional relationships were constantly changing. The language they produced also took account of the new medium of communication, the telephone, not to mention radio. The 1930s saw a clear emergence of a cinematic language that was able, simultaneously, to create space for local characteristics, aspirations of unity, and the need to not exclude relationships with other parts of Italy and the rest of the world.

Screenwriters fulfilled a dual role during the decade that led up to the war: on one hand, they knew how to show off Italy's wealth of linguistic possibilities, thus transgressing the autarchic mandates of the regime, which sought to eliminate linguistic diversity; on the other hand, they made the language of emotion accessible to the people and made it possible for that language to circulate. For all intents and purposes, the early screenwriters were also the architects and planners of a linguistic and narrative system defined by characteristics that were as fragile as they were distant from the regime's expectations. This system still felt the weight of previous models but centrifugal forces also exerted their pressure, pushing it in a multitude of directions.

During the 1930s, thanks to a profound change in the approach to writing and a new awareness of the power of language and the perception of Italian unity through the portrayal of the Italian landscape, cinema's contact, so to speak, with the present and with reality became more continuous. Although Blasetti's early films felt the influence of Soviet style and theory, they were more closely aligned with poetics and bywords of writers like Maccari and Soffici. These films wanted to be the visual singers of authentic Italian faces and the places where average Italians planted their roots. While Italy's potential as a setting for film was opening up in its entirety, the spaces were actually getting smaller and smaller. As filmmakers began to make use of the country's geography and history in their attempt to create a new Italian identity that matched the characteristics and nature of the regime, Sicily began to play an important role. The first to see Sicily as the ideal setting for neorealism were the critics and aspiring directors who contributed to the review *Cinema* and who rallied around Visconti. Just as America was seen through the eyes of Pavese and Vittorini, Giovanni Verga's Sicily—as dreamed and imagined by Visconti, Giuseppe de Santis, Mario Alicata, and Antonio Pietrangeli—became cinema's bridge and connective tissue to the artistic and literary tradition. In film, just as in literature, the renewed interest in Verga's writings had become a password, and *verismo* had become the magic word for those wanting to equip themselves to portray reality.

For Visconti and De Santis, who wrote their treatment based on Verga's short story "L'amante di Gramigna" ("How Peppa Loved Gramigna" or "Gramigna's Lover," a story later made into Lizzani's *L'amante di Gramigna* or *The Bandit*) and first conceived their adaptation of his novel *I Malavoglia* (*The House by the Medlar Tree*, later Visconti's film *La terra trema*) in the early 1940s, the idea of going to Sicily meant heading toward a reality in which every gesture and every drama could unleash their primitive energy, nearly allowing them to attain the sacred value of Greek tragedy. The pendulum did not swing toward history, but rather, toward a mythical portrayal of Sicily, elements of which would become part of postwar Italy's iconography and territorial re-definition. For an entire generation of intellectuals who would move south-ward—from Levi to Guttuso, from Visconti to Germi—the voyage became obligatory: theirs was a journey to the motherland and the rediscovery of the lost roots of a primitive world. Only by withdrawing oneself from its circular time could one build one's own destiny anew.

The advent of sound set the production machine in motion again, sending out an irresistible call to dialectal theater groups scattered across the country that had once dominated the town square. They migrated en masse toward the film industry and would become an important subsection of the star system. An accurate survey of the regional provenance of 1930s actors reveals undeniably that almost every Italian region delivered its most representative actors to the soundstage: Angelo Musco from Sicily, the De Filippo brothers and Totò from Campania, Magnani and Fabrizi from Latium, Gilberto Govi from Liguria, Cesco Baseggio from the Veneto, Armando Falconi and Dina Galli from Lombardy, and Erminio Macario from Piedmont.

The first to complete the passage was Ettore Petrolini. In the July 1934 issue of *Scenario*, there are no fewer than ninety-four close-ups of the actor, in which he assumes many poses and expresses a wide range of feelings and emotions. Some have noted that his face was the ideal mask for masks: his was a tragic-before-comic face, capable of rapid transformation from absolute stillness and immobility to total animation, to an articulation and disarticulation of every single part, just as Totò would achieve with his own mask and entire body. Thanks to this face, Petrolini was able to penetrate the fortified citadel of the classics and to assume the likeness of Othello and Hamlet. In doing so, he reversed their image and brought their dramas to the level of the grayest of workaday life. All the while, with equal success, he adapted himself to meet the challenges of both the stage and the camera. While Blasetti did nothing more than film Petrolini's theatrical performance in his *Nerone* (*Nero*), director Campogalliani had him act in *Il medico per forza* (*The Doctor in Spite of Himself*) and *Il cortile* (*The Courtyard*), thus allowing him to reveal his elasticity and mastery of his voice and body, not to mention the absolute unpredictability of his acting and lines.

Petrolini liked to compare his work to that of a thief who ably steals the traits and idiosyncrasies of characters he meets on the street, in cafés, at the movies or in theaters, or even on the screen. He gleaned a great part of his material from the golden years of the star system and the liberty—and D'Annunzio-influenced cinema of the 1910s. Whether through his satire of

Lida Borelli and her sappy sentimentality in films like *Ma l'amor mio non muore!* (*My Love Will Never Die!*), his character Gastone the *viveur* and "100 percent photogenic" artist (a parody of actors like the effeminate Mario Bonnard), or his sketches of characters like the Gigi "er Bullo," or Gigi "the Bully," from Rome (seemingly inspired by Bartolomeo Pinelli's engravings), with his performances, Petrolini created a force field, an alchemic melting pot in which he composed and transformed theatrically and cinematographically derived elements drawn from his observations of everyday reality. Petrolini would become a model for comic acting in decades that followed, from Sordi to Verdone and even Gigi Proietti.

While Petrolini's style was a marked renewal of multifaceted acting, the comics of the 1930s, who demonstrated a perfect ability to integrate elements of stage and screen, embraced a return to genres, to linguistic specialization, to variety, and to different character types, gestures, and masks. With comics like Totò, Govi, Macario, and Sergio Tofano, Italian cinema saw a massive grafting and transformation of theatrical elements in cinema. Thanks to screenwriters like Metz, Marchesi, Zavattini, and Tofano himself, and to gag men plucked from humor magazines, lines drawn from classic jokes abounded on the cinematic scene, but these writers also introduced surreal plays-on-words, nonsense, and paradoxical situations that would help reshape the internal dialogical and communicative functions of a consistent space in the system.

Totò was the second comic superstar who would redefine 1930s acting by bringing his variety-show moves and jokes to the screen. But above all, he did so by using his body, a perfect example of Edward Gordon Craig's theory of the Über-marionette. Totò could apparently break the laws of physics: his body seemed completely double-jointed, and he could move every limb independently and in perfect asynchrony. More than anyone else in his generation, Totò had a genealogic tree that seemed to stretch back to the night of time, incorporating the ancestral fame of characters like Pulcinella and Sciosciammocca, the shrewdness of Zanni, the forcefulness of the plautine masks, and Capitan Fracassa from the *commedia dell'arte*.

Directors who fished in theatrical spawning waters had no problems when it came to expressive talent: their job was subordinate to the needs of the actors and it consisted in seamlessly showcasing their acting ability. Mattoli's work was exemplary in this sense. He brought to the set his previous experience as a theatrical director and he rapidly achieved success by mixing theatrical, cinematographic, and vaudevillian codes. With every film, he reached wide audiences by sounding comic and sentimental chords. But it would not be until the 1940s that Mattoli would bring two actors—Fabrizi and Magnani, who had been praised by the journal *Cinema*—out from conventional space and make them break new air in his film *L'ultima carrozzella* (*The Last Wagon*), He illuminated their faces with natural light and he asked them to reinvent themselves by throwing off the chains of their theatrical careers. Mattoli took part in the systemic change that was happening. He changed the way he worked by taking a natural approach that was in harmony with the young actors who hoped to reinvent Italian cinema. Such artists considered his work a negative model to be avoided at all costs. Reviewer Gianni Puccini would attack Fabrizi and films like *L'ultima carrozzella* in the pages of *Cinema* with the same violence and reasoning that he would reserve for his criticism of Fellini's early work in the postwar era.

During this period of transformation, Fabrizi's contribution would become a defining element. He worked not only as a star of the screen but throughout the entire creative process of the film, providing the story and developing the screenplay with the director. He also contributed to the screenplays for *Avanti c'è posto* (*Before the Postman*, 1942) and Bonnard's *Campo de' Fiori* (*Peddler and the Lady*, 1943), films that shared their atmosphere with *L'ultima carrozzella*. Together with Rossellini in *Roma città aperta* (*Rome, Open City*), Fabrizi learned how to use his body and voice but he also mastered silence and facial expressions as a means to communicate far-reaching messages.

The case of Fabrizi was the first and most macroscopic in a system that was breaking apart and rebuilding itself by allowing other characters to bring their knowledge and skill to the scene. Without resorting to preexisting repertoires of portraits of the Italian, these individuals were put to work building the new system based on entirely new codes.

When, in a famous advertising campaign of 1926–27, Metro Goldwyn Mayer first used its slogan, "More Stars than in Heaven," thus asserting that the MGM stars were diamonds in the sky above Cineland, there seemed to be no visible trace of the Italian comet that had streaked across the same sky and disintegrated in the early 1920s.

In the 1920s, the glorious cluster of Italian stars exploded when it came in contact with the postwar atmosphere, shattering into a tide of fragments soon destined to leave collective memory. The void of Italian stars would soon be filled by American actors who—just as MGM's triumphant slogans proclaimed—marched on Rome on the eve of Mussolini's rise to power. Their army was led by Douglas Fairbanks, John Gilbert, Norma Shearer, and Joan Crawford.

Vittorio de Sica's rendition of "Parlami d'amore Mariú!" ("Maria, Let's Talk about Love") in *Gli uomini che mascalzoni . . .* (*What Scoundrels Men*

Are!, 1932) and Elsa Merlini belting "Oh, come sono felice, felice, felice . . ." ("Oh, I'm so happy, happy, happy . . .") in *La segretaria privata* (based on István Szomaházy's *Privatsekretärin*, *The Office Girl* or *Private Secretary*) can be credited with erasing the demimonde from the horizons of Italian moviegoers once and for all. Such performances brought these new Italian actors closer to the audience and they showed how the space on the screen perfectly mirrored the space of life in Italy. At the same time, the star system had yet to undergo a palingenesis and metamorphosis. As Italian cinema was crossing the threshold of sound, the new Italian film actors—with their everyday body language, their way of smiling, dancing, and typing on a typewriter— transformed the silver screen into a faithful mirror and accomplice of the new dreams of the Italians, who were timidly breaching the threshold of their country's industrialization. More than anyone else, De Sica played a crucial role in the renewal of the 1930s star system. Many would follow in his footsteps, like Assia Noris, Isa Pola, Gino Cervi, Maurizio d'Ancora, Fosco Giachetti, and Roldano Lupi. Some time later, there was a more ambitious attempt—which met with modest results—to launch Isa Miranda and Amedeo Nazzari, stars capable of shining even in the international firmament, into orbit.[35]

Toward the end of the 1930s, two concurrent factors helped to push the star system upward and to make it shimmer once again: the birth of Cinecittà and the 1938 Alfieri Law, which protected and encouraged Italian film production and pushed American producers out of the Italian marketplace. No matter how hard Italian filmmakers tried to generate a star system that could serve as a surrogate for the sudden disappearance of the American divinities, the void created by their absence soon became all too clear, as did the fact that Italian faux-Hollywood products shone like brass.

In 1936, 65 percent of Italians said they preferred American cinema while 16 percent preferred Italian cinema. Little changed in 1938: 63 percent of Italians still said they liked Hollywood. Even the viewer who had been blinded by autarchic ideology and the most obtuse of critics could not deny that Irasema Dilian and Lilia Silvi were not comparable to Deanna Durbin and Shirley Temple and that Sandro Ruffini was no William Powell. Gary Cooper and Greta Garbo and myriad deities of the screen and familiar heroes could not be cancelled from the collective consciousness by decree, nor did they assume enemy status, even if it was inevitable that actors like Maria Mercader, Doris Duranti, Leda Gloria, and Maria Denis would be adopted as the angels of the Italian family's dinner table conversation.[36] The Italian movie-going public had already become accustomed to wearing rabbit's wool and drinking karkade (products promoted by the fascists, the one because it was produced in Italy, the other because it came from Italy's colonies in Africa) and it decided to accept the new light of Italian stars as Italians slowly became fond of and learned to love actors like Alida Valli, Massimo Girotti, Gino Cervi, Rossano Brazzi, Andrea Checchi, Doris Duranti, Elisa Cegani, Luisa Ferida, Paola Barbara, and Clara Calamai, among others.

Anna Magnani and Aldo Fabrizi were entirely anomalous: they had been plucked from the stages of variety theaters and they would act as ferryboat captains for professional actors who were entering a new and unknown dimension as they began to play characters in whom there seemed to be no distinction between art and life, screen and reality. Their faces were inscribed with the signs of pain, the light of hopes, and the collective expectations of the Italian people.

The Journey and Themes of Cinematic Propaganda

In the early 1930s, the fascist regime changed its tactics: ruralist ideology was abandoned and any reference to fascist intimidation tactics was expunged as policymakers attempted to create the image of a pacified, harmonious Italy that was dominated by a petit-bourgeois ideology. At the same time, celebrative and monumental policies were implemented as the government sought to bridge the past and the present.

With his populism and utopian aspirations for equality, Blasetti found himself out of synch with respect to the regime's new leanings when he delivered his interpretation of the Risorgimento with his films 1860 (*Gesuzza the Garibaldian Wife*) and *Vecchia guardia* (*Old Guard*).

From the moment that the government began to lend its strong support to the Italian film industry, Freddi and the top tier of the regime did not want the revolutionary epic to be celebrated with *strapaese* (overly nationalistic) tones: "The Regime," Freddi would later write, "certainly had no need for digging up elements that could bait or provoke damaging reactions."[37] Despite his unveiled disapproval of the film, Freddi himself recounted how *Vecchia guardia* was met with considerable success in Germany: "Director Blasetti and the little star were even received by Hitler with great fanfare accompanied by celebrations and news coverage."[38] Before Blasetti, Giovacchino Forzano had attempted to relate the nation's history from World War I to the fascist conquest of power with *Camicia nera* (*Black Shirt*, 1933), an overarching fresco that combined fiction, documentary filmmaking, and futurist influences.

Beginning in 1935, fascism seemed to ask the film industry to create stories that would help to construct a monument to the present in the form of a synthesis of Italy's millenarian history. Luis Trenker's *Condottieri* (*Giovanni de Medici: The Leader*, 1937) can be interpreted in the light of this, as can films like Carmine Gallone's spectacular *Scipioine l'Africano* (*Scipio Africanus: The Defeat of Hannibal, Scipio the African*, or *The Defeat of Hannibal*, 1937), the only film on ancient Rome for which no production expense was spared during Mussolini's entire "imperial" period. In *Condottieri*, the director constructed the figure of leader drawing from Nordic mythologies and mountaineering, elements extraneous to fascism. But at any given moment, it is easy to read the story of Giovanni delle Bande Nere, the famous Renaissance mercenary, as a forerunner of Mussolini and nascent fascism. *Scipione l'Africano*, on the other hand, was a film to which the regime gave its unmitigated support in terms of production, although the results were largely disappointing. In this work, the director's mobilization of the masses, the language of the actors and their acting, and his camera moves revealed a kinship that was closer to the history of opera than that of cinema. His excessive use of shots of extras lined up in their tunics, their arms raised in the Roman salute, the lavish orchestral score, and the overstated theatrical acting even made audiences laugh.

With the onset of war in Ethiopia, requests for direct propaganda began to arrive again from all parts: Freddi himself implemented policies for state control of the film industry based on the "interests of cinema within the framework of the Nation's interest" and a mobilization of militant intellectuals followed.[39] After directing *Sentinelle di bronzo* (*Sentinels of Bronze*, 1937) in Africa, Romolo Marcellini went to Spain where, together with journalist Gian Gaspare Napolitano, he made *Los novios de la muerte* (*The Lovers* [*Bridegrooms*] *of Death*, 1937). In the eyes of fascist intellectuals, Africa and Spain opened new horizons that had always been denied to the executors of war and they allowed them to assert their role as the legitimate singers of fascism's enterprises.

In fictional films, starting in 1935 with films like *Passporto rosso* (*Red Passport*) up through Camerini's *Il grande appello* (*The Last Roll-Call*), ruralist ideology was salvaged as a mirage that offered jobs and redemption for thousands of landless farmers. In Genina's *Squadrone bianco* (*White Squadron*, 1936), the most erudite and sophisticated film from a formalist perspective made during this era (similar to the French Foreign Legion films),[40] the antibourgeois polemic culminated in the exaltation of heroics and military sacrifice.[41] Documentaries also found a place next to fictional works. In the case of Corrado d'Errico's *Cammino degli eroi* (*The Path of Heroes*, 1936), the film tried to depict the war in Ethiopia as a major public works project.

After Ethiopia, Italian filmmakers rushed out to cover the war in Spain. Besides the film by Marcellini, who would also make *L'uomo della legione* (*The*

Man from the [Fascist] Legion, 1940), there were other notable documentaries like Giorgio Ferroni's *Arriba España, España Una, Grande, Libre!* (*Onward Spain! Spain, United, Great, and Free!*, 1939) and Genina's *L'assedio dell'Alcazar* (*The Siege of the Alcazar*, 1940), perhaps the most spectacular and best-made film on the Spanish civil war. After returning from Spain, Ferrori made *Ebbrezza del cielo* (*The Thrill of the Skies*, 1939), a passionate story about a young group of glider pilots in the city of Asiago (where the plateau is ideal for gliders). After a series of failed attempts, they ultimately manage to build a flight-worthy glider. In the film, their triumphant return from Spain becomes a pretext for celebration of their accomplishments with a series of flashbacks. The film ends with the first Italian experiment with color aerial shots of the Asiago plateau.

During this same period, Alessandrini made fictional films like *Cavalleria* (*Cavalry*, 1936) and *Luciano Serra pilota* (*Luciano Serra, Pilot*, 1938). These films offered a new model for the fascist and pre-fascist hero. It drew more from the tradition of the romantic hero and moviegoers could identify with them more than any before. In *Cavalleria*, Savoy militarism is viewed—albeit by stretching the truth—as an ideal antecedent for fascist thuggery.

With Italy's entrance into the war came the first explicit calls for the development of propaganda filmmaking. But during this period, the very intellectuals and facilities that the fascists had planned to gather began to go missing.[42] Despite its openly propagandistic intentions, navy commander Francesco de Robertis's *Uomini sul fondo* (*Men at the Bottom [of the Sea]*, 1942) was respectfully admired by the men of neorealist cinema for its dry style, its ability to make objects speak, and the immediacy of its verisimilitude.[43] Together with this and Robertis's subsequent films, other notable works include Genina's *Bengasi* (*Benghazi*, 1942); Esodo Pratelli's *Gente dell'aria* ([*National Fascist Association of*] *People in Flight*, 1942); *I tre aquilotti* (*The Three Pilots*, 1942), directed by Mattoli and written by Vittorio Mussolini, the Duce's brother; Baffico's *I trecento della settima* (*The Three Hundred of the Seventh*, 1943); and Vergano's *Quelli della montagna* (*Soldiers on the Mountain*, 1943). These documentary-style films were often surprisingly well made and they had a remarkable ability to recount heroic exploits in an atmosphere that gave little room to a triumphant and bellicose spirit.

The last—but not least—contribution to war propaganda would be Roberto Rossellini's three titles, *La nave bianca* (*The White Ship*, 1941), *Un pilota ritorna* (*A Pilot Returns*, 1942), and *L'uomo della croce* (*Man with a Cross* or *The Man with the Cross*, 1943), films that celebrated the navy, air force, and infantry, respectively.[44]

Following his contribution to the screenplay for *Luciano Serra pilota*, Rossellini quickly revealed his ability in storytelling as he sought to muster powerful rhetorical figures with any means possible. His Catholicism positioned him outside the warmongering contingent and his anti-spectacular choices were perhaps a reflection of the directorial ethics to which he would remain bound for the rest of his career. His demure style, the immediacy of his frames, and the dramatic sense that he created by approaching his characters with a quasi-documentary style were not out of step with regime's directives. At the same time, his filmmaking did not exalt fascism's bellicose power. Instead, his films revealed a war in which heroism was a form of individualistic expression, a war in which one participated because of a sense of duty but also in which idealism was fleeting. During this period, Rossellini was among the most willing to make propaganda films, albeit after his own fashion. The first such work was *Un pilota ritorna*, written by Tito Silvio Mursino, Vittorio Mussolini's penname. The next was by Asvero Gravelli. Gravelli was not just any fascist: he was a *gerarca* (hierarch) in the fascist party (that is, a top-tier leader) and editor-in-chief of *Antieuropa*, the "anti-European" fascist journal. He wrote *L'uomo della croce* to celebrate Father Rignaldo Giuliani, winner of the Italian Gold Medal for heroism and star of fascist propaganda. Rossellini finished the film in 1942 but it was released the following year, just before fascism was to fall. In the months that followed, Rossellini would be ostracized not so much for his political stance as for his unreliability in respecting production schedules. This allowed him time to reflect and to make choices based on a conscience shaped by the war. He would head down a path shared by millions of Italians. It would be no easy task to shake off the memory of these three films and hail Rossellini as the father of the new Italian cinema immediately following the completion of *Roma città aperta* (*Rome, Open City*).

Among other propaganda films worth remembering, Albani's nostalgic and anachronistic *Redenzione* (*Redemption*, 1942, story by Roberto Farinacci) exalted the campaign of fascist intimidation in Cremona in the 1920s.

As far as drama was concerned, Alessandrini achieved thrilling success with his diptych *Noi vivi* (*We the Living*) and *Addio Kira!* (*Goodbye Kira!*), based on the Ayn Rand novel, which had been translated into Italian by publisher Baldini e Castoldi in 1938. In these films, the Soviet Union's horrors, torture, and abuses of power and Stalin's purges serve as a papier-mâché backdrop on which the director projects more than a few unsettling fears and perceptions of imminent catastrophe for the Italian nation. The film reached the top of the box office thanks to performances by Alida Valli and Rossano Brazzi. Alessandrini also made *Lettere al sottotenente* (*Letters to the Second Lieutenant*, 1942, screenplay by Alba de Cèspedes), a drama that, like many other films from this era, revealed the perception of imminent doom.

For all intents and purposes, Mussolini and fascism's day of judgment was near and brought with it decisive choices for everyone. Many had already opened their eyes, although the majority of the men of Italian cinema would only take a stand after fascism's fall. None of this happened overnight, but the events weighed heavily on Italians' consciences. This was true even for those like the men of Italian cinema, who lived in fictitious worlds.

A Silver Screen Rife with Dreams

As a group of young antifascist intellectuals rallied around the journal *Cinema* and attempted to establish the coordinates of the new poetics of cinema, Cinecittà's standing army chose to flee from the present. It opted instead to seek refuge in a world where it could deposit the hopes, expectations, and desires of a country that was no longer pushed toward the future by warmongering. During this period, the theme of escape on the screen became a symphonic motif that unified midlevel production. It expressed the collective need to move away from the bywords of fascism and to impugn a war lacking any truly meaningful motivation. In the years leading up to the war, poor and middle-class Italy had been forced to don synthetic fabrics like Lanital, Lunesil, Filital, Cocafil, Cisnivea, and Cisalfa. But the country had never abandoned its dreams and its desire to cover itself with banknotes and debts. In 1938, it began to march behind flags that displayed the faces of actors like Alida Valli, Amedeo Nazzari, Lilia Silvi, Rossano Brazzi, Fosco Giachetti, Assia Noris, Luisa Ferida, Massimo Girotti, and Maria Denis, among others. This was an Italy that felt dissatisfied and betrayed in its expectations. In the moment that the restrictions began and the future seemed darker and darker, these Italians did not abandon their dream to live elsewhere (perhaps in Hungary), to carve out a small place for themselves where they could desire furs and tailored suits, silk stockings, luxury, and Grand Hotels where the superfluous triumphed.[45]

If we study these films by grouping them into homogeneous subsets, we can examine the discrepancies between the dreams proposed by the silver screen (caressed, as it were, by the eyes of millions of women) and the material reality of life in Italy during this period. There is no doubt, however, that these dreams became surrogates for those offered by Hollywood. Such subsets created the conditions for the fusion of the viewer's desire and the bodies on the screen described by Roland Barthes in *A Lover's Discourse: Fragments*: "I want to be the other, I want the other to be me, as if we were united, enclosed within the same sack of skin, the garment being merely the smooth envelope of that coalescent substance out of which my amorous Image-repertoire is made."[46]

Leafing through brochures published by the ENIC, ICI, and Cinevita, one is struck by the wealth, lavishness, and opulence: "Jole Voleri, the most elegant actress of the screen in the most elegant film of the season," declares an advertisement for *La danza dei milioni* (*The Dance of Millions*, 1940). The female lead of *Un marito per il mese d'aprile* (*A Husband for the Month of April*) is presented as "Mara, a young beautiful millionaire," who "meets a hot-blooded South American on a steamship." In *Pierpin* (with a story about an actress named Pierpin), "The silks and velvet vied with one another to entice the ladies with their multicolored patterns, their shine, and their softness." In *L'ultimo ballo* (*The Last Ball*), "Signora Marcus, known by her friends as the 'beautiful Titta,' will soon celebrate her fortieth birthday. Ever surrounded by a regiment of suitors, she lives for nothing but frivolity: balls, parties, tennis matches."

On the eve of war, Italy enthusiastically embraced the new prophets of cinematic ritual. These soothsayers turned Nostradamus inside-out, predicting windfalls of thousands upon thousands of lire a month in films like Carlo Borghesio and Mario Soldati's *Due milioni per un sorriso* (*Two Million for a Smile*, 1939), Dino Falconi's *Vento di milioni* (*Millions in the Wind*, 1940), Camerini's *Centomila dollari* (*One-Hundred-Thousand Dollars*, 1940), and Guido Brignone's *Miliardi, che follia!* (*Billions, It's Crazy!*, 1942). In just a few short years, thanks to screenwriters like Giudo Fiorini, Gino Sensani, Antonio Vlaente, Virgilio Marchi, and Vinicio Paladini, Cinecittà had managed to create a world on the screen more real than reality. Millions of moviegoers cast their gaze on the bodies, furs, and worlds created for their female leads by directors like Mattoli, Neufeld, Bonnard, D'Errico, Camerini, Mastrocinque, and Gallone. There is no hiding the fact that certain dreams fed the collective consciousness by creating a instantaneous placebo effect that proved extremely useful in the hardest of times.

Today, these films are an excellent source of information in measuring the desires of middle- and lower-middle-class Italians during the period that spanned the advent of sound up to the world war. Dresses, stockings, jewelry, furnishings, attitudes, and small climbs up the social ladder spoke of an active reality in the collective imagination that was expanding in opposition to the worlds and horizons laid out by fascism. It was a fragile reality but fundamental for the creation of illusory worlds where Italians could take refuge and find a moment of relief.

It is difficult to find any individuals or groups wearing black shirts in propaganda films from this era, and even more arduous to discern language or metaphors borrowed from the vocabulary of war. In situations, dialogues, and bon ton of comedies made during this period, no Italian wearing a black shirt can be found. As if by some law of *contrappasso* (Dantean poetic justice) with respect to the 1938 adoption of Hitler's race laws in Italy, the films made from 1938 to 1943 created a quarantine and an embargo that stopped all infiltration or contamination by fascist germs.

The so-called *telefoni bianchi* (white telephone) films (which I prefer to call *cinema déco*) have been studied in recent years by scholars like Alberto Farassino, Valentina Ruffin, and Pier Marco de Santi.[47] As I have shown in previous works, during the years leading up to the war, these films seemed to respond to Italians' true great expectations. The average Italian aspired not to conquer the world but rather to have a stable job with guaranteed pay and a modern, well-furnished home. This genre reached its peak during the war years with highly successful films like Neufeld's *Mille lire al mese* (*A Thousand Lire a Month*, 1939), Mattoli's *Ore 9 lezione di chimica* (*Schoolgirl Diary*, 1941), and Jean de Limur's *Apparizione* (*Apparition*, 1943).

These films ignored linguistic convention and seamlessly mixed hundreds of foreign words with local dialects.[48] When you lived for a few hours in worlds that could have been created by Gio Ponti; when you had seen your heroine get into a stylish car of the day like the Cabriolet Viotti Gran Turismo; when you had seen her sit in an imitation Mies Van der Rohe tubular chair; when you had seen her prance around a living room furnished with Venini glass fixtures created in Murano by Archimede Seguso, Ercole, Barovier, Napoleone Martinuzzi, or Carlo Scarpa; when, in the face of those who forbade foreign words, you found yourself wanting to wear a *tailleur*, to offer a drink to a very chic miss, to get into a taxi driven by a chauffeur, to sip a vermouth, to pay with a check, to let your sex appeal explode as you danced a foxtrot, it was difficult to return to the real world, no easy task to make do with the food rations, the fear, the trauma, the military catastrophe on all fronts, and the grief that struck the entire nation.

Today, the silver screen offers us a detailed portrait of the average pacifist Italian's wartime impulses and changes in attitudes, hopes, dreams, needs, expectations, and living standards.

The ideology of lavishness—with no reference whatsoever to what was actually happening in Italy at the time—can be found in many titles from this period. In Mattoli's *Lo vedi come sei . . . lo vedi come sei?!* (*Take a Look at Yourself . . . Just Take a Look at Yourself!*, 1939), two cousins deplete an inheritance of millions by auctioning off millions of banknotes for just 2 lire. In *Centomila dollari*, the proud autarchic Lilly refused to accept a check for 100,000 dollars offered her by a rich American in exchange for a dinner by candlelight (this was an evident allusion to the government's decision during the early 1940s to ask the country to make sacrifices for the imminent conflict). These films could sense the storm that surrounded them but they sought with all means to keep it out as they continued to evoke contemporary American and European films.

Even when set elsewhere in conventional locations (Budapest, for the most part), these comedies always kept the viewer in a familiar, tangible world, a friendly and hospitable space that left drama outside. For example, when actress Alida Valli tried to sell an encyclopedia in *L'amante segreta* (*The Secret Lover*), viewers could easily recognize the famous *Enciclopedia Treccani* edited by fascist ideologue Giovanni Gentile. For almost five years, because its reality was so familiar to Italians, a world that lay seemingly right around the corner, Hungary would serve as a magical place, an ideal refuge for their dreams.

Formal Beauty

Despite attacks by critics who flew the flag of realism, during the 1940s Italian cinema saw the emergence of a series of films that were immediately labeled *calligrafici* (calligraphic—intended in the etymologic sense, that is, "beautifully written"). Unjustly, many directors of such films have long suffered a quasi mark of infamy due to reductive and negative criticism.[49] The same criticism has also been aimed at the works produced and the quality achieved by those who worked at the Centro Sperimentale and Cinecittà.

The debut works of directors from this period—like Mario Soldati, Luigi Chiarini, Renato Castellani, Alberto Lattuada, Ferdinando Maria Poggioli, and Luigi Zampa—show their literary, artistic, and cinematic culture. They did not reveal (apparently) any strong ideological or pedagogical intentions. They were, however, driven by a strong ethical tension and their will to assert cinema's expressive autonomy. They championed aesthetic function and, at the same time, they sought to link cinema to all of the arts.[50] The common literary references from this period were drawn from nineteenth-century Italian writers like Fogazzaro and De Marchi and from nineteenth-century Russian and French literature. These directors wanted to achieve a style that allowed them to create a perfect fusion and a cross-contamination of different artistic and expressive languages. Their artistic intentions subjugated all other possible functions of cinema.

Such films were unafraid to reveal their sources and to endorse the umbilical relationship between cinema and literary and artistic traditions. These were intellectual films, free of any significant acts of submission or compliance with the regime, films that could compete with contemporary foreign cinema.

These were works that drew from the artisanal, Renaissance workshop tradition that had been passed down to Cinecittà. Many writers contributed—often significantly—to these films, including Corrado Alvaro, Emilio Cecchi, Francesco Pasinetti, Vitaliano Brancati, Mario Bonfantini, Umberto Barbaro, Ennio Flaiano, Ettore M. Margadonna, Leo Longanesi, and, last but not least, Giacomo Debenedetti, who was never credited because of the race laws.

From a moralistic point of view, these works oscillated between incense and holy water, between damnation and carnal desire. From a figurative point of view, they borrowed heavily from French directors like Renoir, Carné, Feyder, and Duvivier and from German and American cinema as well. Thanks to camera operators like Massimo Terzano, Ubaldo Arata, and Carlo Montuori and to top screenwriters and costume designers like Virgilio Marchi, Gino Sensani, and Antonio, these films mixed elements drawn from the Tuscan *macchiaioli*, pre-Raphaelites, and symbolists with the best of European cinema.[51]

The first to seek the spotlight aggressively was Mario Soldati, with films like *Dora Nelson* (1939), *Piccolo mondo antico* (*Old-Fashioned World*, 1941), *Malombra* (1942), *Tragica notte* (*Tragic Night*, 1942), and *Quartieri alti* (*In High Places*, 1943). Beyond his linguistic and figurative ability, Soldati deserves praise for being among the first to place psychologically and dramatically complex female characters center stage.[52] The same can be said of Chiarini and his films *La bella addormentata* (*Sleeping Beauty*, 1942), *Via delle cinque lune* (*Street of the Five Moons*, 1942), and *La locandiera* (*The Inn Keeper's Wife*, 1943). Chiarini was a theoretician of "absolute form" and he showed a remarkable ability to create new worlds through his excellent use of sets, costumes, and photography. His works were charged with a sensuality that enshrouded the atmosphere and objects on the screen, even though his style seemed immediately to become academic and not live up to his talent as a director.

Films made during this period by Lattuada, Poggioli, and Castellani revealed personalities that belonged to a world that had already been widely depicted. In films like Lattuada's *Giacomo l'idealista* (*Giacomo the Idealist*, 1942) and *La freccia nel fianco* (*The Arrow*, 1943), Poggioli's *Addio giovinezza!* (*Goodbye to Youth!*, 1940) and *Il cappello del prete* (*The Priest's Hat*, 1943), and Castellani's *Un colpo di pistola* (*A Pistol Shot*, 1942) and *Zazà* (1942), the directors used sets and realities created on the soundstage to explore inner conflicts and to show the collapse of a world and the sense that future events that would bring purification.

This group's humanistic orientation and the fact that it lacked any form of populism isolated it from the rest of Italian cinema. The label *calligrafici* would act as a sort of sanitary cordone. Regardless of the critical ostracism that would continue to grow even after the war, these filmmakers helped to assert the director's role as an author and orchestrator of a highly skilled, experienced, and professional team.

A Progressive Shift toward Reality

The 1933 article published by Leo Longanesi in the magazine *L'Italiano* might as well have been undersigned by the founding fathers of neorealism: "One must take the camera to the streets, to the courtyards, barracks, and train stations. All that is needed to make a logical, natural Italian film is to go out into the street, stop anywhere, and observe what happens for a half hour."[53]

Over the course of the 1930s, the Italian landscape would become the natural backdrop for the director's ideological and stylistic choices and his affiliation. Looking back today, it is clear that from the outset of the 1930s, these filmmakers set out—and not only as tourists—to discover "one thousand and one" Italys, from the country's stereotypes to its people's varied ways of life.

At the same time, it is important to remember that the winning formula was not always that of rural, proletarian country life. Italy in 1930s cinema aspired to the models created by Camerini: its films were populated by middle-class office workers, stenographers and secretaries, and it featured models of prosperity and social pacification as required by the regime.

The path toward realism first trodden by Camerini diverged from Blasetti's. One could even say that at the beginning of the 1930s, those who wanted to head down the trails of realism were faced with a three-pronged fork in the road. On one hand, there were those led by Barbaro. These young cineastes had studied at the Centro Sperimentale or they had worked as critics or editors for the journal *Cinema*.[54] Fortified by Pudovkin, they awaited the advent of the messianic individual. On the other hand, Blasetti took it upon himself to celebrate the everyman soul of fascism. Finally, there was the path taken by Camerini, who chose to explore urban space and the outskirts of the big cities and who also examined the geography of collective petty desires.

Slowly, the horizons of the visible began to expand. Some year before *I bambini ci guardano* (*The Children Are Watching Us* or *The Little Martyr*), Francesco Pasinetti made *Il canale degli angeli* (*The Canal of the Angels*, 1934), set in a poor neighborhood in Venice, a story of adultery as seen through the eyes of a child who becomes a silent, sympathetic witness to a family drama. In 1933, German director Walter Ruttmann's *Acciaio* (*Steel*) was an attempt to meld visual elements drawn from the German avant-garde with the regime's need to celebrate Italy's industrialization in epic terms.[55] The same can be said of *La fossa degli angeli* (*Tomb of the Angels*, 1937), shot in the marble-rich Apuan Alps in Liguria, a film hailed by Giacomo Debenedetti as a "symphony of quarries."

Other films that can be included in this group are Materazzo's *Treno popolare* (*Tourist Train*, 1933), Ivo Perilli's *Ragazzo* (*Boy*, 1933), Brignone's *Passaporto rosso* (*Red Passport*, 1935), Marco Elter's *Le scarpe al sole* (*Alpine Love*, 1935, based on the novel by Paolo Monelli [translated into English with the title *Toes Up*]), Amleto Palermi's *Porto* (*Port*, 1935), Baffico's *Terra di nessuno* (*Nobody's Land*, 1938), and Carlo Campogalliani's *Montevergine* (also known as *La grande luce* [*The Great Light*] 1939), among others.

A group of films made in the early 1940s, long considered precursors to neorealism, marked the true moment of confluence and maturation of the cinematic experiences examined up to this point. Today, we rightly consider these works as part of the same process, even though they were the product of a different poetics, ethics, and culture: Blasetti's *Quattro passi tra le nuvole* (*Four Steps in the Clouds*); Mario Bonnard's *Avanti c'è posto* (*Before the Postman*, 1942) and *Campo de' fiori* (*Peddler and the Lady*, 1943); Palermi's *I bambini ci guardano* (*The Children Are Watching Us* or *The Little Martyr*, 1940) and *La peccatrice* (*The Sinner*, 1940); Gianni Franciolini's *Fari nella nebbia* (*Headlights in the Fog*, 1942); and Mattoli's *L'ultima carrozzella* (*The Last Wagon*, 1943). Of course, Visconti's *Ossessione* obviously represents the culmination of the poetics and theories shared by a group of filmmakers—not to mention the comet of future Italian cinema.[56]

On one hand, the group that surrounded Visconti (Gianni Puccini, Mario Alicata, Giuseppe de Santis, Massimo Mida, and Antonio Pietrangeli) and Visconti himself were directly influenced by French cinema (Visconti worked with Renoir). On the other hand, they looked to literature and American film as a powerful model to which they aspired. They also chose to assume the role of inheritors of the *verista* literary tradition. Giovanni Verga in particular would serve as a fertile element.

Ossessione was the fruit of a set of congruent forces and the widespread desire to create a new Italian cinema. Through the powerful construction of the images, through the dramatic and constantly connotative use of black-and-white contrast and tone, through its patches of breathing landscape that served as an accomplice and witness to characters Gino and Giovanna's passion, *Ossessione* marked the advent of a new era in the eyes of most critics. With two articles published in *Film* ("Neorealismo" ["Neorealism"] and "Realismo e moralità" ["Realism and Morality"]) christened an individual for whom he had waited fifteen years: "This is a piece of Italy never before seen . . .

Finally, we have been given *Ossessione*, the artistic depiction of an anguished reality as opposed to fixed-formula archeologies and entertainments."[57]

The wait was over: from the moment it was first screened publicly, *Ossessione* became a rallying cry and a powder keg that accelerated the fragmentation and transformation of Italian cinema. It also forced many directors to take sides and make choices that would allow them to wash their hands of their previous conduct.

Everything began with *Ossessione*: the true renewal of the iconographic repertoire and the creation of a new connection between the figurative arts, the national culture, and what was happening in Italy at the time. Federico Zeri was the last but not the least to recognize Visconti's role as the comet of the new Italian cinema:

> [His] repertoire of characters, frames, locations, and visual cues was rooted in a vast terrain of figurative culture, where Jean Renoir's cinematic France and the impressionist painters alternate with the Italy of the nineteenth-century naturalist painters . . . But art critics have yet to conduct such an investigation. The chain of events started by Visconti and the perception of Italy created by cinematography unfolded under our very eyes, with such richness and variety that our cinema can be considered a guide to contemporary art.[58]

The Cinema of Salò

Salò represents more of a subchapter than a bona fide chapter in the history of Italian cinema. In terms of production, nothing happened in Salò that did not occur shortly thereafter in the new Italian cinema, which was born amidst the ruins of war and fueled by the spirit of an Italy that wished to be reborn and to redeem itself.

Although research in the past twenty years has offered a more complex and balanced view of the Republic of Salò, there have been no new results in regard to cinema.[59] Freddi was the first to gather together the republic's artistic forces. After September 8 (the date when the armistice with the Allies was announced), he decided to move the capital of Italian cinema to Venice and begin filming again. The fascists of Salò attempted to create a Cinecittà surrogate using inexistent monies and officials who had remained in the background for years. This was a period of compromise, of double-crossing, of politics and alliances forged with one eye on the unpredictable outcome of the conflict.

At the end of June 1945, Dr. Rosario Errigo delivered a report (never before published) to the Honorable Franco Libonati, undersecretary of the press and information, who had sent Errigo to evaluate the state of the republic's film industry. Today, this document offers a firsthand account of the available equipment, the monies invested in production, the box-office figures, and the fascists' dreams to give life to a new capital of Italian cinema in Venice.

> The renewal of film production began in Venice early last year with the opening of a new soundstage installed by Cines in the Giardini [the Public Gardens] with equipment owned by Cinecittà and another installed by Scalera Film on the [island of] Giudecca . . . During the same period, the Istituto LUCE installed a small developing and printing lab in Venice, but its operation has been sporadic.
>
> This new film production has received financial support from the Ministry of Popular Culture's resumed liquidation of the branches designated by bill 1061 passed on June 16, 1938, intended to aid films already in production. They have received additional support in particular through funds newly allocated by the legislative decree of March 20, 1944 . . .
>
> In accordance with the said decree, the Independent Credit Bureau for Film at the Banca Nazionale del Lavoro released a special fund of 52,500,000 lire earmarked for the management of the same company with the concession that advances for film production would not exceed 50 percent of the cost of each film.

Fernando Mezzasoma, who had been appointed head of the Ministry of Popular Culture of the Republic, swiftly sought to rebuild the film industry—albeit on a smaller scale—in Venice. A few months prior, the industry had been dismantled by the Germans and by the war. The few documents at our disposal reveal that he had little faith in the propagandistic powers of cinema; he awarded few grants and gave few green lights for the production of fictional films. He also did little to deal with the overall problems of production and distribution. His attitude toward fictional films is illustrated perhaps by his response to a grant request from Vittoria Film for *Diritto alla vita* (*The Right to Life*), a film backed by Giorgio Venturini, then chairman of the Ministry of Entertainment.

"In my opinion," Venturini had written, "the moral content and guaranteed artistic caliber of this film are such that it should be included in the seven titles that will be financed with the remaining funds." In his letter dated January 9, 1945, Mezzasoma answered: "It cannot be financed because it is not propaganda. Finance it yourself."[60]

At the same time, it is important to note that Venturini, whose background was in theater, had little experience in the field of cinema. He was sailing without a compass, getting by with modest means and strong opposition from Luigi Freddi and the toughest and fanatical fascists.

Nineteen films were put into production, with grants ranging from 1,700,000 lire for Piero Ballerini's *Fatto di cronaca* (*Ripped from the Headlines*) to 4,750,000 lire for Giorgio Ferroni's *Senza famiglia* (*Without Family*).

Mezzasoma's primary concern was that of giving new life to the Cinegiornale LUCE (LUCE Newsreels), a creature beloved and controlled by Mussolini from its birth until the end of the 1920s. Following interim-commissioner Giuseppe Croce's brief tenure, its former head Nino d'Aroma was appointed president. A closer look at this small subset will prove invaluable because it marks the moment that actual production in the Republic of Salò began. On one hand, these films were intended to hide the truth; on the other hand, they help us to understand the actual circumstances in which they were made.

Production offices were set up in the Bonvecchiati hotel near St. Mark's Square. While filmmakers were waiting to use the pavilions in the Public Gardens for developing and printing, they continued to send the negatives to Turin, risking bombardment along the way and absorbing high costs. Seventy-one persons—including technicians, journalists, photographers, and camera operators—produced an installment of *Giornale Luce* once a week in Venice. They were paid 10,000 lire a month. Not all of them shared the fascist faith. Some of them, like Rino Filippini, allowed themselves to be recruited as production staff with the promise that they would not be forced to work on propaganda films. The forty-five installments of *Giornale Luce* produced from October 11, 1943, to March 18, 1945 (numbers 374 through 428), often left the war in the background and focused instead on sports or world events. They also featured a wide range of pieces on arts and crafts, like the different engraved metallic buckles in Switzerland used to adorn the traditional suspenders worn in the various cantons, or wood carvings in the Val Gardena, or store-window mannequins in Denmark.

Early coverage of the war and the new political situation began between the first assembly of the Republican Fascist Party in Castelvecchio (in the province of Verona) with installment 380, December 1943. A special installment, number 386, was entitled "L'Italia s' è desta. 9 febbraio XXII: cronache del giuramento dell'esercito repubblicano in tutta l'Italia" ("Italy Has Awoken [from the first line of the "Inno di Mameli," "Mameli's Hymn," the Italian national anthem], February 9, XXII [twenty-second year of fascist rule, that is, 1944]: Reports from the Swearing in of the Republican Army across Italy"). From this moment on, although there was no coverage of the front, there would be stories on the bombardment of works of art, monuments, and churches in Rome and in the north, including the destruction of the Tempio

Malatestiano burial chapel in Rimini and the church of the Eremitani in Padua; the bombing of cities like Mestre and Treviso; the swearing in of new recruits; battalions with names like "Barbarigo" and "Aosta"; soldiers, infantrymen, sailors, and alpine troops shipping off for the front; and memorials for the fallen and visits to the wounded and mutilated. Every so often, viewers saw images of the infantry's attacks on Tito's partisans in Slovenia. The producers of these reels were careful to downplay the ferocity of these clashes and to emphasize that, as soon the valiant soldiers had taken the village and "purged it of the partisans' treachery . . . tranquility and jobs" would soon be restored (*Giornale*, number 395). News reel number 400 was entitled "Roll Call for the Discharged" and, borrowing from the parable of the prodigal son, it told the story of "roughly 50,000 discharged soldiers who have chosen to return to work and to fight. They have responded to the call of the Fatherland and have flooded Provincial Military Command Posts and barracks."

The partisans would make an appearance, just a few reels later, in number 410, the only newsreel produced by the Republic of Salò to mention the civil war that was taking place. This film is all the more striking because of its violent tone. The partisans did not count discharged soldiers among their ranks, the newsreel reported. They were instead "authentic assassins paid by our enemies . . . bastards, whose cowardice has led them to betray the Fatherland, bastards paid for their services by foreigners." This newsreel was also one of the few (two in all) to mention the Brigate Nere (Black Brigades), the Italian counterparts of the German SS. In the light of their poor performance, the filmmakers of Salò quickly chose to veil them in a propitious silence.

In general, and especially in the final months of the war, the Republic of Salò newsreels shunned news from the front and concentrated instead on the homeland front, covering speeches by fascist military chaplain Father Eusebio in Milan and Venice; a visit by fascist *gerarca* Alessandro Pavolini to the I Brigata Nera Mobile (the 1st Black Brigade Mobile Unit); the typical day in the lives of the troops like those of the 10th Mas Battalion; and festivities for the first anniversary of the Fasci republicani (Republican Fascist Party). Mussolini appeared as well, albeit sporadically, in homeopathic doses: presenting a battle flag to a legion of the Guardia Nazionale Republicana (National Republican Guard); reviewing a parade of the 10th Mas; commemorating the seventh anniversary of D'Annunzio's death at the Vittoriale monument. During the eighteen months before he was captured, the highlight of Mussolini's epiphany was reported in newsreel number 418, which covered his days in Milan and his speech at the opera; a rally in Piazza San Sepolcro; and his visit to the Legione autonoma mobile Ettore Muti (Independent Mobile Legion "Ettore Muti"), a unit notorious for torturing its prisoners. Aside from such coverage, the guiding force of the newsreels produced in Venice was silence: there was no mention of the tribunals in Verona, the fascist government's "socialization" of Italian industry, or the Linea gotica (Gothic Line) that divided the Republic of Salò from liberated Italy. And, of course, there was no reference to the Allies' advance.

In February 1944, just in time for the christening of three soundstages built on the grounds of the Biennale pavilions at the Venice Giardini, cameras and other equipment arrived in Venice from Prague, where they had been stored after being confiscated by the Nazis at Cinecittà. The Germans had taken the equipment from state and privately owned studios, claiming that they were trying to protect them from bombardment.

With marked understatement and lucid awareness of the difficulties that he faced, Venturini christened the modest studio lot in his inaugural speech of February 22: "That which you see before is certainly not Cinecittà [Cinema City]. Call it 'Cinema Village' if you like, but rest assured that careful city planning has taken into account substantial future expansion. Remember: even the great city of Rome was born on a small square furrow [plowed by Romulus]."[61]

Even more difficult was Venturini's attempted recruitment of actors, technicians, directors, and employees. For all intents and purposes, it was a failure. Osvaldo Valenti and Luisa Ferida were the only ones who departed willingly for the north. Names like Doris Duranti, Emma Gramatica, Elena Zareschi, Nada Fiorelli, and Olga Solbelli simply were not enough to send a tiny, however bright, star system into orbit in the Venetian sky. As far as screenwriters were concerned, Corrado Pavolini and Alessandro de Stefani headed north and Venetian Francesco Pasinetti worked as a screenwriter on Fernando Cerchio's *Buona fortuna* (*Good Luck*). As far as directors were concerned, only B-list names—Piero Ballerini, Mario Baffico, Francesco de Robertis, Carlo Borghesio, Fernando Cerchio, Ferruccio Cerio, and Flavio Calzavara—answered the call. "There's no use hiding it," wrote Mino Doletti, "the directors have gone missing."[62]

Nearly twenty films went into production in 1944. For the most part, the filmmakers carefully avoided propaganda and chose instead to tackle sentimental topics, comedy, and melodrama, films like Ballerini's *Un fatto di cronaca* (*Ripped from the Headlines*), Ferroni's *Senza famiglia* (*Without Family*, a film released in two "episodes"), and Baffico's *Ogni giorno è domenica* (*Every Day Is Sunday*). The following films also began production during the first months of 1945: Cerio's *Rosalba*, Ballerini's *L'angelo del miracolo* (*The Angel of the Miracle*), Cerio's *Posto di blocco* (*Check Point*), Baffico's *Trent'anni di servizio* (*Thirty*

Years of Service), Dino Hobbes Cecchini's *Fiori d'arancio* (*Orange Blossoms*), and De Robertis's *I figli della laguna* (*Children of the Lagoon*).

A few months after the *cinevillaggio* opened in Venice, it was already clear that fascist critics were not pleased with Venturini's management. The most violent attack came in the form of a late 1944 report to Mussolini (entitled "La cinematografia italiana a Venezia" ["Italian Cinema in Venice"]) by Asvero Gravelli.[63] In the days leading up to fall of Salò, filmmakers Francesco Pasinetti and the young Glauco Pellegrini worked on a strategy to make Venice the new center of film production immediately after the conflict's end (since the Roman film industry had been dismantled in the meantime). Working with antifascist forces, they planned to resume production there, with as little disruption as possible. In May 1945, Pasinetti and Pellegrini, who were working as representatives of the Ufficio tecnico per il cinema del Comitato di liberazione nazionale (National Liberation Committee Film Industry Technical Office), sent a report to the Allies' Psychological Warfare Branch in which they absolved Venturini and credited him with having stopped the Germans from taking cameras and other equipment with them as they retreated from Italy. They also commended Venturini for the fact that only one propagandistic film had been made under his tenure (this film, *Aeroporto* [*Airport*], they pointed out, had been green-lighted by the Germans).[64] Venturini's absolution was shortly followed by the government's decision to heal all wounds as soon as possible in the name of national unity and the country's reconstruction. But Pellegrini and Pasinetti's dream did not last long after Italy's liberation. Although Venice continued to be an ideal set for fictional and nonfictional films and documentaries, it would never be developed into a capital for film production.

3

ᴗ From Neorealism to *La dolce vita* ᴗ.

Rebuilding Italian Cinema from Scratch

In 1945, shortly after Italy's liberation, an article in *Mondo Nuovo* (*New World*, the country's first American-edited illustrated magazine) provided a snapshot of Italian cinema's death and resurrection:

> Producing a film in Italy is like building a house beginning with the roof . . . And yet films continue to be made on the soundstages. It is a wonder that only now, without the means of yesterday, Italian cinema continues to reflect the country's soul . . .
>
> Yesterday, Cinecittà was so luxurious. Today, it is a refugee camp. As if that were not enough, most of the equipment was taken to the North. The only remaining cameras and searchlights were hidden by some well-intentioned filmmakers. And what about the lighting? There are constant power outages. Film, materials to build sets, costumes, and makeup have become a problem. It is difficult just to find these things. But films continue to be made.[1]

In shooting *Roma città aperta* (*Open City* or *Rome, Open City*), neorealist filmmakers reinvented production methods: "No film had more difficulties to overcome than *Città aperta*. A makeshift soundstage was built in an old pavilion once used for dog racing. The dialogue was recorded after filming because there was no sound recording equipment."

This is the first article that describes the physical birth of neorealism. Through its depiction of the soundstage and re-creation of the sets, it immerses us in a surreal but still conventional working space: all previous production standards had been overturned; less prevailed over more, absence over presence. The stage was bare. The same studio that had once "broken one hundred" was now starting over from scratch.[2] In just a few months, one of the most efficient and advanced centers for film production had been dismantled.

And yet, just when the system seemed on the verge of collapse, signs and symptoms of renewal began to multiply. From the very same space that had been destroyed, a will to live emerged. As if by sheer determination and will, filmmakers relied on what little strength they still had to find a plan and an objective.

Before a single new film was made, these manifestations of life and the shared will to be reborn converged to create the Associazione nazionale industrie cinematografiche ed affini (ANICA [National Association of Film and Related Industries]). Founded on July 10, 1944, ANICA comprised approximately ten persons, with Alfredo Proia as its first president.

ANICA rose from the ashes of the Federazione nazionale fascista industriali dello spettacolo (FNFIS [National Fascist Federation of the Entertainment Industries]), founded in 1926. The group represented the interests of producers, distributors, and operators. This continuity was highly important because the first entertainment industry agency was born under fascism. As its identity began to emerge during this period, it launched a series of initiatives aimed at consolidating production and creating technical, artistic, and competitive guidelines. These included separation from political objectives. The agency also sought to protect commercial cinema in Italy from American colonization.[3]

With the birth of ANICA, producers attempted to establish relations with political and diplomatic bodies. A year after its founding, Riccardo Gualino (president of LUX) asked the government for a tax reduction and direct subsidies. The producers believed they had the right to be part of plans for reconstruction. Inasmuch as they were able, they also sought to oppose Hollywood's Psychological Warfare Branch and the American diplomats who aimed to obstruct the renewal of Italy's film industry.[4] In the face of adversity and despite the overwhelming shortage of resources, Italian cinema went back to work. It had been reborn as a field of contradictions and became the winning diplomatic card for Italy's rehabilitation (at the war's end, Italy was "impotence personified")[5] and its rapid reintegration into the international community. In the eyes of the world, Italian cinema was a symbol of the people's will to be free. It also represented a direct means to become acquainted with the Italian people.

Italian cinema had nothing to hide. It wanted to reinstate its power to view and to witness, to reestablish its moral dignity and visibility in a poor but vibrant country that fascism had tried to conceal. From the outset, the press revealed moralistic concern regarding the world's perception of certain graphic scenes from *Roma città aperta* and *Paisà* (*Paisan*). "Why should we send such images of Italian women to the world?" asked the young critic Gian Luigi

Rondi in *Tempo*. "Won't the returning [American] soldier have enough to say about them?" he wrote in reference to a scene from Rome in *Paisà*.[6] His voice would be joined by a chorus of mounting criticism and concern.

The Americans had transformed Cinecittà into a refugee camp. Filmmakers had had to hit the streets: they built new sets wherever they could and shot using whatever film they could find. They showed that Italy—despite its wounds and lacerations—was an extraordinary natural backdrop and that its people could be the stars of infinite storylines. The silver screen became the moviegoer's mirror and the depository of a country's collective hope to move forward. More than in any other moment in the history of Italian cinema (save perhaps for its birth), film had become the medium where fiction and reality blended together. All previous theories on editing, the autonomy of cinematographic codes, and acting had been brushed aside by the unique situation. The catastrophe of the war had led to the transmigration of the country's soul. The camera revealed how cinematic time penetrated the real-time lives of Italians. Rossellini, De Sica, and Zavattini redefined the filmmaker's pact with the viewer. They asked their audiences not to watch but rather to see as in the etymological sense of the Greek *idein*, to see with the mind's eye, to witness, and to share.

This newborn cinema was the child of secular and Catholic spirits that—at least at the time—were willing to help one another along a common road.

"Italy is waiting for its Balzacs, its Tolstoys, its Gorkys," wrote Carlo Lizzani in *Il politecnico*, the socio-political review published by Elio Vittorini.[7] But it would be film that gave Italy the new singers of its collective tragedies and its new ethos, born of wartime suffering and the spirit of the struggle for liberation. Postwar Italian cinema found those singers—along with some of the most important twentieth-century Italian personalities—when it began to annul directorial individuality. The neorealist director was considered an anonymous figure whose voice—like that of a Homeric narrator—was inspired by a Muse. In this case, the voice was a collective one.

From 1945 on, the neorealist masterpieces—even the first by Rossellini and De Sica and later, those by Antonioni and Fellini—were based on true stories. Each of these films was the genuine product of "made-in-Italy" creativity. They were the first authentic Italian products that would pave the way for other Italian triumphs in fields like fashion, design, gastronomy, and architecture. These films produced a carefully crafted Italian imagery and renewed faith in the aesthetic, artistic, cultural, and humane quality of everything Italian. They were a key element in the adoration of Italian products that, beginning in the 1960s, would lead to the development of many industrial sectors in Italy.

At the end of the 1940s and throughout the 1950s and 1960s, hundreds of art-house and genre films established cultural models, values, and ideals that have helped Italy—even in the most trying moments of its history—make cinema a focal point of its identity. Even more so than diplomacy, cinema has been instrumental in creating recognition for Italy abroad.

It may be that this great international scope, resonance, and influence was attained only when the country's economic, political, and industrial energies hit rock bottom. This was true even when the Americans were intent on dealing the decisive blow to a pained industry whose hopes for rebirth were next to nothing. Admiral Stone, the director of the PWB (Psychological Warfare Branch) in Italy in 1945, held that Italian cinema had been "invented" by the fascists. For this reason, he asserted, it needed to be suppressed. He also believed that all of the elements that gave shape to this "invention" needed to be suppressed, including Cinecittà. There had never been a "film industry" in Italy, he claimed.

Twenty-eight films were produced in 1945. In 1946, that number went up to sixty-two, and in 1947, the industry slowly began to regain the market, accelerated by a 1949 law that reactivated incentive mechanisms and prize money, created credit subsidies, and limited imports. In 1945, a number of directors got back to work: Righelli with *Abbasso la miseria* (*Down with Misery*), Gallone with *Avanti a lui tremava tutta Roma* (*Before Him All Rome Trembled*), Brignone with *Canto, ma sottovoce . . .* (*I Sing, but Softly . . .*), and Bonnard with *Addio, mia bella Napoli!* (*Farewell, My Beautiful Naples*). There were others as well: Ferroni, who had worked under the fascists at Salò, De Robertis, and Carlo Ludovico Bragaglia. These directors had enjoyed long careers and they wanted to continue telling stories. They were inspired by the same narrative models they had always used, but they also breathed the air of change around them and immersed their stories in contemporary problems. There were also plenty of grand film-operas, or stories constructed around a singer: Tito Gobbi, for example, starred in *Avanti a lui tremava tutta Roma*, Mario Costa's *Il barbiere di Siviglia* (*Barber of Seville*, 1946), and Giacomo Gentilomo's *O sole mio!* (1946).

Directors who had been fascists or who had sided with the Republic of Salò were not banished. During fascism and this important transitional moment (and even during the Cold War), Italian cinema was always held together by a spirit of unity, tolerance, and the will to move on and absolve directors of their ideological sins. This was true for actors and technicians as well—everyone who might be useful in the filmmaking process.

With each passing year, it became clear that the Italians were catching up to Hollywood and the hundreds of films the Americans had dropped into the market since the end of the war.[8] Although Italy did not play a central role in American strategy and diplomacy in postwar Europe, Italian cinema was a primary objective. As early as 1943, the United States was willing to forget how Italy had represented a constant threat to peace and stability in Europe. In a personal letter dated November 1943, to Wesley Jones of the State Department, Percy Winner, director of operations in Italy, observed that a generation of fascism had not been able to destroy the Italian identity. A good example, he wrote, was that Italians had remained a religious people throughout the fascist era. It was the Americans' duty, he believed, as their friends, to help the Italians return to their moral and political origins without interfering in their choices.

In the Americans' view, the country was to be aided in every respect and every sector except for cinema because the fascist contamination of the industry had been too strong. The United States believed that open markets were the answer to reviving the Italian economy. The big Hollywood studios tried to circumvent State Department directives by taking advantage of the crippled Italian film industry. Italian distributors and operators (at least, the then five hundred functioning theaters) welcomed the Americans, who dumped hundreds of old films into the Italian market in the hopes of averting the Italian film industry's comeback.

The Italians were at the end of their rope. Even the most basic resources were lacking. But they were ready to take whatever was dished out. In fact, the industry's rebirth was stimulated by "disappointment in American films."

A comparative analysis of distribution in the regions liberated by Allied forces shows how various social and geographical categories reacted differently to American films. The support of the Catholic Church would prove to be a determining, and even necessary, factor—although not unconditional. Within the framework of new political alliances, the Church and its enormous organizational apparatus was decidedly in favor of American cinema. For many films, it loosened its belt of moral judgment and used any means possible against Italian films, many of which were prohibited in Church-run theaters.

Even those producers who were working again alternated between supporting the free market and the industry's requests for protectionist legislation that would limit the number of foreign films and subsidize the Italian film industry. Those producers who had come of age during the final years of fascism realized that they could play an important role in representing Italian culture and film in the new political climate. Their strength grew as a result of the success of Rossellini and De Sica. Despite American opposition, producers felt confident that they possessed the necessary support and resources to reestablish an industry that could help the Italian government.

During the postwar period, the Italian government was faced with the problem of guaranteeing the continuity of state-run institutions. Although there was no purging of directors and technicians who had worked during the fascist era, American forces liquidated the LUCE institute in 1947 (the American armed forces had requisitioned the greater part of LUCE's property and returned it in the late 1960s) because of its connection to the fascist regime and the consensus among Italians that its memory needed to be erased. However, the commissioner of the liquidation, Tommaso Fattorossi, took roughly twelve years to complete his work and none of the overseeing officers seemed in a hurry to liquidate the agency. In the late 1940s, because of efforts to facilitate the industry's revival, LUCE was still allowed by law to produce newsreels and documentaries, and it was also able to reopen its film laboratories and printing facilities.

In May 1958, a presidential decree created a new autonomous agency of cinema that would absorb both Cinecittà and LUCE. This marked the beginning of a new era in the agency's history that continues to this day. Today, LUCE oversees production, distribution, and operation, as well as film conservation and study, including an archive of films and photographs.

By 1947, following the success of the earliest neorealist films, there were clear signs of internal renewal. The most popular films on the market were those with Erminio Macario, like Carlo Borghesio's *Come persi la guerra* (*How I Lost the War*, 1947) and *L'eroe della strada* (*A Hero from the Street*, 1948), and the musicals produced during this period. Co-productions made it possible for Italian cinema to reorganize and gain momentum. Producers identified what the public wanted and were able to create films that had cultural value but also offered entertainment and star power to the consumer.[9]

As early as 1946, ANICA asked the government to include Italian cinema in its trade negotiations with other European countries. The agency was determined to aid productions that would create a "Latin front" in the war against the Hollywood invasion. The next step was to forge alliances with other European production companies. By the end of the 1950s, at least half of all the films made in Italy were co-productions with companies based in other European countries.[10] In 1947, ANICA established a relationship with the Motion Pictures Export Association and in April 1951, a deal was struck limiting the number of American films that could be released in the Italian market. The accord also stipulated that some earnings would be reinvested or put in a fund to finance Italian films. In 1948 and 1949, deals were made for co-productions with France, West Germany, and Spain, and in 1954, the Soviet Union. These agreements soon led to the creation of a European market for film that helped to expand film production in those countries that ratified the accord. It also made it possible for films to travel freely between those countries. The enormous international success of De Santis's *Riso amaro* (*Bitter Rice*) and its star Silvana Mangano paved the way for other Italian pin-up girls during the 1950s.

In 1949, Italy produced 76 feature-length films, 104 in 1950, 201 in 1954, and 167 in 1959. It is important to remember that in 1946, Italian films earned a mere 13 percent of the total box office. By 1954, that figure had grown to 34 percent. After the war, Italians embraced the cinema of their liberators. But by the 1950s, Italian films were enjoying great success at home.

The Italian film industry's reentry into the market was facilitated by a series of government measures that encouraged producers to move away from neorealist themes. Until the beginning of the 1950s, there was no ministero dello spettacolo (minister of entertainment). When Giulio Andreotti was the undersecretary to the prime minister and liaison with the film industry, government officials, film producers, and operators began to work together to enhance the Italian film industry's ability to compete with Hollywood on Italian soil. In exchange, the government asked the industry to cool its ideological themes and to suppress embarrassing subject matter. On the other hand, such films were not having much success with audiences. When I conducted research for the first edition of my *Storia del cinema italiano* (*History of Italian Cinema*) in the 1980s, I discovered that Andreotti was pursuing his own vision of Italian cinema. He did so by creating legislation to help it get back on its feet and by encouraging co-productions. My study of American archives revealed that he was often consulting opposing forces: the Americans wanted complete control of the market; the Italian government did not consider the film industry a priority during reconstruction; and Italian distributors were already happy with profits from American films. Andreotti caused a furor with his comments in an article published in the journal *Libertas* in 1952. In this essay, he asked Italian directors and, in particular, De Sica, to make more films about illustrious figures of Italian history. This memory of Andreotti, the ogre who sought to destroy neorealism, has endured, while few remember him as a benevolent figure who made a significant contribution to the protection and renewal of Italian film production.

The expansion of Italian cinema was clearly desired and favored by the Italian government. The renewal of Italian cinema and its genres was fundamental in winning over audiences and creating a market ready to grow in terms of supply and demand. But the success of the Italian approach to production was not due to an overarching political-economic plan. It was the result of a fortunate convergence of decisive factors.

The success of neorealism was short-lived: Visconti's *La terra trema* (*The Earth Trembles* or *The Earth Will Tremble*) was a disaster at the box office , as were Rossellini's films that followed *L'amore* (*Ways of Love* or *Woman*). The biggest box-office films in the postwar period were musicals, dramas, action films, and comedies. In the early 1950s, Raffaello Matarazzo's brilliant films also generated sensational ticket sales: his *Catene* (*Chains*) made almost 600 million lire, and *I figli di nessuno* (*Nobody's Children*) made nearly 1 billion lire. These and similar films were immensely successful along with the many comedies that borrowed sketches and jokes from Italian vaudeville, satirized living conditions, and showed off girls' beautiful legs. As a result, the scales tipped in favor of market demand. This wave of films contributed to the demise of neorealism's commercial viability. Although neorealism had its moment as a core element in Italian cinema, it was ultimately opposed and hindered by the allocation of government subsidies to other genres.

Many mourned the passing of neorealism and many battled to keep it alive—some more wholeheartedly than others—as a cinematic model. Today, the panorama of international cinema reveals how neorealist films from the postwar period continue to represent a model for film production and for ethics in filmmaking. Neorealism has clearly shaped international cinema, from American films to those made in the Third World. During the postwar era, there was practically no country that was not influenced to some degree by Rossellini's and De Sica's masterpieces.

Italian comedies started out quietly and with low expectations. But they soon began to replace the vaudevillian entertainment that was often presented to Italian theatergoers before the screening of a film. Before long, the comic genre was a fundamental element in Italian film production, thanks to the success of films starring Erminio Macario and Totò: Mattoli's *I due orfanelli* (*The Two Orphans*, 1947), *Fifa e arena* (*Fear and Sand*, 1948), *Totò al giro d'Italia* (*Totò Tours Italy*, 1948), and *I pompieri di Viggiù* (*The Firemen of Viggiù*, 1949), and a few years later, the series launched with Luigi Comencini's *Pane, amore, e fantasia* (*Bread, Love, and Dreams*, 1953) and Dino Risi's *Poveri ma belli* (*A Girl in Bikini*; *Poor But Beautiful*; or *Poor But Handsome*, 1956).

Although critics generally snubbed Italian comedies because of their facile jokes and unoriginal situations, these films—with their double entendres and parodies of everyday life and situations—touched upon important aspects of Italian life. They tended to focus on common attitudes and contradictions, and they offered a remedy to the overwhelming challenge faced by the ordinary man during the postwar period.

Commercial cinema and genre films—from operas to dramas, from comedies to mythological films—played a central role in the history of Italian cinema for more than twenty years. They represented a keystone that was destined to grow and take on an increasingly important role. The Italian comedy would become an industry yardstick, a model for co-productions, and a perfect example of a genre that could create demand and then satisfy the market. Comedy directors consistently aimed for higher production value in the acting, set design, costumes, soundtracks, cinematography, and screenwriting.

During this period, the comics—Totò, Eduardo e Peppino de Filippo, Aldo Fabrizi, Erminio Macario, and Carlo Campanini, to name a few—enjoyed great success because they no longer needed masks to enter into their characters: Italian audiences already knew and identified with their characters and their escapades.

Even as overall quality improved, comedies began to suffer by the mid-1950s as consumer culture and industrialization began to sweep away the models that had inspired Italian comic films. A number of factors had a direct impact on the crisis of Italian comedy: in 1954, television became a competitor;[11] no new regulatory legislation was approved; and direct and indirect censorship became rampant[12] so that many films sat on the shelves while others, like *Totò e Carolina* (*Totò and Carolina*) were severely edited;[13] lastly, Italian consumers began to spend their money elsewhere.

During this period, ever-generous fortune again rewarded an Italian film. Pietro Francisci's *Le fatiche di Ercole* (*Hercules* or *The Labors of Hercules*, 1958) earned ten times its cost for the production company, Galatea Film, which would produce other important epics.[14] Thanks to Hercules, Maciste, and Ursus, the chains of cinematic colonialism were broken at the close of the 1950s, the balance of power with Hollywood began to change, and for the first time, box-office scales tipped in favor of Italian cinema.

It is impossible to identify trends or approaches among the different producers included in the 180 partnerships registered with ANICA in 1950.[15] At the same time, there is a clear picture of competing forces at different stages of development and examination of the group of survivors that reveals their competitive, standardized strategies.

By the time American producers went to Italy to make Mervyn LeRoy's *Quo Vadis?* in 1951, Cinecittà was back at work. The period that followed was among the studio's most happy and creative.[16] Although Italy never had movie moguls that rivaled the Hollywood players, there were many great Italian producers like Gualino, Angelo Rizzoli, the Lombardos, Carlo Ponti,

Dino de Laurentiis, Luigi Rovere, Salvo d'Angelo, Peppino Amato, and Ruggero Guarini, not to mention Turi Vasile, Sandro Ghenzi, and Neapolitans Natale Montillo, Fortunato Misiano, and Roberto Amoroso. These producers made it possible for filmmakers to break new ground and to interact with the social, political, cultural, and economic life of Italy.

The first producer to achieve public acclaim was Gustavo Lombardo (whose son Goffredo began to work with him in 1949). He was able to revitalize his production company thanks to Raffaello Matarazzo's films.[17] The Lombardos mainly put out technically and dramatically sophisticated films that were intended for a wide audience. But they also produced films by Lattuada, Fellini, and De Santis.

The LUX strategy was to be low-budget and low-risk by packaging high-quality art films with cultural content. Following the war, Gualino, still company president, encouraged adaptations from literary and theatrical works. Some films made during this period by Germi, Castellani, Zampa, and Soldati had social themes inspired by political writers like Don Luigi Sturzo, Antonio Gramsci, and Gaetano Salvemini. Carlo Ponti and Dino de Laurentiis began their careers at LUX, where they sought to create working methods that could compete with Hollywood. They played a fundamental role in Italian cinema's expansion in terms of production and entertainment value. They helped the industry overcome the crisis of the mid-1950s, and in the decade that followed they helped it reach the greatest moments in its history.

The Shooting Star of Postwar Italian Cinema: Neorealism

"At present, there is no doubt that Rome is the capital of cinema in Europe, if not the world," wrote Jean-Georges Auriol in 1948.[18] Ten years later, Jean-Luc Godard would write: "All roads lead to *Rome, Open City*."[19] For a few years, the rhythm of international cinema was effectively synchronized to the tempos of *Roma città aperta* (*Rome, Open City*), *Sciuscià* (*Shoe-Shine*), and *Paisà* (*Paisan*). Thanks to a handful of films, Italian cinema suddenly became the guiding light of cinematic artistry and a legitimate political and diplomatic representative of a country that was returning to the international stage.[20]

After the film was screened at the Teatro Quirino in Rome in September 1945, Italian critics' responses to *Roma città aperta* were mixed.[21] Some had moralistic reservations, like Luigi Comenicini in *Lettura*; others offered an ideological response, like Alberto Vecchietti in *l'Avanti!*; Antonio Pietrangeli wrote a technical-stylistic critique in *Star*; Pasquale Prunas offered an aesthetic critique in *Sud*, an ambitious biweekly published in Naples.[22] In *Quarta Parete*, Mino Caudana wrote that Rossellini "will have his day of reckoning upon the Last Judgment" because he did not capture the terrifying, horrific atmosphere of Rome. He was applauded by Umberto Barbaro in *l'Unità*, by Alberto Moravia in *La Nuova Europa*, and by Indro Montanelli in *Il Corriere d'Informazione*. In *Il Giornale del Mattino* (September 23, 1945), Ermanno Contini called the work "a film of exceptional artistic value." Carlo Lizzani and Mario Gromo both opened their reviews with "Finally!"[23] When the film came out, even the reviewers with a negative outlook managed to see in Rossellini the messiah they had awaited and they forgot his contribution to war propaganda.

Roma città aperta received a warm response from Italian audiences. Abroad, it triumphed everywhere it went, beginning one evening in New York in February 1946 at a screening organized by the Italian Welfare League (who helped to keep it in theaters for two years). At the Cannes Festival, it received rave reviews. In issue 72 of *Lettres françaises*, November 15, 1946, Georges Sadoul wrote: "I am certain that if Italian cinema continues to live up to its current promise, it is destined for the role played by expressionist cinema in the 1920s in the first postwar period."[24] Jean Desternes commented, "These films are great because they buttress and support their plots with pure truth. They catch life in the act and even the smallest detail is authentic. [In these films] cities actually open up before our very eyes."[25]

In the pages of *Ciné-club* in 1949, Sadoul remembered his emotion when he saw Anna Magnani suddenly appear "with her unkempt hair and big black eyes" in *Il bandito* (*The Bandit*) when it was screened at Cannes: "neorealism and Magnani irrupted into our postwar world." While Rossellini seemed to enjoy greater legitimacy in Italian reviews of *Paisà*, his vision and his message of unity met with opposition from antifascist forces that began to splinter just a few months after the end of the war. French and American critics, however, recognized and celebrated the birth of a new international phenomenon in the films of Rossellini, De Sica, Vergano, De Santis, and Lattuada. They also saw a possibility for Italy and its people to redeem themselves:

> Yes, when we saw *Paisà*, we saw the authentic Italy, the Italy that we love, not the Italy of hysteric braggarts, not the Italy of Mussolini and his castor oil . . . We saw the Italy of the people, the farmhands, the frontlines of factory workers, the Italy of beauty and misery . . . The Italy of Garibaldi, of the antifascists and partisans. *Paisà* is a film about the liberation of Italy but it is also a cinematic revelation. This is the cinema we have been waiting for and that we hope for.

It is a sensational surprise that such revolutionary art comes from the country where fascism was born and that it comes from the poorest country, where technical resources are so scarce.[26]

French critics unanimously embraced Italian cinema without ever bringing up Italy's past political sins. When Louis Chauvet published a review of *Quattro passi tra le nuvole* (*Four Steps in the Clouds*) in *Le Figaro* (April 11, 1947), he wrote that with films like *Roma città aperta*, *Paisà*, and *Sciuscià*, Italian cinema "is about to become the leader in European cinema." André Bazin, who wrote some of the most enlightening pages about Rossellini and De Sica and was among their most impassioned defenders,[27] wrote that *Quattro passi tra le nuvole* was confirmation of his "admiration for the new school of Italian cinema."[28] More than any other, the *Revue du cinéma*, edited by Jean-Georges Auriol, played a fundamental role. Besides a series of enthusiastic reviews of single films by De Sica, De Santis, and Lattuada, this publication also devoted an entire and now legendary issue (issue 13, May 1948) to Italian cinema with a keystone essay by Antonio Pietrangeli.[29]

For a long time, neorealism was the only cinema to circulate in Eastern Europe. After the 1920s Soviet films of Eisenstein and Pudovkin, Italian neorealism would become the model for South American cinematography. It was evident, wrote Auriol of Italian cinema, that "there are intentions and concerns hidden in the spirit of American and European cineastes but visible in their work. These results were absent before such artists had discovered Italian film." In an essay on perceptions of Italy abroad, Robert Paris underlined how European audiences had been unaware of Italian cinema until *Roma città aperta*.

[The film] was a revelation. Finally, a series of things had found expression in a language close to the European language . . . European audiences had finally found that which the great novelists—aside from Joyce (but who reads Joyce?!)—had not been able to give them: a way of speaking and expressing the focus, if not the invention, of a new style of storytelling that came to be— perhaps involuntarily and among other attributes—the only valid equivalent of American literature's Faulkner and Dos Passos.

Even if neorealism's power began to wane by the end of the 1940s, its effects continued to show themselves, rippling far and wide in Italian film production, American cinema, and Third World film, for which it had become a northern light, a production model, and a moral guide. Even in smaller countries, like Finland, where the first neorealist film, *Ladri di bicicletta* (*Bicycle*

Thieves or *The Bicycle Thief*), was first shown only in 1952, critics (beginning in 1950) recognized the importance of works by Rossellini and De Sica as foundational models. At the same time, they also recognized the Italian identity in these films (this was the case of a 1950 series of articles published by Eugen Terttula, who had lived in Italy for a month and who lamented the absence of Italian films on Finnish screens).

In 1953, in the pages of the Bogotá weekly *La semana de cine*, Gabriel García Márquez wailed violently like a rejected and wounded lover when he wrote that Italian cinema, after the wave of neorealism, was now "the worst in the world."

By the end of the 1940s, neorealism had become a driving force in many countries, even in commercial productions. The legacy of comic films with Walter Chiari and Silvana Pampanini, like *Lo sai che i papaveri* (*Poppy*), endured in Latin America, for example, in works by Manuel Puig and Edgardo Cozarinsky. The same can be said for the immigrant community of North America, who gathered around the television in search of traces of home, as Martin Scorsese has recounted in *Il mio viaggio in Italia*. In order to understand the Italian cinema phenomenon in the world, it is important to look beyond the neorealist masterpieces. Genre films also made an important contribution to the perception of Italians in the world.

On one hand, there was Italy, the country of poverty, but a country full of life capable of transmitting its excessive vital energy, thanks to the screen itself above and beyond its limitations. On the other hand, these images deposited themselves in the image bank of directors and filmmakers around the world. Their effects would soon appear everywhere.

In the 1950s, Giulio Cesare Castello's book *Cinema neorealistico italiano* (*Italian Neorealist Cinema*), based on a series of radio shows, clearly showed the influence that Italian neorealism had had on movies like *La bataille du rail* (by René Clement, 1946), *The Naked City* (Jules Dassin), *The Quiet One* (Sidney Mayers), *The Little Fugitive* (Ray Ashley, Morris Engel, and Ruth Orkin), *Marty* (Delbert Mann), *Bienvenido, Mr. Marshall!* (Luis G. Berlanga), *Muerte de un ciclista* (Juan A. Bardem), *Raíces* (Alazraki), and *Do Bigha Zamin* (Bimal Roy), not to mention the films of Cacoyannis, Käutner, Kaneto Shindo, Jacques Becker, Louis Daquin, and Jean-Paul Le Chanois.[30]

For nearly fifty years and even today, all of the great directors of the generations that would follow those who debuted in the 1940s, from Godard and Truffaut to Glauber Rocha and Wim Wenders, from the Taviani Brothers to Bertolucci, from Nelson Pereira Dos Santos to Wajda, Coppola, and Scorsese, have recognized their debt not only to Rossellini, Zavattini and De Sica, and Visconti but also to De Santis, Lattuada, Germi, and Zampa. While

George Lucas has discussed the fundamental role played by Cottafavi's and Francisci's films in the imagery of his own work, he has also allowed us to establish a connection between Hans Solo and Obi-Wan Kenobi's adventures in space and the feats of Hercules and Maciste.

Thanks to some of the masterpieces and the dozens of commercial titles, today we can still understand the rhythms and development of Italian cinema and society. These films give us a sort of vocabulary of the Italian journey from the founding of the Italian Republic after the war until the present. In these films we recognize certain directors who were capable of depicting the country's soul.[31]

With time, the characters' words, their shared gestures, and their hopes for the future became emblematic (like Francesco in *Roma città aperta* who says, "We are fighting for something that must come to be, that cannot not come to be . . . The road may be long and hard, but we will get there and we will see a better world. And most important of all, we will see our children!"; or Anna Magnani's desperate cry as Pina in the same movie, "Francesco! Francesco!"). These characters represented the first living monuments to the Resistance from the civilian population of Europe. Rossellini's films were works of global reach. Through their dramatic depiction as well as their contradictions, they united and divided and acted as a hyphen, a breakwater, and a break from the past.

When Rossellini finished shooting, Italy was still divided in two: not only did he capture an irreversible process in its embryonic state, he also revolutionized the codes of dramatization; he returned man's greatness to the camera; he restored visibility to every aspect of reality and dignity and self-awareness to all of his characters; he reinvented and rediscovered the most elementary forms of communication; he revived cinema's role as a tool of human communication and the collective conscience. Cocteau said that in Rossellini's films, for the first time in Italian cinema, one saw the world "through the eyes of a man who made himself one of the people and through the eyes of a people who identified with the world as seen through the eyes of the man."[32]

In a recent autobiographical essay, Alberto Asor Rosa recounted an emotional childhood moment when the audience and the actors seemed to be perfectly integrated, an exceptional and never-before-seen sensation of tangible fusion between real life and the life re-created by cinema:

> But the most extraordinary cinematic experience of that strange winter of transition was another one. In the avalanche of films that came from the other side

of the Atlantic, every once in a while, a film made in the streets of home managed to slip in here and there—no one knows how. One afternoon—I do not remember what brought us there—we went to see a movie in a crowded theater on the outskirts of the city, in the heart of my neighborhood, between Piazza San Giovanni and Piazza dei Re di Roma. The very title of the film brought to mind our city and our experiences in the preceding months. It was a story about Rome during the German occupation. I believe that this was a unique experience in the history of cinema.

This film overturned all the rules of American movies. The audience was no longer prompted to dream about what could happen in a situation analogous to the one it saw on the screen. Instead, the audience saw itself or what it had been up until a few months prior. In the theater, there were the same people with their cheap clothes and pale faces, with their cheekbones showing from hunger, their cork-soled shoes falling to pieces, their suits made of light cotton, their worn jackets. This was the same poverty of the characters, a short distance away, who were telling their humble story on the screen. And this story was more or less the same story of the audience in the theater, or their closest friends', their relatives', their neighbors'. They had acted it out themselves in the streets of Rome; in the dusty backyard gardens of the outskirts; in the mammoth public-housing apartment buildings, the ubiquitous cafés large and small; with the snarling Germans and fascists and their guns around every corner; under the domination of oppression and fear; with the underground quivering of revolt; with persecution, raids, and the terror of torture and death.

And so it was: when had you ever seen or when would you ever see such a thing again? It is one thing, I imagine, to happen upon that film many months later in some theater in Los Angeles or Soho. It is another thing to see that film by chance in a theater in the outskirts of Rome during a gray winter, as it mirrored real events as they unfolded: the audience, in other words, myself, us, my mother, the woman who lived upstairs from us, the druggist from the pharmacy on our corner, the old lady who worked at the front desk of our building, the electrician who made sure our lights worked, the railroad worker with one leg shorter than the other, the pensioner who lived in the basement under the stairs . . . We were all there, with wide eyes and mouths agape. We saw all the very same damned things that had happened to us just a few terrible months before.[33]

Even though no one had endorsed him as such or conferred such a title upon him, in the eyes of the critics and the public, Rossellini was the leader of a small group of filmmakers who were without means, plans, or a common ideological position. Despite their uncertainties and their sense of collective

guilt (shared by the majority of Italians), they had managed to portray a tragedy and the will to rise up again. It was a magical, unique moment—as Italo
Calvino observed—in which destinies, directions, and the voice of a people
intersected and mixed spontaneously with their culture: "Filled with stories
to tell; each had his own; each had lived an irregular, dramatic, adventurous
life; we snatched the words from each other's mouths."[34]

By virtue of transitivity, Calvino's self-observations ("anyone who started
writing then found himself handling the same material as the nameless oral
narrator") apply to neorealist screenwriters and directors. They were the natural inheritors of an oral tradition that some, like Cocteau, compared to *The
Thousand and One Nights*: "[The films labeled 'neorealist'] were made by oriental storytellers. Like the Orient, Italy lives in the street. The caliph, instead
of disguising himself as one of his people, disguises himself as a camera. He
seeks out the mysterious plots which occur in the streets, in the houses. In
Miracle in Milan, De Sica carries the oriental tale to extremes."[35]

As Italian cinema got back on track, there was a growing need to reappro-
priate the eye's power to move toward the discovery of the visible and to invent
a language capable of telling its story. Even more important was the need to
find a confluence between pathos and ethos. This vision aspired to be ecumeni-
cal. Efforts focused on grafting the everyday moment into the course of history.
Heroes became what Pierre Sansot called the have-nots: a humankind whose
acts would always be invisible, whose voice and whose world were to be illuminated and observed for the first time in representational detail.[36]

Neorealist screenwriters seemed intent on abandoning their presence,
their writing, and the cultural filters they used to draw from reality. They left
the headlines behind as they pushed toward worlds and social realities that
had never been considered before. During the postwar period, a linguistic
polyphony of voices was documented and mixed together in films, from Sicily
to Piedmont, from Campania to the Veneto. Now uncensored, writers began
to use dialects and "regional" Italian in their films. Most significantly, audiences began to hear the voices of figures who had always been marginalized
from the screen because they had never been deemed worthy. Thanks to Zavattini and Amidei, but also Tellini, Fellini, Sonego, and all the other storytellers who drew their tales from oral culture, the traditional stars of movies
lost their function and their centrality as the stories became looser and without any direction or intention. It would not take long for the confines of
reality and the visible to become indistinguishable.

Although not for long, screenwriters and directors felt invested in their
role as interpreters of history and their mission to document the reconstruction of the country. Together with the above names, we should also remember

Ivo Perilli, Maccari, Piero Tellini, Flaiano, Margadonna, and Suso Cecchi d'Amico. In any case, if we wish to give Caesar his due (and by Caesar, I mean Cesare Zavattini), it is important to note that even before the war's end, Zavattini was obsessed with the notion of rebirth and by the need to generate energy—twice as much as in the years leading up to the war. In his mind, cinema was a leading means for change.

Neorealism discovered that there was no distinction between the public and the private. As directors sought out people in unknown regions, they documented previously unheard-of forms of verbal and physical communication and man's interaction with his environment in all its varieties, shapes, and forms. They were capable of making a stare, a silence, or an object speak.

During the most active phase of this project when the greatest faith was placed in the united effort of the new poetics, Zavattini managed to foresee that anyone, even beginning with the simplest of microcellular realities, could achieve the most free and autonomous storytelling universes. Narrative and linguistic systems exploded as a result of the faith in cinema's ability to tell all stories, to celebrate the greatness of the everyday, to sing epic tales of common actions and feelings, and to imitate all languages. Such belief gave screenwriters the thrilling sensation that they could tell any tale and give free rein to an invention capable of finding all visible realities and pushing beyond to explore dreams, the imagination. Thus, they could perceive the spaces that lie outside the confines created by reason and the experiences of the senses. However circumspect and full of contradiction, they were pushing themselves to explore that "beyond" indicated by Pirandello as early as 1915 in his *Quaderni di Serafino Gubbio operatore* (*Shoot!* [*Si gira*] *The Notebooks of Serafino Gubbio, Cinematograph Operator*). Federico Fellini, Tullio Pinelli, and Ennio Flaiano played a fundamental role in this movement, as did Michelangelo Antonioni. But above all, it was in the perception of changes in mentality and in its self-fashioning as a privileged space, where many stories flowed into one another, that postwar cinema began to show its true possibilities. Beyond the directors' will and intentions, cinema abandoned the soundstage and traveled through the spaces of socialization in a disorderly and arbitrary manner. It showed previously unseen aspects of reality and it facilitated the free and involuntary circulation of the signs of collective history.

Directors like Rossellini, Visconti, Germi, Blasetti, Camerini, Castellani, Zampi, and Soldati lived together for a few years in the same field of tension. But as much as they confronted subjects, asking for their self-representation, the weight of literature still came to bear on them, even though it was distributed in an entirely different manner. In the case of Visconti, it even touched upon the deepest structures of his cinema. He chose as his point of reference not the written word, but rather, the oral tale, its epic forms, and its direct translatability.

Beginning with *Roma città aperta*, neorealism gave birth to a new way of seeing man and his relationship with, to borrow Longhi's phrase, "his circumstances." Like the needle of a compass, neorealism was destined to guide the shared thematic and narrative choices of many directors born between the two world wars.

But in terms of iconography and iconology, it is difficult to identify the defining elements of a stylistic lingua franca. Italian cinema got back on track with Rossellini and his *Roma città aperta*. By its very nature, this film created a new way of seeing, of contextualizing and redefining how humankind and objects would be depicted; this was accomplished by putting the camera at eye level. The camera was drawn to stationary images and to the clear-cut, close observation of the relationship between an individual and his surroundings. Rossellini's gaze and his unassuming approach were not imposed on him by production limitations. They were not intended to convey or impose ideological knowledge or imperatives: as a director, his point of view never coincided with that of his characters; he never acted as a deus ex machina in their dramatic or narrative destinies. The popular epic tradition was transmitted orally by storytellers and balladeers. In the movie camera, it found its most illustrious medium. Rossellini used a sort of *sermo humilis*, thanks to which every image restored the complexity of the flux of existence with immediate simplicity. All knowledge, every rule and paradigm of films, had been swept away. The camera's eye became an added organ that the director could use to see in the sense of the Greek *historein*, to bear witness.

Rossellini demonstrated that anyone could film by simply inserting himself into the flux of collective history and by isolating moments without any particular preliminary constructions. By doing so, one was obliged to see images that had been previously left out of the frame.

The Zavattini–De Sica team also worked along these lines. But although their cinema was theoretically based on unmitigated spontaneity, their first postwar film reintroduced the rules of acting, soundstages, and meticulous preparation for each scene and the composition of the frame. Compared to Rossellini, Zavattini and De Sica were a screenwriter-director team that wanted not only to show their characters' point of view but also to make the audience feel the characters' emotions through the eyes of another, a child or an elderly person; they wanted audiences to view the world through virgin eyes and to experience the wonder of such a perspective. Rossellini's style was too narrow for De Sica, who wanted his frames to be charged with pathos, but without resorting to previous models of frame composition. Visconti, rather, and similarly, De Santis, Lattuada, Castellani, and Germi would be the ones to revive meticulously detailed visual composition of figures in space. With Visconti, nothing was spontaneous or natural. Everything was the product of his visual and cultural erudition. Even when he went to Sicily to film the fishermen of Aci Trezza, every element in the frame corresponded to a preexisting *ratio* and a need to create concordances between visual chromatics and the musical tempos of various scores in his stories. Visconti's gaze derived from pictorial tradition: he saw the world through the lens of his musical and visual knowledge and his characters came to life thanks to his gaze. While his colleagues opted for reducing and subtracting elements, Visconti sought to add and overlap. Nothing was left to chance in his films.

The faith in cinema's ability to tell anyone's story, to celebrate the greatness of the everyday, to sing epics of commonplace feelings and acts, to reproduce all languages, and to explode narrative and linguistic systems gave screenwriters the exhilarating sensation that they could write anything. They felt that by opening the floodgates of creativity, they could find undiscovered visible realities and then push further, exploring dreams, the imagination, and spaces that lay beyond the confines of reason and the sensory experience.

From the outset, neorealist cinema and the people who defined it did not want it simply to be the recording and mimesis of the existing world. This is clearer today than it has been in the past. Neorealism deconstructed traditional storytelling but it sought to depict and explore the many dimensions of the real, including dreams, the fantastic, and the imagination. Directors and screenwriters invented a new ethic of seeing. They reaffirmed, or rather, affirmed the primacy of ethics over politics as they sought to portray the shared values, diverse elements, and unknown dimensions of their country.

With a choral voice, postwar cinema depicted the dynamics and transformation of Italians' lives—a "public diary" of their attitudes and collective mentality. It was a diary written by a collective "I," a register and ledger where profits and losses were annotated along with the pointless dissipation of energies, difficulties, and hardships, pain, and resignation together with optimism and a will to start over again.[37]

Compared to postwar cinema in other countries (including the United States), Italian cinema deserves credit for its ability to show the country and its story from the ground up. It did so by trying to focus on the proletarianization of the middle class and the middle-classization of the proletariat through the progressive process of economic and social upward mobility and progressive dissolution.

Undoubtedly, there were some cornerstone works in which the spirit of the era and the historical moment were concentrated (from Rossellini to *La dolce vita*). These films were destined to shape the geography and design of postwar imagery. Some films took on a testamentary value with regard to certain events or periods. They became surrogates, in some cases taking the place of traditional historical sources. In the case of *Roma città aperta* and *Germania anno zero* (*Germany Year Zero*), certain sequences have allowed subsequent generations to come in direct contact with the profound spirit of the Resistance movement in Europe.

When considered as macro-systems, the great and small films of the postwar era helped define and transform the Italian citizen's life and mentality as he passed from reconstruction to the Cold War, from the economic miracle to the *anni di piombo* (the terrorism of the 1970s), from a phase of research and discovery of a thousand and one Italys to the years in which the perception of a nation, its sense of identity, and its shared values would disappear forever. This road ran like a parabola, hitting its highest point at the beginning of the 1960s.

Within this macro-set, Luciano Emmer's works served as a bridge between the first phase, which was dominated by a high, tragic style, and the second, which was much lighter in style. From *Una domenica d'agosto* (*Sunday in August*, 1950) and *Parigi è sempre Parigi* (*Paris Is Always Paris*, 1951) to *Le ragazze di Piazza di Spagna* (*Three Girls from Rome*, 1952) and *La ragazza in vetrina* (*Girl in the Window* or *Woman in the Window*, 1960; a film so butchered by the censors that he was driven to abandon his career as a director), Emmer attempted to take the story apart and multiply its stories and their flow. The tales mixed in such a way that their events became indistinguishable from one another. Their role was to register ways of life, horizons made of expectations and attitudes, perceptions of the future, economic opportunities, and consumer trends among everyday people—a preview of future sociological investigation and census-taking that would be offered later by Italian institutions like Doxa, Istat, and Censis.

Italian postwar cinema has been widely recognized for its masterworks and its genre films, from Totò's comedies to Matarazzo's cinematic operas, from musicals to mythologies. Over the years, this terrain has been repeatedly re-explored and scholars have aptly sketched many connections and relationships. The field has expanded, its gaze being cast no longer on just a handful of monumental films, but rather on the entire set and system. Many individuals, previously confined to the shadows, and many genre films have enjoyed well-deserved reconsideration. Interestingly (and encouraging for those studying postwar film), there exists much forgotten terrain still to be fully explored, just as was the case for silent film until recently.

One of these areas is the vast and nearly unknown, sprawling territory of the documentary, which has only recently begun to bloom thanks to small, isolated studies. The LUCE institute, for one, has begun to reissue Pasinetti's documentaries. As a result, this master of visual storytelling has been rediscovered together with his ability to transfer and metabolize *vedutista* painting with the movie camera. I myself have made sporadic forays into this territory thanks to the opportunity of seeing so many important documentaries together by directors like Francesco Pasinetti and Michelangelo Antonioni, Vittorio de Seta, Florestano Vancini and Luciano Emmer, Francesco Maselli and Valerio Zurlini, Ermanno Olmi and the Taviani brothers, Franco Piavoli and Gianfranco Mingozzi. And yet, I have never embarked on such an endeavor. This field deserves study, but also requires an overarching approach in order to correctly understand the relationship between the documentary and fictional cinema and the latter's place in the framework of European documentary films.[38] If pressed to disclose the most fruitful inroads and still untouched zones for research, I would have no hesitation in suggesting the Italian documentary as a topic of study, in all of its dimensions, rather than aiming at the few remaining unexplored zones of silent film. In the case of the latter, the material that has emerged provides sufficient elements to understand its larger context.

During the 1940s and 1950s, the documentary's golden age, a number of directors—Dino Risi, Luigi Comencini, Giulio Questi, Carlo Lizzani, Gillo Pontecorvo, Renzo Renzi, Michele Gandin, Giuseppe Ferrar, Virgilio Sabel, Giorgio Trentin, Carlo di Carlo, and Silvano Agosti—completed apprenticeships and acquired traits that would define their successful careers. The documentary taught them how to see and master all the aspects of the creative process and film production; it showed them how to use visual language and encouraged them to explore the realities surrounding them. They discovered trades that were about to disappear and daily acts that defined the history of a place or an economy. Documentaries instructed them how to journey through space and time, to breach zones once considered taboo, and to come in contact with archaic realities, magical rituals, and underdeveloped areas a stone's throw away from some of the country's most advanced ones—some of them inspired by Ernesto de Martino's book *Sud e magia* (*Magic and the South* [*of Italy*]).[39] The first true contact with the hidden, unknown realities of Sicily, Sardinia, Apulia, and Basilicata came about thanks to a few memorable documentaries by Luigi di Gianni and Vittorio de Seta. In addition to Pontecorvo's documentary *Giovanna* (1954), the first contact with the daily reality of the lives of the workers came about with documentaries by Ermanno Olmi, where Pier Paolo Pasolini and Tullio Kezich are listed in the credits: *La diga sul ghiacciaio* (*The Dam Over the Glacier*, 1953), *Michelino I B* (*Little Michele, First Class B*, 1956), *Tre fili fino a Milano* (*Three Wires All the Way to Milan*, 1958), and *Un metro lungo cinque* (*One Meter by Five*, 1961). Documentaries on art by Luciano Emmer, Roberto Longhi, Umberto Barbaro, and Carlo Ludovico Ragghianti also produced positive results.[40] Italian documentaries drew upon neorealist testimonials and Zavattini in particular, not to mention the great masters of documentary filmmaking like Joris Ivens and Robert Flaherty. These films allowed the viewer to come in contact with themes that cinema had repressed from its visual horizon, but they also made it possible to access the realities of industry long before fictional cinema did so. More than one director experimented with the syntax, meter, and rhythm of this genre as they explored subjects that would later be developed into fictional films. This was the case for Olmi, De Seta, and Vancini, among others. There have been a few studies of these films, but for the most part they have been disappointing because they were solely descriptive in nature.[41] The attempts to simply restore some of these films (under the aegis of the Associazione Philip Morris cinema project) have shown the high quality achieved by Antonioni, Comencini, Maselli, Petri, Risi, Vancini, Questi, Zurlini, and Visconti, among others.[42] The best results have come from focused research like that conducted on a series of similar documentaries produced by the Italian government and subsidized by the Office of the Prime Minister during the 1940s.[43] To date, no one has studied the industrial films produced for Italy's big companies like Fiat, Oliveti, Montedison, and the Ferrovie dello Stato (National Railway).[44] Here, we can find works signed by Risi and Emmer, Rossellini and Pontecorvo, Folco Quilici and Massimo Mida, Bruno Munari, and Virgilio Tosi and Michele Gandin, among others.

Among the most memorable documentaries made during the 1940s, some stand out thanks to the effect they had on the dynamics, style, and social and cultural content of Italian cinema in the decades that followed: Antonioni's *Gente del Po* (*People of the Po River*, 1943) and *N.U.* (*Nettezza urbana* [*Metropolitan Sanitation*], 1948); Risi's *Barboni* (*Vagrants*, 1946) and *Buio in sala* (*The Lights Go Down in the Theater*, 1949); Emmer and Gras's *Isola nella laguna* (*Island in the Lagoon*, 1949); Maselli's *Bagnaia paese italiano* (*Bagnaia, an Italian Town*, 1949) and *Bambini* (*Babies*, 1951); Lizzani's *Nel Mezzogiorno qualcosa è cambiato* (*Something Has Changed in the South*, 1950); Renzo Renzi's *Le fidanzate di carta* (*Pin-Up Girlfriends*, 1951); Florestano Vancini's *Delta padano* (*The Padanian Delta*, 1952) and *Tre canne un soldo* (*A Dime for Three Reeds*, 1953); Valerio Zurlini's *Pugilatori* (*Boxers*, 1951) and *Mercato delle facce* (*The Market* of Faces, 1952); Giulio Questi's *Donne di servizio* (*Maids*, 1953); Pontecorvo's *Porta Portese* (*Porta Portese* [*Roman Flea Market*], 1954); Valentino Orsini and the Taviani brothers' *San Miniato luglio '44* (*San Miniato, July 1944*, 1954); and Vittorio de Seta's *Isola di fuoco* (*Island of Fire*, 1955).

Among all the documentary filmmakers, Folco Quilici deserves special attention for his ability to conceive a documentary as an integral part of fictional cinema, a place of planetary adventures in which visual storytelling was a perfect substitute for the epic dimensions of oral storytelling. His imagery released powerful mythical forces with the terrestrial globe as the backdrop and visual horizon. His first feature-length film, *Sesto continente* (*The Sixth Continent*, 1954), heralded an uninterrupted fifty-year run of works in which he was able to unite a spirit for adventure, discovery of the near and the distant, curiosity and scientific precision, and a knack for high-level reporting and poetic fire. These qualities would accompany him in every step of his exceptional career.[45]

Beginning in the 1960s, the poetics of the *nouvelles vagues*, together with the advent of television and the new opportunities created by television advertising, reduced the importance of the documentary and its effect on directorial development. Although there were documentaries that marked significant moments in certain directors' careers and shaped their style and their interests, today the phenomenon is more fragmentary and arbitrary. Documentaries are now limited to specific fields and merit attention within the overall framework of the industry of culture and the transformation of the media universe.

Among the territories that have yet to be explored, the least known and the most ghettoized is animation, in part because it is considered a childish genre but also because its greatest period of splendor took shape in the age of television. Contributions to the study of animation have been made by Gianni Rondolino[46] and Giannalberto Bendazzi,[47] who, in recent years, has devoted himself to the study of animation with greater continuity than any other scholar. There have been a few articles and essays here and there in specialized journals,[48] like *L'ufficio moderno*, *Sipra*, and *Il fotogramma*, but animation has never truly enjoyed the attention it deserves. Italian animation was born in 1949 with Anton Gino Domeneghini's *La rosa di Bagdad* (*The Rose of Baghdad* or *The Singing Princess*) and Nino and Toni Pagot's *I fratelli Dinamite* (*The Dynamite Brothers*), both in color. The first of these were released after nearly ten years in the making while the second was the only time the Pagot brothers experimented with cinema because the commercial results were disastrous.

As I have already mentioned, the true story of Italian animation is inexorably linked to Carosello's twenty triumphant years on television.[49] During this period, animation houses grew and reached new heights in technology and creativity: for example, the Gavioli brothers' Gamma Film,[50] Paul Film, Bruno Bozzetto Film, and Pagot Film, to name a few. Carosello became a laboratory and a launching pad for many directors who wanted to try their luck on the big screen.

In 1961, the Gavioli brothers made *La lunga calza verde* (*The Long Green Stocking*), based on a Zavattini treatment, a film that celebrated the events leading up to the unification of Italy. But it was Bruno Bozzetto who scored the first hit with audiences in Italy and abroad when he made *West and Soda* (1965). The film's success was due to the innovative style of the images, its rhythm, and its creativity in terms of the characters and soundtrack. Each of these elements was inspired by Sergio Leone's westerns. Even his second feature-length film, *Vip, Mio fratello superuomo* (*The Super VIPs*, 1968), enjoyed great success. Bozzetto made more breakthroughs in Italian animation than any other director. His most famous character is Signor Rossi, whose daily misadventures at the hands of modernity were depicted in dozens of shorts. The demise of Carosello was a catastrophe for Italian animation, and suddenly all of its energy seemed spent.

In recent years, the only individual in Italian animation to emerge with poetic and creative vigor has been Enzo d'Alò, who made his first feature-length animated film, *La freccia azzurra* (*How the Toys Saved Christmas* or *The Blue Arrow*), in 1996. His *La gabbianella e il gatto*, based on the novel by Luis Sepulveda, enjoyed immense success with audiences (earning nearly 8 million Euros at the box office). This work had all the elements of even the best Walt Disney productions.

Rossellini's Journey: Nobility, Faith, and Modernity

The theory and poetics of neorealism were not the child of a collaborative project perfected on the drawing board; today, neorealism appears to have been the result of an "involuntary trend" and a "field of tensions"[51] that was larger than in the past and cohabited by individuals who moved in various directions. Pasolini called it a phase of "vital crisis."[52] To the directors, it seemed that the visible, its surface, and its depth unfolded under their view. Their task was to comply with the will of things and to document their weeping. Different types of directors shared the same space, descending into the streets to see and retell the interchangeable stories of characters without stories whom the war had transformed into representatives of everyone's story. They drew from the same source to give different shapes to stories told through images. The neorealist container changed continuously like a kaleidoscope, giving life to a series of films defined by elements that did not match up with the properties and limits of the container itself.

Thanks to Rossellini, cinema freed itself from the literary, theatrical, and figurative traditions that had conditioned its path. French critic Serge Daney observed that, thanks to the torture sequence in *Roma città aperta* (*Rome Open City*), the birth of modern cinema was clearly recognizable: the spectator's eye was forced to see realities that had been previously hidden away or considered intolerable. Cinema no longer had to draw upon the major arts but rather it was cinematic writing that modified and influenced the different forms of artistic writing. Directors discovered entirely new forms of communication: silences, voids, landscapes, and objects all began to speak as significance and function were rediscovered in meaningless elements and even the smallest act became noble.[53]

The neorealist gaze was inclusive and overarching. It sought to give a voice to every Italian dialect and to embrace all of Italy, extending its reach as far as possible. *Paisà* (*Paisan*) and *Il cammino della speranza* (*Path of Hope* or *The Road to Hope*) told the stories of journeys that spanned from Sicily all the way to the north of the country.[54] The idea was to move around without any plans and to enter arbitrarily into people's homes so that the camera could show their reality in a natural way. Zavattini had been thinking of a journey through Italy since 1944. For him, the fertile Po River Valley was the cradle of Italian civilization: "The Po River is the father and the mother; it is life, it is the earth."[55] He saw the South, instead, in terms of its unchanging ways and the theatricality of its rituals.[56] Visconti went to the town of Aci Trezza in Sicily to use authentic fishermen when he shot *La terra trema* (*The Earth Trembles* or *The Earth Will Tremble*), based on Giovanni Verga's *I Malavoglia* (*The Malavoglia* or *The House by the Medlar Tree*).[57] Conceived as the first part of a trilogy of the common man, and inspired by Renato Guttuso's painting and Ivens and Flaherty's cinema, *La terra trema* is a journey southward to the roots and mothers of Italian and Mediterranean culture.

Arbitrariness, improvisation, the everyday quality of set designs, and a large margin for error were all elements that shaped neorealist poetics and mythology for future generations. But they were not just myth: they were very real factors linked to early working conditions. Directors were forced to plan their shoots in accordance with a certain range of possibilities. Because of film shortages and precarious financing, Rossellini had to invent a new working method. In regard to his contradictory ideological system and his conversion from fascism to antifascism, it is important to keep in mind that such transformation was common among middle-class Catholics who shunned violence but who fluctuated between consensus and the so-called gray zone, between commonsense opposition to the regime guided by their moral compass and a war that they had to live day by day. We must also account for the added value that made *Roma città aperta* a milestone in the history of cinema. Decades after its release, this film continues to speak to us without losing any of its power.

With *Roma città aperta*, the director and screenwriters (Amidei, Fellini, and Alberto Consiglio) tried to show how antifascism had been widespread among the Roman population. A shared sense of objective guided the actions of Don Pietro, Pina, and Manfredi the engineer. The only collaborator seems to be the prefect of Rome, a slave to the will of the Nazis. While no dominant ideology emerges in the film, there is the utmost respect for the different forces at play. Rossellini was interested in the common folk. For him, the struggle played out in churches, on rooftops, in tenements—all the vital spaces that man is called upon to defend. The maturation of the common man's conscience takes place at the moment in which fascist and Nazi violence appears on his horizon—moments that touch upon an otherwise dormant dignity within him. The film's international success had a boomerang effect on Italian critics who sanctified the director, maestro, and flag-bearer of the new cinema.

Shot in 1946, *Paisà* (*Paisan*) was conceived for the American market. Written in part by Klaus Mann,[58] the film was constructed around six different but perfectly balanced episodes. In this work, the psychology of the individual is sacrificed for the sake of an overall framework and the film's geographic itinerary becomes a moral high ground and testimony to collective redemption.

In *Paisà*, the plurality of the episodes and of the points of view is a plurality of judgments put into progressive focus by a hitherto unknown reality. With each episode, the viewer comes into closer contact and better understands as the Americans and Italians intermingle, until they ultimately die.

As if passed through a funnel, Rossellini's view of the world became more and more concentrated. With *Germania anno zero* (*Germany Year Zero*), made in 1947, all hope was lost. It was impossible to reconstruct from the rubble where no form of solidarity could exist and life was governed by the laws of the jungle. In this film, the camera follows the main character, Edmund, as he wanders aimlessly in search of understanding and comfort from a world that has forced him to kill his father. With nothing to hold on to, no help, and no response, he decides to throw himself into the void. The finale conveys the director's profound personal and ideological crisis: in a moment of extreme ideological pressure, Rossellini decided to dock in a free port where he could continue his research. In 1946, he made two short segments for episodic film *L'amore* (*Ways of Love*): *La voce umana* (*The Human Voice*), based on the play by Jean Cocteau, and *Il miracolo* (*The Miracle*). In these episodes, there is something new with respect to the entire body of his expressive and thematic research up until that point: a need to find new answers to the meaning of life. This Eucharistic element in Rossellini would soon be revealed by Catholic critics across the globe.[59]

With a screenplay written together with Fellini and the controversial figure, Father Felix Morlion, Rossellini's *Francesco giullare di Dio* (*Francis, God's Jester* or *The Flowers of St. Francis*) was one of the biggest disasters of the postwar era. But, together with *La terra trema* (*The Earth Trembles* or *The Earth Will Tremble*), it ushered in a simpler and more harmonious use of the camera. This film's perfect symmetry among its parts is striking, as is its harmonic *cursus*, and the repetition and variation of actions and themes.

From this moment on, Rossellini's films were shaped by the presence of Ingrid Bergman: *Stromboli* (1950), *Europa '51* (*No Greater Love* or *The Greatest Love*, 1951), and *Viaggio in Italia* (*Journey to Italy*; *Strangers*; or *The Lonely Woman*, 1952). Rossellini's camera was no longer satisfied with the merely visible as the director reflected on individual solitude, existential emptiness, and the silence of God. For Rossellini, the visible was an allegory and metaphor for an outer space where the individual sought answers to the meaning of life and destiny. In these films, he traveled the roads that many other European directors would later follow and proved himself to be a guide and explorer in production, style, content, and expression. Rossellini should be admired for his tireless research and obsessive need to look forward. He never rested on his laurels and continued to brave uncharted waters.

When his partnership with Ingrid Bergman ended, he made *La paura* (*Angst; Fear;* or *I Don't Believe in Love Anymore*, 1954), a film in which Rossellini seemed absent. A short while later, he went to India, where he recovered his self-confidence together with his expressive potential and a visual virginity that allowed him to answer more than one of the questions he had asked so obsessively in previous years. His return to Italy and the release of *Il generale della Rovere* (*General Della Rovere*, 1959), awarded a Golden Lion in Venice, allowed him to recover the reputation he had lost with audiences and critics. He was once again acclaimed as a maestro of Italian cinema. The struggle for liberation and civil war, themes that he had repressed for a decade, now returned as a central inspiration for Italian directors as the country was undergoing a phase of important transformation and democratic growth.

The Fables of De Sica and Zavattini

During the happiest moments of their partnership, De Sica and Zavattini, two very different personalities, gave life to a body of creative work in which they explored the visible in the human soul to depths never before reached: they knew how to tell workaday stories and profound stories. The end of the war gave both of them the sensation that they were watching the world unfold before them. "The reality of the situation was extremely rich. You just had to know how to see it," Zavattini once said. After a while, thanks to him, neorealism gained the added value of a retroactive poetics.

Zavattini, without any official title, assumed the role of leader. His need to say and to do was so great that it aroused energy in others and it transformed the energy present in the surrounding reality. His influence reached every level of the production system. He managed to work across the entire field as he created a framework and fabric of relationships between the directors and all the layers of Italian cinema. He offered himself as a guide and midwife. He was a humble but gregarious man who labored over the wires, motors, and transmission belts of thousands of projects, first in Italy and then, beginning in the 1950s, all over the world.[60]

With *Sciuscià* (*Shoe-Shine*, 1946), Zavattini and De Sica launched one of the most creative and fertile partnerships in the history of cinema.[61] Zavattini cooked up treatments by the dozen, and tried to insert them into a framework of individualized and group poetics. The war pushed him to harness his imagination and the surreal, fantastical aspect of his personality, even though there was already a strong symbolic component in *Sciuscià*. The set for the film was built partially on a soundstage, including the interiors and the backgrounds. But the camera seemed to capture the authentic life of the main characters, Pasquale and Giuseppe, and their desires, their dreams, and their imagined future.

Sciuscià was an immediate international success. De Sica knew how to put the camera on the level of his characters. He was able to charge every image with intense emotion, although he never used Rossellini's detached approach. Instead, he sought to show his emotional involvement and indignation as a man and a citizen. In any case, *Ladri di biciclette* (*Bicycle Thieves* or *The Bicycle Thief*, 1948) was his greatest international success, thanks in part to an Oscar. The story advances through a series of related micro-events. Each is charged with meaning and pathos because the viewer becomes immediately involved with laborer Ricci as he searches for his stolen bicycle. The narration is enclosed within a code of gestures and glances that Ricci exchanges with his son Bruno. The story's tension derives from the disproportion between the cause and effects of the social drama that develops following the theft of a bicycle—a magical helper and a necessity for survival. Today, more than any other neorealist director, De Sica is admired for his maieutic talents. Using actors taken from the streets, he was able to obtain inimitable, unforgettable performances. But perhaps he appeals to us also because of his ability to make a seemingly insignificant story into a dramatic adventure.

In his next work, *Miracolo a Milano* (*Miracle in Milan*, 1951), De Sica took his camera to Milan as he decided to enter the territory of the fable and give greater leeway to Zavattini's creations and the search for a way out from the constrictions of reality. Rich with references to the cinema of René Clair and the painting of Grosz and Chagall, the apologue showed the impossibilities faced by poor people. But it also showed how the dream of a fairer distribution of wealth would never be fulfilled for the great masses of Italy. The movie achieved this using a visual writing style, a rhythm, and a lightness never before seen. "All we need is a little plot of land to live and to die" is the refrain of the tramps' hymn. But they will not get even the little they have asked for and their entire community is forced to depart aboard a broomstick and head toward a land where "Good day really means good day." The film's ending is at once a criticism of a historical defeat and an act of hope.

With *Miracolo a Milano*, Zavattini revived the power of utopian imagination with a fable that in no way can be traced back to canonical realism. During those years, realism was increasingly laden with ideological and literary models. Zavattini's realism, on the other hand, was an exceptional and aberrant example that was condemned and, for the most part, refuted.

In the next film, *Umberto D.* (1952), De Sica and Zavattini returned to the exploration of the real and the workaday. Retiree Umberto D. Ferrari was played by an illustrious Italian linguist, Professor Carlo Battisti, who happened to be enlisted for the part. The character is forced to live on his meager salary of 18,000 lire per month. Thanks to his ability to make even the most workaday acts rife with drama and tragedy, he provoked violent, indignant reactions from government officials (after seeing *Umberto D.*, Giulio Andreotti, then minister of culture and future prime minister, famously lashed out against neorealism in the pages of the weekly *Libertà*). But the film also produced a similar reaction in the common viewer, who preferred to repress this type of problem. The drama unfolds through a linear narration that follows and decomposes the most common of actions. The viewer arrives at the perceptive threshold of a human reality, a profound exploration of solitude, and a desperate vindication of the right to live with dignity. In all likelihood, cinema had not and has not since reached such depths.

Zavattini and De Sica's journey was made up of highs and lows. On one hand, Zavattini wanted to give life to film-essays and investigative films with *Siamo donne* (*Of Life and Love* or *We, the Women*, 1953) and *Amore in città* (*Love in the City*, 1953). On the other hand, the Italian-American co-production green-lighted by David O. Selznick, *Stazione Termini* (*Indiscretion*; *Indiscretion of an American Wife*; *Station Terminus*; *Terminal Station*; *Terminal*

Station Indiscretion; or *Terminus Station*, 1953), resulted in a film in which Zavattini and De Sica's presence is barely perceptible.

Following their happy return to the joy of storytelling with *L'oro di Napoli* (*Everyday's a Holiday* or *The Gold of Naples*, 1954) and *Il tetto* (*The Roof*, 1956), a story that could have been drawn from the early years of neorealism, they made *La ciociara* (*Two Women*), a film that won an Oscar and that showed off Sophia Loren's ability as an actress. They also made *Il giudizio universale* (1961), a work in which they seemed to want to explore new territory by creating a moralistic fable. With this film, they rediscovered their shared love for telling stories, social commentary, black humor, and indignation.

Visconti: Ideology and History

Following World War II, critics saw Rossellini, De Sica, and Visconti as the leading men of a post-Risorgimento oleography who rode together. Later, each had to go his own way and, eventually, certain directors betrayed the tenets of neorealism, shared at heart but never written down in any official, mutually agreed-upon document.

Visconti, the last to enter the game—although he had done some of the cinematography for Mario Serandrei's *Giorni di gloria* (*Days of Glory*, 1945)— went off on his own. Critics treated him more respectfully, even when they found it challenging to group him within the theoretic and poetic canons of neorealism and realism.[62] Stylistically and culturally, no director is more respected than Visconti, who has been spared the harsh attacks commonly delivered by critics. But the ideological and artistic expectations have always been greater in regard to his work.

After spending some years working in theater, staging memorable productions and making a significant contribution to the renewal of theatrical repertoire and directorial modalities, he made *La terra trema* (*The Earth Trembles* or *The Earth Will Tremble*, 1948), an overture to a Sicilian trilogy first conceived in 1941.[63]

His development was a symphony—a figurative tapestry in which each image was composed formally through a series of plastic, chromatic, aural, and musical relationships. Each work alternated between lyrical and dramatic movements. Visconti was Rossellini's antithesis: nothing was left to chance, nothing was spontaneous. Like the fatalist Giovanni Verga, Visconti endowed his characters with the cognizance of their exploitation and the strength to grow, fight back, and change the state of things. His editing was a question of rhythm and every frame was filled with resonant signifiers, as if the director were horrified at the thought of emptiness and therefore tried to align every single gesture with the meaning of collective suffering. It took three years to complete *Bellissima* (1951). With this film, he showed his professional ability through the depth of his characters and his skill in observing them and their relationship to their environment. The subject was neorealist, as was the backdrop for this film, but the narrative structure was not—nor were his formal and stylistic choices, which aimed to recompose the story using more traditional models of storytelling. The dream of Maddalena Cecconi (played by Anna Magnani) was the highest vanishing point where the desires of working-class Italians seemed to focus in the early 1950s. Maddalena sets out on her quest, hoping to see her daughter fulfill her own frustrated desires. But when the finish line is in view and the wheel of fortune spins in her favor, she turns down the offer.

During those years, Italy's poor were still reeling from the country's reconstruction, but, for the first time entertained desire for what was beyond their immediate needs. Movies, illustrated serial novels, and cinematic serial novels were their dream factories, as in Fellini's *Lo sceicco bianco* (*The White Sheik*, 1952) or Antonioni's *La signora senza camelie* (*Camille Without Camelias* or *The Lady Without Camelias*, 1953). These works represented an idealized point of passage toward possible changes in social status. With cruelty and heavy-handed morality, Visconti dismantled the cinematographic dream machine.

The unforgettable opening scene in *Senso* (*Livia* or *The Wanton Countess*, 1954), shot in the Fenice Theater in Venice, marked a decisive shift from neorealism and reconnected Italian cinema with opera, literature, and nineteenth-century art. *Senso* was Visconti's attempt to link together a reading of the Risorgimento, the writings of Antonio Gramsci, the nucleus of his own world, and Verdi's operas, which until then had remained in the margins of Visconti's films. From the 1950s on, this work became a rite of passage for generations of critics. The first was Guido Aristarco and his essay in *Cinema Nuovo*, perhaps the greatest piece of his career.[64] While Aristarco recognized Visconti's nineteenth-century literary sources, his analysis did not repatriate him to theater and opera, fields in which Visconti proved to be one of the most innovative interpreters in Italy.

For Visconti the director, *Senso* was a tapestry of cultural threads that neorealism had kept separate.[65] It also represented an autobiographical projection: even today, viewers find it striking for its awareness of the end of a world to which both characters belong. Visconti continued to develop this world with *Il gattopardo* (*The Leopard*, 1963) and films that would follow.

Beginning with *Senso*, after he had explored the possibilities of color and the contamination of codes, Visconti unleashed his taste in set design and began to cast his increasingly decisive gaze in the direction of nineteenth-century literature and decadence. Dostoyevsky was the source of the story for *Le notti bianche* (*White Nights*, 1957). This film was shot entirely on a studio lot and had a dreamlike quality. Visconti's theatrical style disappointed the majority of critics who had followed his career up to that point. But this work also reaffirmed Visconti's masterful talents and his ability to control every element in the frame.

The Choral Voice of Giuseppe De Santis

For the generation of critics who first wrote for the journal *Cinema*, Giuseppe De Santis was the leading personality of the time and the filmmaker from whom they expected immediate masterpieces.[66] He made his debut in 1947 with *Caccia tragica* (*The Tragic Hunt* or *The Tragic Pursuit*), a film that shed light on his taste for wide pans, expansive camera moves, storytelling through a collective "choral" voice, and a fixation with epic narration. More than any other filmmaker of the postwar period, he believed that cinema should be a choral narrative, a source of inspiration, and an independent language. But he also saw it as a means for understanding and transformation, and he sought to create an Italian middle ground between Soviet cinema and American culture.

His second film, *Riso amaro* (*Bitter Rice*, 1949), marked his greatest domestic and international success.[67] It was a perfect hybrid of the great cinematic and photographic models, cinematic serial novels, and workaday culture. De Santis mixed high and low culture in order to reach the largest audience possible and to communicate using all expressive and dramatic means in the language of cinema. One of the defining features of his work was the attention to body language and the presence of historical and societal signs on the body, combined with the explosive power of nature, which De Santis underscored by making Silvana Mangano the first Italian diva of the postwar era.[68] Few of his peers knew how to cast their gaze and dominate space with a camera like De Santis. For him, neorealism meant *not* hiding the camera, its moves, and the editing. He wanted to celebrate each element of the cinematic experience by making the stories as lifelike and credible as possible. He and Rossellini took entirely different roads: De Santis's journey celebrated cinema as a powerful tool full of emotion—and as a story of stories.

In the films that would follow, from *Giorni d'amore* (*Days of Love*, 1955) to *Non c'è pace tra gli ulivi* (*No Peace Under the Olive Tree* or *Under the Olive Tree*, 1955), *Uomini e lupi* (*Men and Wolves* or *The Wolves*, 1957), and *La strada lunga un anno* (*The Year Long Road* or *Road a Year Long*, 1958), he tried to achieve the perfect integration of the female body and the physical space it inhabited: De Santis was among those directors who used the camera to show their great love of women.[69] Set in Ciociaria, where he was born, *Non c'è pace tra gli ulivi* covers many of the themes dear to De Santis, including the shepherds' living conditions and the parallels between the rugged land and the harsh life there. With *Roma ore 11* (*Rome 11:00*, 1952), he abandoned rural life and made a ripped-from-the-headlines film set in Italy's capital. The women in the story are indicative of the massive migration to urban centers taking place at the time. Somewhere between *Roma ore 11* and *Un marito per Anna Zaccheo* (*A Husband for Anna*, 1953), a crack appeared in De Santis's filmography that was never repaired.[70] None of his subsequent films enabled him to regain the reputation he had lost. Almost unanimously, the public, critics, and industry alike found him guilty of excessive ideology and made him the scapegoat for the sins of neorealism. He was ostracized by decree and left the business prematurely.

Fellow Travelers of Neorealism

For some time, everyone hopped on the neorealist bandwagon. All that was needed were certain common elements—even if merely thematic—and an Italian film was categorized as neorealist. At a certain point, there was an attempt to create a discipline, but by that time everyone had taken separate paths, diverting from the initial direction.[71]

The war and the Resistance were common themes in the films made between 1945 and 1946. Vergano's *Il sole sorge ancora* (*Outcry*, 1946) was an ideologically charged film that sought to portray the war from the combatants' point of view, illustrating the dangers of a rapid loss of hope that society would be transformed. For most directors, the passage from fascism to antifascism occurred painlessly and without them having to confess their sins or make retribution through expiation.[72] Any Italian filmmaker who did not sign on with the Republic of Salò was absolved, and in general, a plenary indulgence was applied, even for the few who went to the north of Italy—in other words, to the German side, following the 1943 armistice. Giorgio Ferroni, for example, belonged to the Republic of Salò and made fascist propaganda films. But in 1946, he made *Pian delle stelle*, named after the site where partisans had sought refuge in the Dolomites, a film produced by a partisan association in Padua.

Even Alessandro Blasetti, who had made some of the earliest films under the fascist regime, made a film about the war. In *Un giorno nella vita* (*A Day in the Life*, 1946), he adapted his style and the story to the changing times without giving up control in his direction of the actors, set design, and cinematography. The new men of Italian cinema still saw him as a father who deserved the utmost respect, recognition, and admiration. In the years that followed, he made colossal films during Cinecittà's resurgence, like *Fabiola* (1949) and *Prima comunione* (*Father's Dilemma*, 1950). The latter was a successful collaboration with Zavattini that allowed Blasetti to ease back into the team of neorealist filmmakers. With *Altri tempi* (*In Olden Days*; *Infidelity*; or *Times Gone By*, 1952) and *Tempi nostri* (*A Slice of Life* or *The Anatomy of Love*, 1953), he heralded the new trend of episodic films. With *Peccato che sia una canaglia* (*Too Bad She's Bad*) and *La fortuna di essere donna* (*Lucky to Be a Woman* or *What a Woman!*, 1955) he explored new directions in comedy, parallel to Comencini's films. By the end of the decade, with *Europa di notte* (*Europe by Night* or *European Nights*, 1959), he launched a new trend by editing together clips of shows from Europe's most famous nightclubs.

Camerini had a more checkered career. After the war, he had to depend on the generosity of Italian cinema as he found himself subjected to a new set of rules. In 1946, he directed *Due lettere anonime* (*Two Anonymous Letters*), an operatic film immersed in the atmosphere of the times. During the 1950s, he made two other spectacular films, *Ulisse* (*Ulysses*, 1954) and *La bella mugnaia* (*The Miller's Beautiful Wife* or *The Miller's Wife*, 1955), a remake of his *Cappello a tre punte* (*Three Cornered Hat*, 1935). But, unlike Blasetti's ground-breaking works, his filmmaking had lost something and his films seemed to rest on the laurels of the past.

The directors examined in this chapter were part of a small group of filmmakers who were disparaged for their excessive interest in visual writing and their reluctance to use cinema as a means to change the world. The extraordinary formal quality of their films, their perfect metabolism of cinematic codes, and their use of color over black and white as an means of expression were branded and condemned by militant critics who considered them negative elements detrimental to neorealism. There was a clear-cut continuity of judgment in between the pre- and postwar periods. Above all, there was an absolute preference for ideology over aesthetics and style. Many of these directors had no obvious ideological affiliation and they would become constant targets during the 1940s and the Cold War. Although critics did not recognize their directorial talent, their ability to translate literary culture into cinematic language and their facility to assimilate elements of German, French, Russian, and American cinema reaped rewards at the box office from audiences who appreciated their capacity to optimize all elements of cinema.

Among those directors who debuted in the early 1940s, Alberto Lattuada felt the need to see the reality of war-torn Italy with optimism—without turning his back on his literary background and his love of Carné, Renoir, and French and expressionist cinema. When in Lattuada's 1946 film *Il bandito* (*The Bandit*), the war veteran (played by Amedeo Nazzari) stated, "There'll be work to do until the year 3000," his words marked a new cinema unfolding in Italy— one that had to be invented and rebuilt from scratch. After directing *Il delitto di Giovanni Episcopo* (*Flesh Will Surrender*, 1947, based on Gabriele d'Annunzio's novel, *Giovanni Episcopo*), Lattuada made one of his masterpieces, *Il mulino del Po* (*The Mill on the Po*, 1949), based on the novel by Riccardo Bacchelli. Epic in its narrative scope, the film represents a coming together of neorealism with an attempt to invent a new iconography using the knowledge and forms of cinematographic language. In the 1950s, after directing *Luci del varietà* (*Variety Lights* or *Lights of Variety*, 1950) with Fellini, Lattuada had to come to terms with the laws of the market. At the same time, he wanted to develop his gaze, which was starved (to the point of being bulimic) for images. His eye was capable of observing even the smallest elements of reality, and he enjoyed the gifts of youth and beauty, especially when distributed generously by nature. Along with this vision came his interest for "the humiliated and the offended," which resulted in his film *Il cappotto* (*The Overcoat*, 1952), another high point in his directorial career and an extraordinary dramatic performance by actor Renato Rascel. Four years after the theft of the bicycle, the theft of the overcoat, as Micciché has observed, became "a metaphor for the social nightmare that has beset the entire country at different times and in different ways."[73] As producers recognized that the times were changing, they encouraged Lattuada to incorporate erotica in his films. Their urging led to his *La lupa* (*She-Wolf*, 1953) and *La spiaggia* (*Riviera* or *The Beach*, 1954),[74] both passionate love stories about diehard social prejudices in an Italy racing toward modernization in its values and ways of life. He then made *Guendalina* (1957) and *I dolci inganni* (*Sweet Deceptions*, 1960) about adolescent sexual discovery. Lattuada's visual writing style has probably never been fully appreciated: his rigorous composition of the frame, his mastery of all the elements of cinema, and his ability to create an almost physical relationship between the camera's gaze and the actors. In retrospect, Lattuada might be compared to director Max Ophuls in terms of his narrative elegance and his ability to make the most of his actors and all the elements within the frame.

Compared to Lattuada, Mario Soldati had a much more varied career. While Lattuada moved constantly upward, Soldati seemed to travel downhill. With *Le miserie del Signor Travet* (*His Young Wife*, 1946) and *Policarpo ufficiale di scrittura* (*Policarpo*, 1959), Soldati established himself as a talented, erudite director, but eventually, the allure of literature captured him, and he lost his faith in cinema as a means of expression.[75]

Like Soldati, Luigi Zampa had a varied career. Unfortunately, the remarkable stylistic and thematic cohesiveness of his films has been forgotten. He is remembered today primarily for his comedies, a genre for which critics have little love or respect. But he has every right to be counted among the great masters of neorealist filmmaking. In his films, Zampa used style as a vehicle for social commentary born of indignation.

With *Vivere in pace* (*To Live in Peace*, 1946), Zampa tried to distance himself, emotionally and ideologically, from the war and to advance the cause of universal pacifism. With *L'onorevole Angelina* ([*The Honorable*] *Angelina*, 1947), Zampa dove decisively into the waters of neorealism. Throughout his career, he was never afraid to reveal his directorial presence in his films and to give voice to the common man's feeling of disenfranchisement and distrust in the government and its institutions. From *Anni difficili* (*Difficult Years* or *The Little Man*, 1953) to *L'arte di arrangiarsi* (*The Art of Getting Along*, 1953), the themes of protest, civil indignation, and dark comedy (derived primarily from a six-film partnership with Vitaliano Brancati) became mixed with Zampa's intention to paint a fresco of Italian vice and virtue—within a society dominated by dishonesty, corruption, backroom politics and lobbying, opportunism, organized crime, and a growing Italian nostalgia for the thugs of fascism. *La romana* (*Woman of Rome*, 1954), based on the novel by Moravia, was less successful and edgy. Brancati's premature death in 1954 opened a creative void and deep-rooted crisis in Zampa's cinema.

Renato Castellani also moved toward neorealism without abandoning his strong views on directing and storytelling. *Mio figlio professore* (*Professor My Son*, 1946) seemed to breathe the same air as films by Lattuada and Soldati, while in *Sotto il sole di Roma* (*Under the Sun of Rome*, 1948) and *È primavera* (*It's Forever Springtime* or *Springtime in Italy*, 1950), a realist evolution had clearly occurred. His *Due soldi di speranza* (*Two Cents Worth of Hope* or *Two Pennyworth of Hope*, 1951) was central to his growth as a director. At the time, leftist critics (and as a result, subsequent critics and historiographers) have wrongly branded this film as the father of ideological dissolution and so-called pink neorealism. His characters' only legacy, also captured in his later films, *Giulietta e Romeo* (*Romeo and Juliet*, 1954) and *I sogni nel cassetto* (*Dreams in a Drawer*, 1956), was that they had heart. They acted toward each other out of instinct and without thoughts of the future. Their downfall was their lack of ideological awareness. They had neither the will nor the teleological leanings to construct their own destiny.

Even though the ideological tension of his works subsided (in direct relation to the social reality and context in which his characters moved), the emotion and visual tension remained unchanged. Throughout the 1950s, these films spoke to Italian audiences and are considered emblematic of that age.

More than any of the other newcomers, Pietro Germi looked to the models of American cinema and sought to transplant them in an Italian context. Germi is another case of forgotten talent. By the same token, he has enjoyed a great deal of critical attention in recent years. His bibliography has grown so quickly that it could soon overtake the rather modest number of works devoted to De Sica.[76] Germi was a director who loved to put his stamp on genre films through his remarkable ability to create atmosphere and to draw out the relationships between his characters. He was an anti-conformist director who cannot be grouped among the militant, leftist directors, nor among those of the right. Following his debut film, *Il testimone* (*The Witness*, 1945), he moved to the LUX team, where he used the same technicians as Castellani, Zampa, and Lattuada. Among his contemporaries, he had the greatest natural ability for storytelling and gave his films epic overtones as he borrowed from mythology. His second film, *Gioventù perduta* (*Lost Youth*, 1947), adapted elements from American film noir for a story that showed the disasters brought upon the most recent generations by the war. *In nome della legge* (*In the Name of the Law* or *Mafia*, 1949) was a *film d'auteur* where Germi showed his mastery of dialogue, characters, and sets in the style of John Ford. His *Il cammino della speranza* (1950), written by Fellini and Tullio Pinelli, traveled the length of Italy from south to north, illustrating the country's dialectal barriers by following a group of clandestine Sicilian immigrants who leave the infernal mines of Sicily behind and head to the promised land of France. The main character, Saro (a reincarnation of father Aeneas), and his companions never feel any connection to the land that they pass through. The only roots that they recognize and their only possible identity lie in Sicily. In Naples, Ciccio, their guide, tries to abandon them. In Rome, they are arrested by the Carabinieri. In the North, they are received as foreigners. For them, Italy is a hostile country inhabited by ferocious peoples: in the northern region of Emilia-Romagna, the residents of a small village yell racial epithets at Barbara ("What are you saying, you dirty southerner [*terrona*]? Sounds like Abyssinian! Darkie!"). France, on the other hand, is seen by them as heaven on earth.

Germi suffered from an identity crisis at the outset of the Cold War. Like Lattuada, Soldati, and Fellini, he dismissed the logic of antithetical frontlines. During the 1950s, with *Il brigante di Tacca del Lupo* (*The Bandit of Tacca del Lupo*, 1952), *Il ferroviere* (*Man of Iron* or *The Railroad Man*, 1955), *L'uomo di paglia* (*A Man of Straw*, 1957), and his adaptation of Gadda's novel, *That Awful Mess on Merulana Street, Un maledetto imbroglio* (*The Facts of Murder*, 1959), he tried to maintain stylistic and ideological control of his films and with each one, he adapted them in harmony with his characters' ethics and trials.

Bellissima

"After all, what is acting? Huh? If I think that I'm someone else . . . If I pretend to be someone else . . . Now, that's acting."

If pressed for the most memorable moment of postwar Italian cinema, I would have to choose this classic scene from *Bellissima* in which Margherita Cecconi, played by Anna Magnani, puts on her earrings, fixes her hair in the mirror, and reflects on how easy it is to step into someone else's shoes. This scene captures the new style of acting created by neorealism as conceived by Zavattini and put into practice by De Sica and Rossellini. They were absolutely convinced that anyone could become the central character of a story and could be made into a star without paying too high a price. In effect, neorealism also affirmed the right and the opportunity to play oneself, to act on screen by living one's own life. But with *Bellissima*, we are witness to a moment of change and an attempt to exploit—artistically and commercially—this golden trend of stars who were born by accident but became standard-bearers for all cinema.[77] Here, we also witness the rebirth of and quest for a new feminine identity, as Giovanna Grignaffini clearly showed in her *Racconti di nascita*.

The potential for study of the postwar star phenomenon in Italy is divided into two contiguous but distinct fields. The first would be to work on the mimesis, perfect fluidity, and mirror-image relationship between screen and audience. The second would be to work on the films themselves, along with consulting the films' peripheral texts and contexts by examining industry publications and articles (illustrated in such magazines as *Hollywood*, *Festival*, and *Novelle Film*), photographs, letters, the changing processes of classification, the flux of desire, and the different approaches to depiction of the body.

The star phenomenon had no rightful place in the poetics and practice of neorealism. For many actors, the move from studio work (based on theatrical conventions) to realist working methods happened seamlessly. But for others, it was a watershed moment that brought about profound changes and suddenly revealed previously unknown talents and potential. Visconti and screenwriter Zavattini depicted the movie industry "dream machine" and its destructive power in moralistic and even Pirandellian terms. In doing so, they captured the dynamics of an irreversible process on film.

Until that moment, one of the greatest achievements of postwar Italian cinema was linked to its capacity to put everyday people center-stage. Their stories became the reflection of a collective condition: thanks to this type of cinema, wrote Pasolini, "the world became the subject / made no longer of mystery but rather history." In certain films by Rossellini, De Sica, and Visconti, the discovery of the perfect fluidity between screen and audience produced the illusion that they had discovered a winning formula.

In terms of the expressive process, the use of nonprofessional actors can be seen as a high point in the history of international cinema. In terms of the acting machine, however, it was a mandatory but unconvincing step that had to be quickly abandoned to allow Italian cinema to regain its ability to compete in the market. Despite memorable performances by Rinaldo Smordoni, Franco Interlenghi, Lamberto Maggiorani, Enzo Stajola, Francesco Golisano, Carlo Battisti, and Maria Pia Casilio, among others, the attempt to replace professional actors in the name of unmitigated, perfect, natural empathy failed in just a few short years. The star system went back into motion and tried to assimilate the lessons learned from neorealism. Filmmakers believed in finding and recruiting new faces everywhere: in stores and businesses, beauty contests, cafés and restaurants, even on the street. They used all means at their disposal to imitate and compete with American cinema. Of all of these actors, only Franco Interlenghi, following his debut in *Sciuscià* (*Shoe-Shine*), would enjoy a long career. He reached his greatest heights in films by Emmer, Duvivier, and Antonioni, and when he played a young man in Fellini's *I vitelloni* (*The Young and the Passionate*, 1953), he found the role for which he would always be remembered. The overpowering appearance of a Botticellian Venus in the rice fields, Silvana Mangano, with her black stockings and tight-fitting shorts, marked Italy's move toward Hollywood and paved the way for shapely women who would become stars of the screen.

Italian producers discovered that attractive Italian actresses not only conveyed the country's underdevelopment, pain, and misery but were also lucrative in foreign markets. They were quick to use beauty as a national asset and they tried to repeat the process by discovering and promoting new faces and new bodies, from Lucia Bosé to Eleonora Rossi Drago, from Silvana Pampanini to Yvonne Sanson, Gina Lollobrigida, and Sophia Loren. These faces and these bodies, as well as many others, were destined to enjoy mass appeal in the hearts and minds of audiences.

Throughout the 1950s there was a genuine blossoming of the star system that managed to keep American cinema in check. It allowed certain actresses to unseat American stars in the minds of Italians. They would become the new ambassadors of Italian cinema in the world. By the mid-1950s, Gina Lollobrigida (Blasetti coined the term *maggiorata* [bombshell or shapely, buxom woman] for her) and Sophia Loren would eclipse the others. For a while, Silvana Mangano held her own next to Loren, but she was uncomfortable in the spotlight. Unlike other Italian postwar bombshells, she made it clear that she had climbed the Mt. Olympus of stardom only by chance and that her reason for staying there was survival. In any case, there had never been such a phenomenon since the time of silent movies in Italy.

Although Anna Magnani was part of the star phenomenon of that era, her career would be better analyzed in terms of her cinematic sovereignty in twentieth-century film and the fire that fueled her characters' passions. The star phenomenon flourished in part thanks to her, but it was ultimately based on the exhibition of physical attributes that Magnani—by virtue of genetics—did not possess.

The sex symbols of postwar Italian cinema offered ideals of beauty based on excessive natural gifts and the triumph of "naturalism." Gina Lollobrigida, riding a burro with her skimpy, tattered dress in *Pane, amore, e gelosia* (*Bread, Love, and Jealousy* or *Frisky*, 1954), was the ultimate icon of this trend. They relied on new and golden standards of measurement that highlighted the prosperity of the bosom, ample hips, and, most important, the aggressive exhibition of the body (which would remain covered for the most part until the next decade when the bikini triumphed). Throughout the 1950s, women were the most coveted cinematic prize. The first challenge to men's hold on the world began with performances by Anna Magnani and then Gina Lollobrigida, Sophia Loren, Lucia Bosé, Silvana Pampanini, and Marisa Allasio in a series of films by Risi, beginning with *Poveri ma belli* (*A Girl in a Bikini*; *Poor But Beautiful*; or *Poor, But Handsome*). Until then, men still wielded nearly unlimited power in the family and the workplace. While these actresses were admired above all for their physical beauty, there were others as well who were admired for their looks, like Giulietta Masina and Franca Valeri.

After a series of trial runs in Italy whereby they obtained their full-fledged status as stars, Lollobrigida and Loren left for the United States in hopes of rising even higher in the international arena (the former had already become a star in France in two spellbinding performances with Gérard Philipe in *Les Belles-de-nuit* [*Beauties of the Night*] by René Clair and *Fanfan la Tulipe* [*Fanfan the Tulip*] by Christian-Jaque in 1952). For Loren, this was an opportunity to grow and achieve a greater awareness of her talents. For Lollobrigida, it was a near disaster because she proved incapable of drawing previously unrevealed dimensions of her repertoire as an actress. And for Alida Valli, her postwar trip to America did little to help her career, despite the fact that she worked with Hitchcock and Orson Welles (nor did traveling to America bring added success to Vittorio Gassman). Valli returned to Italy to find a truly important role awaiting her as the Countess Serpieri in *Senso* (*Livia* or *The Wanton Countess*). But, after that part, even though there were some exceptions, Italian cinema no longer had need of her star charisma and it never again took advantage of her talents as an actress.

As far as the men were concerned, there was Nazzari, who was immediately reintegrated into postwar Italian cinema and who enjoyed a five-year wave of success together with Yvonne Sanson in Matarazzo's operatic films. There was the rise of a group of comics headed by Totò. And there was the continued success of Alberto Sordi and Marcello Mastroianni. For a time, there were some attempts to exploit and counterpose young actors with gym-sculpted physiques like Maurizio Arena and Renato Salvatori, the "poor but beautiful" stars of Risi's films. Thanks to co-productions, hybridization also took place between European and American stars. The new made-in-Italy star system helped significantly to reconquer international markets. This period provided the new generations of actors the opportunity for professional growth.

Toward the end of the 1950s, bodybuilders imported from America began to appear on the scene: Gordon Scott and Gordon Mitchell, Ed Fury and Brad Harris, Mickey Hargitay and Mark Forest. For a moment, they seemed to encroach on the success of Italy's female superstars. For a few years, Italy, a country that had exported muscle-bound actors during the era of silent films, was forced to recruit them in gyms and male beauty contests on the other side of the Atlantic. These characters were inexpressive and entirely unable to act, but they offered their muscles, "swollen with protein, butter, and honey, but without any strength," according to writer and director Duccio Tessari.[78] In fact, Steve Reeves proved unable to lift Virna Lisi in the air. In any case, they were not the ones who drew the public's attention. Audiences came to see them portray heroes who could overcome nearly any obstacle through the use of strength.

The 1950s came to a close with the emergence of new forms of male stardom provided by the antiheroes of comedies and the future monsters of the 1960s. Mastroianni, Sordi, Gassman, Tognazzi, and Manfredi showed such power as actors that they were able, in just a few short years, to take on nearly any role, to change masks with extreme ease, to wear a thousand different costumes, and to give life to a thousand different faces—old and new—of the Italian whose life was beginning to be transformed by the economic miracle of the 1960s.

The Rebirth of Genre

Over the course of decades, there have been delicate oscillations in the perception of Italian cinema among different generations. Although today, at the beginning of a new millennium, the younger generations have lost practically all contact with current Italian cinema and with its history and memory, critics in the 1940s and 1950s concentrated their focus on *films d'auteur*. Thanks in part to French critics and in part to new related fields of awareness, the 1960s saw attention shift from the highest planes of film production to the lowest. As a result, there was renewed interest in the emotive capital of cinema and the attempt to subvert the system of relationships and values. Even when such revisiting was also born of the need to give a balanced overview of the cinematic panorama, it helped shed new light on films and directors previously confined to the shadows.[79] Together with reparations to directors who have been forgotten or who were never taken into consideration, it is important to consider the creative input made by all those who contributed to the production of a film, from costume designers and camera operators to character actors and set designers. In genre films, these elements really shone and were exploited to the fullest. Such artisanal knowledge would become the cornerstone of Italian cinema, allowing it to endure over time and to overcome even the most dire crises. The disappearance of genre films over the past twenty years represents a grave weakening of Italian cinema's creative heritage and its specialized forms of knowledge.

It is important to note, however, that during those years when Italian cinema was considered a crucial weapon in the battle of ideas, critics (even the ones who had read Antonio Gramsci's splendid pages on popular literature) were careful not to cheer too loudly for films by Gentilomo, Mattoli, Matarazzo, and Mastrocinque, to name just a few. Nor did they recognize that this type of production had re-established a strong network of media connections with illustrated serial novels, magazines, Puccini and Verdi operas, cartoons, vaudeville, *commedia dell'arte*, and so on. It had also established unprecedented connections with audiences living in farming communities, small towns, and the outskirts of big cities, where theaters often showed second- and third-run films.

Perhaps the strongest and most obvious umbilical chord with Italian culture was the film-opera that Carmine Gallone made immediately following the liberation of Rome, *Avanti a lui tremava tutta Roma* (*Before Him All Rome Trembled*, 1946), starring Anna Magnani. In this film, the director mixed operatic arias and the staging of operas with the stories of resistance fighters and the antifascist struggle.[80] By marrying these themes, Gallone was able to resurrect his career in the wake of the formal expulsion that sidelined him for a few months. With this film he would become the director of operatic films par excellence, able to translate operas into the language of cinema and bring complete works, their music, and their stories to the screen. Together with Magnani and Fabrizi, the first true operatic film stars of the postwar period were Tito Gobbi—who starred in *Torna a Sorrento* (*Come Back to Sorrento*, 1945) by Carlo Ludovico Bragaglia, in which he sang *Rigoletto*, and in *O sole mio!* (1946) by Gentilomo—and Gino Becchi, Beniamino Gigli, Nelly Corradi, Ferruccio Tagliavini, and Gino Sinimberghi, among others. These performers found success with audiences in the years that followed, thanks to cinematic adaptations of the operatic canon.

From 1946 to 1947, five operatic films were produced, from Rossini's *Il barbiere di Siviglia* (*Barber of Seville*) to Donizetti's *L'elisir d'amore* (*The Wine of Love*) and Verdi's *Rigoletto*, not to mention many other titles drawn from the operatic canon, more or less directly, like Max Neufeld's *Il tiranno di Padova* (*The Tyrant of Padua*, 1946) and Gallone's *Addio Mimí!* (*Her Wonderful Lie*, 1947). There were also biographical films about famous musicians, like Camillio Mastrocinque's *Il cavaliere del sogno* (*Donizetti* or *The Life of Donizetti*, 1946), in which the director staged a romanticized biography of Gaetano Donizetti. Of all the biographical films, the most memorable was Matarazzo's *Giuseppe Verdi* (*The Life and Music of Giuseppe Verdi* or *Verdi, the King of Melody*, 1953), in which the director used the figure of Verdi to resurrect the ideal archetype that he had found in characters played by Amedeo Nazzari beginning with his film *Catene* (*Chains*).

Save for a few exceptions, critics refused to embrace the so-called *filmelodramma* (operatic film). Nor did they accept the producers' educational intentions. Then, when the quality of the recordings, the acting, and the directing had such convincing and spectacular results, film writers came to pay more attention, thanks in great part to critic Beniamino del Fabbro. During the 1950s, new technologies and Cinemascope color made it possible to deliver quality in terms of the music, directing, and acting. In many instances, no one seemed to miss theatrical production values and the many operatic films produced during this period allowed viewers to hear—directly or indirectly—a number of operas, from Clemente Fracassi's *Aida* (1953) and Gallone's *Casa Ricordi* (*House of Ricordi*, 1954) to Flavio Calzavara's *Rigoletto e la sua tragedia* (*Rigoletto and His Tragedy*, 1956). Although the production value of these films was good—if not great—they did not obtain the success their producers had hoped for, and they marked the decline of the genre.

Just as producers of operatic films had sought to exploit classical music, it did not take long for others to employ a hybrid of traditional Italian music crossed with the foreign rhythms of boogie-woogie, rock, the mambo, and the cha-cha-cha. At the height of the 1950s, Ettore Giannini made what could be considered a truly unique work, *Carosello napolteano* (*Neapolitan Carousel* or *Neapolitan Fantasy*, 1953). With this film, Giannini revived a show that had already toured Europe. Although based on popular Neapolitan songs, this important and original work was rich with iconographic and popular references to the period between the two world wars. It covered a historical arc that spanned a few centuries and sought to capture the soul of Naples through the spirit of her songs. Almost unanimously, foreign critics, who saw the film at Cannes in 1954, received it triumphantly and praised its portrayal of Italian characters and local colors.[81]

In the mid-1930s, Giacomo Debenedetti, in an enlightening article on the relationship between cinema and intellectuals, had made an early comparative analysis of the functions of cinema and those of nineteenth-century opera. In his study, he underlined their shared lineage, parallels, and characters: "As entertainment, social phenomenon, and—we can even say—public service, cinema fulfills a function analogous to that carried out by opera during the nineteenth century, particularly in Italy . . . The analogy between the function of cinema and that of opera as entertainment lies in their repeated yearly offering of a relatively unchanging, canonical repertoire of emotions and sentiments, etc., and all in all, unchanging content."[82]

As opera continued its evolution, Raffaello Matarazzo played an integral role, capable of transferring and adapting themes, situations, ideology, and morals to a world that wished to conserve the laws of the past even as it collided with change and modernization. All of Matarazzo's films were based on operas. In particular, his trilogy, *Catene* (*Chains*, 1950), *Tormento* (*Torment*, 1950), and *I figli di nessuno* (*Nobody's Children*, 1951), carried the entire genre and obtained results that nobody could have imagined. These films revealed how much working-class audiences depended on literary models and the nineteenth-century feuilleton. In the years that followed, Matarazzo provided the groundwork for Gentilomo, Bonard, Mario Costa, Genina, and others who made films that deserve renewed consideration today, like Cottafavi's *Una donna ha ucciso* (*A Woman Has Killed*, 1952), Genina's *Maddalena* (1954), and *Traviata '53*, also by Cottafavi. These films represent the evolution and perfect development of opera in the modern drama of failed communication and existential solitude, themes for which Antonioni had already provided some important examples.

Today, it may still be blasphemous to compare Matarazzo and Visconti. But it is important to recognize that they both drew from the same sources and inspiration, even though the stylistic results were different for each: the former aimed for the cheap seats in the balcony, while the latter set his sights on the stage and box seats. When Luchino Visconti staged Gaspare Spontini's *La vestale* for the opening of La Scala on December 7, 1954, he made the following declaration in reference to his film *Senso* (*Livia* or *The Wanton Countess*): "*Senso* is a romantic film clearly influenced by Italian opera . . . Its characters make operatic declarations. This is highly important to me. Even in real life, there are operatic characters, like the illiterate shepherds of Sicily . . . [In this film] I transferred the sentiments expressed on the stage in Verdi's *Il trovatore* into a story of war and rebellion."

For at least five decades, Italian workers and farmers filled the movie theaters in the country and the outskirts of the big cities. They were fully capable of evaluating, interpreting, and understanding the relationship between opera and other cinematic genres. Between the 1940s and 1950s, this audience was witness to the full integration of cinema and the various layers of opera. In an article on folk music that he published at the beginning of the 1950s, Renzo Renzi showed the parallel between folk singers and their audiences and popular films and their audiences, pointing out that folk singers could draw from a thousand-year-old tradition of popular narratives: "The audience cried for real. It cried real tears. This was the same audience that cheered Matarazzo's films *Catene*, *Tormento*, and *Torna!* [*Come Back!*]: these incredible adventure stories depicted life's injustices with faith in the triumph of honesty and basic emotions."[83]

The destiny of the main character in Matarazzo's *Catene* was inexorably linked to that of the heroines in films like *Cieca di Sorrento* and *Genoveffa di Brabante*. The many elements of the narrative structure seemed to be scattered along the same lines that had been established by a common plot derived from the nineteenth-century *grand opéra* and feuilleton. For many years, working-class audiences embraced these films. In doing so, they lent their support to a type of cinema that would undergo slow transformations. This cinema never completely died; it has, in fact, recently been resurrected on television.

Beyond the Surface of the Visible: Fellini and Antonioni

Although the influence of literature began to diminish with neorealism, Italian cinema began to feel the weight of culture, the figurative arts, iconographic models, and existentialist thought. Fleeting, incomparable elements came to

replace the certainties of real data. Directors realized that the data of perception were no longer sufficient to fulfill the dimensions of the visible. It became
clear that often the essential component was the invisible lying behind the
visible. Little by little, objects and shapes began to take on enigmatic, disturbing characteristics. Thanks to Antonioni and Fellini, the visible was now
presented in infinite dimensions, slowly deconstructed and no longer providing certainty. With few exceptions, reality continued to be offered to viewers
in the poverty and wealth of black and white.

Even in his early films, Fellini had drawn from a personalized repertoire
he had accumulated in his memory. In these works, he had given shape to
ectoplasmatic figures that fluttered in a dimension suspended somewhere between reality and dream. Fellini and Antonioni unhinged the coordinates and
conditions that delimited creative space and the construction of the signified
and the signifiers of the postwar period. They sought to construct works that
were no longer measurable by the meter of the theory and poetics of neorealism and realism.

Antonioni saw the world vis-à-vis his mind and rational thought. But
unlike Visconti, who metabolized all the arts, he appropriated and moved past
the avant-garde and continued to push toward a world that measured itself
by different indicators. In a certain sense, his imagery could be considered a
counterpoint to Visconti's vision: to the same degree that Visconti was obsessed by a *horror vacui* and tended to fill his images with the greatest number
of historical and psychological elements, Antonioni managed to create a sort
of emptiness in the space that surrounded his characters. And he did so in
such a way that there was a correspondence between their inner void and
discontent and the absence of possible connections with their environment
and the persons surrounding them. Fellini saw the world with a third eye: an
inner eye that fished for images in the subconscious, in dreams, and in memory.
Even when he observed the present, Fellini remained a director with a foot
in either world, his imagery always suspended between the experience of reality and a reality drawn from dreams and fantasy. These different modalities of
seeing and the different paths of these directors' careers illustrate the complex
iconosphere of Italian cinema and the difficulties in developing a single direction of study (even if considered to be the winning one).

In contrast to neorealist culture, Fellini came to the set with the simplicity of a self-taught director and a relatively anomalous library of references
that was clearly influenced by existentialism and psychoanalysis, although one
of the recurring themes among critics was that Fellini's readings of such fields
of thought were shallow.[84] Until that point, his contributions to Rossellini's

screenplays had been limited to those situations in which reason and the visible were insufficient to explain reality.

After working ten years as a screenwriter, Lattuada promoted Fellini to co-director for *Luci del varietà* (*Variety Lights* or *Lights of Variety*, 1950). With this and the first film in which he had total control as director, *Lo sceicco bianco* (*The White Sheik*, 1952), Fellini found his inspiration in the lowest forms of popular, town-square entertainment.

Camera operator Ubaldo Arata once noted resentfully that when Fellini worked as Rossellini's assistant director, he liked to position "the camera at the level of a hunchback," or, in other words, he continuously shifted the camera from the classic positions. For Fellini, vision had always been linked to its etymological meaning, "to aim," "to gaze," and "to show," and he always maintained a sort of primitive wonder in everything he filmed. Every time he happened to see something he had never seen before, vision became a "miracle" for Fellini.

From the outset, Fellini, like a magician, told stories born of his own experiences. Every theme, figure, character, and motif began to levitate and to move back and forth from autobiographical memory and collective memory. In his first films, *Lo sceicco bianco* and *I vitelloni* (*The Young and the Passionate*), he sculpted his figures with the gusto for construction one might find in a homespun puppet theater, as he identified and circumscribed the roles and functions for each person. Fellini quickly showed himself to be a director capable of constructing, out of experiences and circumscribed realities, a genuine cosmogony that expanded infinitely.

In *I vitelloni*, he made his first return to his hometown, Rimini. In this placentary and familiar reality, Fellini formed a narrative structure subject to an important deconstruction: the story was fractured into five minimal events, each distinct but interchangeable. Beginning with *La strada* (*The Road*, 1954) and Gelsomina and Zampanò, Fellini's characters emerged as the fruit of the subconscious. In this film, Fellini took the point of view of his main character, creating an image of the world and of the real in the form of a mysterious, magical, and entertaining carnival show. In doing so, he managed to make this carnival-show world overlap with the world of a traveling carnival show. Gelsomina seemed to speak every language save for the normal ones: she spoke the language of the mentally ill, she heard things, and she heard language in nature, but communication with others presented difficulty. Fellini's soundtracks were composed by Nino Rota: even though he had worked for over twenty years as a film composer, it was at this moment that he began to create melodies from which the images seemed to gush. These compositions were destined to become elements that directly evoked the overarching spirit of the film. The melodies of *La strada* and *Il bidone* (*The Swindle* or *The Swindlers*, 1955, a work that should be considered a key element in the Fellinian universe inasmuch as it foreshadows the narrative and stylistic structure and modalities of *La dolce vita*,) converged in *Le notti di Cabiria* (*Cabiria* or *The Nights of Cabiria*, 1957)—a universe expanded, releasing a growing creative energy that never lost continuity with its previous experiences.

By the end of 1959, Fellini completed *La dolce vita* (*The Sweet Life*), a work that represented a turning point. From this moment forward, he began to approach his images using a technique similar to that of the masters of American action painting. In an almost physical sense, Fellini poured himself into an object, stopping short of destroying it. In doing so, he channeled his life energy into the images. In international cinematic imagery, some of his images have become public domain, like Anita Ekberg and Mastroianni in the Trevi Fountain. *La dolce vita* was a grand social and cinematic fresco that served as a bridge in the history of Italian cinema, concluding one phase and heralding a new era, covering a lot of ground in terms of new tendencies and trends in international moviemaking.

Even during that phase of neorealism, when a newly constructed heritage needed to be administered and multiple voices needed to be congregated into an ideological and expressive amalgam that was anything but homogeneous, Michelangelo Antonioni could be considered a dissonant voice in the chorus. Although his point of departure was the same, he proudly vindicated his different approach from his very first documentary, *Gente del Po* (*People of the Po River*, 1943): "This is my only presumption: I went down the path of neorealism on my own. Visconti was making *Ossessione* and I was just a few feet away making my first documentary . . . Everything that I have done, good or bad, started there."[85]

To the same degree that Fellini sought to unleash his visionary energy, Antonioni was a visual architect and a builder of spatial relationships between dissimilar elements, persons, and things.

As a neorealist, he was not interested in themes as much as in choices of vocabulary and visual strength. His directorial debut, like Fellini's for that matter, was received by critics as yet another sign of a growing diaspora, a dispersal and deconstruction of the neorealist body. From the very first frames of *Cronaca di un amore* (*Chronicle of a Love* or *Story of a Love Affair*, 1950), we are faced with a fleeting, spectral dimension. In Antonioni's symbolic urban space, shadows are disturbing totems projected onto the characters.[86]

With his debut film, he tried to establish a distance from his characters and their environment. This approach allowed him to capture signs, symptoms, and clues that served to form a diagnosis of his characters' inner turmoil. In his films, Antonioni digested the spirit and lessons of Camus' *L'étranger*. Even Italian geography acquired a new and important meaning in Antonioni's work.

As early as 1952, when other directors were beginning to move in a more articulated direction, in step with Italy's changing time-space coordinates and reality, Antonioni transgressed their notion of ideal space by shooting two of the three segments in *I vinti* (*The Vanquished* or *Youth and Perversion*) in France and England. With this film, he declared that he wanted to discover the many facets of the individual, the kaleidoscope of appearances and illusions, the fragility of sensations, and the trickery of logical and perceptive data. Antonioni never tried to balance the books by revealing all the logical connections and concatenations between a series of facts and clues: instead of real space, he sought to measure internal distances.

La signora senza camelie (*Camille Without Camelias* or *The Lady Without Camelias*, 1953) moved within an illusory cinematic dream. More than anything else, this film helped Lucia Bosé, a salesgirl turned movie star by accident, to refashion herself after Louise Brooks in Genina's *Prix de beauté* (1930). *Le amiche* (*The Girlfriends*, 1955), based on Pavese's novel *Tra donne sole* (*Among Women Only*), seemed to be Antonioni's mandatory next step: Pavese's mythologies were set aside in the screen adaptation and Antonioni focused on the rituals of neurosis and the emotional emptiness prized by the bourgeoisie of Turin. *Il grido* (*The Cry* or *The Outery*, 1957) was a break from his previous work and a sort of prologue to the films he would make in the 1960s. In reviewing this film, critics found it hard to accept a proletariat incapable of establishing a balanced relationship with life. They found the main character overwhelmed with emotion and lacking any type of social integration.

Beginning in the 1950s, Antonioni exposed the principles of his poetics and quietly continued to reaffirm them, avoiding any clashes with critics and neorealist directors. His break from the group happened progressively, and its consequences have never been fully studied.

The 1950s Generation

Neorealism developed and traveled in multiple phases. The first was the lift-off and entry into international orbit. This phase ended quickly because the initial impetus ran out and the movement met with attrition and resistance from opposing forces. Once neorealism entered the atmosphere of the Cold War and the long, triumphant power of the Christian Democracy following the 1948 elections, the neorealist body entered a second phase. It settled and began to expand its territory and then exploded. The fallout of the resulting fragmentation affected the entire surface of international cinema. In terms of narrative and visual approach, the umbilical cords that connect the neorealist fathers and subsequent generations have never been severed.[87] The energy may have waned, but it has continued to touch personalities that differ greatly from one another. This legacy is attributable to a platoon of screenwriters who scoured the Italian landscape and history for singular and significant events, however small. They were authentic recorders of the conditions in even the smallest particles of the social body. Thanks to their humble soldiering (among them, only Zavattini would ever fully enjoy the limelight), they created a new continuity and exchange between reality and cinematographic fiction.

Thanks to screenwriters like Zavattini, Amidei, Flaiano, Ennio de Concini, Suso Cecchi d'Amico, Ruggero Maccari, Age and Furio Scarpelli, Piero de Benardi and Leo Benvenuti, Ettore Scola, Tullio Pinelli, Rodolfo Sonego, and Ettore Margadonna, a new working method was created. It incorporated all aspects of filmmaking and allowed for a continuous overflowing, assimilation, digestion, and circulation of ideas and narrative approaches.

For some camera operators and directors, the light of neorealism was an important although superficial point of reference: for example, Genina's *Cielo sulla palude* (*Heaven over the Marshes*, 1949) or Curzio Malaparte's *Cristo proibito* (*The Forbidden Christ* or *Strange Deception*, 1950). But the neorealist spirit guided the debut of directors like Carlo Lizzani, who, thanks to a new formula of collaborative production, was able to make *Achtung! Banditi!* (*Attention! Bandits!*, 1951). From the outset, Lizzani showed himself to be a director of action films rather than psychological, cerebral films. Courageously, he went against the grain as he attempted to keep the memory of the Resistance and the partisan struggle alive and to curb its rapidly growing mythology and rhetorical transformation. Even when they did not allow him to tell stories dear to his heart, the films that would follow—from *Cronache di poveri amanti* (*Chronicle of Poor Lovers*, 1954) to *Lo svitato* (*He Has a Screw Loose*, 1956) to *Esterina* (*Little Esther*, 1959)—showed off his professional skill, his flexibility, and his ability to champion "little" history and its small but significant events within the context of history with a capital H. His great directorial talent and open-mindedness allowed him to help his actors and the stories and to create a continuity between themes that generally swayed between the headlines and history.

Nonetheless, these were hard times for those who came of age with the journal *Cinema* during its early run: paradoxically, these years were tougher than wartime for filmmakers, even though, thanks to expanded production, no one was silenced by political pressure. But true opportunity and the reality of the situation were far below what had been expected and promised.

Former *Cinema* critics Gianni Puccini and Antonio Pietrangeli, leaders in their field, met a similar fate. Of the two, Puccini doggedly managed to carve out some space as a director. His debut was a costume drama, *Il capitano di Venezia* (*The Captain of Venice*, 1952), and then, at the end of the 1950s, he made a series of comedies: *Parola di ladro* (*Honor Among Thieves*, 1957), which he directed with Nanni Loy; *Il marito* (*The Husband*, 1958); *Carmela è una bambola* (*Carmela Is a Doll*, 1958); and *L'impiegato* (*The Employee*, 1959). To an extent, these films played a part in the transformation of the genre and they documented the first significant changes in Italian society.

Antonio Pietrangeli was among the first critics of his generation to direct. But, beginning with his first film, *Il sole negli occhi* (*Empty Eyes*, 1953), he laid out the themes and stylistic traits that would accompany his career until his untimely death before his fiftieth birthday in 1968. Pietrangeli was a director who explored the world of women with great sensibility and intelligence. He sought to tell the story of its integrity and generosity and the high costs of achieving even partial emancipation from male supervision and power.[88]

Mauro Bolognini also made his debut in the same period. He cooked up no less than nine films, mostly comedies, between 1953, when he made *Ci troviamo in galleria* (*I'll See You On the Balcony*), and 1959, when he made *La notte brava* (*Bad Girls Don't Cry* or *On Any Street*). Based on a novel by Pier Paolo Pasolini, *La notte brava* sent Bolognini down a path that would lead to the greatest expression of his ability to re-create literary texts on the screen. In this film, he borrowed from period paintings to reconstruct and explore the different psychologies and environment of post-unification Italy.[89]

At the age of twenty-five, Francesco Maselli made his debut with *Gli sbandati* (*Abandoned*, 1955). With this film, he sought to adapt the lesson of neorealism to a different way of contemplating personal and collective histories. He used a love story to x-ray the bourgeois attitudes during the final phase of the war and the struggle for liberation. During the 1950s, these themes were considered taboo. But the most striking thing about his film is his stylistic maturity and his knowledge of film above and beyond Italian cinema. At the Venice Film Festival, critics hailed this work as the birth of a great director.

Valerio Zurlini's *Estate violenta* (*Violent Summer*, 1959) was similar in its themes and conclusions albeit different in terms of its point of view and opinions. Zurlini had debuted a few years earlier with a cinematic adaptation of Pratolini's novel *Le ragazze di San Frediano* (*The Girls of San Frediano*, 1954). This Italian adaptation of Claude Autant-Lara's *Le diable au corps* (*Devil in the Flesh*, 1947) focused on the story of a boy's sexual initiation with an older woman. But the setting was the historical events that occurred during the summer of 1943, between July 25 and September 8 (when Italy surrendered to the Allied forces).

The end of the decade marked the debut of Gillo Pontecorvo and Francesco Rosi. Pontecorvo's first feature-length film, *La grande strada azzurra* (*The Wide Blue Road*, 1959), was based on Franco Solinas's novel *Squarciò* (*Squarciò the Fisherman*). Unlike Maselli's debut film, Pontecorvo's first work was not received enthusiastically by critics, who pigeonholed him as a would-be De Santis.

Francesco Rosi, who had already worked as Visconti's assistant director on *La terra trema* (*The Earth Trembles* or *The Earth Will Tremble*), enjoyed a much stronger debut that gave a taste of things to come in his career. His *La sfida* (*The Challenge*, 1958) was based on a true story that took place in present-day Naples. Rosi was able to give the episode a tragic dimension and to utilize the lessons of neorealism together with American film noir. At the same time, he melded the single event with the sociological context while making its presence felt in every moment of the film. With *I Magliari* (*The Magliari*, 1959), he reaffirmed his ability to enrich a neorealist approach, which he had mastered, with a deepened sociological awareness, a civic passion, and his faith in cinema as a weapon—elements that Italian cinema seemed to have lost during the 1950s. Rosi was one of the few Italian directors who worked on the timelines and multiple dimensions of film, making time-space elements the crux of his research. In Rosi's films, the representation of time was never linear, but rather, a relationship of coexistence of multiple timelines. In the Southern Italy of his films, time did not exist: his timelines mixed and blended together the reversibility and irreversibility, circularity and linearity, dynamics of modernity and the static reality of mythology. The forces he examined drew their energy from mythological time and from the circular time of an agrarian culture. He sought to project those forces toward the more advanced frontiers of modern society and to subject them to the rules of that society.

In film after film, Rosi observed and depicted Southern Italy's singular sense of time. In doing so, he measured time in Italian society as a whole by using the South's unique meter and rhythm and projecting it onto the rest of Italy.

Within the firmament of postwar Italian cinematic genres (some brighter than others, some more enduring than others), actor Totò shone like a star endowed with its own light, capable of illuminating an entire genre all by itself. Totò managed to lend his famous face to the success of countless "instant films," in spite of their modest production value. Many critics, he once said, scolded his directors for using him as the same character in every film. "Why should they use a different one every time? I have used this character in *commedia dell'arte* farces, in variety shows, in cabaret acts, in magazines, in comic operas, in dialectal prose and in movies. I am so fond of it. It's my dearest possession."[90]

As Roberto Escobar recounted in the most original and intelligent profile of Totò to be published in recent years, Fellini, an admirer of Totò, once declared that Toto's character "was so grand" and so "wonderful," that no film could contain it. The best the camera could do, he said, was simply to report it. Totò was Totò as Pulcinella was Pulcinella, the classic character of the *commedia dell'arte*.[91]

Totò made over one hundred films following World War II, for the most part with directors who simply operated the camera. But he also worked with directors like Rossellini, De Sica, Blasetti, Zampa, Fabrizi, Steno, Monicelli, Pasolini, and Bolognini. Mattoli made the most films with Totò (sixteen), followed by Mastrocinque, Sergio Corbucci, and Bragaglia.

Totò was the perfect embodiment of Edward Gordon Craig's notion of the Über-marionette. Not only was Totò remarkably agile, possessing the ability to move and articulate his body and face as if independent from one another, but they often seemed to be disconnected from the elementary forms of discursive syntax, struggling to construct a structured relationship between one another. Totò wore a mask that fought to adapt to determined roles: his strength and his genius derived from the unpredictability of his gestures and vocabulary, elements that allowed him to break all the rules, to reveal the absurdity of bureaucratic rigmaroles, laws, and regulations, forms of injustice and dissimulation achieved through the use of superior language skills or a uniform and title. Even though he was guided by an anarchic spirit that compelled him to oppose the abuses of everyday life with every means at his disposal, Totò depicted a gallery of Italian characters without ever abandoning his own. They were poor, always hungry, often scheming, but deep down they were honest victims of a history to which they were forced to pay a heavy personal toll. With film after film, the viewer accompanied Totò on his journey through an Italy that was changing: *Il ratto delle Sabine* (*The Rat of the Sabines*, 1945), *Napoli milionaria* (*Side Street Story*, 1950), *Guardie e ladri* (*Cops and Robbers*, 1951), *Siamo uomini o caporali?* (*Are We Men or Corporals?*, 1955), *Destinazione Piovarolo* (*Destination Piovarolo*, 1955), and many others. But these films were also a journey into a linguistic container that gathered, distorted, and parodied all forms of language.[92] The journey took place among a series of peoples who inhabit the Italian peninsula but have entirely different ways of life and modes of communication. Totò adapted to each linguistic and cultural situation through opportunism and shrewdness by utilizing his exceptional knack for survival.

Genre Films Set Out to Conquer the International Market

Based on the novels by Giovanni Guareschi and directed by Frenchman Julien Duvivier, the highly successful *Don Camillo* series is perhaps the most significant example of a microcosm that participated in the life of much more expansive systems. But it owed its equilibrium to the fact that the forces in conflict within it never showed any centrifugal tendencies. This series of films was produced during the hottest years of the Cold War and its tolerant view maintained a perfect balance between the two opposing forces. To the credit of its producers, *Don Camillo* distilled the complexity of the political-anthropological-social reality in Italy into a Catholic-communist dialectic. It did not depict religion and ideology from a Manichean point of view, but rather, as complementary and necessary faces of the very same reality. And it did so in the shadow of the bell-tower in a tiny little town in Emilia-Romagna. Through cinema, this out-of-the-way place took on the central and exemplary value of an Italy touched by modernity but still capable of retaining its original characters. The *Don Camillo* films represent a sort of micro-genre and a first attempt to extend and portray contrasts and contradictions that animated and shaped the coming together of the old and the new democratic regimes. But they were also a sign of the widespread need to simplify life and to reestablish community and recognized, immovable values.

After the immense success of Riccardo Freda's *Teodora, imperatrice di Bisanzio* (*Theodora, Slave Empress*, 1953) and Pietro Francisci's *La regina di Saba* (*The Queen of Sheba*, 1953), it would take five years for Francisi's *Le fatiche di Ercole* (*Hercules* or *The Labors of Hercules*, story by Ennio de Concini and Francisci) to reopen the way for mythological fantasy-adventure films. This film gave forceful new momentum to commercial production. "The advent of this genre," wrote Vittorio Spinazzola, "marked the definitive disappearance of films devoted to the dramatic pangs of love felt by characters wearing modern garb."[93]

The genre would continue to develop unthreatened by competition, and the box-office results were impressive: such films brought hundreds of millions of viewers to second- and third-run theaters, where they typically paid 100 to 200 lire for admission. With a budget under 300,000,000 lire, *Le fatiche di Ercole* would earn almost 900,000,000 domestically. In the United States alone, it made 130,000 dollars, an astronomical sum at the time. By the end of the decade, filmmakers raced to make mythological films: in 1960, of the fifteen fantasy-adventure films produced, eleven earned more than 400,000,000 lire. A few titles, like Francisi's *Ercole e la regina di Lidia* (*Hercules Unchained* or *Hercules and the Queen of Lydia*), Carlo Campogalliani's *Maciste nella valle dei re* (*Maciste the Mighty* or *Son of Samson*), and Cottafavi's *La vendetta di Ercole* (*Goliath and the Dragon* or *Vengeance of Hercules*), would bring in over 800,000,000 lire at the box office.

The success of these films was also due to the fact that with a few hundred lire as the price of admission, you could reinforce a vision of the world in which the forces of good and evil were clearly divided. Viewers directly identified with heroes who defended the ideal of good governance, justice, and freedom. Most significant, these films provoked the unleashing of impulses and urges hidden in the collective subconscious. As Domenico Paolella wrote, they served as a proven, low-cost "psychoanalysis of the poor."[94]

In a glowing article published in the September 1959 issue of *Cahier du cinéma* ("Prélude à Cottafavi"), Michel Mourlet explicitly accused Italian critics (who were "lost in the haze of neorealism") of critical blindness when it came to the genius of Vittorio Cottafavi, whom, only a few years later, he would call "the only one to triumph in making a historical film, a genre in which Kubrick, Ray, Mann, and, most recently, Minnelli have failed."[95] The Italian critics' answer left no doubt regarding their unwillingness to promote such commercial films to the level of *film d'auteur*: "We have carefully searched *La vendetta di Ercole* for a sculptor, poet, republican, aesthete, technician, the great director of actors ... It was in vain. We watched the whole film carefully. Sadly, we found no trace of a sculptor, poet, nor any technique."[96]

Their failure to appreciate commercial films and their inability to recognize the gems and nuggets of genius in the mishmash of derivative and poorly made films were certainly not the worst sins of Italian critics during those years. Indeed, today Vittorio Spinazzola's series of articles on commercial cinema (gathered in the volume *Cinema e pubblico* [*Cinema and the Public*]) still represents a defining moment: before they began to reveal their limitations insofar as commercial genres, Italian critics would expose their shortsightedness and the inadequacy of their critical approach when they wrote about internationally acclaimed directors Antonioni and

Fellini. No one would ever hail these reviewers as prophets of the new forms of cinema in Italy.

Erudite directors like Cottafavi never hid the importance of entertainment value in their full-immersion approach to mythology. Nor did he conceal his lack of accuracy. In his films, Cottafavi sought to explore female psychology and to examine forms of good governance, the practice of democracy, and the fears of the present day, in particular the threat of atomic war. With *La rivolta dei gladiatori* (*The Warrior and the Slave Girl*, 1958), *Messalina, Venere imperatrice* (*Messalina*, 1959), and *Le legioni di Cleopatra* (*Legions of the Nile*, 1959), Cottafavi paradoxically seemed more interested in the exploration of the female mind rather than the slave's body.

Mythological adventure directors from this period created truly spectacular cinematic gems through their irony and sacrilegious spirit, absolute love of storytelling, exemplary parsimony in respecting their small budgets (consequently reducing the number of costumes), and accurate chromatic studies that helped to make these films works of pictorial art: from Cottafavi's *La vendetta di Ercole* (*Goliath and the Dragon* or *Vengeance of Hercules*)—with its three-headed Cerberus, the centaur, and the giant bat (conceived by Carlo Rambaldi)—to *Ercole alla conquista di Atlantide* (*Hercules Conquers Atlantis; Hercules and the Captive Women; Hercules and the Conquest of Atlantis; or Hercules and the Haunted Women*, 1961, also by Cottafavi), and Gentilomo's *Maciste contro il vampiro* (*Goliath and the Island of Vampires; Goliath and the Vampires; Maciste Vs. the Vampire; or The Vampires*, 1961). They used boiling polenta to create an active volcano, a few buckets of water for a storm, and corny lines like "It was a truly titanic enterprise!" in the final scene of *Arrivano i Titani* (*My Son, the Hero; Sons of Thunder; or The Titans*). This spirit brought these films to life. They were conceived, as Ennio de Concini has noted, mostly for a barrel of laughs.[97]

Internationally, these films were well received by critics and audiences alike, even though in Italy their only affirmation came from their success with the general moviegoer. Among the many historical-mythological films made during this period, there are others worth remembering: Campogalliani's *Il terrore dei barbari* (*Goliath and the Barbarians*, 1959), Sergio Leone's *Il colosso di Rodi* (*The Colossus of Rhodes*, 1959), Jacques Tourneur and Bruno Vailati's *La battaglia di Maratona* (*Giant of Marathon*, 1959), Ferroni's *La guerra di Troia* (*The Trojan Horse; The Trojan War; or The Wooden Horse of Troy*, 1962), Freda's *Maciste all'inferno* (*Maciste in Hell* or *The Witch's Curse*, 1962), and Fernando Cerchio's *Totò e Cleopatra* (*Totò and Cleopatra*, 1963).

In 1961, one of the most fertile years for the genre, thirty-three fantasy-adventure films were made, and in 1964, that number grew to forty. But only two years later, these muscle-bound heroes disappeared entirely from the screen: tunics and swords were replaced by pistols, machineguns, and ponchos worn by the new taciturn heroes of westerns made in Spain or Southern Italy.

Comedy Grows Up

Thanks to a series of successful debuts by comedy directors during the 1950s, the production quality of comedies began to rise progressively and irresistibly over the course of about fifteen years until the genre became one of the industry's guiding forces. At the outset of the 1950s, comedies were improvised using *canovacci* (plot outlines in the manner of the *commedia dell'arte*). But just as eighteenth-century Venetian playwright Carlo Goldoni had adapted the *canovacci* into polished comedic scripts, Italian directors began to craft their screenplays. From Comencini's *Pane, amore e gelosia* (*Bread, Love and Jealousy* or *Frisky*) and *Pane, amore e fantasia* (*Bread, Love and Dreams*) to Risi's *Poveri ma belli* (*A Girl in Bikini*; *Poor But Beautiful*; or *Poor But Handsome*), the storylines for these films became more and more elaborate as they incorporated elements from rapidly changing Italian society. The success of Risi's *Poveri ma belli* in particular seemed to establish the Goldonian treatment as a winning formula.

These films looked to Beaumarchais and Goldoni for their pedigree and inspiration, but their success was due to their ability to be in perfect synchronicity with the changes that were taking place in Italy. The stories embraced the spirit of reconstruction, the emergence of youth culture, and the desire for new models of socialization, as they recognized that youth culture was the springboard for these changes. Shortages and underdevelopment (problems that had been sweetened by the natural gifts of Gina Lollobrigida and Sophia Loren) were not entirely repressed. But consumerist models and attention on the role and interrelations of the individual were the main focuses. Perhaps more than any other film, Monicelli's *La grande guerra* (*The Great War*) marked Italian comedy's move toward a new identity and more sophisticated production. Just a year earlier, *I soliti ignoti* (*Big Deal on Madonna Street*), also by Monicelli, offered moviegoers a heroic-comic film, a parody of chivalrous romance and an Italian take on the "great caper." In the end, the crooks never get their hands on the Holy Grail, nor do they get the loot they are after. All they get is a crummy bowl of pasta and beans, *pasta e faglioli*.

Thanks to the talented team of Roman screenwriters, Amidei, Sonego, Age and Scarpelli, Scola, and Maccari, comedy became one of the primary ways to tell the story of the coexistence of an old and a new Italian identity. At the same time, it also showed the illustrious family tree of Italian comedy, reaching back to Boccaccio, sixteenth-century Italian theater, sixteenth-century playwright Ruzante (Angelo Beolco) and the *commedia dell'arte*, and dialectal theater.

Beginning with *La grande guerra*, actors and comedians were asked to modify their role in film. A more exact mimetic ability was required, but at the same time it had to be more expansive and flexible. Actors needed to be able to draw on a wider range of registers, from physical and verbal comedy to notes of high drama. In any case, the two heroes of *La grande guerra* were the front line of an army descendant from Ruzante. They moved in every direction of history, pushing back and forth between the two wars, searching for a moment of respite and dignity whereby they could attenuate the historical meaning of their defeat. The process of acquiring a moral conscience— the genre's backbone in the years that followed—became one of the greatest manifestations of the ideological growth and the ambitions of the genre.

"I was wrong," says the German sergeant at the end of the film. "I thought they had more pluck."

"War is not their forte," answers the captain. "The only pluck they have is the kind they make with onions in Venice. Before long we'll be eating that, too."[98]

This was a decisive moment—not just in this film but in Italian comedy as a whole. Faced with this insult, the soldiers Busacca and Giacovazzi feel that it is no longer possible to defend their lives at any cost if their lives have lost their meaning. When they reveal their identity (they had disguised themselves as German soldiers), they effectively disassociate themselves from the army of cowards among whom they had hidden. They had embraced the age-old tactic of dressing up like someone else out of opportunism, out of habit, cowardice, and laziness: by virtue of revealing their true identity, they suddenly break from their old ways. These characters are the fruit of the *commedia dell'arte*, and they helped shape the face of the new Italian. They forced Italians to question and react to the transformation of their identity and the new inroads of thought opened by the works of director Luigi Zampa and screenwriter Vitaliano Brancati. With these films, Italians began to reflect on the changes that had accompanied their sudden new sense of well-being. In their giant steps toward unimaginable wealth, Busacca and Giacovazzi had thrown off their rags together with their sense of altruism, their respect for others and for the law, their solidarity, their honesty, and their willingness to sacrifice.

Despite the negative attitude of the most authoritative Italian critics in the daily newspapers and specialized journals, comic directors became aware of the genre's potential during the 1950s. Thanks to Monicelli, Comencini, Risi, Bolognini, Pietrangeli, Puccini, Steno, and others who reaffirmed their personal style in film after film, comedy met the 1960s aggressively and with a mature self-awareness. It no longer had to hide its ambition to play a more essential and strategic role in an industry that was competing with Hollywood.

4

⌣ From the Boom Years to the Years of Terror ⌣·

Years of Growth, Years of Crisis

In 1960, the Italian film industry enjoyed greater profits than ever before: 160 films were produced, of which 66 were co-productions (61 with France); exports exceeded 20 million dollars; box-office receipts grew and the number of filmgoers, which peaked at 800 million viewers, remained stronger in Italy than in any other European country.[1] Suddenly, Italian cinema had reached the peak of its success. There were a number of good reasons to rejoice, including the international success of co-productions like *La dolce vita* (*The Sweet Life*), *La grande guerra* (*The Great War*), and *Il generale della Rovere* (*General Della Rovere*).[2] Of course, the real value of any single element must be judged in the context of the overall picture. But the euphoria of the moment caused many to overlook any negative signs.[3] At the outset of the 1960s, the revival of the film industry seemed to overshadow any losses due to the crisis of the construction industry. Even the creation of the Bureau International du Cinéma made it possible for Italian cinema to play a leading role, with the other national film industries in the background.

The farther they aimed their sights and the greater the challenges they faced, Italian filmmakers delved deeper into a new recessive cycle and structural mutation. During the early 1960s, producers began to realize that in order to meet new challenges, their products had to live up to the technical standards established by their American competitors. As a result, they recognized that they needed to overcome an Italocentric view of the world in order to create films that would be acceptable on an international level.[4] It soon proved to be a winning formula: challenge American cinema on its own turf by reinventing the western—changing its narrative models, its rhythms, its composition, its mythologies, its ethos, and even its geography.

From the 1960s through the mid-1970s, the Italian film industry found success with artistic and commercial films, and it enjoyed an extended boom in markets throughout the world, thanks in part to the westerns produced in Italy during that period. But such success was short-lived and would soon dwindle precipitously.[5] The initial phases of this recession were due to an unfavorable economy and the competition from the music and television industries. The failed passage of legislation that would have redefined the industry also contributed to the decline. In just one year, from 1964 to 1965, the number of films produced in Italy was cut in half: from 214 to 121 titles. On the other hand, year after year, the industry also saw a growing malaise among filmgoers.[6] After ten years, ticket sales were down by more than 200 million. This trend would continue for years.

The industrial take-off caused Italians to move away from farming just as the film industry was laying down roots in the smaller towns. Cinema would not die, of course, but small-town community screenings would all but disappear. Still, Italy managed to keep ticket sales higher than the rest of Europe, where the number of filmgoers was reduced by 80 percent in just a few short years.[7] In light of the situation, co-production again proved the best defense and offense in changing the balance of power.[8]

With the 1965 passage of new film industry legislation, the Italian government increased revenues in box-office profits, creating one of the highest tax rates in all of Europe. At the same time, the percentage of returns to producers decreased, and thanks to delays in disbursements, the producers ceased to function as the industry's immune system. The so-called Corona Law also damaged the industry by favoring the Istituto Luce as the producer of partially and fully government-funded documentaries, short-length films, and feature-length films. The idea was to bring some order and take away some types of production from the de facto monopoly of studios that were protected by some politicians. On paper, the lawmakers' intention was praiseworthy, inasmuch as they were trying to favor directorial debuts and quality films. But the new reality quickly proved ruinous for many small, specialized businesses that were forced to close—save for a few exceptions—without paying back their investors. At the same time, the criteria for government funding set forth in article 28 of the new law did not always promote quality and original subject matter. Yet, thanks to this new regulation, there was a changing of the generational guard and the government became the first true production house in Italy.[9]

During the first decade of article 28, five films a year were subsidized by the government, while the next decade, the number averaged twenty-five. This modest figure was not sufficient to give aspiring filmmakers the boost and confidence they needed, and it was much lower than the number of state-funded films in France.[10] In one of the articles of the new law, number 55, a first attempt was made to regulate the relationship between film and television. This was one of the legislation's two provisions that would help to slow the drop in ticket sales.

At the end of the 1960s, the number of tickets sold just exceeded 500 million. As a result, theaters began to close by the hundreds. The new private channels on television began to reap the fruits of a different type of collective consciousness. Television began to shape the new tastes in cinema of the Italian filmgoer, and it forced a new visual and communicative vocabulary on the public, together with new screen icons. The Italian film industry's star system no longer seemed able to generate the appeal that the new stars of television could. On television there were athletes, singers, politicians, and talk-show personalities.[11]

Another problem was public and private television's vampirism with respect to cinema. The crisis was also fueled by the fact that national production was unable to organize itself and create the alliances and connections that would allow Italian producers to withstand the unbridled attack of American multimedia groups and the process of globalization. During the 1970s, even though people were watching more films thanks to private television broadcasts and the advent of videocassettes, the role of cinema waned in the collective consciousness. Following World War II, cinema opened up and helped create new worlds and horizons. Cinema was in step with the rhythms and the desires of a country reconstructing itself. Now it was forced to fit into the funnel of the television era, and it appeared to be reaching the end of its run.

Beyond the early 1970s, the twenty years that would follow were marked by a dramatic and nearly irreversible process whereby the Italian market lost its clout and began, more and more, to be just another consumer of cinema and television produced in the United States.

By the end of the 1960s, all the creative energy and efforts to invent new forms of cinema and to explore new narrative and stylistic horizons came to an abrupt stop. From the very beginning of the decade, as theaters began to disappear, so did the big studios. The demise of Titanus during the mid-1970s was not due to films like those of Olmi and Pasolini, but rather, to the bad reception of some its co-productions, namely, Aldrich and Leone's colossal *Sodoma e Gomorra* (*Sodom and Gomorra*) and Visconti's *Il gattopardo* (*The Leopard*).[12]

Eitel Monaco's reign as president of ANICA (Associazione Nazionale Industrie Cinematografiche Audiovisive e Multimediali [National Association of the Film, Recording, and Multi-Media Industries]) spanned from 1949 to 1971. During that period, nearly every sector of the industry grew. Although there were a few crises, overall there was uninterrupted growth that included some veritable triumphs. But when the new president, Carmine Cianfarani, began his mandate, he could no longer count on his predecessor's socio-economic and cultural infrastructure, which had remained stable for more than two decades. His presidency, which continued into the mid-1990s, was marked by profound changes and seemingly incessant shakeups that would visibly and dramatically damage the entire film industry.

As the industry of culture underwent deep transformations, cinema lost its status as the greatest of secular rituals and was no longer a necessary luxury.[13] Year after year, tens of millions of viewers began to desert cinema and focus their consumption and free time elsewhere.[14]

The 1960s: Memorable Vintages and Bumper Crops

The films made in the 1960s were memorable for their quantity and quality, their experimentation and innovation, their continuity and renewal of traditional cinema models, and their powerful expansion of Italian cinematography in the world market. The top four box-office titles of 1960 were La dolce vita (The Sweet Life), Rocco e i suoi fratelli (Rocco and His Brothers), La ciociara (Two Women), and Tutti a casa (Everybody Go Home). The public began to embrace cinematic masters who previously had been confined to Cineclub and Cineforum, and it was becoming clear that the quality of demand was beginning to shape and enhance the quality of film offerings.

The year 1960 was an exceptional vintage in which the producers themselves began to believe in the power of good film over bad film. During the years that would follow, Italian cinema seemed to possess an inexhaustible creative energy, capable of giving birth to an entirely new group of talented filmmakers without forgetting its masters or directors of previous generations. Journalists were not able to take stock of what was happening; even the most illustrious critics were in a state of shock after viewing the works of Fellini and Antonioni. They continued to write about cinema's new incompleteness and fragmentation, but they were unable to understand the profound change that had taken place in its narrative and iconographic models. Genre films aided the emergence of artisanal directors, who had already been promoted to the rank of "director with a capital D" by the foreign press. During the 1960s, four generations of directors were working under conditions of expressive and creative freedom, with economic opportunities and an unprecedented connection to their audience. Producers invested more money than ever before and the established masters, as well as their up-and-coming counterparts, defended their art while not forgetting the audience they had won over.

During this period, Cinecittà's artisanal atelier reached its creative pinnacle. A variety of elements, which had worked independently until then, came together, aiding one another in conquering the international audience. For over a decade, the success of Italian cinema was interwoven with syndromes of omnipotence and by a spirit of adventure, embraced by an increasingly literate audience who pushed filmmakers to explore new territory. Producers were even willing to give a camera to theater actors like Carmelo Bene, who made no fewer than five feature-length films in just a few short years;[15] or to painters like Mario Schifano, Alberto Grifi, and Gianfranco Baruchello; or to independent filmmakers like Piero Bargellini and Silvano Agosti, who had studied editing at the Moscow Cinema Institute; or to Gian Vittorio Baldi, who worked not only as a director but also as a producer and instructor of cinema. Movie cameras were handed over to persons who would make only a single film, like Gianni Da Campo, who landed a success in 1966 but then took up teaching instead. They were given to documentary filmmakers like Vittorio de Seta and Ermanno Olmi, and to writers like Pier Paolo Pasolini, Alberto Bevilacqua, and Enzo Siciliano, not to mention young critics like Maurizio Ponzi. There was room for everyone, and toward the end of the decade, thanks in part to Rossellini who led the way, television began to experiment with its first artistic works.

During the years that followed World War II, a new visual vocabulary emerged, redefining even the most elementary forms. The 1960s would prove to be the years of the greatest experimentation, freedom, and expressive riches. Not everything in the cauldron was made of gold, but the average qualitative level was the highest of all time. Every element of filmmaking would undergo profound changes: narrative models and storytelling forms, vocabulary, editing, acting techniques and photographic technology, the exploration of new uses for music and sound, makeup, and the attention to detail in historical reproductions. The results can be found on every level of the system, from the more or less successful debuts of directors like Tinto Brass, Silvano Agosti, Bernardo Bertolucci, Brunello Rondi, Gianfranco de Bosio, and Gian Vittorio Baldi, to genre films in which in many cases new ground was broken in photography, sound, editing, syntax, and temporal rhythms. It was an extraordinary laboratory of filmmaking.

Among the hundreds of first-time filmmakers, many are worth remembering: Olmi and Pasolini, Bertolucci and Ferreri, the Taviani and Petri brothers, Damiani, Scola, Wertmüller, De Seta, Agosti, Orsini, Caprioli, Salce, Bellocchio, Mingozzi, Vancini, Gregoretti, Montaldo, Bene, Baldi, Nelo Risi, Brass,

Leone, Cavani, Brusati, Corbucci, Magni, Enrico Maria Salerno, and many others.[16] In the years that followed, on the cusp of the 1960s and 1970s, scores of others would also debut: Amelio, Greco, Citti, Avati, Ponzi, Del Monte, Argento, Di Carlo, Ferrara, Giannarelli, Giraldi, Bevilacqua, Battiato, Marco Tullio Giordana, Brenta, Bertolucci, and Moretti. It is impossible, given the limited space, to list them all. For a more complete list, see my earlier works, Micciché's essays, and the catalogue edited by Adriano Aprà and Stefania Parigi, who offer a much more detailed and comprehensive picture.[17] Above all, I hope that the new generations of film scholars will study these periods, which seem to interest them less than the era of silent films.

It is important to remember that all elements of the system were working together with unprecedented efficiency: technicians, screenwriters, production designers, costume designers, composers, stars, character actors, and camera operators. As of yet, no one has studied these creative units, how they functioned together, and what a gift they were to Italian and international cinema.

To a greater extent than their forefathers, the newcomers believed in film as a work of art. They sought to make their first films with the greatest artistic freedom and control over the creative process. Filmmakers like Olmi, for example, did not merely conceive the story but also wrote and directed their films, even working as camera operators and editors. Following in the footsteps of Cesare Zavattini and the New Wave directors, filmmakers made movies unhindered by production restraints and without marketing concerns.

Thanks in part to the works produced by the École du regard and the Gruppo '63, a greater number of potential narrative models emerged, and the story no longer had to unravel along traditional lines. Just as stories had been constructed, they were now being "deconstructed." Linear development was now being replaced by exasperated repetition and narrative fragmentation that required the reader-viewer to reconstruct and reinterpret the text. This was a period of crisis for movie characters: like characters in novels, they were increasingly replaced by other narrative elements.[18] Syntax, prosody, rules and modes of classical editing, iconography, and iconology were all being reexamined and freely reassembled in new combinations. The narrative system was subjected to serious shakeups, but it did not collapse—nor was it destroyed. The expression "poetic cinema," as defined by Pasolini, found a new following, while "prose" cinema reached its widest audience ever with lofty subject matter, and experimental cinema found its exegetes and singers of its praises among the critics.

As far as the signifier was concerned, most directors used cinema to interpret the poetic and theoretical advances and new forms of thought and art that had appeared in Europe in recent decades. But this is not to say that they overlooked the signified and its fecundity and vitality in a tradition that embraced the social and political functions of cinema. The new "tide" of Italian directors was the least affected by the Oedipal complex that gripped Europe, and it was less inclined—in theory and practice—to break with the cinema of its forefathers.[19] The very concept of "director" had expanded to include (together with often international acclaim) even those of genre films. The critic's playing cards had been radically reshuffled, and even the most open-ended and complex game was possible. The ideological compass that had long guided the critics in previous years had now been demagnetized and many magazines suddenly found their editorial power diminished. Harsh criticism was undoubtedly still easy to dole out, but prior models for comparison were suddenly no longer viable. Authority and charisma were no longer recognized and were even the subject of derision, as in the case of Fellini's *Otto e 1/2* (*Eight and a Half* or *Federico Fellini's 8*, 1963).

Monumental History and Memory Revisited

Thanks to a new political climate (both national and international), the need to revisit recent history was greater than ever. Italians shared a desire to reflect on the one hundred or so years that had passed since their nation's unification in 1861, on its personalities and stereotypes. Suddenly, Italian filmmakers embraced the history of unified Italy through the eyes of characters who had always been considered victims, not heroes, mere bystanders who were just part of the landscape. For the first time, filmmakers began to deal with taboo subjects and historical figures: fascism; the Resistance; the conditions of factory workers; the role that fascists played in acts of retaliation and massacres during the final two years of World War II; and the Italian Socialist Republic or Republic of Salò (named after the city on Lake Garda where it was founded), a last-ditch puppet fascist government installed by the Nazis after the Italians officially surrendered to Allied forces.[20] The heritage of neorealism was vital to this process, but there was also a pressing need to be in step with the present and to open the cinematic tradition to new cultural phenomena and trends. The earliest films of this period helped renew the entire directorial landscape without cutting the umbilical cord of the postwar heritage and without silencing the directors of prior generations. With the advent of the Center-Left movement, the weakening of the anticommunist *cordon sanitaire*, and the fall of many taboos, the Catholic and communist presses began to undergo a process of secularization. Beginning in 1960, German machine-gunners rattled away in literally tens of films that were to reopen repressed pages of recent history. The attention was focused on the fascists at their sides, and there was no cover-up of the responsibility and active role that Italians had played in the civil war following Italy's "liberation" by the Allies. Even though it was too early to use the term *civil war* to describe what was happening Italy and the Republic of Salò from 1943 to 1945 (Claudio Pavone's book *Una guerra civile* [*A Civil War*] was published in 1991), Italian cinema began to depict and stick its fingers into this wound. Deep lacerations were reopened and painful pages of history were reread with an articulate but conflicted intent to reflect on those events. A great number of films made during the 1960s and early 1970s used the symbolic date of September 8, 1943 (when Italy's unconditional surrender to the Allies was announced), as their backdrop in a quest to retell the difficult choices faced by the "boys of Salò." The film's acceptance of the complexity of this historic moment represented the first respectful investigation into the reasons for the defeat and the motivations of those who chose to continue the war alongside the Nazis. *Tiro al piccione* (*Pigeon Shoot*, 1961), based on the novel by Giose Rimanelli, was the most anti-conformist film in this sense, and Giuliano Montaldo was the first director who tried to tell the story of a young man who had pledged his allegiance to Salò. With his *Sacco e Vanzetti* (*Sacco and Vanzetti*, 1971), Montaldo would reach the highest point in his career, combining civil passion, ideological and emotional commitment, and superb cinematic ability. But even *Il terrorista* (*The Terrorist*, 1963) by De Bosio is still amazing to watch today, thanks to the attention to detail, the balance, and the realistic historical approach to the various political forces in Venice during the months of Salò.[21]

Many directors were attracted by political, historical, and civil subject matter: from Florestano Vancini's *La lunga notte del '43* (*The Long Night of '43*, 1960) to Lizzani's *Il gobbo* (*The Hunchback of Rome*, 1960) to Pontecorvo's *Kapò* (the story of a Nazi prison Kapo, a prisoner in charge of a work gang, released in 1960) and his *La battaglia di Algeri* (*The Battle of Algiers*, 1966). Directors like Comencini, Monicelli, Risi, and Salce tried to probe the memory of a past that refused to pass through the lens of drama and even comedy— that is, they used cinema as Freudian transfer of revolutionary expectations that had been betrayed or otherwise unfulfilled. Gianni Puccini and Nanni Loy abandoned comedy to direct films like Puccini's *Il carro armato dell'8 settembre* (*The Tank Crew of September 8, 1943*, released in 1960) and Loy's *Un giorno da leoni* (*A Day for the Courageous*, 1961) and *Le quattro giornate di Napoli* (*The Four Days of Naples*, 1960), in which they used a multiplicity of voices to retell the struggle for freedom in a national-populist vein.

The repressed memory of the struggle for freedom and the war would greatly influence the years that followed 1960. Even Totò, the great Neapolitan actor and comedian, would be drafted for these films: Corbucci's *I due marescialli* (*The Two Marshalls*, 1961) and Steno's *I due colonnelli* (*The Two Colonels*, 1962). War movies from this period are particularly interesting because they attempted to reread (then) recent history as epic; at the same time, directors were trying to keep pace with historiographic debate and the new sensibility of the times.[22]

As far as its take on the present was concerned, Italian cinema begrudgingly decided to join modernity. The ranks of the so-called apocalyptic intellectuals among Italian directors swelled, to borrow Umberto Eco's phrase, while the integrated, that is, believers in the positive aspects of the mass media, were few. In any case, screenwriters from nearly all film genres were mobilized. Italy in its moment of change became the favorite source for material, but it also became a source of fear and negative transformation as well. In Italian film, the advent of modernity was often considered to be a moment of crisis, and at very least, it was always viewed from the bottom up. On the other hand, the farmer's world was always seen in terms of its progressive alienation from the country's path toward industrialization and the factory, themes that were taboo until the 1960s, when directors began to examine them.[23] In *Rocco e i suoi fratelli* (*Rocco and His Brothers*), the world of the factory workers is the backdrop for a tragic tale. The director, Olmi, shows this world from within, drawing from his own experience and from the novels of the same era by Paolo Volponi and Ottiero Ottieri. The viewer is thus witness to the anthropological mutation that took place together with the industrialization of Northern Italy and the traumatic changes that the farmers had to endure as they became part of the industrialized world. Suddenly, there were literally tens of films—from Lizzani's *Esterina* (*Little Esther*, 1959) to Olmi's *Il tempo si è fermato* (*Time Stood Still*, 1960) to Gregoretti's *Omicron* (1963) to Monicelli's *I compagni* (*The Organizer*, 1963)—in which proletarians and workers were featured characters and "social" roles became more and more significant. The viewer passed through the gates of the factories, and the factories themselves absorbed the cityscape and refashioned it in their own image.[24] It was not much, but it was already something.

For a cinematic tradition that has always favored Rome as its backdrop when recounting the adventures of the Italian middle class, the world of factory workers in Northern Italy was relatively unknown. Its discovery was met with anthropological curiosity. In some instances, Italian directors sought to depict the emotions of their subjects, while in others, attention was placed upon their ideological conscience and their difficulties in adapting to a new environment. By the 1970s, films like Petri's *La classe operaia va in Paradiso* (*The Working Class Goes to Heaven*, 1971), Wertmüller's *Mimí metallurgico ferito nell'onore* (*The Seduction of Mimi*, 1972), Scola's *Trevico-Torino* (*From Trevico to Turin*, 1973), Comencini's *Delitto d'amore* (*Somewhere Beyond Love*, 1974), and Monicelli's *Romanzo popolare* (*Come Home and Meet My Wife*, 1974) gave us direct access to the world of the workers, who seemed increasingly atypical and ever more psychologically disturbed. These characters were forced to budget their emotions before they calculated their salaries, and they were no longer controlled by organized labor. These comedies were not just a reflection of the present—they also presented both the superficial and deepest changes the characters were facing. This now historic window on the world of the workers has yet to be fully analyzed.

By the same token, the worker depicted on the screen during the early 1970s did not reflect Italy's economic development.[25] Instead of glorifying their struggles, Italian cinema sought to depict the characters' dissociation, the deterioration of their once strong ideological fabric, their discovery of their private emotions, their rage, and the various types of organized and disorganized protest. During the so-called *Anni di piombo* (literally, the "years of lead," or rather the "gun-slinging years"), when Italy found itself in the grips of international and domestic terrorism, the working conditions of Italian factories were restructured and an entire social species of Italian workers seemingly disappeared. Italian cinema defended and documented the stories of these persons, who had always lived on the margins of the frame.

The early 1960s were also the years when the concept of the Italian state began to disintegrate on imaginary as well as very real levels. The Italian state was all but absent from the lives of its citizens during the period immediately following World War II: any representation of its institutions would have been too risky then. By the beginning of the 1960s, it had been transformed into a power that was dominated by dark forces that plotted against the citizens themselves: Petri's *Indagine su un cittadino al di sopra di ogni sospetto* (*Investigation of a Citizen Above Suspicion*, 1970) and *Todo modo* (*One Way or Another*, 1975); Damiano Damiani's *Il giorno della civetta* (*The Day of the Owl*, 1968), *Confessione di un commissario di polizia al procuratore della repubblica* (*Confessions of a Police Commissioner to the District Attorney*, 1971), and *Perché si uccide un magistrato?* (*Why Does One Kill a Magistrate?*, 1975); and Rosi's *Cadaveri eccellenti* (*Illustrious Corpses*, 1976) and *Tre fratelli* (*Three Brothers*, 1981).

During a roughly fifteen-year period, there were so many films that dealt with the theme of polis, that is, good and bad governance, that the critics began to call them genre films and made them the target of often violent attacks.[26] These were years when the nation's critical and ideological sense of direction began to fail, and at the same time, critics and filmmakers were racing to outdo one another while artistic "political films" were in the sights of everyone's guns. The films made by Rosi, Petri, Orsini, Vancini, Pontecorvo, Damiani, the Taviani Brothers, Bellocchio, Montaldo, Maselli, and others represent a fundamentally important source for understanding this period in Italian history, from the deaths of Pope John XXIII and Palmiro Togliatti to the murder of Aldo Moro.

These were years when all certainty seemed to disintegrate and when the political parties became less involved in citizens' lives. There were revolutionary pulsations and Oedipal rebellions. Some of the films made during this period winced at the sight of antigovernment movements while openly showing sympathy for the Third World and the struggles of other peoples. Nonetheless, they were able to raise doubts and to ask difficult questions. They pondered the necessity to decipher a fleeting present and to reveal the uncertainties behind every choice. They recognized the people's diminishing faith in organized politics. Italian cinema once again felt like it was an integral part of a progressive political movement, but then suddenly it found itself in the middle of no-man's-land, where it was no longer clear where the attacks were coming from and who its enemies or allies were. As a result, political films were forced to disguise themselves as genre films or to reveal their solidarity—more or less explicitly—for violent forms of political upheaval.

There was a popular slogan among some of those belonging to the left, who no longer recognized Italy's historically sanctioned political parties: "neither with the state, nor with the Red Brigades." Many political filmmakers took an antigovernment stance without endorsing the cause of terrorists. They did so by producing characters that represented the state as concentrated evil. The importance of their films was increased by the fact that the films produced in Italy between 1966 and 1976 captured a moment of wide-reaching change in ideological models, infrastructure, the people's sense of ideological belonging, and leftist directors' ability to interpret history. This is clear in films like Pontecorvo's *La battaglia di Algeri* (*The Battle of Algiers*, 1966) and *Queimada* (*The Mercenary* or *Burn!*, 1969); Bellochio's *La Cina è vicina* (*China Is Near*, 1967); the Taviani Brothers' *San Michele aveva un gallo* (*Saint Michael Had a Rooster*, 1971) and *Allonsanfàn* (1974); Montaldo's *Sacco e Vanzetti* (*Sacco and Vanzetti*, 1973) and *Giordano Bruno* (1973); Amelio's *La città del sole* (*The City of the Sun*, 1973); Maselli's *Lettera aperta a un giornale della sera* (*Open Letter to an Evening Newspaper*, 1970); Orsini's *I dannati della terra* (*The Damned of the Earth*, 1968); Ansano Giannarelli's *Sierra Maestra* (1969); Petri's *Todo modo* (*One Way or Another*, 1975); Rosi's *Cadaveri eccellenti* (*Illustrious Corpses*, 1976); and literally dozens of other films set in the past or present.

The spirit of 1968 rubbed off on directors and screenwriters who shared similar experiences and who were trying to stay in touch with the spirit of the times. They did so in a wide variety of ways, even using period movies to deliver their message.[27] When we look carefully at the shared spirit of dozens of films during this decade (the same spirit present in genre films), we see how cinema was harnessed to light the revolutionary flame and to become a model for ideals and ideologies. But it was also the object of a Freudian transfer of impulses that could not be acted upon in society.

Even in westerns like *Quien Sabe?* (*A Bullet for the General*), *Requiescant* (*Kill and Pray* or *Kill and Say Your Prayers*), and *Se sei vivo spara* (*Django, Kill . . . If You Live, Shoot!*), it is not hard to detect revolutionary leanings that even conjoin the cause of the Indians and Catholicism. During the first wave of protests, directors and screenwriters focused on establishing ties between the institutions, the student rebellion, and the revolutionary aspirations that preceded them (as in *Indagine su un cittadino al di sopra di ogni sospetto* [*Investigation of a Citizen Above Suspicion*]). The films from this period are replete with verbal Freudian transfer (including Samperi's *Cuore di mamma* [*Mother's Heart*], 1969, and Mingozzi's *La vita in gioco* [*Life at Stake*], 1972), but symbols and symbolic colors were the primary indicators of the revolutionary pulse. As in scenes from Togliatti's funeral in the finale of Pasolini's *Uccellacci e uccellini* (*Hawks and Sparrows*, 1966), red flags—as an ideological, iconological, and idealized leitmotiv—can be seen in a group of films that dealt with historical subjects spanning the entire arc of unified Italy (that is, from 1861 on). Garibaldi's followers wave red flags during the battle scenes in *Il gattopardo* (*The Leopard*) and red flags ring loudly—as if by synesthesia—even in Rosi's black-and-white film *Salvatore Giuliano*, and in particular during the Portella della Ginestra scene (where a group of Sicilian workers is fired upon in a right-wing response to the communist coalition victory in island elections in 1947). There are red flags in films like *Chi lavora è perduto* (*Who Works Is Lost* [that is, "Those Who Work Are Lost"]); *La Cina è vicina* (*China Is Near*); *Amore e rabbia* (*Love and Anger*, 1969); *Lettera aperta a un giornale della sera* (*Open Letter to an Evening Newspaper*); *Allonsanfàn*; *Romanzo popolare* (*Come Home and Meet My Wife*); *Libera, amore mio!* (*Libera, My Love!*); and in the second part of Bertolucci's *Novecento* (*1900*, 1976), in which the Resistance celebrates its deification with the largest red flag ever to appear on screen. At a certain point, the red flags used in protest marches no longer allowed the spectator to discern the protestors' political affiliation. In many cases, there were fewer and fewer workers and farmers waving those flags. Looking back, it appears that the revolutionary dream had taken on literary qualities in cinematographic imagery during the second half of the 1970s. It was much closer to Pasolini's "a dream of something" than it was to Marxist-Leninist texts. Farsightedness made it difficult to see what was about to happen and to unravel and understand its ideological dynamic. This phenomenon afflicted Pontecorvo's films until *Ogro* (*Operation Ogre*, 1978), in which he tried to use examples from other historical moments or places to develop his view of the present.

Rosi was certainly the best director in terms of interpreting the economic, political, and institutional history of postwar Italy. With a reformist's point of view and without ever chasing after the revolutionary movements, his films show how Southern Italy has set the pace for the rest of the country by subjecting it and forcing it to meet the South's needs.[28] Francesco Rosi created his own way of understanding reality through the medium of film. He did so using an unrelenting, direct visual writing style inspired by Visconti and American cinema on one hand, and on the other hand, by models of journalistic and juridical investigation.

In *Salvatore Giuliano* (1960), Rosi employed a *narratage* technique clearly based on Welles's *Citizen Kane*. It showed how political power and the Mafia worked hand in hand, their leading figures often being the same. Sicily and Southern Italy had become a laboratory where contemporary politics had begun to resemble ancient rituals, myths, and societal models. Rosi's films are destined to be cited as historical sources no less important than reports prepared by Italy's anti-Mafia commissions. In the future, they will be useful in understanding the ascent of the Mafia's power and its national and international collusions.[29] His socially and politically themed films will continue to speak and to maintain their spark thanks to his visual writing style, his sense of rhythm, his ability to gauge actors' talent, and his perfect blend of ethics, civil passion, and mastery of cinematography.

The Comic Epic of the Boom Years

During the economic boom of the 1960s, as Italian society began to change, Italian comedy became the depository of the country's fears and hopes. There is no path in Italian cinema that has not passed through comedy along the way. Studies of Italian comedy reveal how the Italian comedy macrosystem has touched every facet of film production: finance, language, narrative models, and even the Italian star system. From approximately 1960 to 1975, Italian comedy became a creative workshop where regularly disparaged narrative forms were revitalized: it represented a crossroads of creativity and inventive production during this period. With time, Italian comedy also became the genre destined to grow more than any other. In doing so, it revealed unforeseen depth and richness of meaning. It fueled the Italian star system, whose light had begun to dim on the screen. This genre would ultimately be used by scholars who preferred it to the so-called political films that had become outdated with younger generations. Its characters move and act without being mere voices of the screenwriters. Comedy films were unique, and they lent themselves to varying interpretations. In political films, on the other hand, meaning was guided by the writers and could only be digested when the viewer could understand the film's references and underwrite its more evident messages.

La grande guerra (*The Great War*, 1959) was the first comedy to enjoy lavish production.[30] Its expressive and linguistic sophistication became a standard for the entire system of production in Italian cinema. This was a sort of promotion for a genre that had been confined to the lower rungs of production. Comedy thus became a "super-genre," attracting important investments and experimenting with new narrative models. As a broad new field of linguistic possibilities was explored, the heavens opened for the first time for a male-dominated group of stars. With the advent of Italian comedy, screenwriters like Age, Scarpelli, Sonego, Scola, Maccari, Benvenuti, De Bernardi, and Zapponi began to reinterpret the figure of the common man using Zavattini's technique of "shadowing" the character. In a sense, they stretched the viewer's gaze from the present back to the near past and even to the nineteenth century. They used ill-shaped lenses to shed light on certain never-before mentioned traits of the Italian. They accentuated his old and new vices, from his political pragmatism to his personal victimism, from his everyman-for-himself attitude to his lack of civic and national duty and lack of respect for the law. But then at just the right moment, these writers would reveal his few surviving virtues, endearing this familiar monster to the viewer. The new leading character of Italian comedy was no longer the humiliated and easily intimidated office worker who found himself entrapped in the vortex of a story much bigger than him. He was now a small man beginning to climb the social ladder with all means available to him. He was ready to sell his soul, if only to better his social and economic status.[31]

The comedic heroes of the 1970s wore new masks, and even when they donned the old ones, their ethical character seemed to incorporate the public good when they were faced with difficult choices.[32] Italian comedy not only documented the deep, negative transformation of Italians and the loss of their value system. In the more ambitious films, the leading characters rediscovered an ethical sense that they seemed to have lost.

Misery and rags were long gone: the common-folk characters of an Italy about to enjoy an economic boom had new backdrops. They had greater ability and were better-spoken: they spoke proper Italian instead of dialect and they were quick to adapt to their new economic condition. They drifted into contact with other persons, often arriving at a progressive indifference to others' misfortunes. Their blindness with respect to their cultural reality is embodied in lines of dialogue:

> "Is that really a national monument? What's taking you so long to tear that ugly thing down and build a nice little building like the other ones around here? Tear down the ancient ruins and build a modern-looking building." (from *La bella di Lodi* [*The Beautiful Girl from Lodi*, 1963], directed by Mario Missiroli and written by Alberto Arbasino)

> "I'd give the Sistine Chapel for an electric stove!" (from Mario Camerini's *Via Margutta* [*Run with the Devil*, 1960])

Comedy had become the quickest—and least sophisticated—vehicle for telling the stories of Italians' newfound economic freedom that would have been unimaginable a few years prior. Italians' new mobility and their contact with other regions caused their dialects to mix. Roman dialect was no longer the "guiding" dialect of film dialogue. A new "formal" Italian emerged: an offspring of television, popular music, magazines, and cinema (Pasolini called this new language "neo-Italian" in 1965).[33] The hegemony of 1950s Roman dialect reached its peak in films like *I soliti ignoti* (*Big Deal on Madonna Street*). But by mid-1960, Northern dialects were used more frequently in films. The new breed of Italian businessmen, who had built their fortunes from the ground up, spoke a "regional" Italian. Thanks to these new entrepreneurs, the geography of Italian film moved northward for the first time in its history. They were a perfect counterpoint to the worker, even though their characters were rarely developed beyond rough sketches. Comedy (and other genres) had no intention of cutting the umbilical cord with Southern Italy. Filmmakers sought to show its primitive, archaic, violent, backward, and underdeveloped nature. Between 1960 and 1963, depictions of Southern Italy clearly began to change not only in films like Germi's *Divorzio all'italiana* (*Divorce Italian Style*, 1961) and *Sedotta e abbandonata* (*Seduced and Abandoned*, 1963) and Lattuada's *Il Mafioso* (*Mafioso*, 1962), but also in films like Rosi's *Salvatore Giuliano* and *Le mani sulla città* (*Hands Over the City*, 1963). Even laughter took on a tragic twist and directors began to forcefully make a distinction between Sicilian history and Italian history.

The comic genre grew thanks to intelligent screenwriting, the extraordinary talents of the actors, and producers who began to invest more and more money in comedies.

From 1960 to 1975, comedy earned the right to be considered highbrow, with films by directors like Comencini, Monicelli, Risi, Scola, Wertmüller, Loy, Salce, Pasquale Festa Campanile, Luigi Magni, Pietrangeli, Zampa, and Germi, who had managed to carve out a common space for themselves where they could exercise complete creative freedom in coming up with storylines. During this period, the lessons of the master filmmakers began to bear fruit in a workshop atmosphere among directors. They found true joy in working together, their friendships, and their shared creative participation. I believe that the climate on the set of the comedic film was indicative of the optimism and solidarity that this family-workshop of filmmakers shared.

These were years of euphoric production when all aspects of the industry seemed to be functioning optimally. Treatments and screenplays for comic films were prepared by writers like Age and Scarpelli, Maccari, Benvenuti and De Bernardi, Scola, Sonego, Zapponi, and Zavattini, among others, and then—in the mid-1970s—by Vincenzo Cerami, who returned to Italy after an apprenticeship in America. The comic genre slowly expanded and even cast its gaze toward the past with films about important events in Italian history. There were films about the workers' struggle of the late nineteenth century; films about World War I or the two decades of fascism; and there were movies that took a closer look at contemporary anthropological, cultural, and social changes in Italy. These movies allowed Italians to relive their past and to reflect on their gains and losses in near real time. Viewers laughed at characters in costumes or uniforms and they were amused by the originality of the performances. But the true force behind the comic mechanism lay in the fact that these films called on their audience to recognize the present in their own past and to measure everything against a standard of "overall quality." A new morality permeated film production on every level. Characters (like Silvio Magnozzi in Risi's *Una vita difficile* [*A Difficult Life*], 1961) had to give up the old ways and stereotypes that had grown out of laziness, cowardice, and opportunism, and then had to make life-changing decisions—for the most part, they made the right ones, even if only at the last minute.

A secular spirit and even anti-clerical and anti-papal themes (for example, in Luigi Magni's films) can be found in many movies from this era. Some would attribute this to the fact that Romans, whose city still represents the center of the Italian film industry, had been subjected to the ill effects of religious influence in politics for centuries.

Ever careful not to glorify the economic boom of the 1960s, directors and screenwriters observed the transformation of the country and its people through the lens of a microscope. Suddenly, it became clear that the classic image of the poor Italian and the idyllic countryside had been contaminated; the "good-hearted" Italian species had been transformed into self-serving social climbers—monsters controlled by the triumphant civilization of consumerism. Risi's film *I mostri* (*15 from Rome* or *Opiate '67*, 1963) was the first of a long series of films to combine an extraordinary gallery of portraits of Italians during a process of rapid transformation. Episodic films would decisively crystallize this genre and this format would ultimately become a highly successful one for Italian directors, some of whom used it to produce small masterpieces.

In *films d'auteur* and genre films alike, there was a generally negative attitude regarding the boom and its fallout: the new divisions between the haves and the have-nots, the damage created by economic growth, the unrecognizable countryside, the breakdown in communication, and the development of cannibalistic competitiveness. In Franco Brusati's greatest film, *Pane e cioccolata* (*Bread and Chocolate*, 1973), the scope extends beyond Italy's border, using comedy as a vehicle for indignation. The film exposed the daily racism in civilized Switzerland experienced by Italian emigrants. Here the victim is at once jolly and tragic: not only is his citizenship revoked, but he also loses his right to belong to society—and even his right to simply be human.

When exposed to new stimuli, Italians developed a desire to change everything, together with a new aggressiveness in whatever situation they found themselves. This can been seen in films like Risi's *Il sorpasso* (*The Easy Life*, 1962), De Sica's *Il boom* (*The Boom*, 1963), and Risi's *Il gaucho* (*The Gaucho*, 1964) and *Il tigre* (*The Tiger and the Pussycat*, 1967). In these movies, social interaction was reduced to tribalism and the struggle for survival. Everything had changed too quickly to foresee the negative consequences. During the early years of Italy's economic "miracle" of the 1960s, money became an obsessive leitmotiv on the horizons of rich and poor—proletarians, members of the middle class, and industrialists alike—as evidenced in Brusati's *Il disordine* (*Disorder*, 1963), Salce's *La cuccagna* (*A Girl . . . and a Million*, 1962), Fulci's *Colpo gobbo all'italiana* (*Getting Away with It the Italian Way*, 1962), and Petri's *Il maestro di Vigevano* (*The Teacher from Vigevano*, 1963). Riches could be easily obtained during those years and people often did so with no regard for the law. This was one of the primary causes of the rapid change in values and in moral and social models, as depicted in movies like Rossellini's *Anima nera* (*Dark Soul*, 1962) and Risi, Comencini, Bolognini, and Franco Rossi's *Le bambole* (*The Dolls*, 1965). During this phase of accelerated transformation, women paid the highest price in films like Zurlini's *La ragazza con la valigia*

(*Girl with a Suitcase*, 1962), Pietrangeli's *La parmigiana* (*The Girl from Parma*, 1963) and *Io la conoscevo bene* (*I Knew Her Well*, 1965), and Monicelli's *La ragazza con la pistola* (*Girl with a Pistol*, 1968)—even though many female leads found the strength to stand up for themselves.

The memories of Italians' hunger, ignorance, underdevelopment, social backwardness, and back-breaking work in the field had been left behind and erased. People wanted to get rich at any cost ("She would sell an eye . . . It's not as if I *told* her to sell an eye, for God's sake! She's free. It's not as if we were living in the time of slavery" [*Il boom*]). The newly rich showed off their wealth with lavish parties, banquets, and receptions ("Until the other day she was just a nobody, and now she can't go to the bathroom without her mink coat" [Pietrangeli's *Il magnifico cornuto* (*The Magnificent Cuckold*), 1964]). People who had risen from rags to the greatest of economic and political riches became the featured characters in films made during this period.

Consumption had become more important than anything else. In the 1960s, Italian cinema told stories of illusory opulence built on quicksand. Working-class as well as upper- and lower-middle-class Italians sought increasingly to camouflage their poor beginnings as they humbly joined the world of consumption. They began to travel for the first time and to experience mentalities other than their own, new forms of social organization, and different sexual mores. The Italians of this era were ill informed but curious, and they had a good dose of tolerance with respect to others. Sonego was perhaps the screenwriter most sensitive to this type of problem.[34] But the story of the new Italian epic was told first and foremost by directors like Gian Luigi Polidoro, who made *Le svedesi* (*Swedish Women*, 1969), *Il diavolo* (*The Devil* or *To Bed or not to Bed*, 1962), *Una moglie americana* (*The American Wife* or *Run for Your Wife*, 1964), and *Una moglie giapponese?* (*A Japanese Wife?*, 1968). This was true as well in the case of actor and—above all—director Alberto Sordi who made *Fumo di Londra* (*Smoke over London*, 1966), *Un italiano in America* (*An Italian in America*, 1967), *Finché c'è guerra c'è speranza* (*While There's War There's Hope*, 1974), and *Un tassinaro a New York* (*A Taxi Driver in New York*, 1987). In these and other films, the no-longer-poor Italian sought his fortunes in North America and other continents, his cardboard suitcase tied with string under his arm. His new station did not stop him from realizing that the rapidity of change had been excessive and the road behind him had been littered with emotional ruin. For him, economic well-being was obtained in exchange for an emotional desert and the abandonment of more than one of his ideals and values.

Another important theme developed by comedy was the rapidity of changes in sexual mores, the crisis of sexual identity, and the new openness with regard to ever-expanding horizons of decency. Last but not least, the environment also became a theme dealt with in films during this period: the unbridled construction was reshaping the Adriatic, Amalfian, and Sardinian coastlines, and the Italian landscape in general was being desecrated by growing trash heaps and development.

Then, all of a sudden, something broke. Films no longer wanted to or knew how to make people laugh. Films became unsettling and made people uneasy with their images of human and environmental abandon and degradation. They showed faces ever more sad and gloomy in gems like Lattuada's *Venga a prendere il caffè . . . da noi* (*Come Have Coffee with Us*, 1970), Comencini's *Lo scopone scientifico* (*The Scientific Cardplayer* or *The Scopone Game*, 1972), and Monicelli's *Un borghese piccolo piccolo* (*A Very Little Man*, 1970), based on Cerami's novel of the same title. These characters were unable to keep up with a society whose rules were changing and whose ideological and moral standards were being turned inside out.

There is no doubt that 1970s comic films began to lose their luster and knack for lashing and taunting a society that had nonetheless maintained a strong value system. Even though Italian filmmakers seemed to take less pleasure in telling their stories, it is also true that 1970s comedies represent perhaps the most stirring snapshots of these sad, aging monsters (for example, in Monicelli's *Amici miei* [*My Friends*], 1975): the ungluing of Italy's social fabric; the recession that followed the boom and its effect on the weakest and most disenfranchised classes; the collapse of traditional family relationships; the advent of new forms of a secular religion and—above all—a new sexual religion; the total loss of trust in the government and politics; the return to subhuman living conditions for entire social groups; depression; a material and emotional deficit throughout Italian society; a breakdown in social communication; and a flood of insecurity and fear. Many comedies from this period seem to have been contaminated by horror films. However much Italian directors pined for the euphoria of the previous decade, the comedies made during the 1960s—and even through 1975—provide us with an overview that could have been used in an annual report of sociological statistics documenting the transformation of Italian society.

Even though newspaper and magazine critics were slow to recognize the artistic achievement of Italian comedies, they began to give them higher marks. No more failing grades and a slight attenuation of the negative evaluations, with a few reservations, of course. In many cases, the Italian critics forced the directors to retake their exams, but Italian comedies started to receive some attention abroad, thanks to a few positive articles published in French magazines. Of all the film genres of the 1960s, Italian comedy marked an important success for the industry on domestic screens but struggled to make it outside of Italy's national borders.

The Monsters: Fathers and Sons

Of all the fathers of Italian comedic films, Monicelli was the first to up the ante for the rest of the crowd. His dramatic and visual ambition had never been seen before in Italian comedies, and he was not afraid to tackle tough historical and epic themes. In the early 1960s, Monicelli started his own production company in order to have complete freedom in making his films and to maintain their artisanal production values—a defining feature of the genre.[35] His film *La grande guerra* (*The Great War*) marked his initial attempt to make a historical film. He followed up with *I compagni* (*The Organizer*, 1963), a film about the nineteenth-century workers' protests in Turin. His emotional and ideological approach to this work seemed greater than in his previous effort. The film is an accurate and pulsing portrayal of the early socialist movement in Italy and a realistic depiction of its first struggles. In *L'armata Brancaleone* (*For Love and Gold*, 1966), he unleashed his skill for storytelling and his joy in giving life to a comic-book story that spoke of the present-day and of Italians' road to riches—an economic miracle within reach of everyone. Borrowing models from the epic poems of the Renaissance and mixing them with elements from popular cartoons, puppetry, and Don Quixote, Monicelli followed the escapades of Brancaleone of Norcia, a knight who, with his ragged army, set out to reconquer the Holy Land. Four years later, he would make *Brancaleone alle crociate* (*Brancaleone at the Crusades*, 1970). This film was not as good in terms of the narrative itself, but much more historically accurate in its imagery, sets, and costumes (by Mario Garbuglia and Ugo Pericoli). Monicelli proved to be the most talented of the Italian comic filmmakers. He was especially gifted at making anthropological observations of that species of Italians known as "born losers," who, despite all odds, have the strength to move on with their lives. During the tumultuous year of 1968, he was back in the limelight with *La ragazza con la pistola* (*Girl with a Pistol*), in which he tried to tell the story of a Sicilian girl in England who must abandon the medieval customs of her homeland as she becomes accustomed to the liberties of the Anglo-Saxon lifestyle. Although he was not entirely immune to the crisis of the Italian comedy during these years, he was the most prolific of the comic directors in renewing and ennobling the genre. From 1975 to the present, he has made nearly twenty-five films. He has always seen the world in dark tones while exploring a wide range of subjects. Among these titles, some of the best have been *Il frigorifero* (*The Refrigerator*), his segment in *Le coppie* (*The Couples*, 1970); *Vogliamo i colonnelli* (*We Want the Colonels*, 1974); *Amici miei* (*My Friends*, 1975); *Viaggio con Anita* (*Lovers and Liars* or *A Trip with*

Anita, 1978); *Temporale Rosy* (*Hurricane Rosy*, 1979); and *Speriamo che sia femmina* (*Let's Hope It's a Girl*, 1986). Perhaps the best film was his *Un borghese piccolo piccolo* (*A Very Little Man*, 1976), his comedic manifesto and homage to the end of an era and to all of its filmmakers. In this film, he seemed to capture the ineffable character of Italians during this period and their irreversible loss of all positive traits.

Like Monicelli, Luigi Comencini also told the story of antiheroes and their moral struggle in his film *Tutti a casa* (*Everybody Go Home*, 1960), in which a group of Italian soldiers return home after the Italian armistice with the Allies on September 8, 1943. Alberto Sordi's unforgettable performance as second lieutenant Innocenzi gave us a classic portrait of the Italian left helpless following General Badoglio's signing of the armistice. As he finds his way home, Innocenzi also discovers the moral strength to choose sides. Among the fathers of Italian comic films, Comencini seemed to care the least about territorial borders and limitations. It is no coincidence that in his subsequent films—*A cavallo della tigre* (*Jail Break* or *On the Tiger's Back*) and *Il commissario* (*The Police Commissioner*)—he would try to break new ground. He would finally establish himself as a great director with his adaptation of Carlo Cassola's bestseller *La ragazza di Bube* (*Bebo's Girl*). Comencini received his first international recognition as a master filmmaker during the 1960s and 1970s thanks to films like *Incompreso* (*Misunderstood*), *Infanzia, vocazione, prime esperienze di Giacomo Casanova, veneziano* (*Giacomo Casanova: Childhood and Adolescence*), *Le avventure di Pinocchio* (*The Adventures of Pinocchio*), *Lo scopone scientifico* (*The Scientific Cardplayer* or *The Scopone Game*), *Mio Dio, come sono caduta in basso!* (*How Long Can You Fall* or *Till Marriage Do Us Part*), *L'ingorgo* (*Traffic Jam*), *Voltati Eugenio* (*Eugenio*), and *Cuore* (*Heart*). He became the first comic director to enter the pantheon of master filmmakers of the postwar era (thanks in great part to the work of Jean Gili).[36] His films are marked by his ability to employ all of his narrative skills in sharing his vision of the world and his sensibility with the viewer. He lovingly explored faraway, mysterious worlds that were always full of pain and childhood fears.

Dino Risi was a director remarkably similar but by no means identical to Monicelli and Comencini (a mystery akin to the Holy Trinity). Unlike the latter two, Risi was less interested in creating moralistic parables. He preferred to use his disaffected lens to capture and record the transformation of the urban and geographical landscape of Italy and its people.[37] The first film in his tetralogy, *Una vita difficile* (*A Difficult Life*)—together with *Il sorpasso* (*The Easy Life*), *La marcia su Roma* (*March on Rome*), and *I mostri* (*Opiate*)—was the story of the consummate Italian, from the liberation by the Allies to the economic boom of the 1960s. It chronicled the Italian's diminishing hopes and his acceptance of every type of compromise. Even when he was creating a story much wider in scope, Risi always seemed to find immense pleasure in sketching his characters with pointillist caricatures. Gathered together, they made for a compact gallery of figures who appeared strong but in reality were fragile, full of ideas for the future while trailed by a series of emotional and professional disasters. Risi always shined when working with a short story where swift observation tied an entire emotional, psychological, professional, and social situation together with deft touches. Vittorio Gassman was the ideal actor for Risi's cinema; they would make almost twenty films together.

In his films set in the 1960s—*I mostri* (*Opiate*), *L'ombrellone* (*Weekend Wives* or *Weekend, Italian Style*), *Il giovedì* (*The Thursday*), and *Il Gaucho* (*The Gaucho*)—Risi used a new style of editing that was a precursor to today's music video. His accelerated technique borrowed from the rhythms of rock music and from the songs of popular Italian singers and singer-songwriters like Mina, Gino Paoli, and Celentano. This new form of visual storytelling, in which the music determined the pace of the story and its visual syntax, allowed him to capture the true spirit of the era. More than any of his fellow directors, he was able to gauge the slightest changes in the temperature of his times. He seemed perfectly attuned to every new catch phrase, fads, ritual, and tic—of both young and grown-up persons alike. Of all the 1960s filmmakers, he was the most detached and the least prone to making "message" movies. But a turning point in his career came in the early 1970s when he made *In nome del popolo italiano* (*In the Name of the Italian People*, 1972) and *Mordi e fuggi* (*Dirty Weekend*, 1973), thanks in part to the support given him by Zapponi. These films were openly ideological in their content. With *Profumo di donna* (*Scent of a Woman* or *Sweet Smell of Woman*, 1974), Risi broke new ground by attempting a rich psychological profile of an emotionally fragile character who has used aggression and dissimulation to mask his problems. By the mid-1970s, Risi's touch and vision began to show signs of nostalgia. For the first time, his approach to his characters betrayed his affection and understanding of their drama. He seemed to relate to their desire to fall in love at an old age. They were unafraid of being ridiculed or humiliated in films like *La stanza del vescovo* (*The Bishop's Room* or *The Bishop's Bedroom*, 1977, adapted from the novel by Piero Chiara) and *Primo amore* (*First Love*, 1978).

With *I nuovi mostri* (*The New Monsters* or *Viva Italia!*, 1977), Monicelli, Scola, and Risi went back in time (like a Dumas novel) to take a look at a group of characters who had come of age during Italy's economic boom. In the directors' view, the results of their life journey had been disastrous. The new monsters were physically and morally repulsive. These new faces of Italy left the viewer with no choice but to turn away in disgust.

Risi's latest works were no longer shaped by the lightness of his touch, by his sympathy for rascals who had some redeeming qualities, and by the sharpness of his gaze that allowed him to move beyond the present. As for many of his fellow directors from this period, the "years of lead" meant a loss of any faith in the legibility of the present.

A member of the generation that followed Risi's, Etttore Scola resembled a medieval apprentice to a painter who had spent at least seven years mixing paints. Over the course of his apprenticeship, he wrote jokes for humor magazines, worked for screenwriters Age and Scarpelli, worked as a "gopher," and worked on treatments and screenplays of literally dozens of films before becoming a director.[38]

Together with Maccari, Scola wrote the story and screenplay for *Il sorpasso* (*The Easy Life*) and he was directly involved in the production of comedies from the early 1950s through the early 1960s. His debut would come in 1964 with *Se permettete parliamo di donne* (*Let's Talk about Women*), a film comprised of nine portraits of women using Pietrangeli's films as a model. In his second film, *La congiuntura* (*Hard Time for Princes* or *One Million Dollars*), he went back to themes dealt with in *Il sorpasso*. With even stronger resolve, he sought to expose the phenomenon of illegal transfer of capital abroad.

His *Riusciranno i nostri eroi a ritrovare l'amico misteriosamente scomparso in Africa?* (*Will Our Heroes Be Able to Find Their Friend Who Has Mysteriously Disappeared in Africa?*, 1977) was an adaptation of Conrad's *Heart of Darkness* using colorful Roman characters as the film's stars. The southern-born Scola seemed to always seek out the exotic: he headed to the uncharted northern region of Veneto to make a film after Genoese Pietro Germi and Venetian Tinto Brass showed him the way. He set *Il commissario Pepe* (*Police Chief Pepe*, 1969) in the city of Vicenza, showing off his new talents as a social explorer. In the process, he exposed a world of perversions, corruption, and vice by the smiling face of respectability, Catholic power, and the churchman's frock. But even in his early films, Scola proved to be a true perfectionist, always careful to surround himself with the most creative energy in Italian cinema. He had camera operators like Carlo di Palma, Pasqualino de Santis, and Luciano Tovoli; editors like Ruggero Mastroianni, Kim Arcalli, and Raimondo Crociani; production designers like Luciano Ricceri; composers like Morricone, Bacalov, and Armando Trovaioli; and costume designers like Gabriella Pescucci.

In the early 1970s, he made a quasi-experimental film on the difficulties faced by a southern Italian boy who had emigrated to the capital of the Italian automobile, Turin: *Trevico-Torino (Viaggio nel Fiat-Nam)* (*From Trevico-Turin, a Journey to FIAT-nam*). This work was influenced by contemporary activist films, and in particular, by Godard's films. But Scola's chief interest was that of following the main character's wanderings through a world that is at times a jungle, at others a maze, a fortress that will not allow him entry. With many obstacles to overcome, the main character has trouble understanding even simple communication and codes of behavior that seem foreign to him.

In 1974, when Italian comedy was in a general state of decline, Scola was at the height of his career when he made C'eravamo tanto amati (We All Loved Each Other So Much), a journey through the hopes and dreams, compromises and disappointments of four friends, spanning the time of their armed struggle in the Resistance to the present day. With this film, it was as if Scola had suddenly shifted gears and embraced the legacy of his teachers as he continued to explore Italian history and the emotional life of Italians.

Among his best efforts was Una giornata particolare (A Special Day, 1977): on the very day that Hitler came to visit Italy, in a towering low-income housing project emptied out for the occasion (re-created by Luciano Ricceri and filmed by Pasqualino de Santis), a housewife finds herself at her wit's end and out of touch with her own body; the fascist police watch a homosexual man headed for prison; they meet by chance and for a short while they manage to put their loneliness aside and to rediscover true intimacy, conversation, and emotional and physical contact with one another.

Scola's previous films had made use of Brechtian alienation and the unity of place, time, and action. With this and subsequent works, he would apply such lessons to his examination of history. Just as he used a low-income apartment in Una giornata particolare, he used a middle-class apartment to tell the story of different generations of the same family spanning nearly an entire century in La famiglia (The Family, 1987); in La terrazza (The Terrace, 1980), he used the scene as the backdrop for a group of intellectuals who, unable to understand the present, engage in gratuitous and affected dialogue. But he also used public spaces to examine more varied types of characters: a ballroom in Ballando ballando (Le Bal [The Ball], 1983); a movie theater in Splendor (1989); a restaurant in La cena (Le Dîner, 1998); two shops in 1938, side by side on the same street, one run by a Jewish family when Italy adopted Hitler's race laws, in his recent film Concorrenza sleale (Unfair Competition, 2001). Structural unity has allowed Scola to take an original approach to historical subjects. Directly and indirectly, he used music, props, costumes, and his actors' facial expressions to re-create historical moments in time. Spanning the years of the fascist regime through the years of the current Italian Republic to the present, Scola touched upon some of the happiest moments in Italian history while depicting the some of the most traumatic changes faced by the Italian people. Aside from Il viaggio di Capitan Fracassa (Captain Fracassa's

Journey)—a film similar to Fellini's *E la nave va* (*And the Ship Sails On*), in which he metaphorically described Italian cinema's arduous voyage toward its death—Scola has always taken the minimalist road and has always chosen to examine a cell that represented the entire body. His films *Che ora è* (*What Time Is It?*, 1989) and *Mario, Maria e Mario* (*Mario, Maria, and Mario*, 1993) are prime examples of this. He has also taken great risks, as in the case of *Il mondo nuovo* (*La Nuit de Varennes* or *That Night in Varennes*, 1982), in which he returned to picaresque themes. In this film, he made an explicit homage to neorealist screenwriter Sergio Amidei by developing a correlation between the flight of Louis XVI and Victor Emanuel III's disgraceful departure from Rome after having dismissed Mussolini at the end of July 1943.

Nanni Loy can be counted among the directors who have elevated the genre of comedy films in Italy. More than any Italian filmmaker, he has teetered between comedies and dramatic films of greater scope and ambition. As an assistant to director Luigi Zampa, he absorbed the filmmaker's approach and quickly showed his talent in directing actors on the set. After a few collaborations as co-director with Puccini on *Parola di ladro* (*Honor Among Thieves*, 1957) and *Il marito* (*The Husband*, 1958), he tried to repeat the success of *I soliti ignoti* (*Big Deal on Madonna Street*) with a sequel, *L'audace colpo dei soliti ignoti* (*Fiasco in Milan*, 1959). He followed up with two ambitious historical epics: *Un giorno da leoni* (*A Day for the Courageous*) and *Le quattro giornate di Napoli* (*The Four Days of Naples*). In 1967, he decided to try his hand at a domestic comedy with *Il padre di famiglia* (*The Head of the Family*), an adaptation of Risi's *Una vita difficile* (*A Difficult Life*), but told from a woman's perspective. Loy's sense of humor was perhaps the most Anglo-Saxon among his contemporaries, at least when he favored irony and skepticism over superficial laughs. This can be seen in his reflections on the difficulties of man's daily struggle for simple survival in films like *Rosolino Paternò, soldato* (*Operation Snafu* or *Situation Normal, All Fouled Up*, 1970) and *Café Express* (1980). He also put a comic spin on American and Italian bureaucratic absurdity in *Detenuto in attesa di giudizio* (*Why*, 1971).

Another director who earned the right to be included among the group of great Italian comedy filmmakers was Luigi Magni, who had a true knack for historical film and a remarkable ability to make his workaday characters move with emotional power onscreen. His cinema gracefully spanned the arc of Roman and Italian history, from the Punic Wars to the Risorgimento: *Nell'anno del Signore* (*The Conspirators*, 1969), *Scipione detto anche l'Africano* (*Scipio, the African*, 1971), *In nome del papa re* (*In the Name of the Pope King*,

1977), *Arrivano i bersaglieri* (*The Bersaglieri Are Coming*, 1980), and *La carbonara* (2000). With their folksy style, his films made nineteenth-century Bartolomeo Pinelli's drawings come to life and revived the soul of nineteenth-century Roman poets Pascarella and Trilussa.

Pasquale Festa Campanile was one of the era's most prolific filmmakers and writers. Over the course of his career as a director and screenwriter, which began as a co-director with Massimo Franciosa, he would make over fifty films. His success in making sophisticated soft-porn comedies about changing Italian sexual mores went beyond mere voyeurism. Of all the directors who began their careers with lofty ambitions, he was the one who took the road of facile verbal vulgarity and eroticism. His films deserve to be studied as a body of work because—if for no other reason—they served as a link between different film genres of that era. Among his more successful and memorable films were *La costanza della ragione* (1965), *Il merlo maschio* (*Secret Fantasy*, 1972), *Rugantino* (1973), *Cara sposa* (*Dear Wife*, 1977), *Il corpo della ragassa* (*A Girl's Body*, based on the novel by Gianni Brera, 1979), *Il ladrone* (*The Good Thief* or *The Thief*, an adaptation of the director's novel, *Il ladrone*, 1980), *Nessuno è perfetto* (*Nobody's Perfect*, 1981), *Bingo Bongo* (1982), and *La ragazza di Trieste* (*The Girl from Trieste*, 1982).

Lastly, Luciano Salce, a fine and often sardonic actor and screenwriter, also deserves mention for his impressive filmography. Besides *Il federale* (*The Fascist*, 1961) and *La voglia matta* (*Crazy Desire* or *The Crazy Urge*, 1961), he will be remembered above all for having directed the mid-1960s Fantozzi movies. His intelligent and often sophisticated humor happily embraced the facile elements of the vaudevillian entertainment that typically preceded the projection of a film in the early days of cinema. He opened the door to what would be 1970s Italian comic films.

From Stars to Starlets

By the close of the 1960s, women had dominated the Italian star system for nearly a decade and some had even ascended the Mt. Olympus of international stardom. These were the years when cinema exalted the body and the new canon of feminine beauty. But suddenly men began to wield more power. From this moment on, past categories could no longer be applied to Italian stardom. The explosion of new celebrities created a galaxy of shining stars so great that it would ultimately diminish each one's luster. This phenomenon was born of a newfound collective desire to covet objects other than the faces of Italian cinema. Television and the announcers and presenters of quiz and game shows became the new focal point. Television personality Mike Bongiorno's beautiful assistant, Edy Campagnoli, would end up competing with Sophia Loren and other emerging stars of the new Italian cinema. As early as the 1950s, movies had been based on songs by performers like Luciano Tajoli and Claudio Villa. Now, singers like Domenico Modugno, Mina, Celentano, Gianni Morandi, and Al Bano would enjoy success in film and television as well. In other words, beauty and youth were no longer the only criteria for celebrity.

As the mass media underwent this transformation, a small group of actors managed to monopolize Italian stardom by playing a wide array of roles and showing off their immense talent. Marcello Mastroianni was first and foremost among them, appearing in films by Visconti, Monicelli, Fellini, Bolognini, De Sica, Antonioni, Germi, and Petri, and then by Risi, Zurlini, Scola, the Taviani brothers, and even Tornatore and Archibugi. He also appeared in a number of foreign films in which he became the new icon of the Italian lover. The press even went as far to call him the reincarnation of Rudolph Valentino. Of all the actors during this period, Mastroianni was the one who wore his celebrity with a sense of humility. Ever surprised by his success, he was by far the most flexible and malleable of the Italian actors of this era. He seemed able to enter easily and seamlessly into characters and to give life to a gamut of emotion using only nuance and nearly imperceptible overtones.[39]

The four monsters of Italian comedy—Gassman, Sordi, Tognazzi, and Manfredi—became the embodiment of good looks, virility, and sexual ambiguity. With equal nonchalance, they could don the garb of the proletariat and the bourgeoisie, a priest's frock or an eighteenth-century costume. They gave life to characters ranging from a crippled violinist to a film director in crisis to a conniving bricklayer suffering from overwhelming jealousy.

Of these four musketeers, Vittorio Gassman was the D'Artagnan, an impetuous braggart who broke into the Italian comedy scene after roughly ten years and twenty unnoticed parts in Italian and Hollywood movies (although *Kean*, in which he starred and co-directed in 1956, is an important movie inasmuch as the role of the English lover of the limelight was the ideal vehicle for his talent).[40] Suddenly, he gave up his career as a stage actor and director and started making comedies. He really began to take off when, in the same year, he appeared as Peppe the washed-out boxer in *I soliti ignoti* (*Big Deal on Madonna Street*) and Busacca in *La grande guerra* (*The Great War*).

Of the four of them, however, Alberto Sordi would land the best roles, the most varied and the most articulate characters. In the made-for-television *Storia di un italiano* (*Story of an Italian*, 1979), he assembled clips of his most important roles. The result was an anthology that showed how his characters told the story of Italy.

Sordi was the legitimate heir of Petrolini, an actor who, for many years, made Roman dialect the lingua franca of Italian cinema. He defined the now archetypal role of bully of the tough streets on the outskirts of Rome; the Roman bureaucrat and office worker; the shrewd Italian; the Italian mama's boy who suffered from Peter Pan syndrome; he played opportunists, masters in the art of self-preservation. His characters were somewhat dishonest, but in the end, they were always likable—people found everywhere in postwar Italy. Like a sponge, Petrolini absorbed the rapid social, sexual, and ideological changes that were taking place in Italian society. He seemingly metabolized elements of the new mentality and was able to convey a strong emotional connection in the characters he portrayed. Like Totò's films, Sordi's movies (and in particular those written by Sonego or directed by Sordi himself) told the Italian's daily story of change and resistance to change, of vices, neuroses, and a few virtues—chiefly the virtue of being able to endure the harsh lot that life had handed the Italian without his ever giving up. In the course of the twentieth century, the people of Italy had been heroes, killers, and victims; some suffered from heroes' syndrome, others were paralyzed by cowardice; some had sacrificed everything in the name of money, others had committed amazing acts of altruism and generosity.

Ugo Tognazzi was brought into the first-string team of comics following a long run in vaudevillian revues and variety shows when he and Raimondo Vianello scored a big hit with their television program *Un due tre* (*One, Two, Three*, 1958–59). On their show, they employed socio-anthropological satire and impeccable comic timing to create a memorable series of male and female characters who performed jobs soon to be obsolete in the new Italy.[41] This duo was broken up by Luciano Salce who cast Tognazzi as the lead character in *Il federale* (*The Fascist*) alongside Georges Wilson, one of the greatest actors of the Théatre National Français. Salce then gave him a more contemporary role in *La voglia matta* (*Crazy Desire* or *The Crazy Urge*), in which he played a forty-something professional man who falls madly in love with a sixteen-year-old. With these two roles, he made a name for himself as a comic-dramatic actor, and he would ultimately land a part together with Gassman in *La marcia su Roma* (*March on Rome*) and *I mostri* (*Opiate*).

While Gassman was trying to lighten up his image after playing so many tragic roles, Tognazzi was doing just the opposite and sought out the most demanding dramatic roles he could get. He was cast in a number of roles by Marco Ferreri: in *Il professore* ("The Professor"), Ferreri's episode in *Controsesso* (*Countersex*); *L'uomo dei cinque palloni* (*The Man with the Balloons* or *Break up*); *L'ape regina* (*The Queen Bee* or *The Conjugal Bed*); *La donna scimmia* (*The Ape Woman*); and *Marcia nuziale* (*The Wedding March*). He would later work with several directors, including Pasolini and the Taviani Brothers, Scola, Monicelli, Lattuada, and Bertolucci. Tognazzi never hesitated to play repulsive characters; his roles never evoked the sympathy and forgiveness that Sordi was able to create with the characters he portrayed.

The last to arrive on the comedy scene was Nino Manfredi, who earned his place as a leading man courteously and respectfully. Every time he was in-frame, it was as if he apologized for the nuisance. His alienated acting style made him the most Brechtian of the postwar stars. He was the best at showing weakness and fragility in every aspect of his roles, but his characters were also educated and civilized. He could make every one of their inner strings reso-nate. While Gassman yelled and slapped, Manfredi responded passively, with silence, his requests and his presence just barely whispered. After a memorable performance alongside Sordi in the role of the ill-suited gondolier who had fallen in love with Marisa Allasio, his first big break came with a Spanish film, *El Verdugo* (*Not on Your Life*, directed by Luis Berlanga, 1963). This role al-lowed him to show off the bizarre, bitter elements of the born loser. Over the arc of his career, he created a gallery of roles. Some of the most memorable were his portrayal of the little soldier in *Avventura di un soldato* (*A Soldier's Adventure*, the silent segment of *Amore difficile* [*Of Wayward Love* or *Sex Can Be Difficult*]); Marco in *Il padre di famiglia* (*The Head of the Family*); an immi-grant in *Pane e cioccolato* (*Bread and Chocolate*); Nale in De Bosio's *La Betía* (*In Love, Every Pleasure Has Its Pain*); and a conman in *Café Express*. He also had some great cameos (the most famous as Geppetto in Comencini's *Pinocchio*). With time, his acting became more and more refined.

After spending a few years as Antonioni's Muse, Monica Vitti came to be associated with a group of comic actors when she began to utilize her ex-traordinary linguistic ability and her talent in mime. She funneled this energy, previously kept at bay, in roles at times puppet-like and purposely disarticulate, at times powerfully erotic. Her greatest successes in comedy were in films like *La ragazza con la pistola* (*Girl with a Pistol*), *Dramma della gelosia, tutti i particolari in cronaca* (*Jealousy, Italian Style* or *The Pizza Triangle*), *La supertestimone* (*The Best Witness Ever*), and *Polvere di stelle* (*Stardust*).

Sophia Loren's Oscar for her role as Cesira in *La ciociara* (*Two Women*), when she was just twenty-six years old, made her a true international superstar.[42] She would be the last true diva of Italian cinema to be endowed with the required aura and classic attributes of glamour and beauty. Thanks in part to her collaboration with Mastroianni and De Sica, who cast her beside Mastro-ianni in one her most memorable roles as Filumena Marturano in De Sica's adaptation of Eduardo de Filippo's *Matrimonio all'Italiana* (*Marriage Italian-Style*), she would enjoy her long run without competition from younger actresses. Even today, her star power and beauty continue to land her challenging roles (she was recently cast by her son Edoardo in his *Between Strangers*, 2002), but she is also prone to make less-flattering commercial appearances, like her testimonial for a brand of prosciutto in Emilia-Romagna or her support for the "ultima buona azione della lira" campaign.[43]

Today, Gina Lollobrigida's star has begun to fade. Although considered gorgeous at the outset of the 1960s, her looks do not match up with today's canons of beauty and she cannot seem to find directors or screenplays that could do her justice in her maturity.

As the 1950s faded into the 1960s, Silvana Mangano continued to make memorable appearances in films like *La grande guerra* (*The Great War*) and *Jovanka e le altre* (*Five Branded Women*). Even though she did nearly everything she could to stay out of the limelight and to devote herself exclusively to her family, in later years she could still captivate moviegoers in films by Pasolini and Visconti.

During the 1960s, besides Claudia Cardinale, Stefania Sandrelli, and Monica Vitti, other starlets would make their debuts and attempt to embark on the road to superstardom. Virna Lisi, Catherine Spaak, Sandra Milo, and Ornella Muti combined beauty and talent but did not seem to possess the "Midas touch."

Together with Giancarlo Giannini, and in more recent years Michele Placido and Sergio Castellitto, Gian Maria Volonté is an actor who seemed more a product of the Actor's Studio than a homegrown son of Italy, where, throughout the 1950s, new actors were generally graduates of the Accademia d'arte drammatica (Academy of Dramatic Arts). He had an extraordinary ability to step into historical roles, like Sicilian union worker Salvatore Carnevale; a Venetian partisan in De Bosio's *Il terrorista* (*The Terrorist*); oil tycoon Enrico Mattei; anarchist Nicola Sacco; gangster Lucky Luciano; writer Carlo Levi; politicians Enrico Berlinguer and Aldo Moro; and journalist Eugenio Scalfari.[44] Besides these memorable portrayals, he also played bad guys in Sergio Leone's early westerns. Where Mastroianni created his characters by using less, Volonté would add more and more elements to his, either distorting them or attempting perfect mimicry. Like Giannini, Volonté spent a lot of time preparing for his roles.

But Giannini preferred portraying persons who never really existed. He liked building his characters from scratch. Whether Sicilian mafiosi or working-class heroes, truckers or luxury yacht sailors, they always gave the viewer an idea of their past from their first appearance onscreen. As a result, moviegoers always felt compassion for them and their struggle for survival.

During the 1970s, Bud Spencer and Terence Hill became superstars thanks to their appearances in westerns and their action-film-slapstick-comic-duo routine reminiscent of Laurel and Hardy.

Today, Italian cinema has more than a fair share of young but veteran actors who have already demonstrated remarkable talent: from Claudio Amendola to Stefano Accorsi, from Francesca Neri to Margherita Buy, from Sabrina Ferilli to Nancy Brilli and Chiara Caselli, from Raoul Bova to Sergio Rubini and Laura Morante, Kim Rossi Stuart, Alessandro Gassman, Luca Zingaretti, and Valerio Mastandrea, among others. But aside from Roberto Benigni, Monica Bellucci, Valeria Golino, and Anna Galiena (who, thanks to their strong personalities, have had no trouble working with foreign directors), Italian cinema produces few superstars. Italian stars now come from television and politics, soccer and motorcycle racing, pop music and auto racing, musicals and fashion—but not from movies.

There is no lack, however, of celebrities adored by the public and recognized for their talent. Besides the short list above, there are actors like Diego Abantantuono, who made his debut onscreen in the 1980s, Massimo Boldi, Luca Barbareschi, Fabrizio Bentivoglio, Valeria Bruni Tedeschi, Roberto Citran, Maria Grazia Cucinotta, Licia Maglietta, Isabella Ferrari, Lucrezia Lante della Rovere, and Amanda Sandrelli, to name a few. Abantantuono has shown some superstar qualities, but any census of Italian actors today points not to a group of superstars, but rather, a genuine school of talented young actors often underutilized by Italian cinema.

The early 1980s saw an Adriano Celentano "phenomenon." He moved gracefully between film, television, and music. A number of comic actors— Carlo Verdone, Francesco Nuti, Massimo Troisi, Roberto Benigni, Massimo Boldi, Teo Teocoli, and Christian de Sica, among others—had their first break on television. Current Italian superstardom must be studied as a crossover, hybrid phenomenon in which cinema no longer plays a forward position, but rather, a wing or, in some cases, is even forced to watch from the bench. One of the fundamental reasons for this is that the television screen took over cinema's function as Italy's myth-making machine. Another primary reason is that directors began to play the starring role on the silver screen, which also had become smaller. The new generations of film directors became less and less adept at exploiting their actors' ability and seemed more reluctant to share center-stage with their actors. This explains why so many successful actors have wanted to become directors, thus validating the scientific law of progressive incompetence.

Stardom in Italian cinema has become unpredictable and relatively incapable of self-generation. There is no comparison with the past superstars of Italian cinema. Today, the opportunities to appear on television have multiplied exponentially. The resulting phenomenon of television's Vanna White and co-host divas has been based on the performers' overall incompetence. The stardom of days gone by was monumentalized in scope (Loren was a prime example of this). Today's celebrity has been merely super-sized. There is room for everyone in front of today's millions of digital video cameras. Zavattini's dream seems almost to have come true, if only by giving life to reality shows like *Il grande fratello* (*Big Brother*), *Operazione Trionfo* (the equivalent of *American Idol*), and *Saranno famosi* (*Fame*).

Western, Horror, Political, and Erotic Films: The Genre Films

Unlike the English-speaking countries, Italy has never had a tradition of bona fide horror films. During the three decades when silent films were produced in Italy, the only horror movie made was *Il caso Haller* (*The Case of the Baron Haller*, 1933), with a storyline inspired by Dr. Jekyll and Mr. Hyde. But then, suddenly, among the many films that were produced during the magical year of 1960, five horror movies stood in the last two rows of the class photo: Mario Bava's *La maschera del demonio* (*Black Sunday*; *The Demon's Mask*; *The Hour When Dracula Comes*; *House of Fright*; *The Mask of Satan*; or *Mask of the Demon*), Ferroni's *Il mulino delle donne di pietra* (*Drops of Blood*; *The Horrible Mill Women*; or *Horror of the Stone Women*), Renato Polselli's *L'amante del vampiro* (*The Vampire and the Ballerina* or *The Vampire's Lover*, the first Italian film to portray real vampires), Pietro Regnoli's *L'ultima preda del vampiro* (*Curse of the Vampire*; *Daughters of the Vampire*; *Desires of the Vampire*; *The Last Prey of the Vampire*; *Last Victim of the Vampire*; *The Playgirls and the Vampire*; or *The Vampire's Last Victim*), and Anton Giulio Majano's *Seddok l'erede di Satana* (*Atom Age Vampire*). These films are worth watching as they are indicative of the new commercial trend in Italian cinema during the 1960s, combining a number of disparate elements that were in decline by the end of the 1950s. When Terence Fisher released his *Dracula* in 1957, Italian cinema was in a phase of rapid growth: it seemed only logical, from a financial point of view, to produce near perfect imitations that were virtually indistinguishable from the original. The genre would ultimately be forgotten because it lacked any identity or continuity with the Italian tradition of filmmaking.[45]

It is a pity that of all the commercial genres from this period, horror movies have not received the critical attention they deserve. And yet it is by creating new rules and breaking the old that a genre of storytelling assaults censorship and expands the dark, irrational zones of modernity and advanced civilization.

By the end of the 1960s, horror films, like westerns, were colored by ideological (although not politicized) leanings drawn from the youth culture's challenge to the establishment. Film critics have never really shed light on this fact. In any case, some of these directors—Riccardo Freda, Antonio Margheriti, and Mario Bava—would soon become Italian cinema's most nationally and even internationally recognizable figures. Already working in the early 1960s, Renato Polselli, Camillo Mastrocinque (a do-it-all director), Mario Caiano, Lucio Fulci, and Massimo Pupillo should also be remembered in this group. Bava and Freda had been inspired by the low-budget horror titles produced by Hammer Films in the 1960s. They showed remarkable attention to detail in creating the visual construct of every frame, in the use of sound effects and soundtrack, and in their emphasis on symbolism and a vast array of sexual psychopathologies. It did not take long for them to use the genre to create a number of highly articulate films. Cinema could express all of our repressed desires, said Barbara Steele of this period in Italian cinema, of our suppressed obsessions, "from incest to necrophilia," an affirmation of the connection between "sex and death."[46]

Sexual desire, perverted and deviant eroticism would open the way—thanks in part to the easing of censorship laws—to horror movies that seemed to have no limits in the 1970s by directors like Argento, Fulci, Alberto de Martino, Luigi Cozzi, and Joe d'Amato.

The horror genre was soon divided into two schools. On one hand, there were those who chose to remain within classical settings. They preferred accurate re-creations of Gothic castles enveloped in fog. On the other hand, there were those who focused on contemporary Italy. The latter sought to create macabre worlds derived from current psychopathologies. Together with accurate set construction and cinematography, music began to play a more important role. Scores for horror films were written by composers like Roman Vlad, Carlo Rustichelli, Riz Ortolani, Giorgio Gaslini, Pino Donaggio, Manuel de Sica, Franco Mannino, and Ennio Morricone. Mario Serandrei was the editor on many of these films in the 1960s. Ennio de Concini and Bernardino Zapponi wrote a lot of the screenplays. Carlo Rambaldi worked as a special effects artist for Bava, Ferroni, and Fulci, and Vittorio Storaro, Luciano Tovoli, and Luigi Kuveiller were among the top cinematographers. During this period, a great deal of important work was done in the possibilities of black and white and in expanding the limits of color. A number of experimental elements from these films would ultimately find legitimacy in later *film d'auteur* productions. Perhaps more than any other genre, Italian horror films made the greatest use of the industry's craftsmen. The early themes of Italian horror movies mixed desire for immortality with a thirst for blood; they combined the myth of eternal beauty with passion and unbridled sexuality, often coupled with syndromes of omnipotence that sought to fulfill the darkest of yearnings.

The first Gothic film produced in Italy was Freda's *I vampiri* (*The Devil's Commandment; Evil's Commandment; Lust of the Vampire*; or *The Vampires*, 1957). It was shot in just twelve days on the Cinecittà lot. It is a story of pseudo-vampirism: an elderly aristocrat woman has discovered that the blood of young women is an elixir for eternal youth, so she begins to kidnap them and suck their blood.[47] Freda was convinced that horror and terror should be sought not in costumes and papier-mâché sets but in our everyday lives.[48] Over the course of his career, he achieved his ideal of pure horror with two important films, *L'orribile segreto del Dr. Hichcock* (*The Frightening Secret of Dr. Hichcock; The Horrible Dr. Hichcock; The Horrible Secret of Dr. Hichcock; Raptus; The Secret of Dr. Hichcock; The Terrible Secret of Dr. Hichcock*; or *The Terror of Dr. Hichcock*, 1962) and *Lo spettro* (*The Ghost* or *The Spectre*, 1963). Freda wanted to break all the rules. He wanted to push the envelope of monstrosity ("an assassin should be a monstrous assassin"), of violence, hate, and themes like necrophilia, and he did so to an almost unsustainable level.[49] Freda firmly believed in what he was doing. "Vampires exist," he once said. "There is not a moment that they are not lurking around us . . . Being a vampire means living near someone younger than you and, unbeknownst to him, sucking up the best he has to offer, his intelligence, his life spirit, and, above all, his freshness, the freshness of his ideas, feelings, and reactions."[50] Mario Bava, on the other hand, was more interested in the supernatural, and he tried to sprinkle his films with irony, even though *La maschera del demonio* (*Black Sunday; The Demon's Mask; The Hour When Dracula Comes; House of Fright; The Mask of Satan*; or *Mask of the Demon*) is one of the most macabre Italian horror films ever produced.[51] Irony was the staple element of the horror genre, and was widely used in westerns and mythological films as well. Like other directors of horror films, and particularly the earlier years of the genre, Bava used it to temper the frightful mood. This was one of Italian horror's trademarks and in no way did it diminish the quality of the final product. In his annual report for the 1988 issue of *Film Guide*, Lorenzo Codelli included Bava's *I tre volti della paura* (*Black Christmas; Black Sabbath; The Three Faces of Fear*; or *The Three Faces of Terror*) in his list of the ten best films made between 1963 and

1968. If Mario Bava's films do not represent a "milestone" in cinema history, as Codelli has noted, he at least created his own "niche."

In 1962, Bava began work on *La ragazza che sapeva troppo* (*The Evil Eye* or *The Girl Who Knew Too Much*). Set in Rome, it was the story of nighttime murder committed at one of the most famous tourist destinations in the world, the Spanish Steps. With this film, he unknowingly laid the groundwork for Argento's later films. The following year, Bava made *La frusta e il corpo* (*The Body and the Whip*; *Night Is the Phantom*; *Son of Satan*; *The Way and the Body*; or *What*), a film in which he tackled the subject of sadomasochism. Bava had a remarkable ability to create an entire sequence shot (plan-sequence) with elaborate camera moves that draw the viewer into the story and make the supernatural seem very real.

Save for a few exceptions, the earliest horror films were plagued with bad screenplays and cheap makeup, so bad in some cases that they produced a comic effect. But this has been the case for all commercial genres.

In 1963, the third father of horror Italian-style, Antonio Margheriti (using the pseudonym Anthony Dawson) made his first film, *Danza macabra* (*Castle of Blood*; *The Castle of Terror*; *Coffin of Terror*; *Dimensions in Death*; *Edgar Allan Poe's Castle of Blood*; *The Long Night of Terror*; *Tombs of Horror*; or *Tombs of Terror*). The viewer immediately identifies with the film's main character, who powerlessly watches a series of murders, each more horrible than the last. Although the film was cut by censors (who, among other things, eliminated the lesbian scenes—the first ever in the history of Italian cinema), the film maintains a dark, sick mood from the initial frames to the very last. Not long after its release, Margheriti spent a few short weeks making *La vergine di Norimberga* (*Back to the Killer*; *The Castle of Terror*; *Horror Castle*; *Terror Castle*; or *The Virgin of Nuremberg*), a film in which he made a connection between horror and recent history, and in particular, to Nazism.

In the years that would follow, a healthy assortment of titles would pave the way for Italian horror: films like Margheriti's *I lunghi capelli della morte* (*The Long Hair of Death*, 1964) and *Contronatura* (*The Innaturals*; *Screams in the Night*; or *Unnaturals*, 1969); and Bava's *Terrore nello spazio* (*Demon Planet*; *The Haunted Planet, The Haunted World*; *The Outlawed Planet*; *Planet of Blood*; *The Planet of Terror*; *The Planet of the Damned*; *Planet of the Vampires*; *Space Mutants*; or *Terror in Space* 1965), *Operazione paura* (*Curse of the Dead*; *Curse of the Living Dead*; *Don't Walk in the Park*; *Kill, Baby . . . Kill!*; or *Operation Fear*, 1966), *Diabolik* (*Danger: Diabolik*, 1968), *Quante volte . . . quella notte* (*Four Times That Night*, 1969), *Il rosso segno della follia* (*An Axe for the Honeymoon*; *Blood Brides*; *Hatchet for the Honeymoon*; *The Red Mark of Madness*; or *The Red Sign of Madness* 1969), and *Cinque bambole per una luna d'agosto* (*Five*

Dolls for an August Moon or *Island of Terror*, 1970). There were also other important films like Mario Caiano's *Amanti d'oltretomba* (*Lovers Beyond the Tomb; Lovers from Beyond the Tomb; Night of the Doomed;* or *Nightmare* Castle, 1965) and Massimo Pupillo's *Cinque tombe per un medium* (*Cemetery of the Living Dead; Coffin of Terror; Five Graves for a Medium; Terror-Creatures from the Grave;* or *Tombs of Horror*, 1965) that were part of this unstoppable crescendo of madness, violence, sadomasochism, and every form of sexual perversion imaginable.

Then, in 1970, Dario Argento made his debut with *L'uccello dalle piume di cristallo* (*The Bird with the Crystal Plumage, Bird with the Glass Feathers; The Gallery Murders; Phantom of Terror;* or *Point of Terror*), a film that left critics unimpressed.[52] As for the directors that came before him, women would be the object of desire in his films, the lead character, and the victim par excellence. With his early films, Argento was compared to Alfred Hitchcock. The analogy is useful but not quite on the mark. Like Leone, with whom Argento and Bernardo Bertolucci co-wrote the screenplay of *C'era una volta il West* (*Once Upon a Time in the West*), he painstakingly conceived each frame of his films. By virtue of being his own camera operator, Argento also became the killer in his films, in perfect synchronicity with his panting breath as he lurked ever closer to his victims.

Through the use of excessive amounts of blood and extreme brutality, Argento was a pioneering force in splatter (so called in Italy), slasher movies. In the second half of the 1980s, this genre would enjoy a great wave of success in Italy with cartoons like *Dylan Dog* and Tiziano Sclavi's short stories.

From his *Quattro mosche di velluto grigio* (*Four Flies on Gray Velvet* or *Four Patches of Gray Velvet*, 1971) to *Profondo rosso* (*Deep Red; Deep Red Hatchet Murders; Dripping Deep Red; The Hatchet Murders;* or *The Sabre Tooth Tiger* 1975), his films also paved the way for American directors of action films like Brian de Palma, David Lynch, and David Cronenberg, who would imprint their brand of violence on screens across the world.[53] By the late 1970s and early 1980s, in films like *Suspiria* (*Dario Argento's Suspiria*, 1976), *Inferno* (*Dario Argento's Inferno*, 1980), and *Tenebre* (*Under the Eyes of the Assassin* or *Unsane*, 1982), Argento began to explore black magic, parapsychology, extrasensory perception, and the fine line between life and death. In the 1990s, he returned to classic tales like *La sindrome di Stendhal* (*The Stendhal Syndrome* or *Stendhal's Syndrome*, 1996) and *Il fantasma dell'Opera* (*Dario Argento's The Phantom of the Opera* or *Phantom of the Opera*, 1999).

Thanks to Argento, horror films received a powerful transfusion (pardon the pun). Literally tens of horror films were made following his success, mostly set in the present with real-life killers taken from the headlines, but also with apparitions of demonic forces, zombies, and the like. The amount of violence and blood onscreen increased exponentially but was no longer used only in conjunction with horror and fright. The home became the principal backdrop for horror that revealed itself as families gathered around their fireplaces. Women were generally the victims and they were often possessed by unspeakable impulses and awful demonic forces. With new directors, the stories took new and different twists: sexuality became more and more important while mystery began to lose its allure. Nothing was barred from the eyes of the defenseless viewer: nymphomania, incest, pedophilia, bestiality, rape, coprophagy, and sadomasochist orgies. Ultimately, hardcore pornography would also become part of the genre. Among the films mapping the new waters of horror in Italy, there are many worth remembering: Giulio Questi's *La morte ha fatto l'uovo* (*A Curious Way to Love*; *Death Laid an Egg*; or *Plucked*, 1968), an Antonioni-esque science-fiction sociological fright movie with Buñuelian sprinklings about the dehumanization of the workplace, genetic engineering, and the death of the working class; Sergio Martino's *Lo strano vizio della signora Wardh* (*Blade of the Ripper*; *The Next Victim!*; *Next!*; or *The Strange Vice of Mrs. Wardh*, 1970); Luigi Bazzoni's *Giornata nera per l'ariete* (*Evil Fingers* or *The Fifth Cord*, 1971); Tonino Valerii's *Mio caro assassino* (*My Dear Killer*, 1971); Martino's *Tutti i colori del buio* (*All the Colors of the Dark*; *Day of the Maniac*; *Demons of the Dead*; or *They're Coming to Get You*, 1971); Aldo Lado's *La corta notte delle bambole di vetro* (also known as *Malastrana* in Italy; *Paralyzed*; or *Short Night of the Glass Dolls*; 1971) and *Chi l'ha vista morire* (*The Child* or *Who Saw Her Die*, 1972); Fulci's *Non si sevizia un paperino* (*Don't Torture Donald Duck* or *Don't Torture a Duck*, 1972); Romano Scavolini's *Un bianco vestito per Marialé* (*Spirits of Death*, 1973); Alberto de Martino's *L'anticristo* (*The Antichrist*, 1974); and Paolo Cavara's *E tanta paura* (*Plot of Fear* or *Too Much Fear*, 1976), with a story by Bernardino Zapponi, music by Ennio Morricone, and a cast that included Corinne Cléry, Michele Placido, and Eli Wallach. It is also worth remembering Pupi Avati's small gem, *La casa dalle finestre che ridono* (*The House with Laughing Windows* or *The House with Windows That Laugh*, 1976). Avati had already directed a series of films set in the Padanian plains of Emilia-Romagna in Northern Italy. These films often tempered horror with comic relief. In films like *Balsamus, l'uomo di Satana* (*Blood Relations*, 1968), *Thomas—Gli indemoniati* (*Thomas and the Bewitched*, 1969), *La mazurka del barone, della santa e del fico fiorone* (*The Mazurka of the Baron, the Saint, and the Early Fig Tree*, 1974), and *Bordella* (*House of Pleasure for Women*, 1976), Avati liked to make the blood resemble Lambrusco, the classic wine of food-mecca Emilia, or *salama da sugo*, a rich sausage cooked in tomatoes, from the city of Ferrara. He would then begin to make other types of films, making nostalgic, action, and period films with a clear inclination toward minimalist storytelling. There were other films worth remembering as well: Fulci's *Sette note in nero* (*Murder to the Tune of Seven Black Notes*; *The Psychic*; or *Seven Notes in Black*, 1977); De Martino's *Holocaust 2000* (*The Chosen* or *Rain of Fire*, 1977); Lamberto Bava's *La bimba di satana* (*A Girl for Satan* or *Satan's Baby Doll*, 1982) and *Per sempre* (*The Changeling 2* or *Until Death*, 1988); Umberto Lenzi's *La casa delle anime erranti* (*House of Lost Souls*, 1989); and Fulci's *La dolce casa degli orrori* (*The Sweet House of Horrors*, 1989).

The use of makeup and special effects grew as horror films began to overlap with thrillers and often crossed the threshold of porn. Little by little, audiences became less and less interested in artisanal films made on shoestring budgets, crafted around dismemberment and a miraculously endless stream of blood. Instead, audiences began to lean toward American cinema and its spectacular special effects. That is not to say that Hannibal the Cannibal is not a direct descendant of the serial killers who brought life to Italian horror in the 1970s. In the years that would follow, the energy of Italian cinema would spill over into American horror, thriller, and slasher films. Directors like George Romero and Brian de Palma, and more recently, Quentin Tarantino, have never curbed their praise for Italian films made during this period; and they have repeatedly claimed to have been inspired by films by Bava, Margheriti, and Freda, and even by Umbero Lenzi and Fernando di Leo. Many Italian wizards of lighting, special effects, and music would suddenly find themselves working in Hollywood. It was as if someone had driven a sharp wooden stake through the heart of Italian horror.

Together with comedy (a genre that has been studied with brilliant results, especially in France), westerns generated the greatest critical interest outside of Italy as they began to take the place of American films on screens around the world. Scores of books have been written on the subject, and in some cases, foreign critics have better captured the magic of Sergio Leone and his critical intelligence than Italians. The expression "spaghetti western" initially had a negative connotation with racist undertones. Over time, its variations have been used to define any non-American western: "paella western," for films made in Andalusia and "Chop Suey Western" for those made in Hong Kong.

In an essay on the relationship between European and American westerns, Lorenzo Codelli pointed to Roberto Roberti's *Vampira indiana* (*Indian Vampire* [*Woman*], 1913) as the prototype for the spaghetti western.[54] Roberto Roberti was, indeed, the father of the leading and most charismatic figure of the genre, Sergio Leone, who was able to bring authentic structural innovation to the western.[55] Together with Leone, Duccio Tessari and Sergio Corbucci also began to incorporate sharpened and violent irony in their westerns. They paved the way for the endless variations that would appear in the nearly five hundred films made over the course of a decade.

In Europe, Germany and Spain had begun to produce westerns by the second half of the 1950s. The success of German westerns in the early 1960s helped the country's film industry emerge from a long slump. A young Italian producer named Alberto Grimaldi was the first to buy rights for such properties, and in 1963 he began producing the films of Joaquin Romer Marchent: *El sabor de la venganza* [Sp.] (*I tre spietati* [It.], *Gunfight at High Noon, Sons of Vengeance*, or *Three Ruthless Ones*) and *Antes llega la muerte* [Sp.] (*I sette del Texas* [It.]; *Hour of Death; Seven Guns from Texas*; or *Seven from Texas*). He then used his earnings to finance some of Italian cinema's greatest masterpieces by directors like Pasolini, Pontecorvo, Fellini, and Bertolucci, among others. Thanks to westerns, Spanish-Italian co-productions were able to bring Italian cinema to the South American market. The setting for these films was almost always the Mexican border. Important sets were built in Southern Spain: in Almeria, in Daganzo outside of Madrid, and in Mazanares near Granada. In Italy, westerns were set in Ciciaria or in certain cases, on the island of Sardinia in San Salvatore di Sinis in the Oristano area.

The follow-up to these colossal productions was *Per un pugno di dollari* (*A Fistful of Dollars* or *For a Fistful of Dollars*, 1964), a low-budget film made by Sergio Leone but credited to Bob Robertson. The film starred a television actor, Clint Eastwood, whose career seemed all but finished.[56] The film was perhaps overly inspired by a film made in 1961 by Akira Kurosawa, and Leone was accused of plagiarism. Nonetheless, the film became one of the all-time greatest successes of Italian cinema. Thanks in part to his previous experience as the director of *Il colosso di Rodi* (*The Colossus of Rhodes*, 1959), Leone was interested in and fascinated by the resilience and power of mythology and its malleability with regard to any type of tale. In the early phase of his career, he was interested in deconstructing the myth of the hero and heroic endeavors, preferring instead to take apart the narrative mechanism only to reassemble it again and again. Then, with each film that he made, he sought to reveal his heroes' motivations. He created characters that were ever more motivated by their idealism. They were capable of conceiving and founding an entire city or following their dreams to change the world while maintaining their ties of friendship.

The first things that Leone changed were the narrative prosody, syntax, and temporal structures of the classic American western. But he also changed its fundamental morality. All of Leone's films are structured around more than one dimension of time: sometimes the duration of an action is extended and the smallest unit of time is decomposed so as to make its duration perceptible and quantifiable to the characters themselves; at other times, action is accelerated by the rapid crackling of the guns as their chambers are emptied. In the earliest westerns, the heroes spoke in monosyllables, communicating primarily with their pistols, never seeming to be motivated by idealism. They were angelic figures who had to maintain a balance between their environment and the situations in which they found themselves; they lived in a world dominated by violence where only the strongest would survive. While the directors of classic westerns preferred not to show bloodshed on screen, shootouts in westerns became true massacres in the 1960s and early 1970s. The audience of classic westerns waited patiently for the glorious final duel in films by John Ford, Anthony Mann, or Budd Boetticher. But viewers quickly became accustomed to the new rhythms imposed on them by pistols and nearly every type of weapon in the hands of Clint Eastwood, Gian Maria Volonté, Giuliano Gemma, and Thomas Milian—not to mention Bud Spencer's and Terence Hill's punching and slapping.

Thanks to the surprising success of *Per un pugno di dollari* and *Per qualche dollaro in più* (*For a Few Dollars More* or *For Some Dollars More*), and then the even more ambitious *Il buono, il brutto, il cattivo* (*The Good, the Bad, and the Ugly*), Leone decided to set his sights on America. In the years that followed, he would produce his most ambitious films and give audiences a taste of his ability as a storyteller and director: *C'era una volta il West* (*Once Upon a Time in the West*); *Giù la testa* (*A Fistful of Dynamite, Duck, You Sucker, Once Upon a Time . . . the Revolution*); and the gangster epic, *C'era una volta in America* (*Once upon a Time in America*). Starting with *C'era una volta il West*, Leone's power in visual storytelling had grown to the point that he felt ready to go head to head with John Ford, even though he was also careful to point out their differences. Like Ford, he was interested in the relationships between the human figure and the space it inhabited and the possibility of guiding the viewer's gaze to distant points on the horizon where heaven and earth intersect.

With memorable performances by actors like Henry Fonda—who helped raise the genre to its greatest heights—and other icons of American cinema, from Jason Robards to Lee Van Cleef, James Coburn, Rod Steiger, Charles Bronson, and then Robert De Niro, Leone's films marked some of the most important international co-productions during a period when Italian directors enjoyed a great deal of latitude with American producers.

Leone's final film, *C'era una volta in America*, was a coming-together of all of his concepts, his cinematic passions from Griffith to Hawks and Coppola, and his life's vision. Oreste de Fornari wrote of this film, "It is unlikely that we will ever see so many myths together" on the screen, "and never again with so much emotion."[57]

The success of *Per un pugno di dollari* had an immediate effect on the industry, and masses of directors began making westerns instead of the mythological films they had made following the end of World War II: Mario Caiano's *Le pistole non discutono* (*Bullets Don't Argue*; *Bullets Don't Lie*; or *Guns Don't Talk*, 1964); Michele Lupo's *Per un pugno nell'occhio* (*Fistful of Knuckles* or *For a Fist in the Eye*, 1964); Corbucci's *Minnesota Clay* (1965), *Navajo Joe* (*Navajo Joe*; *A Dollar a Head*; or *Savage Run*, 1966), *Il grande silenzio* (*The Big Silence* or *The Great Silence*, 1968), *Il mercenario* (*The Mercenary*; *A Professional Gun*; or *Revenge of a Gunfighter*, 1968, conceived by Giorgio Arlorio and Franco Solinas for Pontecorvo), *Vamos a matar compañeros* (*Campañeros*, 1970), and *Che c'entriamo noi con la rivoluzione* (*What Am I Doing in the Middle of the Revolution*, 1972); Mario Amendola and Duilio Coletti; Lucio Fulci's *Le colt cantarono la morte e fu . . . tempo di massacro* (*The Brute and the Beast*, *Colt Concert*, or *Massacre Time*, 1966); and Tonino Valerii's *Per il gusto di uccidere* (*For the Taste of Killing*; *Lanky Fellow*; or *Taste for Killing*, 1966), *I giorni dell'ira* (*Blood and Grit*; *Day of Anger*; *Days of Wrath*; or *Gunlaw*, 1967), *Il prezzo del potere* (*The Price of Power* or *Texas*, 1969), and *Il mio nome è Nessuno* (*Lonesome Gun* or *My Name Is Nobody*, 1973). And there were others as well: Damiani's *Quien sabe?* (*A Bullet for the General*, 1966); Florestano Vancini's *I lunghi giorni della vendetta* (*Long Days of Vengeance*, 1967); Carlo Lizzani's *Requiescant* (*Kill and Pray* or *Kill and Say Your Prayers*, 1966); Sergio Sollima's *Faccia a faccia* (1967); Giulio Questi's *Se sei vivo spara* (*Django, Kill . . . If You Live, Shoot!*, 1967); Franco Giraldi's *Sette donne per i MacGregor* (*7 Women for the MacGregors* or *Up the MacGregors*, 1967); and Tinto Brass's *Yankee* (1966). All of these directors embraced the genre and exploited it symbolically and metaphorically, often with positive results. But their films incorporated current events, not unlike the political films of the same period.

In the complex storylines of these films, as in classic westerns, the main characters no longer faced death only at the end of their journeys. Death seemed to follow them at every moment. In Enzo G. Castellari's *Keoma* (*Desperado*; *Django Rides Again*; *Django's Great Return*; or *The Violent Breed*, 1976), the genre's swan song, death is embodied by an old woman in rags. The lines of her face show utter exhaustion and a lack of will to live. The antiheroes of Italian westerns were given ample time to play before their true test. But these characters still had many obstacles to overcome and rarely did they employ virtue or skill to do so. In many cases, it was the main character himself who no longer had a reason to live.

Italian westerns made abundant—and at times unconventional—use of coffins, cemeteries, and dead bodies. Cadavers were gathered up by bounty killers; churches were desecrated; coffins rarely contained the deceased, but rather money, gold, weapons, and bullets, often serving as makeshift homes and hiding places; cemeteries were used to hide buried treasure and were the ideal backdrop for duels. Solitary gunslingers emerged as the preferred stars, and they became increasingly motivated by social causes, protests, and the Mexican rebellion. They often dreamt of impossible revolutions and ably exploited folkloric genres that previously had been the vehicle of conservative ideals and ideologies.

For some time, westerns seemed to share the militant and student causes of the era's political films, and in some cases became the models for mass militancy.

Contemporary history was seemingly ever-present in these films, observed critic Enzo Natta in 1968. "There is a clear reawakening of the Third World, of a rebellion by the disinherited peoples of the world, the black ghettoes, the militants, and the violent reaction to colonialism in the Congo, Angola, and Latin America."[58]

In films like *Se sei vivo spara* and Giulio Petroni's *Tepepa* (*Blood and Guns* or *Long Live the Revolution*, 1968), directors carefully explored the iconography and rituals of death: massacres, hangings with the condemned suspended upside-down, torture, the spirit of rebellion. Imagery from Nazi tortures and reprisals during World War II was next to unavoidable for this generation of filmmakers. On one hand, it served as metaphorical scenery for the present; on the other hand, it reignited the memory of a near past that refused to be erased.

Between the films of Leone and Tessari and those made in the following decade, the western seemed to become a sort of foreign legion that enlisted mercenaries from all walks of life: directors who had been disinherited by neorealism, displaced citizens, and artisanal directors who were capable of nearly anything.[59] All together, these directors seemed thoroughly convinced of the genre's symbolic power and its ability to retell stories of the present. At the height of 1968, a hardly memorable director, Gian Andrea Rocco, made the right film at exactly right time with his homage to feminism, *Giarrettiera Colt* (*Garter Colt*), shot on location in Sardinia with actress Nicoletta Machiavelli.

As for other film genres, some of the most important composers—Morricone, Riz Ortolani, Luis Enrique Bacalov, Carlo Rustichelli, and Bruno Nicolai—contributed scores.

In a career spanning over forty years, Morricone composed literally hundreds of film scores. But it was with Leone that he reached his highest moments. In these scores, the music was fundamentally linked to the dialogue and at times became the star itself. Morricone's music was an essential element of these films; it became the dialogue of the actors themselves. His sounds took the place of words and foreshadowed action. They became the guiding force that redefined the musical landscape of the western. Where previous soundtracks featured popular ballads, now there were whistles, whips, bells, and Jew's harps mixed with violins, a horse's neigh, and the notes of a harmonica. Morricone created rhythms that no longer had an evocative function. They served to slow down time, to inflate emotion, to observe the decomposition of the action by increasing attention and awareness of even the smallest details. Most important, they dug deep into the characters themselves and at times came to mark their rhythms of life.[60]

Tonino Delli Colli, Carlo di Palma, and Giuseppe Ruzzolini were among the camera operators on these films. And while Adriano Bolzoni, Franco Solinas, and Fernando di Leo were the names most commonly associated with these films, other veterans also had a hand in production: Ennio Flaiano and Suso Cecchi d'Amico, Luciano Vincenzoni, Age and Scarpelli, Ennio de Concini, and Franco (Kim) Arcalli, not to mention Lina Wertmüller, Freda, Margheriti, Mastrocinque, and Squitieri.

On one hand, there emerged a marked emphasis on the motivation for mass murder in these films. Bloodshed and the celebration of the rituals of death became central to the stories. On the other hand, some directors chose the path of bloodlessness in films in which the heroes achieved justice using only their fists. The triumphant pair, Bud Spencer and Terence Hill of the Trinity movies, made its debut in E. B. Clucher's *Lo chiamavano Trinity* (*They Call Him Trinity* or *My Name is Trinity*, 1971). They drew their inspiration from the comic films of Mack Sennett rather than the westerns of the 1940s and 1950s. During its final season, the Italian western absorbed the comic-heroic film's taste for parody, in which heroic endeavors were typically satirized and bloodshed omitted entirely. Brawls took the place of massacres. There were Rabelaisian feasts and showdowns punctuated by slaps in the face and kicks to the rear end. These films attracted a younger audience that had abandoned comedies in the early 1970s, turning its back on the great Italian filmmakers.

Even the directors who truly believed in the power of political films suddenly came to a grinding halt during the era of Red Brigade terror and assassinations of judges, union workers, and government officials. This phenomenon gave

birth to a new popular film genre that began with the films of Petri and Dia-
mani, the so-called *poliziottesco* ("cop thriller" films). Their models were films
like Michael Winner's *Death Wish* (1974) and Don Siegel's *Dirty Harry*, yet
the ideology behind them was entirely different. They told the story of the
disintegration of the urban fabric, the citizen's lack of security at home, the
growing scourge of drugs and delinquency, the escalation of violence, and the
birth of new criminal powers that controlled territories from Sicily all the way
to Milan. As a result, many cities in the south and north of Italy came to
resemble the large urban centers of America.[61] These films were often based
on stories taken straight from the headlines, and they used real events as
examples of how an urban environment could easily degenerate. Action was
the centerpiece of these movies and violence was depicted as something very
real that could happen to anyone, unlike the violence of the westerns that
was shown in an imaginary or metaphorical light. Even a director like Lizzani
decided to make a cop thriller movie. His works, which explored political and
social themes using stories taken from the headlines, led the way for many
others: *Banditi a Milano* (*Bandits in Milan* or *The Violent Four*, 1968), *Barbagia*
(*The Tough and the Mighty*, 1969), *Roma bene* (*Roman High Society*, 1971),
Torino nera (*Black Turin*, 1972), and *San Babila ore 20: un delitto inutile* (*San
Babila-8 P.M.*, 1975). These films told the story of a well-off, industrialist
society that had idly watched the emergence of neighborhoods where an-eye-
for-an-eye was the law of the land and where the police were powerless. Some
directors, like Fernando di Leo—who had made a controversial film about the
decay of marriage, *Brucia ragazzo, brucia* (*Burn, Boy, Burn* or *A Woman on
Fire*, 1968)—produced movies where violence was depicted in all forms imaginable: *I ragazzi del massacro* (*The Boys Who Slaughter*; *Naked Violence*; or *Sex
in the Classroom*, 1969), based on a novel by Giorgio Scerbanenco; *Il boss* (*The
Boss*; *Murder Inferno*; or *Wipeout!*, 1972), *La mala ordina* (*Black Kingpin*; *Hired
to Kill*; *Hit Men*; *The Italian Connection*; *Manhunt*, *Manhunt in Milan*; or *Manhunt in the City*, 1972); *Il poliziotto è marcio* (*Shoot First, Die Later*, 1973); *La
città sconvolta: caccia spietata ai rapitori* (*Kidnap Syndicate*, 1975); and *I padroni
della città* (*The Big Boss*; *Blood and Bullets*; *Mister Scarface*; or *Rulers of the City*,
1976). These works would later be recognized by directors like Tarantino as a
fundamental element in the formation of their own films. Other directors, like
Stelvio Massi, told the stories of cops who—as in Siegel's and Eastwood's
films—were not very different from the criminals they were tracking down:
Mark il poliziotto (*Blood, Sweat, and Fear* or *Mark of the Cop*, 1975), *Mark il
poliziotto spara per primo* (*Mark the Policeman Always Shoots First*, 1975), *La
legge violenta della squadra anticrimine* (*Cross Shot*, 1976), *Poliziotto senza paura*
(*Fatal Charm*; *Fearless*; or *Magnum Cop*, 1977), *Sbirro, la tua legge è lenta* . . .

la mia no! (*Copper, Your Laws are Slow . . . But Mine Aren't!*, 1979), and *Poliziotto, solitudine e rabbia* (*The Rebel*, 1980). A number of cop thrillers were also made by directors of westerns and horror films, from Mario Caiano to Umberto Lenzi, from Enzo Castellari to Giuliano Carnimeo.

Of all the low-budget films made during the 1960s and 1970s, sexy movies guaranteed the highest profit margin. Unlike pornographic films, sexy films had a minimal risk of censorship or screening limitations. As the genre continued to grow, it invaded nearly every other, except for the porn industry itself.

For producers and operators, sexy and pornographic films represented a last-ditch effort to revive their businesses before closing their doors. The genre debuted in 1959 with a striptease in Alessandro Blasetti's *Europa di notte* (*Europe by Night* or *European Nights*). It was then developed in a series of documentaries on nightlife in all the major cities of the world. Later films would investigate sexual behavior in primitive civilizations and the industrialized world. Using a mixture of feigned educational intent and pseudo-documentary techniques, many of these films attempted to push the envelope of social norms by violating visual taboos, even when supposed shots of exclusive nightclubs in Asia seemed to have been made with shoestring budgets in a nightspot outside of Milan or on the beaches of the Adriatic. Low-budget horror films would continue to be more successful, but these cheaply produced documentaries—like Renzo Russo's *Mondo caldo di notte* (*Hot World by Night*, 1962) and Elio Montesti's *Nudi per vivere* (*Strip to Live*, 1964)—promised to show forbidden images and to offer more and more revealing shots of women's bodies.

After *Mondo sexy di notte* (*Sexy World by Night*) the year 1963 saw an explosion of films with titles that included the word *sexy*: Roberto Bianchi's *Sexy follie* (*Sexy Follies*), Mino Loy's *Sexy magico* (*Magical Sexy*), Bianchi's *Sexy nel mondo* (*Sexy the World Over*), Osvaldo' Civirani's *Sexy proibito* (*Prohibited Sex*), Marcello Martini's *Sexy proibitissimo* (*The Most Prohibited Sex*), and Pasquale Oscar de Fina's *Sexy ad alta tensione* (*High Voltage Sexy*). Fake documentaries explored the female body as if it were the landscape of an undiscovered continent. Gualtiero Jacopetti enjoyed a whopping success with pseudo-investigative films in which he sought to document every trace of primitive behavior in modern civilization, including sadomasochist rituals, cannibalism, and peculiar and horrifying foods.

The growth of sexy films continued throughout the 1960s, ultimately becoming part of the cultural landscape. As permissiveness became more commonplace and many taboos fell by the wayside, cinema was not the only medium that played with women's rear ends as a lure. Who can forget the Jesus jeans ad campaign with its peremptory and hardly puzzling slogan: "If you love me, follow me"? Olivero Toscani, one of the most controversial figures of the era, was to thank for that one. Eroticism became part of all forms of media and even contaminated weekly news magazines and serious—albeit backward— national newspapers like *Il corriere della sera*. The overdose of erotic imagery produced some small societal changes but did not affect the deep transformation of the collective consciousness imagined by Pasolini in the trailers for his films, beginning with *The Decameron*. Thanks to the success of *The Decameron*, which earned over 4 billion lire, 1960s erotic films sought out cultural nobility through elaborate costumes that were quickly removed and often also resorted to prestigious literary works for legitimacy.

Pasolini's success paved the way for myriad erotic, episodic films in which Sade and Von Masoch were used as would-be inspiration when, in truth, they were inspired by the songs and atmosphere of army barracks, fraternities, and brothels.

Not long after, Samperi's *Grazie zia* (*Come Play with Me* or *Thank You Aunt*) and *Malizia* (*Malice* or *Malicious*) created the prototype for the soft-porn film that explored vice in the family and the problem of sexual initiation among adolescents. Samperi, following in the footsteps of Bellocchio, had already attacked the institution of family in upper-class Italy. After directors like Bellocchio and Ferreri had cast aside all taboos in their films, the family and the home became the ideal backdrop for horror and the perfect depositories of all known forms of perversion and psychopathological sexuality. The progressive saturation of the market continued for four or five years. After all avenues of medieval and Renaissance storytelling had been exhausted, directors looked inward and brought back the keyhole gaze of maids, nurses, young teachers, and nannies, not to mention stepmothers, young widows, and even career and military women.

Toward the end of the 1970s, pornographic theaters first began to appear in Italy: initially just a handful, then tens and hundreds of them. Unfortunately, for every one of these red-light theaters that opened, at least ten, or even twenty, second- and third-run theaters in small towns and the outskirts of big cities closed. By the beginning of the 1980s, only the first-run theaters were left.

Fathers, Sons, and Nephews

The last period for which an Italian cinematographic class photo could be attempted was that which spanned the 1960s through the mid-1970s. The group was dense and it united directors from at least four generations. But most amazing are the affinities among them, their bloodlines and family trees, open and hidden relationships, innovation and respect for tradition, and the concerted effort to help the entire system grow and to establish a clear directorial consciousness.

Rocco e i suoi fratelli (*Rocco and His Brothers*, 1960), a tragedy in five acts on the ills of being uprooted and the subsequent loss of identity, was the last film that brought Visconti into contact with Italy's general public.[62] Visconti had decided to make a contribution to the debate over the overwhelming phenomenon of internal immigration from the south to the north. He did so by his own fashion, using a short story by Giovanni Testori as the basis for a powerfully operatic fresco: a southern family of five brothers, led by a mother who is both mother and father, takes its chances by leaving its native farmland in search of better luck in the factories of Milan. While the spirit of Gramsci is left to the mercy of the storyline, notes of Verdi and Puccini can be heard throughout this film. The balance among its parts is remarkable, as is the admixture of naturalistic and symbolic elements in the acting and sets. Visconti had extraordinary ability in directing his actors and impregnating every movement and line with meaning. He was a master at revealing the characters' past and future in their faces and in the backdrops against which they moved. This was an astonishing and contradictory film; Visconti had chosen a classical form of storytelling to recount a social and economic phenomenon that had yet to be studied in depth. From a formal and stylistic point of view, Visconti was perhaps more prone to incorporate elements of French cinema and contemporary literature than his peers. Together, his works have an exceptional inner coherence and cohesion even when the subject matter was no longer the lower class, but rather, the aristocracy. The influence of Renoir in his films is clear, but upon closer examination, so is that of Ophüls and Stroheim, Cocteau, and Duvivier. Following the completion of *Rocco e i suoi fratelli*, Visconti would embark on a long cycle of his reunification with the nineteenth-century novel and the world of belonging. Following his perfect gem *Il lavoro* (*The Job*, his segment in *Boccaccio '70*, 1962), in which he parodied Antonioni and alienation, Visconti immediately set out to make his grandiose fresco, *Il gattopardo* (*The Leopard*, 1963). The direction, production, acting, and camerawork in this film were spectacularly powerful. It is among the greatest examples of stylization and narrative ability in the entire history of Italian cinema. Of all the characters, Prince Salina was perhaps his most authentic alter-ego. But the novel itself—its structure, meaning, and ambience—had been his true inspiration. As if to refute Proust, Visconti unfolded his imagery entirely, thus releasing his powers of synaesthesis and his remarkable ability to enhance the power of dialogue. Tomasi di Lampedusa's novel and other literary texts (including some operas) offered a perfect world from which Visconti could extract sound and noise, tactile sensations, visual emotion, and fragrance. Through his cinematic versions of these works, he could re-create the fragrance of an era and bring a story to sigh out loud.[63]

A comparison of the original text, literary adaptation in the screenplay, and the final choice shows how the conversion of verbal signs into visual signs tends to eliminate any unpredictable elements. In the process of final visualization, it preserves and empowers those signs present in the screenplay. This was underscored by the fact that the narrator comes to identify with the character in the story. More here than in *Senso* (*Livia* or *The Wanton Countess*), Visconti was paying homage to a world that was disappearing—but also to a new world, just emerging. He did so by celebrating the beauty and youth in characters Angelica (Claudia Cardinale) and Tancredi (Alain Delon) as absolute values. *Il gattopardo* is a monumental film and the greatest manifestation of Visconti's sophistication and vision of the world. Even decades after its release, foreign filmmakers would continue to be inspired by it (think of Martin Scorsese's *The Age of Innocence*, 1993). No Italian directors attempted a similar production, especially after it contributed to the closing of Titanus. With *Vaghe stelle dell'Orsa* (*Sandra of a Thousand Delights*, 1965),[64] *Lo straniero* (*The Stranger*, 1967), *La caduta degli dei* (*The Damned*, 1969), *Morte a Venezia* (*Death in Venice*, 1971), *Ludwig* (1973), *Gruppo di famiglia in un interno* (*Conversation Piece*, 1974), and *L'innocente* (*The Innocent* or *The Intruder*, 1976), Visconti continued to pursue an ideal of formal precision and to develop his ability in orchestrating subject matter set against the greatest moments of history. The breadth of his stories put him on par with the very authors from whom he drew: Mann, Proust, and D'Annunzio. But in some of his films (particularly *La caduta degli dei*, *Morte a Venezia*, and *Ludwig*), Visconti expanded his cinematic models and maestros—from Renoir to Ophüls, Sternberg, and Duvivier. Visconti's world was rife with shapes and signs borrowed from all the arts.

But with every film he made, his relationships with authors and directors seemed to become more strained. In many of his interviews, he expressed disdain for some of his colleagues from the 1960s. He appeared to desire solitude in the final part of his career and it became more difficult for him to understand and depict the present. It is now up to the new generation of directors to carry forward his legacy of classic cinema in which nothing is left to chance and the story is precisely structured at every turn.

While Bernardo Bertolucci called Pasolini's first film the reinvention of Italian cinema, Franceso Rosi has been widely recognized for his contributions to the vocabulary, morphology, and syntax of Italian film. Rosi assimilated a great deal of Visconti's cinema, but from the outset, he sought his own path and carefully studied American commercial film genres. With his first film, *La sfida* (*The Challenge*, 1958), he portrayed Naples as a cultural tragedy by removing any picturesque elements in order to "show what was beneath" the city's surface. From the outset, he demonstrated that he had an eye that allowed him to translate the precariousness of Neapolitans' existence, the symbolic meanings of their gestures, their stares and silences, and the relationship between individuals and the cityscape. His intelligence lay in his not wanting to create a perfectly seamless story, but in knowing how to make every act significant. Borrowing from Visconti and Ernesto de Martino, Rosi tried to show the presence of mythology in the landscape and workaday gestures. He was also inspired by folktales. His *C'era una volta* (*Cinderella: Italian Style* or *More Than a Miracle*, 1967), based on Giambattista Basile's *Pentamerone* or *Lo cunto de li cunti* (*The Story of Stories*), is wrongly considered today to be one of his minor works. In his films set in Italy, the irrational power of myth, ritual, and mystery cults was confined to the dark corners of the country's social fabric and was portrayed as a manifestation of madness devoid of any sacral aura. But in *Momento della verità* (*The Moment of Truth*) and *Carmen*, set in Spain, or *Cronaca di una morte annunciata* (*Chronicle of a Death Foretold*), set in South America, he gave these elements a festive and sacral quality. The characters in these films celebrate rituality oscillating between terror and ecstasy, between darkness and light.

Rosi was also inspired by the mythology in literary texts like Carlo Levi's *Cristo si è fermato a Eboli* (*Christ Stopped at Eboli*) and Primo Levi's account of his return from Auschwitz, *La tregua* (*The Truce*). In these works, he found a vibrant message that led him to revisit the protection of every individual's right to life with dignity.

In Italy, mythology has lost some of its splendor with the passing of time. It has become increasingly dark around the edges. As if by a natural metamorphosis, mythology has been transformed into a mystery cult in Italy—in a society that rides the cusp between backwardness and progress: political mystery, judicial mystery, governmental mystery, military mystery, and even economic mystery; mysteries destined never to be solved.

From *Salvatore Giuliano* to *Lucky Luciano*, from *Il caso Mattei* (*The Mattei Affair*) to *Tre fratelli* (*Three Brothers*) and *Dimenticare Palermo* (*The Palermo Connection* or *To Forget Palermo*), Rosi's films dealt with the networks of power and control in Italy, the Mafia, and its web of economic and political ties. In order to ensure its survival through a constant game of intermarriages, intersections, and interchange, organized crime—and by extension, every type of power—co-opts omnipresent forces above suspicion. In his works, an omniscient and all-powerful eye seems to regulate the Mafia-controlled world.

It is difficult to determine to what extent he is a true disciple of Visconti (even though his relationship to him as a director of opera is clear), but Franco Zeffirelli is certainly a descendant. He developed a dual career as an equally successful director of films and operas. He brought literary and theatrical works, from Shakespeare to operas, to the screen. His sets were lavish and meticulously accurate. His actors were top-notch and his films appealed to an international audience. Like Visconti, Zeffirelli was virtually unaffected by the transformations that took place during the last four decades of Italian film history. Over the course of his career, he developed a classical concept of *mise en scène* and direction of actors that he drew from his experience in theater. He was thus able to optimize his use of sets, costumes, lighting, and the composition of every frame (the two films that established him as a world-class director were *The Taming of the Shrew* with Richard Burton and Elizabeth Taylor, 1967, and *Romeo and Juliet*, 1968). At the same time, he satisfied the needs of American producers. At a certain point, he began telling stories that were no longer drawn from theatrical or literary texts. At the end of the 1990s, he made what is perhaps his best film, *Tea with Mussolini* (1999), in which he re-created a moment from his own life in 1930s Florence. In this film, he was able to create just the right balance of attention to detail, emotional involvement, irony, and pleasure in directing some of the great women of screen and stage. An account of Maria Callas during the year preceding her death, *Callas Forever* (2002), was an autobiographical film brimming with memories and passion.

Mauro Bolognini was another director who followed in Visconti's footsteps while using a more malleable visual vocabulary and style and different narrative models. During the 1960s, he reached the height of his career with a group of films. When viewed back to back, they are impressive: for their quality and the diversity of visual techniques; the direction of the actors; the assimilation of figurative, dramatic, and literary works; the director's mastery of all elements of the medium and his ability to tell the story of post-unification Italy through heroes that came from different walks of life, now aristocratic, now middle-class, now proletarian: *Il bell'Antonio* (*Bell'Antonio*, 1960), *La viaccia* (*The Lovemakers*, 1960), *Senilità* (*Careless*, 1961), *Agostino* (1962), *Metello* (1969), and *Libera, amore mio!* (*Libera, My Love*, 1975).

Bolognini was not a director who suffered from imperial illusions. He always took a humble, detached, and servile attitude in his approach to literary texts, considering them a privileged source of inspiration for his works. Bolognini's films must also be considered as a cohesive and continuous body of

work. Inspired by writers like Chelli, Pratesi, Svevo, Pratolini, Brancati, Moravia, Parise, and Pasolini, in the 1960s he began to draw—almost exclusively—
from stories set during the one hundred years of unified Italy. To this mixture
he added his Renaissance-inspired workshop method and an unmatched ability to tell the stories of Italian cities—from Trieste to Venice, from Bologna
to Florence, from Rome to Catania—with a sensitivity that conveyed the soul
of the city itself.[65] Bolognini worked with screenwriters like Giuseppe Berto,
Pasolini, Goffredo Parise, Testori, Pratolini, and Moravia; production designers like Garbuglia, Mario Chiari, Polidori, and Luigi Schiaccianoce; costume
designers like Danilo Donati, Piero Tosi, and Gabriella Pescucci; composers
like Piccioni, Trovaioli, and Morricone; and camera operators like Rotunno,
Nannuzzi, Tonti, and Martelli. In other words, he used only the best and most
creative people available at the time. In many ways, Bolognini followed in
Visconti's footsteps, but with one eye on the ruling class and another on the
emerging classes. His films either cannibalized society or fought to escape the
anonymity that history had imposed on them for centuries. More than anything else, he was fascinated by women: they were the sisters and daughters
of the heroines in Puccini's operas. Bolognini's women had courageously
begun their social ascent; often pitted against history, the results sometimes
left them overwhelmed—but they always managed to assert themselves with
respect to the men in their lives.

Like the main character in Ferdinando Camon's novel La donna dei fili
(The Woman Made of Threads), Bolognini's films were a tapestry of cinema,
history, and eighteenth- and nineteenth-century literature.[66] He systematically interwove all of these elements into a gigantic, panoramic fresco that he
developed continuously. More than any other director, he was able to capture
and depict the history and geography of unified Italy.

Besides being one of the fathers of postwar Italian cinema together with Zavattini, Camerini, and Blasetti (whose Io, io, io e gli altri. . .[Me, Me, Me . . .
and the Others, 1965] is a film worth remembering), Vittorio de Sica was at
the core of an aristocratic group of comedy filmmakers who were at the top of
their game in the 1960s.[67] After years of working frenetically as an actor, with
mixed reviews as a director, he rediscovered his desire and the strength to
make movies again: first with La ciociara (Two Women, 1960, based on the
novel by Moravia); then with a series of vehicle movies created for Sophia
Loren, La riffa (The Raffle, his segment of Boccaccio '70, 1962), Ieri, oggi, e
domani (Yesterday, Today, and Tomorrow, 1963), and Matrimonio all'italiana
(Marriage Italian-Style, 1964). In 1961, just as the "economic miracle" of the

1960s was about to take shape, he made *Il giudizio universale* (*The Last Judgment*), a film that seemed to revive the theme of his *Miracolo a Milano* (*Miracle in Milan*) with more cynicism, spite, and bitterness. His talents as a director were highlighted in the films he made with Sofia Loren, either by herself or paired with Mastroianni. They also showcased his ease behind the camera, using it to enable the actors and facilitate the action without ever revealing his presence. De Sica liked his characters to remain still in the frame, at once constricting them and freeing their dramatic power, physical energy, and sexual charge. Throughout the decade, De Sica's charisma and talent as a storyteller had a visible effect on comedy filmmaking in general as well as its stylistic and narrative development. Following this phase of rediscovered inspiration and blissful creativity, De Sica—perhaps more than any of his peers—began to spread his energy and talent too thin. In the spirit of artisanal filmmaking, he was always too happy to lend a hand to other directors. He failed to take the time to adapt his own cinema to new narrative models. He found himself at a creative impasse and realized that he was losing the very qualities that had driven his cinema from its beginnings. This crisis must have weighed heavily on him and most probably led to his progressive detachment from his longtime collaborator Zavattini.

De Sica left behind a number of successors: first there were all of the comedy directors who would have been unable to exploit their abilities had he not raised the bar with his knack for reading stories in his characters' most mundane acts and his skill in moving so nimbly between comedic and tragic tones. But there were also directors who understood his strength in rereading history through a literary text (like Moravia's *La ciociara* [*Two Women*]) and favoring the human element over ideology at a time when films were becoming more and more political.

Of all the directors who debuted in the 1940s or shortly thereafter, Blasetti's students had the most difficulty. The filmmakers who got their start at the Centro Sperimentale, from De Santis to Puccini and Petrangeli and Lizzani, risked losing their meal ticket if they did not delivery quality films. Puccini's ethic could be applied to many of these filmmakers: "continue to make honest films for honest audiences." Those who did not accept the new standards for production were forced to make advertisements (as in the case of Emmer after the censors massacred his *La ragazza in vetrina* [*Girl in the Window* or *Woman in the Window*], 1960) or to go into television (as was the case of Renato Castellani, who thrived in the new medium). Others had to simply scrape by just to survive. Some young directors, like *enfant prodige* Francesco Maselli, hovered in the shadows (despite his success with *I delfini* [*The Dauphins*], 1960, and *Gli indifferenti* [*Time of Indifference*], 1961), perhaps because of their excessive intelligence and the difficulty in translating their poetic and political sensibility into prosaic films.

For a director like Giuseppe de Santis, three films in twenty years was a less than prolific showing (even though one of these films was *Italiani brava gente* [*Attack and Retreat*], 1964, a considerably demanding and spectacular work). He was determined never to abandon the themes and subject matter in which he believed so strongly. Ultimately, he became one of the few victims of political and commercial censorship in Italy. The history of Italian cinema is more than just the films that were actually made. De Santis was doubtlessly one of the greatest Italian directors, but the 1960s did not see any significant additions to the directorial legacy he had created in the previous decade.

More fortunate than De Santis, Carlo Lizzani was a director capable of a "veritable career in pedestrian filmmaking."[68] He was also a creator of new film genres. He made a series of historical films set during the final years of fascism: *Il gobbo* (*The Hunchback of Rome*, 1960), *L'oro di Roma* (*The Gold of Rome*, 1961), *Il processo di Verona* (*The Verona Trial*, 1963), and *Mussolini ultimo atto* (*The Last Days of Mussolini, The Last Four Days, The Last Tyrant*, or *Mussolini: The Last Four Days*, 1974). He also made an excellent adaptation of Luciano Bianciardi's novel *Vita agra* (*It's a Hard Life*, 1964[69]) and dramatizations of real-life crimes, *Svegliati e uccide* (*Too Soon to Die* or *Wake Up and Die*, 1967) and *Banditi a Milano* (*Bandits in Milan* or *The Violent Four*, 1968). He would continue to make films throughout the 1980s and 1990s at an even pace.

Thanks to De Sica, Pasquale Squitieri made his directorial debut in 1969 with *Io e Dio* (*God and Me*), a heavy-handed editorial on contemporary society that would be followed by westerns in which he was credited as William Redford. Squitieri established his personality as a director with *Camorra* (1972), in which he proved his ability in action films capable of re-creating the world of organized crime in Southern Italy. Like Rosi, he liked to depict the world that he knew and its degenerative social and political fabric. He took on difficult subjects like prefect Cesare Mori's battle against the Mafia during the fascist era or drugs, terrorism, and the most recent forms of organized crime: *I guappi* (*Blood Brothers*, 1973); *L'arma* (*The Gun* or *Sniper*, 1977); *Il Prefetto di ferro* (*The Iron Prefect*, 1977); *Il pentito* (*The Repenter*, 1985); *Il colore dell'odio* (*The Color of Hate*, 1989); and *Li chiamarono . . . briganti* (*Brigands*, 1999), a film on the highway robbers in Southern Italy during the years that followed unification. The exception to his filmography was the biographical *Claretta* (*Claretta Petacci*, 1984), the story of Mussolini's passionately devoted mistress who followed the dictator until the end and was killed with him. Squitieri successfully carried on the legacy of Visconti and Rosi by creating films geared to general audiences and tackling difficult and weighty subject matter. Although he never seemed to reach his greatest potential, the quality of his works never suffered.

During the 1950s, Luigi Zampa was the first director to make historical comedies about the Italian experience. He never lost faith in his work, even when his creative juices flowed less freely. Audiences loved his contemptuous, vitriolic screenplays and Alberto Sordi's memorable performances in movies like *Vigile* (*The Traffic Policeman*, 1960), *Il medico della mutua* (*Be Sick . . . It's Free* or *The Family Doctor*, 1968), and *La contestazione generale* (*Let's Have a Riot*, 1970). Like Germi, he was never afraid to entertain his audience: he had a great sense of rhythm, a terrific sense of humor (bent toward the bizarre), and an unforgiving vision of Italy. Like Germi, he wanted to produce comedies with a "moral." In these films, Zampa exposed and scorned privilege and backwardness, the decline of honesty, human and environmental degradation, opportunism, bureaucratic and legislative absurdities, and Italians' self-serving indifference. But while Germi was exposing classic Italian provincialism in the northeastern region of the Veneto, Zampa's destination was farther away and seemingly foreign to mainland Italy, on the island of Sardinia. In the opening lines of his 1966 film *Una questione d'onore* (*A Question of Honour*), the voiceover informs the viewer: "Sardinia is a land of 24,084 square kilometers [approx. 14,966 square miles], 967,000 inhabitants, 4.5 million sheep, 8,200 boxers, and 36,250 *carabinieri* [Italian paramilitary state police]." Of all the directors who used comedy to depict the stasis and dynamics, frictions and anomalies of a society that refused to change, he was the most Gogolian.

Unlike Zampa, who could not seem to stop the decline of his creative arc during the 1960s, Germi came on the scene during this period and enjoyed his greatest moments of glory.[70] With his Sicilian diptych, *Divorzio all'italiana* (*Divorce—Italian Style*, 1961), which won an Oscar, and *Sedotta e abbandonata* (*Seduced and Abandoned* or *A Matter of Honor*, 1963), and his exploration of Catholic society in the Veneto where he exposed the vices and carnal sins tolerated and absolved by the Catholic institutions of provincial Treviso in *Signore e signori* (*The Birds, Bees, and the Italians*, 1965), he painted a picture of backwardness in the South and the deep North. He showed the survival of tribal and primitive behavior in contemporary Italian society and the self-assured exploitation of religious morality. In doing so, he helped establish enduring regional stereotypes. Were we to search for the presence of well-dissimulated secular spirit in postwar Italian cinema, Zampa and Germi would have to be recognized for their approach in depicting the secularization of the sacred and the difficulties in practicing religion in a society losing all of its moral points of reference. During the final phase of his career, with *Serafino*

(1968), *Le castagne sono buone* (*A Pocketful of Chestnuts*, 1970), *Alfredo, Alfredo* (1973), and *Amici miei* (*My Friends*, 1975), Germi took an anti-ideological high road where his still derisive but melancholic spirit was mixed with a longing for a natural, uncontaminated state of being—a return to existence as a "noble savage."

By the close of the 1960s, the film critic for *Il manifesto*, Italy's communist daily, would write provocatively that "[Antonio] Pietrangeli is the most undervalued Italian director, while Antonioni is the most overrated." Even though the Centro Cinema Città di Cesena has made praiseworthy strides in conserving and publishing his archives and in carefully reevaluating his films, it is fitting that the most significant book devoted to his work is titled *Un'invisibile presenza* (*An Invisible Presence*).[71] During the 1960s, he made a series of films that allowed him to focus on women's emancipation and liberation in society: *Adua e le compagne* (*Adua and Company, Adua and Her Friends* or *Hungry for Love*, 1960); *Fantasmi a Roma* (*Ghosts of Rome* or *Phantom Lovers*, 1961); *La parmigiana* (*The Girl from Parma*, 1963); *La visita* (*The Visitor*, 1964); *Il magnifico cornuto* (*The Magnificent Cuckold*, 1964); *Io la conoscevo bene* (*I Knew Her Well*, 1965); and his posthumously released film, *Come, quando, e perché* (*How, When, and With Whom*, 1969). In these films, he capably created female characters and observed their efforts to adapt to a new social and economic reality. Of all his characters, Adriana, played by Stefania Sandrelli in *Io la conoscevo bene*, has become the most iconic. She was pushed, little by little, to a tragic and desperate end by the persons around her. They considered her a mere sexual object to discard after use.

Embarking on a new phase in his then decades-old career with the energy of a newcomer, Alberto Lattuada made eleven films during the 1960s, on subjects ranging from the sexual problems of adolescence to the adaptation of contemporary as well as sixteenth-century literary works.[72] This rapid pace eventually began to wane, but he never lost his knack for cultured and visually elegant cinema, even when making no effort to hide his taste for voyeurism in revealing the beauty of the female body. His films always maintained close links to European and Italian literature. His adaptations included *Lettere di una novizia* (*Letters from a Novice*, from the novel by Guido Piovene); *La steppa* (*The Steppe*, from Chekov), *La tempesta* (*Tempest*, from Pushkin), and *La mandragola* (*Mandragola: The Love Root* or *Mandrake*, from Nicolò Machiavelli); *Cuore di cane* (*Dog's Heart*, from Bulgakov); and his bizarre masterpiece, *Venga a prender il caffè. . . da noi* (*Come Have Coffee with Us* or *The Man Who Came for Coffee*, from Piero Chiara's novel *La spartizione* or *The Man of Parts*). He also borrowed from history with films like *Fraülein Doktor* (*The Betrayal* or *Fraulein Doktor*), set during World War I. At the same time, he was always in tune with changing attitudes, adolescent angst, self-discovery of sexuality (as in *I dolci inganni* [*Sweet Deceptions*]), and trends that were about to become apparent (as in films like *Il Mafioso* [*Mafioso*], *Sono stato io* [*I Did It* or *It Was I*], and *Le farò da padre* [*Bambina*]). Lattuada alternated between tales intended to educate or serve as an example (*Oh, Serafina!*); stories that confronted environmental or moral problems; and others that depicted the influence of the media, or at least portrayed the symptoms thereof. Of all the so-called calligrapher directors, he proved to be the best at exploring new inroads and developing new high-quality prototypes for comedies, sexy movies, and even mass-appeal titles. His colossal biography *Christopher Columbus* won him an Emmy in 1984.

Renato Castellani's career came to a near-dead stop in the early 1960s. But thanks to television, he made a comeback with two memorable biographies, *Vita di Leonardo* (*I, Leonardo* or *The Life of Leonardo da Vinci*, 1971) and *Giuseppe Verdi* (*The Life of Verdi*, 1982). Unlike Rossellini, Castellani pushed the entertainment value of these films over their educational content. He recognized that television audiences naturally expected a different cinematic approach. Thanks to Rossellini and Castellani, cinematic genres began to migrate toward television and disappeared from theaters; these included literary adaptations but also films with a social message.

The Rossellini Family

Of all the maestros of postwar Italian cinema, Rossellini stood apart from his generation. He always retained his curiosity and love for risk-taking, and he never lost his newcomer's fresh approach. During the final fifteen years of his career, his emphasis was on experimentation. And even though he was not afraid to compromise, his inner restlessness always brought him back to the fold. He slowly abandoned stories for film and began to favor television as a medium to create new forms of recounting history, new dimensions, and new forms of visual storytelling. Rossellini saw history as an attempt to immerse oneself in the past. He based his concept of "total history" on the 1920s French school of *Annales* historians: through the examination of memory and the workaday, he sought to reveal how the past affected present history. At a certain point, Rossellini seemed to embrace a new calling, and he embarked on an entirely new adventure, with the need to free himself from all previous forms of knowledge. Of all of his peers, he was the most restless. Even when he was commissioned to make a film, he always sought to reinvent the medium and explore new possibilities in communication and storytelling.

After *Era notte a Roma* (*Escape by Night* or *Wait for the Dawn*, 1961), a film that breathed the new air of national and international détente, he made *Viva l'Italia* (*Garibaldi*, 1961), a film he was commissioned to make for the centennial of Italy's unification. The latter work would become his model for made-for-television historical films like the lavish production *La prise de pouvoir par Louis XIV* (1966). He would develop these into veritable journeys across human history with *Gli atti degli apostoli* (*Acts of the Apostles*, 1969), *Socrate* (*Socrates*, 1970), *Pascal* (*Blaise Pascal*, 1971), and *Cartesius* (*Descartes*, 1974). He ultimately returned to the birth of the Italian Republic with *Anno uno* (*Italy: Year One* or *Year One*, 1974). Unlike Visconti, who remained virtually the same throughout his career, Rossellini underwent a transformation during the 1960s that marked a new era for Italian directors. He reaffirmed himself as the spiritual father to a new generation of filmmakers who broke onto the scene during those years.

There were many directors who belonged to the Rossellini family of filmmakers.

Ermanno Olmi made his debut with *Il tempo si è fermato* (*Time Stood Still*, 1960) after working for almost ten years making documentaries for Edison Volta, Italy's electric company. A self-taught filmmaker, Olmi was a student of Rossellini's gaze onto the world. To it, he added his ability to emote and to close in on his characters by examining their stories and deciphering the expressions on their faces. His films *Il posto* (*The Job* or *The Sound of Trumpets*, 1961) and *I fidanzati* (*The Engagement* or the *Fiancés*, 1963) took a close and emotionally charged look at the effects of industrialization on agrarian Italy as the economic boom rapidly transformed the country. As if with a magnifying glass, Olmi drew attention to his characters' gestures and facial expressions. He revealed their sense of loss, their feeling of being uprooted, and the difficulties they faced in a world where all the rules had changed. His knowing, powerful gaze captured and communicated the relationship between individual and environment with remarkable precision. After he completed a less than hagiographic biography of Pope John XXIII, *E venne un uomo* (*And There Came a Man* or *A Man Named John*, 1965), and a few films for television, including *I recuperanti* (*The Scavengers*, 1974, based on a story by Mario Rigoni Stern), he made *L'albero degli zoccoli* (*The Tree with the Wooden Clogs*, 1978), a film in which autobiographical and collective memory, evenemential history, and deep history helped create the most inspired monument to agrarian civilization in postwar cinema.

After winning the Palme d'Or at the Cannes Festival, the film became one of the most successful Italian films of all time. But it was also violently attacked by left-wing critics who refuted the story's message of submission to and passive acceptance of one's own destiny. During the tense years of terror-ism in Italy, this film seemed as though it had arrived from another planet, based on a memory that the critics could not tolerate in that form.

Even Vittorio de Seta made some documentaries before debuting with *Banditi a Orgosolo* (*Bandits of Orgosolo*, 1961). This film could perhaps suffice to illustrate a career comprised of just a handful of titles: *Un uomo a metà* (*Almost a Man* or *Half a Man*, 1966); *L'invitata* (*The Uninvited*, 1970); and made-for-television movie, *Diario di un maestro* (*Diary of a School Teacher*, 1972). *Banditi a Orgosolo* deserves a place in the pantheon of documentary films, right next to the works of Flaherty, Ivens, and Grierson.[73] The entire story is told through images: the camera captures the characters' every move-ment as they follow the dictates of centuries-old laws. From the opening frames of the first sequence, showing Sopramonte (a picturesque area outside Orgosolo), the viewer is immersed in an incident where the law is immediately broken. The economy, rituals, and ways of these shepherds have endured for millennia, and the only thing they have taken from modern civilization is the rifle: it helps them hunt but it also facilitates breaking the law.

After a long run as documentary filmmakers, brothers Paolo and Vittorio Taviani debuted together with co-director Valentino Orsini in *Un uomo da bruciare* (*A Man for Burning*, 1962), a biography of Sicilian union organizer Salvatore Carnevale. The following year, the two filmmakers published an essay in the revue *Cinema Nuovo* in which they laid out their cinematic pro-gram. They described their cultural horizon and revealed the tension that pushed them to navigate uncharted seas at a time when ideological certainties were coming apart at the seams. The Taviani films were a mixture of literary culture and cinematic models drawn from Brechtian alienation. But they were also students of Eisenstein's intellectual editing style and believers in ideology as an overarching passion and life choice. Films like *I sovversivi* (*The Subver-sives*, 1967), *Sotto il segno dello scorpione* (*Under the Sign of Scorpio*, 1969), *San Michele aveva un gallo* (*St. Michael Had a Rooster*, 1971), *Allonsanfàn* (1974), and *Padre padrone* (*Father and Master* or *My Father My Master*, 1977, winner of a Palme d'Or in Cannes by a jury chaired by Rossellini) reveal both their stylistic tension and their utopian ideals, their dream of change and their hope for a new age of great social equality. *Sotto il segno dello scorpione* is a polyphonic work. The star is the masses and the story proves how hard it is to subvert reality through words. On the other hand, *San Michele aveva un gallo* is a monodic film focused on a single character whose story takes place in four separate locations. The main character, jailed anarchist Giuio Manieri, carries out an imaginary rebellion in his mind and reaffirms his beliefs in the revolu-tionary power of imagination.

The Taviani brothers' cinema was clearly influenced by early neorealism and particularly by Rossellini. But they were also inspired and enlightened by Chaplin, Bresson, Mann, Goethe, Brecht, Musil, and Pollock. They borrowed elements from the entire cultural spectrum, ranging from psychoanalysis to abstract expressionism and existentialist philosophy. And although they adopted a plurality of styles, irony was often a means of alienation in their films. The style of *Padre padrone* was different from any of the films before it. The film alternates between documentary and highly imaginative lyricality. Loosely based on Gavino Ledda's novel, the story is the character's journey toward liberation. Over the course of the film, he is freed from a state of semi-servitude in a patriarchal society through his acquisition of the Italian language (his father had never allowed him to go to school and as a result, he was illiterate, speaking only Sardinian dialect). The Tavianis' working method, their choice of collaborators, and their creative process constitute an ideal subject of study.

The Tavianis were among the most tenacious filmmakers of their generation. They believed steadfastly in their abilities and they never ceased to defend their creative license. During the 1980s and 1990s they produced their masterpieces: *La notte di San Lorenzo* (*The Night of Shooting Stars* or *The Night of San Lorenzo*, 1980), *Kaos* (*Chaos*, 1984), *Good Morning Babylon* (1986), *Fiorile* (*Wild Flower*, 1992), *Le affinità elettive* (*The Elective Affinities*, 1996), *Tu ridi* (*You Laugh* or *You're Laughing*, 1998), and lastly, their made-for-television adaptation of *Anna Karenina* (2000). When compared with the films of the previous decade, their cinema has greater narrative scope and is more epic in nature. The ideological element always took a backseat with respect to the films' lyricality and epic component. By telling a story from a child's point of view in *San Michele aveva un gallo*, they used her memory and her gaze as a depository for images that seemed drawn from a Homeric epic. This would become a decisive element for the stylistic-narrative turning point for decades to follow. Their films were always about goals to be accomplished, beliefs in an idea; they were about discipline, utopia, and ways of freeing oneself from earthly burdens and ascending to the heavens. In visual, narrative, and rhythmic elements, at times their scope was expansive, enveloping the maximum space possible (as in Ford); at other times it became more concentrated (as in Bresson). Like Michelangelo, the Tavianis were born to practice the art of sculpture in their films, removing the surface to reveal beauty underneath. Even though they seemed to have co-opted Tolstoy's concept of earthly religiosity, they never forgot the joys that life can offer at any given moment.

After beginning his career as part of an exceptional trinity of co-directors with the Taviani brothers, Valentino Orsini released his *I dannati della terra*

(*The Damned of the Earth*, 1967) at the height of the student and antiwar movements of 1968. The film recounts the story of an Italian intellectual who must face the reality of the Third World. Orsini was much less Rossellian than the Taviani brothers. He was perhaps closer to Visconti or De Santis in terms of filmmaking. He was more interested in delivering a clear, unambiguous message than in style per se. He belonged to the generation of directors who still believed that movies could help bring about change. Both *Corbari* (1970) and *Uomini e no* (*Men and Not Men*, 1979, based on the novel by Vittorini) reexamined the partisan movement. By looking into the shadows of the resistance and its short-lived revolutionary spirit, these works cast light on the reverberations that continued to resonate in Italy. His last film was a "private" film, *Figlio mio, infinitamente caro* (*My Dearest Son*, 1984), in which he explored the crises—in particular, drugs—that broke up a family over the course of twenty years.

Director Giuliano Montaldo made an impressive debut in 1961 with his *Tiro al piccione* (*Pigeon Shoot*), a film about anti-conformism and the puppet fascist government in Salò. Like many of his generation, he was motivated by his civil and political beliefs. In 1970, he made one of his most memorable and morally charged directorial efforts, *Sacco e Vanzetti* (*Sacco and Vanzetti*), with a cast that included Gian Maria Volonté and Riccardo Cucciolla. Whether depicting minor or major historical events—like his World War II epic, *Agnese va a morire* (*And Agnes Chose to Die*), based on the novel by Renata Viganò—Montaldo always showed remarkable ability as a narrator. He was equally gifted in period films, like his *Giordano Bruno* and the colossal *Marco Polo*, one of the earliest Italian productions created for an international television audience. In the 1980s, he made *Gli occhiali d'oro* (*The Gold Rimmed Glasses*), based on Giorgio Bassani's novel (translated as *The Gold-Rimmed Spectacles*), and *Tempo di uccidere* (*The Short Cut* or *Time to Kill*, adapted from Ennio Flaiano's novel), a film in which he delved into the realm of the private with unprecedented mastery.

Farthest-left writers attacked directors like Rosi, Petri, Montaldo, and Damiani with a violence unheard of even in the darkest years of the Cold War. For the most part, these critics wrote for the review *Ombre rosse*, published in Turin, and looked to Goffredo Fofi as their guiding voice.

Director Giuseppe Ferrara's films depicted postwar Italian history with remarkable cohesiveness, including a series of unresolved mysteries surrounding the Mafia, religion, and Italian as well as international politics. After receiving a degree in humanities with a thesis on 1950s Italian cinema, he began directing historical documentaries. His breakthrough came in 1970 with *Il sasso in bocca* (*Stone in the Mouth*).[74] Never fearing to test the limits of

politics, law, diplomacy, and religion, he courageously re-created and reinter-
preted the characters that shaped Italian history. His most important works
were *Faccia di spia* (*Face of a Spy*, 1975), *Panagulis Zei* or *Panagulis vive* (*Pana-
goulis Lives*, 1979), *Cento giorni a Palermo* (*A Hundred Days in Palermo*, 1983),
Il caso Moro (*The Moro Affair*, 1986), *Giovanni Falcone* (1993), *Segreto di stato*
(*State Secret*, 1994), and *I banchieri di Dio—il caso Calvi* (*The Bankers of God:
The Calvi Affair* or *God's Bankers*, 2001).

Liliana Cavani, who received her degree from the Centro Sperimentale
in Rome, was one of the most restless and erudite directors of her generation
in both style and content.[75] After making some important documentaries, she
debuted with a full-length film, *Franceso d'Assisi* (*St. Francis of Assisi*), which
portrayed St. Francis of Assisi in an entirely new light. Her Francis was a
slightly depressed protestor and an avid, albeit mad, supporter of "armed broth-
erhood"—the ideal defender of the 1968 student movement. The historical
figures she would depict later in her career, like Galileo and Leo Milarepa,
interested her inasmuch as their teachings were relevant to current issues.
They offered nonviolent models of dissent with regard to the contemporary
establishment. Madness would be the star of the films that would follow: *Oltre
la porta* (*Behind the Door, Beyond Obsession, Beyond the Door, Jail Bird* or *The
Secret Beyond the Door*) and *Al di là del bene e del male* (*Beyond Good and Evil*
or *Seeds of Evil*). Her strongest film, and the one most influenced by Visconti,
was *Il portiere di notte* (*The Night Porter*), a story of sadomasochist violence
with performances by Dirk Bogarde and Charlotte Rampling. In this film, the
memory of Nazism is told through a tale of attraction and repulsion with a
physicality never before seen in her films. Following in the footsteps of Visconti and Pasolini, she displayed an ability to create a diversity of tones and
camera angles at a time when Nazism had become a pretext for breaking the
rules of cinema. Other films worth remembering include *Pelle* (*The Skin*,
1981), her version of Curzio Malaparte's novel; *Interno berlinese* (*The Berlin
Affair*, 1985), an international success; and her renewed interest in St. Francis,
Francesco (*St. Francis of Assisi*, 1989), which she made some twenty years after
the first film.

While Lina Wertmüller may have had less intellectual ambition and fewer
intellectual concerns than Cavani, she had a much freer, more joyful sense of
spectacle. She showed remarkable ability in mastering different styles and was
able to produce comedy and drama with equal energy and passion. Few directors from her generation were able to deliver such a strong creative identity
in the images and stories of their films. This identity is present even in her
lesser works, in which last-minute reworking of the scripts took its toll. Her
debut film, *I basilischi* (*The Basilisks* or *The Lizards*, 1963), seemed to position

her somewhere between Germi and Olmi. The Italian "musicals" that followed starred Rita Pavone, who, together with singer Adriano Celentano, was Italy's pop music idol. Then Wertmüller truly established her identity as a director with a series of films starring Giancarlo Giannini: *Mimí metallurgico ferito nell'onore* (*The Seduction of Mimi*, 1972), *Film d'amore e d'anarchia* (*Love and Anarchy*, 1973), *Travolti da un insolito destino in un azzurro mare d'agosto* (*Swept Away* or *Swept Away . . . by an Unusual Destiny in the Blue Sea of August*, 1974), and *Pasqualino Settebellezze* (*Pasqualino* or *Pasqualino: Seven Beauties*, 1975). The films she made during the 1980s and 1990s did not enjoy the same success, although her *Io speriamo che me la cavo* (*Ciao, Professore!* or *Me Let's Hope I Make It*, 1992, based on the collection of schoolchildren's essays by teacher Marcello d'Orta) is worth remembering, thanks to a balanced performance by Paolo Villaggio.

In his novels, Alberto Bevilacqua aptly created worlds where individual and collective histories mixed with memory, enchantment, passion, and mystery. But he was never able to bring his literary ability to the big screen despite an auspicious start with *La califfa* (*Lady Caliph*, 1970). With film after film, he seemed intent on following in Fellini's footsteps. His attempts at breaching the oneiric dimension included films like *Questa specie d'amore* (*This Kind of Love*, 1971), *Attenti al buffone* (*Eye of the Cat*, 1975), *Bosco d'amore* (*Forest of Love*, 1981), and *La donna delle meraviglie* (*Woman of Wonders*). But, unlike Pasolini, he never convincingly bridged the gap between literature and cinema.

Born in 1922 (the year Mussolini marched on Rome), Damiano Damiani spent roughly fifteen years making documentaries and writing screenplays before making his break-out police thriller *Il rossetto* (*Lipstick* or *Red Lips*), a film seemingly inspired by Germi's *Un maledetto imbroglio* (*The Facts of Murder*, 1959). Damiani was the perfect example of the mid-level director. He was capable of producing commercially successful films and he knew how to reach his audience. He possessed a remarkable ability to dramatize important episodes in Italian socio-political life. He could be categorized somewhere between Rosi and Lizzani: from the former, he gleaned his interest in the Mafia and corruption in the 1960s; from the latter, his taste for dramatizing real-life events. During the 1960s and 1970s, he averaged a film per year. In the twenty years that followed, he alternated between film and television. His first chapter of the television Mafia saga *La piovra* (1983) would become a model for Italian television exports. His perspicacity served him well in portraying historical events. He seemed to favor dramatic action over psychological tension when exposing corruption and iniquity in Italian political and civil institutions. Above all, he loved to navigate uncharted waters, to redefine genres, and to explore new possibilities in previously tested narrative models. He made adaptations of works by writers like Elsa Morante (*L'isola di Arturo* [*Arturo's Island*], 1961), Alberto Moravia (*La noia* [*The Empty Canvas*], 1962, from the novel *La noia* or *Boredom*), and Leonardo Sciascia (*Il giorno della civetta* [*The Day of the Owl*], 1968). He worked with Sicilian stereotypes and he tried his hand at every genre, ranging from westerns to horror films. His films always held the right balance between experimentation and commercial success. The subject matter he chose involved audiences emotionally, with the right mix of spectacle and drama. At a certain point, he began to construct stories around detectives and magistrates: figures who, for better or worse, tried to remain true to themselves and their beliefs at any cost. But repeated commercial success began to take a toll on Damiani's identity as a director over the arc of his career. Nonetheless, many of his films are worth reconsidering today: *La rimpatriata* (*The Reunion*, 1962), a film that, like others during that era, documented the first signs of crisis as Italy's economic optimism began to wane; *La moglie più bella* (*The Most Beautiful Wife*, 1969), Ornella Muti's debut; *Confessione di un commissario di polizia al procuratore della repubblica* (*Confessions of a Police Commissioner to the District Attorney*, 1971); *Girolimoni* (*The Assassin of Rome*, 1972); and *Un genio, due compari, un pollo* (*A Genius, Two Friends, and an Idiot*; *A Genius*; *Two Partners and a Dupe*; *Nobody's the Greatest*; *The Genius*; or *Trinity Is Back Again* 1975).

Franco Brusati's career was much less prolific despite his debut in the melting pot of the Italian *nouvelle vague* with *Il disordine* (*Disorder*, 1963). There is no strong, unmitigated thematic or stylistic common denominator to be found in the films he made over the next twenty years. His most stylistically ambitious and innovative works, *Tenderly* (*Il suo modo di fare* or *The Girl Who Couldn't Say No*) and *I tulipani di Haarlem* (*Tulips of Haarlem*), were box-office failures. But *Pane e cioccolata* would be a hit in Italy and throughout the world. It was a bizarre, surreal, Kafkian ballad about racism in "civilized" Switzerland and the atopia of an Italian emigrant who is not allowed to live—let alone belong—anywhere.

Even if he had not become the cultured representative of 1970s Italian erotic cinema, Tinto Brass would be remembered for his early films: *Chi lavora è perduto* (*Who Works Is Lost*, 1963), a Venetian vernacular variant on the theme of alienation (in which the leading character utters his reprise, "I'm so fed up!" as he wanders the streets of Venice); and *Il disco volante* (*The Flying Saucer*, 1964), the story of Northeastern Italy's troubled integration into modernity, also set in the Veneto. The films that followed revealed his knowledge of cinema, the media, and the arts. These works proved he was capable of creating cinema for the masses: *Col cuore in gola* (*Deadly Sweet*; *Heart Beat*; *I*

Am What I Am; or *With Heart in Mouth*, 1967), *L'urlo* (*The Howl*, 1968), *Nerosubianco* (*Black on White* or *The Artful Penetration of Barbara*, 1968), *Dropout* (1970), and *La vacanza* (*Vacation*, 1971). After two films made in the 1970s, in which stories set in Roman times or during Nazism were a pretext to allow his eroticism to emerge, Brass directed *La chiave* (*The Key*, 1982), a work that heralded a long season of borderline pornography and films that celebrated the beauty of the female body and the joys of voyeurism: *Miranda* (1985), *Capriccio* (*Capri Remembered* or *Love and Passion*, 1987), *Paprika* (*Paprika, Life in a Brothel*, 1990), and *Monella* (*Frivolous Lola*, 1998). But unlike the many confessionals of postwar Italian cinema, his openly chauvinist take on sex was secular and joyous. In one of his latest films, *Senso '45* (*Black Angel*, 2001, based on Camillo Boito's novel), his renewed directorial ambition was expressed through irreverent and even sacrilegious allusions to directors like Rossellini, Visconti, Kubrick, and Fellini. But it was also present in his meticulous re-creation of the final months of the fascist regime in Salò on Lake Garda in the Veneto. Where Visconti had purged his version of its erotic content, Brass visually reintegrated it in his own adaptation of the Boito novel.

With just four titles produced, Augusto Tretti has been the least visible of Italian directors over the past forty years. With his first films (*La legge della tromba* [*The Law of the* Trumpet], 1960, and *Il potere* [*Power*], 1972), made on shoestring budget, he attempted to apply the teachings of Brecht. These works were received enthusiastically by Zavattini, Fellini, Antonioni, and Fortini. Goffredo Lombardo even tried to distribute the first full-length film, but was met with disastrous results. Despite the low output of work, Tretti showed great creative ability and belief in what he was doing. Some might call him the "Italian Ed Wood."

Fellini enjoyed his most creative season during the 1960s. By that time, he had mastered every aspect of filmmaking. Film seemed to emanate from his body. Together with Flaiano, Guerra, and Zapponi, he made a series of works that gave life to recurring, obsessive ghosts. With 8 (*Eight and a Half*, 1963), he reached for great heights, but they became increasingly darker and their message ever more laden with death.

Starting with *La dolce vita*, Fellini began to defend his creative integrity from the rest of the world with every means available, even though he also had his moments of artistic crisis and impasse. He would never again lack coherence and correspondence between his directorial aesthetic and his artistic objectives. 8 was an "open work," a text within a text. From the inner parts of its creative flow, this film was an attempt to document the complexity, mystery, crisis, impotence, and power of artistic creation under the sign of many artistic, cultural guardian angels. The existentialist thought that drove his film in the 1950s gave way to other influences. But this time, even in the title, the narrator became the main character and the whole film took place in first person.[76] Fellini had become part of his own work. He no longer directed his characters from the outside like Visconti. In each film, some of his energy seemed to pour onto the screen. The more complex and expansive the narrative sketch became, the more Fellini moved beyond ordered models of narrative coherence and construction. He loved to lose himself in a labyrinth of dreams, memories, and epiphanies. Never easy to decipher, they came to life in his imagination and then connected themselves in unpredictable and arbitrary ways.

The critics' reaction to 8 was "bewilderment" (wrote Fernando di Giammatteo in the pages of *L'Europa Letteraria*) and confusion. The traditional tools used to interpret films could not be applied. The phantoms of the subconscious had become full-time employees of Fellini's imagery. Together with elements inherited from Pirandello, Dante, T. S. Eliot, and Jung, they were melded in a magical cauldron of imagination into a vastly diversified popular iconography.[77] Once Fellini had crossed over the horizon of the real, he brought an entire imaginary world to the screen. His grandiose frescoes flowed over the banks of codified narrative models, which were suddenly set adrift in their wake. During the 1950s, Fellini decanted popular entertainment, putting it at the center of his stories. In the 1960s, each story became an enormous container in which high and low forms of pop culture mixed together and marched, step by step, toward a final televised destination. At a certain point, the story became obsolete. As the images flowed tumultuously, they accumulated, constructing their significance, all the while maintaining their ambiguity and epiphanic and mysterious meaning. In the review *Arts* (February 20–26, 1963), Dino Buzzati used the expression "masturbation" of a genius to describe the complexity of 8 and its arduous translatability into a discourse even remotely linked to reality. Alberto Arbasino would write in the pages of the daily *Il giorno* (March 6, 1963): "This film is an advanced chapter in the history of novelistic form . . . 8 leaves all of cinema behind it in a heap and reduces it to mere genre. It falls ahead of our own narrative at a most sensitive moment of friction between convention and the avant-garde and gives it a decisive shove in the direction of experimentalism."

Even more so than with *La dolce vita*, this film gave way to the absolute primacy of the image in Fellini's world. Never following pre-established rules, the image came into being and combined with other images taken from various sources: from comic strips, advertisements, serialized photographic romance novels, and Italian vaudeville and variety shows. Dialogue was an added element and the viewer had a completely free hand in decoding the film's meaning. Whether or not he had any clear messages to convey with previous films, Fellini no longer had a clear message to convey, nor did he have a concise vision of the world. His works did not pave new roads to follow. They contained no political or moral goals, even though a ray of hoped glimmered in the endings to many of his films. Although the critics remained divided, they recognized the originality of Fellini's signifiers, the mastery of Rotunno's photography and Rota's soundtracks, and the richness of Gherardi's immensely varied set designs. In the eyes of the critics and international audiences, this innovative film (which won the grand prize at the Moscow Film Festival) placed Fellini in the pantheon of the great visionary directors with Welles, Buñuel, Kurosawa, and Bergman.

Split personalities would reappear in *Giulietta degli spiriti* (*Juliet of the Spirits*), in which, thanks to color, Fellini was able to liberate more of his visionary instincts and images taken from his own subconscious and collective imagination. His use of a female point of view and the stronger presence of irrational and para-psychological elements was not peacefully accepted by the critics, who continued to give him low marks ("Fellini 8-"[78] was the title of Mino Argentieri's review in *Rinascita*). Fellini's imagery was said to be overly geared to a bourgeois audience; his lofty aesthetic too limited; the director himself held hostage by his own ghosts and childhood memories. Such limitations, some said, would never allow him to grow as a director. The title of an essay by Raymond Borde was indicative: "Fellini Should Rid Himself of His Monsters" (*Arts*, October 26, 1965). The films *Satyricon* (*Fellini Satyricon* or *The Degenerates*, 1969), *I clowns* (*The Clowns*, 1970), *Roma* (*Fellini's Roma*, 1971), and *Amarcord* marked figurative and narrative innovation. They ostentatiously combined and celebrated new yet similar forms and figures of Fellinian imagery. Together, they represent a body of exceptionally creative works skimmed from the shadows of illness and his earliest chthonic fears. These films are undervalued and merit study inasmuch as examples of Fellini's expressive and visual experimentation. With *Amarcord*, Fellini taught Italy not to fear upsetting elements in its collective national history. He urged Italians to explore them as a shared heritage that deserved their attention. Personalities like George Simenon were blown away by Fellini's vision and genius and by the multiplicity of potential connections with painting in his work.

There would be no lack of public tributes, honors, and recognition. No other postwar director created such a cohesive series of modern epics and no other filmmaker's career was marked by phases so utterly "distinct" yet still "equal." The critics, on both the left and the right, never entirely embraced his cause. In their eyes, Fellini came to a dead stop by the mid-1970s and could only repeat himself. Beginning with *Toby Dammit* (Fellini's segment in *Histoires extraordinaires* [*Spirits of the Dead*; *Tales of Mystery*; or *Tales of Mystery and Imagination*], 1967) and later films like *Casanova* (*Fellini's Casanova*, 1976), Fellini began to see himself as "a bookkeeper, an account, a provincial playboy who believes that he has lived but was never born; who traveled the world without ever existing; who passed through life like a wandering phantom."[79] A funereal veil was more and more frequently drawn over the scenes of his films. He seemed to be attending a series of good-bye ceremonies, repeated and varied by a series of worlds destined to disappear. With *Prova d'orchestra* (*Orchestra Rehearsal*, 1979), Fellini's imagination moved from catastrophe to catastrophe toward an increasingly apocalyptic horizon without ever losing his creativity. At the same time, certain sequences in *Roma* already gave the impression that Fellini was beginning to conceive science-fiction movies and that he was imagining future scripts dominated by chaotic development and widespread, menacing, and irreversible destruction.

Of all the neorealist directors, Antonioni was the one who chose to explore new narrative and figurative dimensions. He courageously plunged into unknown waters and redefined spatial relationships, the relations between characters and the spaces they inhabited, and the perception of the "empty" and the "filled" as a representation of the characters' dramas. Thanks to his pioneering spirit, his curiosity, the richness of his interpretations, and his literary and artistic interests, he was able to change and enrich the entire history of postwar Italian culture. Antonioni sought to reinstate a visual and cultural heritage drawn from the most varied and eccentric sources; thus he seemed to reinvent all points of reference and every password used by his contemporaries.[80]

Beginning with *L'avventura* (*The Adventure*), he sought to substitute real spaces with spatial experiments that helped measure internal distances.[81] Antonioni toppled all perception of space. In his films, point of view and vision were determined by objects. As perhaps only Robert Bresson had done before him, he sought to capture even the mental radiation that emanated from the characters as they fled normalcy. His imagination lay on the farthest border of postwar cinematographic experimentation. Even communication became precarious in Antonioni, because the reason to communicate had been lost, as had the meaning of words, the value of emotions, and the perception of objects. "There are days when I have nothing to tell you," says Lea Massari in one of the first scenes in *L'avventura*. This would become a chronic state of being in Antonioni's films. His cinema represented the human condition of alienation whereby the individual became increasingly detached from his surroundings and disconnected from his self.

In *L'avventura* and the films that would follow—*La notte* (*The Night*, 1961), *L'eclisse* (*The Eclipse*, 1962), and *Deserto rosso* (*Red Desert*, 1964)— space was reduced, as in a Mondrian painting, to its elementary structures. He then slowly began to expand it with films like *Blowup* (1966) as pure metaphysical painting.[82] The use of color widened the range of Antonioni's expressive and formal possibilities. In his color films, the characters seemed to dissolve into the landscape and become spots of color: "Everything is color. The green and silver water tanks, the black smokestacks . . . the yellow and red-crimson structures, the white milk, the golden yellow, gray, black clouds of gas . . . Nature has been destroyed, raped, humiliated . . . Even our feelings have changed, conditioned by the surroundings, by the landscape, and the color of this background . . . What color are our feelings?"[83]

For Antonioni, cinema was a means to synthesize and reformulate the poetics, theory, and techniques of painting, music, and contemporary aesthetics. In *Blowup*, he centered these elements in the frame and made them a topic of history. As soon as he began to dissolve his characters within their reality, he felt a need to reaffirm his poetics on a much vaster scale. He went to England, the United States, and Spain to make *Blowup* (1966), *Zabriskie Point* (1970), and *Professione: reporter* (*The Passenger*, 1975). There, he found the ideal setting for an individual to reconstruct an identity fragmented and taken away by society. *Professione: reporter* revisited the theme of wandering present in *Il grido* (*The Cry* or *The Outcry*) and the annulment of identity and absence together with the game of death.

The style of Elio Petri's first films, *L'assassino* (*The Assassin* or *The Lady-killer of Rome*, 1961) and *I giorni contati* (*His Days Are Numbered*, 1962), owed much to Antonioni. Jean Gili called him *mal aimé* (because he was chosen by the critics as the scapegoat of political cinema). As a director, he knew how to evolve and to find his own stylistic element. He applied the lessons learned from his neorealist heritage to his baroque narrative and visual abilities. Through a mixture of expressionism, Brecht, and the bizarre, his films brought together "Marx and Gramsci, but also Freud and Reich. He dove into the world of dreams with Kafkian lunges and into the maze that divides being and schizophrenia."[84]

For his debut film, *L'assassino*, Petri put together a top-notch team: Marcello Mastroianni, still reeling from the success of *La dolce vita*, was the film's star; Montaldo was the assistant director; the editor was Ruggero Mastroianni, who sought to re-create the rhythms of Godard's 1959 *À bout de souffle* (*Breathless* or *By a Tether*); the screenplay was written by Pasquale Festa, who had just finished work on the script for *Rocco e i suoi fratelli* (*Rocco and His Brothers*), Guerra, and Massimo Franciosa; Carlo di Palma was the cinematographer and painter Renzo Vespignani the production designer. Structured around flash-backs, this police thriller used its meticulously created imagery as an expression of the characters' psychological makeup.

In 1967, Petri began working with Ugo Pirro, who would help him make the most significant trilogy of his career: *Indagine su un cittadino al di sopra di ogni sospetto* (*Investigation of a Citizen Above Suspicion*, 1970), *La classe operaia va in Paradiso* (*The Working Class Goes to Heaven*, 1971), and *La proprietà non è più un furto* (*Property Is No Longer a Theft*, 1973).[85] *La classe operaia* was attacked by the critics who were busy vying for positions to the left of left-wing. In the journal *Quaderni piacentini* (October 1971), Fofi published a violent review in which he spared no element of the film, massacring it as if in a Django western. Political and revolutionary themes never saved a mediocre film, nor did many of the articles published during those years in journals like *Ombre rosse* (*Red Shadows*). During those restless years, political films seemed overly reformist and compromised by power. The left became so hostile to Petri that during a fiery screening at the Porretta Festival in 1971, Jean-Marie Straub called for *La classe operaia* to be burned. With the help of Brecht, the theater of Artaud, and Gian Maria Volonté's talents as an actor, these films exposed the most significant elements of the Italian political machine and Italian society at the end of the 1960s. They achieved this despite requiring the viewer to read between the lines, and they pulled no punches in examining aspects of Italian society that are no longer comparable to contemporary Italy. Petri's last film, *Todo modo* (*One Way or Another*, 1975), was made on the eve of the 1975 elections. It prophesied the kidnapping and assassination of Aldo Moro, which it interpreted as self-cannibalization intended to exorcise the crisis within the Christian Democrat Party.

Like many other directors, Florestano Vancini made documentaries for roughly a decade before his debut, *La lunga notte del '43* (*The Long Night of '43*, 1960), based on a story by Giorgio Bassani. This courageous film focused on the fascists' responsibility in the reprisals and civil war during the years of Salò. It also revealed how many power structures remained in place as Italy transitioned from fascism to democracy, and in particular, it unmasked those who were part of the so-called gray zone, that is, those who stood by and watched as events unfolded without ever taking responsibility for them.

Following this film, Vancini's career took off with films like *La banda Casaroli* (*The Casaroli Gang*, 1962), *La calda vita* (*The Warm Life*, 1964), *Le stagioni del nostro amore* (*Seasons of Our Love*, 1966), and other films that established him as a serious director. His *Bronte: cronaca di un massacro che i libri di storia non hanno raccontato* (*Bronte: The Story of a Massacre That the History Books Have Never Told*, released as *Liberty* in English) deserves praise for its meticulous documentation, the excellence in dramatic structure, and the director's remarkable ability to tell the story on behalf of the vanquished.[86] Vancini was among the first to examine this period in history. His *Il delitto Matteotti* (*The Assassination of Matteotti*) was also an informative look at the fascist era.

Greatly influenced by Antonioni and Fellini (for whom he had worked as an assistant director on *La dolce vita*), Gianfranco Mingozzi made a series of important documentaries before debuting with *Trio* (1967), a film in which he showed a great capacity to mix different stylistic layers. This semi-documentary film was made with hand-held cameras, overabundant close-ups, and details of bodies and faces reminiscent of Godard (*Une femme mariée* [*A Married Woman*], 1964) and Antonioni. Without giving up his career as a documentary filmmaker, he also explored different roads with films like *Sequestro di persona* (*Island of Crime*; *Ransom in Sardinia*; *Sardine: Kidnapped*; *Sardinia: Ransom*; or *Unlawful Restraint*, 1968), in which he offered an interpretation of the kidnappings in Sardinia connected to the construction industry; *La vita in gioco* (*Life on the Line*, also known as *Morire a Roma* [*To Die in Rome*], 1972); and *Flavia la monaca musulmana* (*Flavia*; *Flavia the Heretic*; *Flavia the Rebel Nun*; *Flavia, Priestess of Violence*; *Flavia: Heretic Priestess*; *The Heretic*; *Muslim Nun*; or *The Rebel Nun*).[87] Guided and mentored by personalities like Danilo Dolci, Ernesto de Martino, Leonardo Sciascia, Salvatore Quasimodo, Zavattini, and Luciano Berio, he tackled difficult subjects like the survival of magical rituals in Salento (Apulia) with *Taranta*[88]; the Canadian Native Americans' abandonment of their homeland with *Il sole che muore* (*The Dying Sun*); emigration and the Mafia with his masterpiece *Con il cuore fermo, Sicilia!* (*A Hard-Hearted Look at Sicily*, 1968–69); and various films about film with *L'ultima diva* (*The Last Diva*, 1981), a look at the life of Francesca Bertini, *Bellissimo* (*Bellissimo: Images of the Italian Cinema*, 1985), and *Storia di cinema e di emigranti* (*Cinema and Emigrants, a History*, 1986). In his films, he has always used young stars to explore Italian history, from fascism to the years of terrorism. Some other important films made by Mingozzi are *La vela incantata* (*The Magic Screen*, 1982); *L'appassionata* (*The Passionate* [*Woman*], 1988); *Il frullo del passero* (*The Sparrow's Fluttering*, 1988); and, more recently, *Tobia al caffè* (*Tobias at the Café*, 2000).

Mingozzi was in search of other worlds: real and imagined, near and far. He sought out cultures both different from and similar to his own. He always looked for a common ground between himself and his subjects and never attempted to conceal his presence or his emotional attachment, nor did he ever stop mixing his rationality with the reasons of his heart and his profound sense of moral duty.

Ansano Giannarelli was another director who devoted most of his career to making documentaries. His most memorable were *Resistenza: una nazione che risorge* (*The Resistance: A Nation Rises Up*, 1976) and *Roma occupata* (*Occupied Rome*, 1980). His feature-length *Sierra Maestra* (1968–69) was one of the better films made by directors whose work was driven by the revolutionary tension of the era. With this film, he wanted to reveal the similarities between Latin America and some of the underdeveloped regions of Italy (primarily Sardinia, where most of the shooting was done). The main character of the film, a journalist, brings to mind Régis Debray, who was arrested after alleged involvement with Venezuelan guerrillas. His dilemma consists in either continuing to believe in the battle of ideas or becoming directly active in the armed struggle. Giannarelli had complete creative control over this film and his camera operator was Marcello Gatti, the cinematographer on Pontecorvo's *La battaglia di Algeri* (*The Battle of Algiers*). Even this film was attacked by militant critics, who continued to act as a mass firing squad. But it was also criticized in journals like *Cinema Nuovo* and *Filmcritica* for its cinematographic weaknesses. In 1987, Giannarelli made *Remake*, with the Locarno Film Festival as its backdrop. This film highlighted his gift for observation, his talent as a narrator, and cinema's important role in understanding life.

Valerio Zurlini's first film came out in the late 1950s. Despite its melodramatic storyline, his second film, *La ragazza con la valigia* (*Girl with a Suitcase*), was a successful expression of his poetic and artistic vision.[89] In this story of stereotypical Italian vacationers during the economic boom of the 1960s, he sketched and captured his characters' emotions just as they were beginning to show, along with their true colors, the hue of their worlds and their moments of self-examination. He had perfected his screenplay by eliminating all unnecessary elements, including aspects of the historical and spatial context. It was as if he had absorbed the techniques of the painter Morandi, whose work he admired so greatly. Jean Gili put it best when he wrote that Zurlini's films capture the landscape like no others: "Italian landscapes and landscapes of the soul."[90] But Zurlini was also one of the hardest directors to picture in the class photo. The films that followed were not as successful: *Le soldatesse* (*The Camp Followers*), based on a novel by Ugo Pirro about the Italian army's missions—military and otherwise—in Greece during World War II; and *Seduto alla sua destra* (*Black Jesus*; *Out of Darkness*; *Seated at His Right*; or *Super Brother*), a Pasolini-inspired work that told the story of African leader Lumumba's assassination and the solitude that surrounded him and all the characters whose stories he retold in this film. Of the eight full-length films he made over the course of twenty-five years, the most significant were *La prima notte di quiete* (*The Professor*) and his masterpiece, *Il deserto dei tartari* (*The Desert of the Tartars*), based on the novel (translated, *The Tartar Steppe*) by Buzzati, a film in which he reached the greatest heights of his compositional research and narrative forms made of empty—instead of filled—spaces.

Of the entire generation of 1960s filmmakers, none stood out like Pier Paolo Pasolini. He was a postwar one-man band, capable of transforming everything he touched into gold, from painting, poetry, and narrative to cinematography. Even his life and death were works of art.[91] It was only natural for him to move from painting to screenwriting. Thanks to his work with Fellini and Bolognini, he was able to apply his vision to moviemaking: with *Accattone* (1961) and *Mamma Roma* (1962), Pasolini discovered the world of images as he attempted to create the perfect cinematic equivalent of paintings by Piero della Francesca, Masaccio, and Masolino—mapping out his own cinematographic iconosphere, with the great art historian Roberto Longhi as his guide.[92] His first films were attempts to transfer the world of his Roman *ragazzi di vita* (street urchins) from the page of his first novel to the screen.

Better than any other medium, cinema suited Pasolini's pulsing, explosive artistic culture, its moods, and its energy. At a certain point, words no longer sufficed to express the meaning in his unmitigated contact with the subject matter and the awesome power of images that could convey the material reality of an idea, its incarnation, and its manifestation of a myth in the close-up of a face. When Pasolini got behind a camera, he lacked the practical experience needed to make movies. But his strong background in figurative art and his firm belief in the translatability of words into images allowed him to reinvent the basic rules and vocabulary that defined the two-dimensional space of film. He thought of himself as a Giotto who created spaces together with the figures that would inhabit them (indeed, he would play Giotto in his *Decameron*). Cinema made it possible for Pasolini to fully exploit his natural tendency to mix styles and forms. With the use of color, these possibilities grew: *La ricotta* (*Ricotta,* his segment in *Ro.Go.Pa.G.*, 1963) was a collage of colors and sounds, dissonance and counterpoint, cinematic and artistic allusions, the sacred and the deconsecrated. It marked one of the greatest moments of creativity in postwar art. With *La ricotta*, Pasolini began to realize that his intellectual direction was no longer connected to the sub-proletarian world with which he had identified for years and from which he had affected his point of view and gleaned his vitality. Of course, the ruffian and the poor *Stracci* represent an *alter Christus* figure, but the director played by Orson Welles is Pasolini himself—a character who understands that he cannot completely become his characters. He can certainly command them using his bullhorn, but his story no longer shares any affinity with his plebeian characters. From then on, he would devote his films to classic works of literature, with Dante and the Gospels as his constant guides. The classics formed a cultural backdrop that allowed him to wander through history and mythology.[93] Through literature and painting, he obsessively searched for paradise lost and a vantage point from which he could cast his gaze on the present and future. His cultural wanderings led him to devour a wide array of texts. But, besides Dante's *Comedy*, he always carried the Gospels with him wherever he went, as in *Il Vangelo secondo Matteo* (*The Gospel According to St. Matthew*, 1964) and *Uccellacci e uccellini* (*Hawks and Sparrows*, 1966). In 1965 he wrote the poem "Alí dagli occhi azzurri" ("Blue-eyed Alí"), in which he prophesied that millions of young men from the Third World would land on Italian shores and conquer the old continent in the name of religion and revolution.

During the final phase of his life, he took on the role of Nostradamus. As the need to talk about himself emerged, tragedy and medieval tales became the systems he would use to give direction and meaning to his peripeties and his need to interpret the present allegorically and figuratively, as in films like *Edipo re* (*Oedipus Rex*, 1967), *Teorema* (*Theorem*, 1968), *Medea* (1969), *Decameron* (1970), *I racconti di Canterbury* (*The Canterbury Tales*, 1972), *Il fiore delle Mille e una notte* (*A Thousand and One Nights*; *Arabian Nights*; or *Flower of the Arabian Nights* 1972), and *Salò o Le 120 giornate di Sodoma* (*Salò, or The 120 Days of Sodom*, 1975).[94]

Pasolini knew that when he entered myth in the first person he was desecrating sacred space. But he managed to avoid the problem through ironic elements that saved him and lessened the gravity of his sins. It is amazing to think that someone like Pasolini—who was not a master of the cinematographic medium—was able to tell stories that gave life to more stories still. Over the past thirty years, his cinematic language and themes have continued to influence directors like Sergio Citti, Luigi Faccini, Nico d'Alessandria and Aurelio Grimaldi, Mario Martone and Marco Risi, Ciprí and Maresco and Pappi Corsicato. Pasolini's life's work and his cinema continue to speak to us thanks to his cultural nomadism, his ability to mix and hybridize all codes, his asystematic working method, and his ability to tap into the pulse and capture the soul of minorities and regional identity. Pasolini had a lucid capacity to see far into the distance, predicting deep-reaching transformations as well as forms of degradation and the loss of light in our world.

Sergio Citti played a fundamental role in guiding Pasolini through the slums of Rome. With his film *Ostia* (1970), he tried to apply his oratorical talents and the world that he knew to the screen. Citti can be counted among the so-called naïf directors, who, with Augusto Tretti as their earliest exponent, would produce waves of successful cinematic "good savages."[95] In 1973,

Citti made *Storie scellerate* (*Bawdy Tales* or *Roguish Stories*) and then *Casotto* (*Beach House*; *In the Beach House*; or *The Beach Hut*) in 1977. Among his later films, *I magi randagi* (*We Three Kings*, 1996) is worth remembering for an appearance made by Roberto Benigni and the imaginative adventures of the three characters. The more recent *Vipera* (*Viper*, 2000), story and screenplay by Vincenzo Cerami, also deserves mention.

After a stint as Pasolini's assistant director, Bernardo Bertolucci made his debut not long after his twentieth birthday with a Pasolinian film, *La commare secca* (*The Grim Reaper*, 1962).[96] His first real film as an artist was *Prima della rivoluzione* (*Before the Revolution*, 1964), a film that he claimed to have made "to close the books" with the city where he and his father were born: Parma. It marks the first in a series of works dominated by the theme of simultaneous self-reflection and examination of his father. Bertolucci was never afraid to make intellectual cinema rife with musical, literary, and cinematic allusions. Even the Godard-dependent and hardly Bertoluccian *Partner* (1968) told the story of the difficulties and ideological alienation faced by the 1968 generation. *La strategia del ragno* (*The Spider's Stratagem*, 1972) and *Il conformista* (*The Conformist*, 1970) marked a turning point where he expanded his repertoire of references and began to assimilate new iconographic and literary sources, ranging from Borges to Magritte, from Edward Hopper to De Chirico and the so-called naïf painters of Emilia-Romagna. Through his collaboration with cinematographer Vittorio Storaro, light and color assumed a decisively important role in his films. Over the long term, Storaro's work was destined to reshape cinematography in general. But it was with Bertolucci that Storaro was able to develop his approach to light as a narrative element. *Ultimo tango a Parigi* (*Last Tango in Paris*, 1972) immediately drew attention from the censors. In Italy, the film was virtually burned at the stake by critics of its explicit sex scenes. The nakedness of the apartment (in which much of the action transpired) was intended to underscore the undressing of the characters' deepest feelings, but audiences made the film a success because they loved their bodies rather than what was inside. With *Novecento* (*1900*, 1976), Bertolucci presented a "historical" film. In a sort of tit-for-tat, he tried to translate his father's poetic legacy to the screen, while adapting lessons gleaned from John Ford and Kurosawa. He used an epic tale, a Verdian opera, and folklore to tell the story of the Po River Valley.

No other director, even among those for generations before him, seemed able to make a film so epic in scope. More than thirty years after its release, it has helped anoint him as one of the greatest maestros of international cinema. He is among a handful of directors who have shaped world cinema over the course of the past thirty years.

Not as prolific as Bertolucci, Gillo Pontecorvo was a slow-working and meticulous director. Six years after his *Kapò* (*Kapo*, 1960), *La battaglia di Algeri* (*The Battle of Algiers*, 1966) told a story of Algerians' struggle for independence. Based on rigorously detailed documentation, the film included action scenes depicting terrorist attacks, images that resonated with an audience sowing new revolutionary dreams. Like many directors and screenwriters of his generation—Valentino Orsini, Giuliano Montaldo, and Franco Solinas, among others—he was disillusioned by Italian postwar politics. He was drawn instead to romantic revolutionary and subversive characters and he was among the first to depict terrorism in films charged with emotional and ideological energy, as in *Queimada* (*Burn!* or *The Mercenary*, 1969). These works would become the models for many South American films. But over the past thirty years, his career has been marked by his inability to produce new works of the same caliber as his *La battaglia di Algeri*. Unfortunately, many of his works have not aged well.

While the Taviani brothers' universe appeared to expand constantly, Marco Ferreri's collapsed like a funnel as he sought out stories seemingly less and less charged with life and desire. More than any other director, Ferreri was obsessed with impending dangers—and by the possibility of so many small catastrophes and apocalypses looming on our horizon. More than any other, he questioned the meaning of human life on earth. There was a self-destructive tendency within him and his progressive failure to find reasons to live pervaded his works, growing even as the horizon became smaller and smaller. After beginning his career working with Zavattini, he went to Spain and immersed himself in late surrealism, making *El Pisito* (*The Little Apartment*, 1959) and *El Cochecito* (*The Little Coach* or *The Wheelchair*, 1960). In his first Italian films, *L'ape regina* (*The Queen Bee* or *The Conjugal Bed*, 1963) and *La donna scimmia* (*The Ape Woman*, 1963) to *L'uomo dei cinque palloni* (*The Man with the Balloons* or *Break up*, 1965), he told bizarre, pseudo-educational stories in which the human race was struggling for survival. Ferreri seemed intent on applying evolutionary theory as he sought to envision life beyond the human race. He was interested in the intermingling and interference of different codes, communication lapses, and what could be called the ecology of sight and communication. In this regard, his *Dillinger è morto* (*Dillinger Is Dead*, 1968) was a manifesto denouncing the communication breakdowns of the late 1960s. It was also one of the few films that ended with the character escaping and being reborn. With *Il seme dell'uomo* (*The Seed of Man*, 1969) he brought his characters to the edge of catastrophe.

In his examination of the challenges of modern living, Ferreri predicted catastrophe for the individual and the couple. With *Liza* (*Love to Eternity* or

La cagna [It.], 1972), *La Dernière femme* (*L'ultima donna* or *The Last Woman*, 1976), *Ciao maschio* (*Bye Bye Monkey*, 1978), and *Storie di ordinaria follia* (*Tales of Ordinary Madness*, 1981), Ferreri developed a post-Darwinian story of the species' struggle for survival. As his career developed, he began to abandon the visual elements that once had tied his work together; he became focused on his characters' dramas, obsessions, and fears as they imagined the future. *La casa del sorriso* (*The House of Smiles*, 1991), *La carne* (*The Flesh*, 1991), *Diario di un vizio* (*Diary of a Maniac*, 1993), and *Nitrato d'argento* (*Nitrate Base*, 1995) marked the end of his career with notes of melancholy and intimism. As Tornatore and Scola had done before him, Ferreri made a film about the passing of cinematic culture with his final film. Made with ramshackle means and minimal resources, *Nitrato d'argento*, chock-full of emotion, revealed his sincere desire to create his own goodbye ceremony.

With his 1965 debut film *I pugni in tasca* (*Fists in His Pocket* or *Fists in the Pocket*), Marco Bellocchio was received with an enthusiasm not dissimilar from the reaction to Visconti's first film. The Buñuel-influenced *I pugni in tasca* revealed his directorial talent and his masterful ability to tell a story and to direct his actors. It also established him as a director who could presage times of protest. With *La Cina è vicina* (*China Is Near*), he used his camera to express his political militancy as he sought to record the actions and convergence of the revolutionary and student movements. Although an entire generation embraced him as its director and northern star, time was not good to him during the initial phase of his career. While rich in ferment and drive, his work was confusing. It was the fruit of the dissociation between a directorial superego and an ideologue who pushed him in opposite directions. And yet few European movies have been as powerful as *I pugni in tasca*, a work that was energized by the youth culture and the swelling protest. This film showed the new generation's break from traditional politics and the imminent beginning of a new phase in the history of Italian life and society whereby political orientation was being lost. It also revealed new ideals inspired by China and South America and how the red and black flags were losing their symbolic value. His highly politicized second film, *La Cina è vicina*, was an attempt to express his cinematic aesthetic. But with this film, Bellocchio already began to lose some of his admirers because of the strong stylistic break from his previous work. In the 1970s, he continued to develop anti-institutional themes with fictional works like *Nel nome del padre* (*In the Name of the Father*, 1971) and documentaries like *Matti da slegare* (*Fit to Be Untied*, 1974). With these films, he used psychoanalytic theory as his guide, paying less attention to stylistic concerns. During the 1970s, beginning with his television adaptation of Chekhov's *The Seagull*, Bellocchio understood that "you can't be angry for your entire life." In the films made during this period, he attempted to articulate his characters' reality, history, and inner world. His earlier and much louder cinema was replaced by works that explored mental illness that resulted from family abuse. But these films—*Gli occhi, la bocca* (*The Eyes, the Mouth* or *Those Eyes, That Mouth*, 1982), *Enrico IV* (*Henry IV*, 1983), *Diavolo in corpo* (*Devil in the Flesh*, 1986), and *La visione della sabba* (*The Sabbath* or *The Witches' Sabbath*, 1987)—also allowed Bellocchio to revisit his cinematic style. The Roman psychoanalyst Massimo Fagioli was a big influence on Bellocchio during these years. In the 1990s, he seemed to reaffirm his ability to tell a story and his directorial and narrative skill as he adapted literary works for the screen like *Il principe di Homburg* (*The Prince of Homburg*, 1996) and *La balia* (*The Nanny*, 1999). All the while, he continued to develop his vision of the world, his relationship with his actors, and his relationship with his characters and their life choices. As Sandro Bernardi has noted, Bellocchio's films over the past twenty years have never been facile.[97] His work continued to be restless and ever more secluded as he sought to perfect his style and to capture moments of truth that could explain the ills of daily living. He wanted to understand the impossibility of accepting laws, conventions, and rules that disabled the individual's authenticity and kept him at the mercy of others.

Salvatore Samperi was similar to Bellocchio in his style of storytelling and his equally furious and Oedipal attack on the bourgeoisie. Following his *Grazie zia* (*Come Play with Me* or *Thank You Aunt*, 1968), one of the most overrated films of the era, he was able to show his true colors, his best and worst, as he explored vice in the family. He told stories of nascent and newly discovered sexuality with repressed Catholic society in the Veneto (a region of Northern Italy) as his backdrop. Like many directors of that era, including Pasolini, Samperi played an important role in guiding Italian cinema toward a pansexualism that touched all genres. With films like his *Malizia* (*Malice* or *Malicious*, 1973, a film that inspired the *Pierino* series with Alvaro Vitali), directors turned away from revolution in the town square and began peeping through keyholes to depict vice in the family and the joys of voyeurism.

The Loss of the Present

By the time of the 1968 crisis and the "years of lead" that followed, as film critics were jockeying to see who could be the more leftist among them, they sent politically themed films intended for mass audiences to the firing squads.

The creative polycentrism and experimentation of the 1960s began to disperse. Competition from television became increasingly stronger and new generations were increasingly less interested in politics. The anthropologic imagery of Italian cinema also began to change. Directors were no longer interested in the stories of middle- and working-class Italians (in truth, Italian cinema had never successfully depicted the world of the workers). It was clear that a genetic mutation had occurred and the beloved monsters of Italian comedies began to appear in a post-human condition. The unified structure of the Italian film industry began to implode and its heritage and its character began to dissolve. The new hybrid beings of Italian cinema were tied to the past by an umbilical cord but they were no longer part of a community defined by spaces, surfaces, and connections.

In the same vein as the papier-mâché recreations of Italy in early twentieth-century cinema, the filmmakers of the 1960s were more interested in Italy's past, its history and the national memory of the previous century, than in its present. Most directors chose to look backward at the past as they tried to capture memories instead of unraveling the enigmas of the present. While their depiction of the present was confused, their portrayal of the past was lucid and clear. This is exemplified by the grandiosity of films like *Novecento*, *Amarcord*, Pasolini's *Trilogia della vita*, Olmi's *Albero degli Zoccoli*, and Scola's *C'eravamo tanto amati* (1974).

Generations of directors have tried to interpret and to access a chaotic and indecipherable present. For many, it was easier to look to the past and revive values that had all but disappeared or the notion of a lost world. The present was increasingly distant, confused, difficult to decipher, and enigmatic. They had lost their sense of belonging: no one knew for whom they were writing or for whom they were filming. Their clarity had allowed the postwar directors to bring every element of the landscape into focus by making it a historical subject. But due to a widespread and nearly pathological shortsightedness, that clarity was lost forever, together with the country's and its people's progressive loss of passion and hope for future.

5

⸱⁓ From the 1970s to the Present ⁓⸱

Metamorphosis of the Landscape

During the 1972–73 cinematic season, 344 titles were produced in Italy, taking in 62 percent of domestic ticket sales. At the time, there seemed to be no reason to worry, even though a wide divide was beginning to emerge between films that made back their production costs (very few) and films that lost money.[1] For every *Ultimo tango a Parigi* (*Last Tango in Paris*, a film that was censored by the Italian courts and a film for which Bertolucci was "sentenced to be burned at the stake," and a film that became the sixth biggest earner in the world), there were hundreds of titles that never broke even. And production houses were barely surviving the run of a film. The success of erotic films and the last wave of westerns brought about a tumultuous and ruinous tide of quickly made films, poorly produced and with even worse acting, titles that struggled to make back their cost in second- and third-run theaters. During the 1970s, the decline of theatergoers became evident and began to accelerate dramatically: hundreds of theaters closed and sales dropped to around 50 million lire per year.[2]

At the same time, the American government decided to offer tax incentives to producers who invested in homemade products. As a result, a new production strategy began to take off in the United States and around the world and would have a devastating effect on production in other countries. American producers began to withdraw their investments in the Italian market, where they had contributed to the renewal and development of Cinecittà during the 1950s. Italian producers were no longer able to make films that featured American stars, the magic helpers often necessary to penetrate the U.S. and other international markets. Italian legislation passed in 1965 encouraged new Italian filmmakers but it weakened faith in the market and shook the otherwise solid industrial infrastructure. It also reinforced the notion that the Italian government should bear more of the industry's risk and loss. At the end of the 1970s, the Italian government's co-productions represented a meager 2 percent of overall production. By the mid-1990s, that figure had risen to 38 percent. In neighboring France, the number of films co-produced by the government dropped from 35 percent in 1970 to 2 percent by the end of the decade.[3]

In 1972, with Francis Ford Coppola's *The Godfather*, the American film industry began its new practice of "saturation selling," whereby the number of distributed prints of big-budget films grew exponentially with the aim of quickly recouping production costs. As a result, smaller films immediately began to disappear and second- and third-run theaters rapidly received a death sentence.

With the new process of market globalization, Italian film production seemed increasingly incapable of organizing itself and creating alliances and connections to repel the unbridled attack of the big multimedia American entertainment groups.[4] During the early 1970s, the politics and power of Italian and European cinema made it possible to compete with the American film industry. But in the decades that followed, the sheer scale and systems of relationships and power changed profoundly: there were no longer any safety nets, internal reference points, or protections. On the international playing field, it appeared that a handful of large groups—similar to the Seven Sisters of oil production—were aiming to shape and control the world entertainment market and to install cinematic productions at the center of an integrated network of communication services.[5]

A truly comparative and transnational perspective is needed to study these decades of economic transformation and changes in the approach to film production.[6]

The game had changed and so had all the rules. As far as the market was concerned, the story of Italian cinema during the final quarter of the twentieth century was a story of progressive marginalization, loss of contact with the expansion of the integrated groups who controlled the new media universe, loss of exposure, and loss of that aura previously guaranteed by the neorealist cinema of Fellini, Antonioni, Pasolini, and Bertolucci. The love of Italian cinema would remain intact outside of Italy but it was distributed in an inconsistent manner. Interest in Italian cinema shifted toward films of the past and tended to favor individual titles produced over the past decades by Bertolucci, Olmi, Tornatore, Amelia, Salvatores, Troisi, Moretti, and Benigni.

Not only did the rules of the game change but so did the interlocutors, the genres, the technology, the sets, the power of the various players on the field, and the channels of film distribution. At the beginning of 2002, the simultaneous release of George Lucas's *Star Wars: Episode I* in roughly fifty theaters marked a new era in the history of technological evolution and film distribution. And it reinforced the power of the new big studios and their strategy of saturating theaters with just a handful of titles.

Over the course of the 1970s and 1980s, as film consumption grew markedly thanks in part to the prevalence of television, videocassettes, and VCRs, cinema's role in the Italian collective consciousness began to ebb.[7] During the same period, film producers began to reflect on the role and power of television with respect to cinema: films seemed naturally destined to be viewed on a television screen even when they did not make it into theaters. In the early 1970s, when the Italian film industry still held a top slot in the international market, the Italian market began to undergo a dramatic and irreversible process of marginalization that—over the course of the next twenty years—would leave it on par with that of the Third World. The Italian market was slowly reduced to playing the role of the simpler consumer of *made in USA* films and television programs. The cinema was no longer the backdrop for the modern world's most important secular ritual: year after year, tens of millions of moviegoers abandoned the movie theater. Third- and then second-run theaters were the first to be affected.[8] By the beginning of the 1990s, the number of tickets sold annually hovered around 90 million. By 1992, that number had dropped to just over 80 million. Growth in sales in 1993 did not lead to a reversal of this trend and in any case did not apply to Italian cinema, which had been penalized and deserted by audience like never before. In the years that followed, new generations of Italians would become disenchanted with Italian cinema, in part because they associated cinematic products with television. Over the next quarter of a century, more than 700 million moviegoers disappeared and functioning movie theaters went belly-up by the thousands. The number of films produced has fallen to a new all-time low in recent years. But more significantly, fewer and fewer films are able to generate top box-office numbers. There are also fewer and fewer producers capable of grandiose thinking, taking risks, and attempting to make films that can compete on an international level: the terrain is too shaky and it lacks storylines that can generate the strength necessary to mobilize the system. Ticket sales have dropped drastically but films are also being distributed in a new way. Consumption is now sprinkled throughout the myriad private television stations that began to proliferate in the mid-1970s. Generations of cinema-dependent and cinephile moviegoers have been uprooted by a new generation of television-addicted viewers who are greater in numbers and less demanding—especially when it comes to advertising. These consumers quickly became the guiding force that decisively shaped the production of images in the world. The passing of power has been gradual but highly visible. As Italian cinema began to face the crisis of the late 1970s, it did so by trying to revise its star system and by fishing for rising television stars.

During the early 1970s, the defection of millions of moviegoers was also due to external factors: the oil and international economic crises, the sense of fear and collective uncertainty caused by a decade of protracted terrorism, and the new and different distribution of consumer goods. Tumultuous and uncontrolled growth of private television set off the rebirth and indiscriminate pillaging of post–silent era cinema. The cinematic patrimony of the entire world, which seemed destined to be forgotten, became newly accessible and it began to circulate in a chaotic and tumultuous manner at all hours of the day and night on all channels—without any attempt to regulate or control it. Because viewers preferred movies over any other type of programming, cinema flooded television schedules. It has been calculated that by the end of the 1970s, thousands of cinematic titles were being transmitted every day by the antennas of countless private television stations. The shape and landscape of film production in Italy and abroad changed drastically. American cinema emerged from a cycle of long crises and embarked on a revival that would lead to its nearly absolute domination of the international market. In Italy, the great producers like Ponti and De Laurentiis began to disappear, emigrate, or lay down their arms. They considered television to be the only true producer of cinema and they made way for small, courageous entrepreneurs who risked everything with each film. These filmmakers, who initially counted on government subsidies, were well aware that they had to cater to niche markets. Their films would appear briefly in a few art-house theaters before being screened at all hours of the night on public and private television stations.

Who were the producers who worked during the final decades of the twentieth century? The slots at the top of the list are held by those who were able to navigate the treacherous waters of the previous decade. Together with his father Mario Cecchi Gori, Vittorio began to finance successful comedies directed by Castellano and Pipolo or by Neri Parenti and Carlo Verdone. There were also Goffredo Lombardo, Alfredo Bini, and Franco Cristaldi, whose son Massimo would follow in his footsteps. Together with Alberto Grimaldi, all of these producers achieved their greatest successes in the late 1960s through the early 1970s.[9] Then came a long list of producers who would also play important roles as distributors before television changed the rules of engagement: Roberto Cicutto together with Mikado, Luigi and Aurelio de Laurentiis, Mario Gallo, Fulvio Lucisano, Andrea Occhipinti, Antonio Avati,

Domenico Procacci, Mauro Berardi, Giovanni Minervini, Tonino Cervi, Silvio Clementelli, Giuseppe Colombo, Giovanni di Clemente, Pio Angeletti, Luciano Martino, Franco Committeri, Francesco Adriano de Micheli, Angelo Bassi, Giovanni Bertolucci, Claudio Bonivento, Gianfranco Piccioli, Mario Orfini, Leo Pescarolo, Enzo Porcelli, Marina Piperno, Angelo Barbagallo and Nanni Moretti, Maurzio Tedesco, Stefano Agosti, Conchita Airoldi, Monica Venturini, Sandro Parenzo, and Italo Zingarelli. Very quickly, the majority of these producers found themselves faced with a fleeting market that was more and more allergic to art films. Beyond a constantly changing audience and a suddenly stagnant market, they were also forced to come to terms with the fact that many of their films were destined to be seen on the small screen of public television.[10] Then there were the producers of the most recent generation, who deserve credit for their belief that the machine could be restarted: Domenico Procacci, Gianni Romoli, Tilde Corsi, Gianluca Arcopinto, Maurizio Tini, and Lionello Cerri. Together with many others, they have attempted to restore the lost art of film production.

At any rate, the truly "great" producers of the final quarter of the twentieth century were RAI and Finivest. Beginning in 1976, RAI produced films by Bellocchio, Olmi, the Taviani Brothers, Fellini, Rosi, Giordana, Avati, Lizzani, Antonioni, Amelio, Moretti, Del Monte, Carlo Verdone, Squitieri, Loy, Monicelli, Comencini, Troisi, Tornatore, Marco Rici, Scola, Maselli, Montaldo, and Wertmüller. Finivest first entered the scene in 1984 as Reteitalia and Penta and it produced films by Moretti, Piscicelli, Tornatore, Dino Risi, Ferreri, Salvatores, Rosi, Luchetti, Argento, Olmi, Mazzacurati, the Taviani brothers, and Maselli.[11] Clearly, these were important editorial choices, regardless of individual titles, and they helped to support directors who delivered superior films. It quickly became evident that the presence of these two colossal producers was necessary to create films intended for European markets. Not only did they help to nurture new talent, but they also made it possible for established directors to work under excellent conditions.

The time has come for scholars of Italian cinema to devote in-depth study to made-for-television films and to recognize these works for their cinematographic virtues. Many masters who made their debut in the 1960s have made films for television without turning their backs on the language of cinema: Olmi, the Taviani brothers, and even younger directors like Zaccaro, Carlei, Sironi (with his series of Commissario [Inspector] Montalbano films), and Alberto Negrin (in particular, his *Perlasca* or *Perlasca: The Courage of a Just Man,* 2002). RAI and Mediaset have produced many important works in recent years. Some of these films have been colossal in scope in terms of both investment and spectacular vision. Even though some of these were intended solely for television, they, too, have every right to be considered part of the legacy of Italian film.

In recent years, the production of dramatizations, series, and mini-series has expanded and in some cases, these works—*Il maresciallo Rocca* (*Marshall Rocca*), *Commesse* (*Saleswomen*), *Linda e il brigadiere* (*Linda and the Brigadier*), *Ultimo* (*Codename: Ultimo*), and *La vita che verrà* (*The Life That Will Come*)— have enjoyed consistent popularity with audiences, in part because they drew from the tradition of postwar Italian cinema and Italian comedy. These works told the stories and depicted the dreams of common Italians by filtering their characters through workaday experiences with which viewers could identify. One important element of their success was the viewer's familiarity with the domestic setting, the direct violation of the characters' privacy, and the public use of private affairs.

In reviewing the films of recent years, it becomes clear how stories set in the present have enjoyed greater success than nostalgic works that revisit the 1950s and 1960s and all the mythologies linked to those decades. The most successful programs seem to tend to give new life—nearly fifty years later—to the depiction of personal stories of common people who have no story—in the tradition of Luciano Emmer's *Una domenica d'agosto* (*Sunday in August*) and *Le ragazze di Piazza di Spagna* (*Three Girls from Rome*) and other works that belong to the genre of so-called *neorealismo rosa* (rosy neorealism).

At this point, let's take a look at the role played by the Istituto Luce in terms of production and distribution.[12]

In 1962, the Istituto became a publicly traded company. Thanks to the international success of Marcellini's documentary, *La grande Olimpiade* (*The Grand Olympics*, 1961), it was able to launch feature-length and artistic productions. In 1965, it became the first producer of children's films, with films like Gianni da Campo's *Pagine chiuse* (*Closed Pages*, 1966), Ernesto Guida's *Un amico* (*A Friend*, 1967), Pino Zac's *Il cavaliere inesistente* (*The Nonexistent Knight*, 1968), Lino del Fra's *La torta in cielo* (*Cake in the Sky*, 1970), Angelo d'Alessandro's *Turi e i paladini* (*Turi and the Paladins*, 1977), Pupi Avati's *Noi tre* (*The Three of Us*, 1983), and Cristina Comencini's *Zoo* (1986). In 1982, the Istituto also became a distributor through Italnoleggio. In the late 1960s, Luce was producing works by well-established directors but it also began investing in up-and-coming and young filmmakers like Lizzani, Pino Zac, Avati, Mingozzi, Paolo Benvenuti, Orsini, Giuseppe Bertolucci, Bellocchio, Bladi, Pasquale Misuraca, Squitieri, Gianni Amelio, Beppe Cino, Monicelli, Wilma Labate, Giovanna Gagliardo, Luca Verdone, Sandro Cecca, Francesco Ranieri Martinotti, Vito Zagarrio, Fabio Carpi, Mario Brenta, Michele Placido, Scola, Peter del Monte, and Francesca Archibugi, among others. By the end of the 1980s, Luce had begun to partner with foreign studios and to distribute internationally, releasing films by Claude Chabrol, Otar Iosseliani, and Theo Anghelopoulos.

In 1994, Luce asked Folco Quilici to direct a series of eighty documentaries devoted to *La storia d'Italia del XX secolo* (*Twentieth-Century Italian History*) with historians Renzo de Felice, Valerio Castronovo, and Pietro Scoppola as consultants. The project marked a new phase for Luce in which the studio began to delve into digital formats and historical footage. Luce operates independently of Cinecittà: in its capacity as a public institution, Luce has a bright future in terms of production, distribution, and the use of Italian archival material.

With growth in consumption and higher standards of living in Italy, cinema seemed to have lost once and for all its status as a public ritual and absolutely necessary privilege. Filmmakers began to lose faith in the profitability of their work. By the end of the 1970s, investors no longer viewed filmmaking as bottom-line profitable enterprise. Not surprisingly, this period saw a proliferation of small producers who resorted to government subsidies. In some cases, the results were praiseworthy, but they were often anemic, asphyxic, and lacking in thematic substance.[13] Such filmmakers deserved encouragement and support, but they certainly were not appropriate for innovative global marketing strategies. A comparison between the generation of Spielberg, Lucas, and Scorsese with that of their Italian contemporaries in the 1970s is seemingly impossible. To compare them would be unfair on all levels. Ties between producers and directors from previous generations became weaker and weaker, as did faith in the potential of cinema as an artistic medium. Experimentation ceased and theaters were empty.

In the 1960s, Italian government subsidies helped to launch the careers of Silvano Agosti, Gianfranco Mingozzi, Fabio Carpi, Emidio Greco, Maurizio Ponzi, Giuseppe Ferrara, Ansano Giannarelli, and Toni de Gregorio. The Taviani Brothers and Carmelo Bene received government aid for some of their early films and subsidies also helped to launch Luigi Faccini, Peter del Monte, Nanni Moretti, Franco Piavoli, Salvatore Maira, Nino Bizzarri, Nico d'Alessandria, Francesca Archibugi, Fulvio Wetzl, Davide Ferrario, Paolo Benvenuti, Nico Cirasola, Silvio Soldini, Sergio Rubini, Michele Sordillo, Antonio Capuano, Guido Chiesa, Pasquale Pozzessere, Aurelio Grimaldi, Lucia Guadino, Vito Zagarrio, Pappi Corsicato, Wilma Labate, Stefano Incerti, Vanna Paoli, and Fulvio Ottaviano, among others. Thus, a relatively meager and low-profile investment by the government delivered a substantial return, allowing a number of notable players appearing to join the team of Italian filmmakers.[14]

Over the past twenty years or so, roughly twenty new filmmakers have emerged (in the 1980s, nearly three hundred directors made their debuts). Even though most of these directors never achieved commercial success and consequently never made a second film, many of their works are worthy of the attention and praise that critics and audiences have failed to deliver. Among these, the women alone account for a significant group of directors: Vanna Paoli, Anna Negri, Antonietta de Lillo, Stefania Casini, Roberta Torre, Isabella Sandri, Angiola Janigro, Nina di Majo, Wilma Labate, Cara Apuzzo, Elisabetta Lodoli, Giovanna Gagliardo, Simona Izzo, Cecilia Calvi, Cristina Comencini, Anna di Francisca, and Laura Belli, among others.

More than ever before, young filmmakers are producing their own films. During the 1980s, even though many of their films were screened and awarded prizes in film festivals, few managed to obtain distribution. In previous decades, nearly every film—whatever the genre—made it to theaters, even though few generated more than paltry box-office sales. *Nostra Signora dei Turchi* (*Our Lady of the Turks*), for example, was screened in art houses even though it never made much money. But at a certain point, it seemed that Italian films without major distribution were being denied this opportunity. The only exception to the rule was Fulvio Wetzl's *Prima la musica poi le parole* (*First the Music, Then the Words*), a film that screened at more than sixty international festivals before it obtained limited distribution in Italy.

For the past fifteen years or so, young Italian cinema has been practically invisible (only a handful of films have managed to generate modest box-office sales at best). Young Italian cinema is a phantom without any shared habitat or stylistic, cultural, or ideological interconnections. Beyond government subsidies, Italian cinema deserves greater attention and it could use an injection of faith. Otherwise, its chronic state of creative autism will remain unchanged and it will continue to be shunned by audiences. Italian cinema has slowly lost faith in its own means and it has lost the self-confidence that was its strength in the most difficult of times. But it has also lost the confidence of art-house owners, who, because of diminishing government support, have been forced overwhelmingly to embrace the blockbuster phenomenon.

The classic producer has been replaced by individuals who have more in common with brokers and traders. Very few are willing to take risks and catastrophic results have discouraged even the most courageous among them. In any case, by the early 1980s, the level of fragmentation had reached hypertrophic proportions: during the 1980–81 season, 87 Italian films were made by 67 production companies; only 2 years later, 112 titles were produced by 84 companies. By the early 1990s, the number of production houses nearly coincided with the number of titles produced (90 companies, 97 films). Television has done little to encourage small production houses and rarely does it throw out a life preserver to directors' first films. Throughout the 1980s, despite a few exceptions to the rule, the Italian film industry gradually drowned and was forced to reduce its margins. It lost its sense of purpose and was no longer able to weave a fabric strong enough to maintain relationships with foreign markets. Comedy and new comedians became the only commodities deemed worthy of investment by high-level operators. At the same time, the industry witnessed the disappearance of the genres that had represented the bread and butter of general audiences. Masters like Fellini, Antonioni, the Taviani Brothers, Olmi, Ferreri, and Scola no longer seemed able to generate audience interest. And in recent years, even the works of Carlo Verdone have disappointed at the box office.

In the mid-1980s, Cecchi Gori began its unstoppable and incomparable rise. Its dominance of the domestic market has been nearly unchallenged. In the short term, its alliance with Berlusconi Communications, forged toward the end of the decade, did not bear the fruits hoped for, neither at home nor abroad. In the early 1990s, it opened Pentamerica, an independent production house located in Los Angeles. But its attempt to challenge the Americans on their home turf has been most disappointing.

The last to arrive on the scene was Reteitalia, a branch of Fininvest's film division. Traditional film producers have never known the financial liquidity enjoyed by Reteitalia: in its first year alone, it invested a figure equivalent to 40 percent of domestic production. Reteitalia's capital was warmly embraced and it quickly became clear that capital was becoming the key element necessary to change the market and a factor in subsequent vertical integration. Because costs are immediately covered by pre-sales to television, the associated producers have not had to struggle to improve the quality of their products. In fact, the exact opposite occurred as Reteitalia took the place of Gaumont Italia, a production company many hoped would create a new generation of young, talented directors. Despite its liquidity, private television has weakened creativity and has begun to transform cinematic products into made-for-television products. In the beginning Reteitalia produced genre films like Il commissario Lo Gatto (Commissioner Lo Gatto, 1986) by Dino Risi, Morirai a mezzanotte (The Midnight Killer, 1986) and Le foto di Gioia (Delirium, Delirium: Photo of Gioia, Gioia's Photograph, Photo of Gioia, or Photos of Joy, 1987) by Lamberto Bava, Puro cashmere (Pure Cashmere, 1986) by Biagio Proietti, and Rimini Rimini (1987) by Corbucci. These films were intended to hasten the directors' passage from cinema to the small screen, and Reteitalia was not concerned with performance in theaters. One exception was Retei-talia's light comedy *Superfantozzi* (*Super Fantozzi*, 1987) by Neri Parenti, which was intended as a theater release. But in 1988 it began to invest in new directors and more serious projects.

Executives of both private and public television companies began to real-ize that foreign products were simply more profitable because the cost was already amortized. In-house production brought with it the risk that the prod-uct would not be sold abroad. It was not until the 1990s that legislation was passed to promote the production of Italian fictional films. The new govern-ment support reversed previous trends and a large number of new directors, actors, and technicians began to wave the television banner. But throughout the 1980s, instead of creating new opportunities and encouraging growth in the film industry, television opted for dependence on U.S. products and on television series in particular. By doing so, television generated enormous sums of money through increasingly profitable advertising sales.

With each passing year, television's weight has grown and, increasingly, it has affected the language of cinema. Today, it seems that many directors see television viewers as their primary audience.

As we cast our gaze beyond television and contemplate the entire audiovi-sual entertainment universe, it becomes clear that we are in the middle of an intergalactic war for the control of production and broadcasting. The level of investment would have been unthinkable even a few years ago. International competition has grown fiercer and twenty-first-century technologies promise the creation of interactive networks, virtual reality, and the globalization of information. All of these processes are destined to produce profound muta-tions in the nature of images and entirely transform the iconosphere, our means of access to new images, and our creative powers. According to studies by ANICA, cinema will become a weaker and weaker pawn in the game to control global information and broadcasting. In the meantime, the film business itself has changed radically: the number of screens has grown thanks to the birth of multiplexes, but the number of tickets sold has not increased proportionately.[15]

Over the past few years, the era of celluloid has rapidly come to an end. Those who did not foresee the rise of digital film now find themselves left behind. Only recently did Cinecittà begin to retool for new technologies. Research and innovation are the key ingredients to an active and competitive role on the international market. On a playing field increasingly dominated by American giants, we must ask ourselves, what can Italy's role be? As the new millennium unfolds, unless we begin to encourage new directors to step forward, there doesn't seem to be much hope for an industry that thinks only in domestic terms.

The Italians' delay in embracing new technology and the disparity in financial resources with respect to the United States have clearly penalized the Italian film industry. But all is not lost. We must continue to believe in and exploit our creative tradition, the raw material of Italian cinema. We must find new ways to make the most of our heritage. We must begin again to weave the threads of international partnerships and we must revive our ability to think in terms of the big picture, even when challenged by modest resources. We must quit the little garden where we have produced films and transform our many individual weaknesses into shared, unifying strengths. We need new forms of distribution and new channels of transmission, including the Internet, which has redefined the entire industry.[16]

Even though the spring of 2001 brought new hope to Italian cinema, the rhythms and realities of the market in the new millennium are not encouraging.[17] There is no new fervor circulating among a new generation of cineastes inspired by decentralization and polytopic production, nor is there a new will to communicate using images superior to any of those produced in the past.

Signs of Loss, Signs of Hope

"Mamma mia, Italian cinema got smaller!" The average Italian moviegoer might say something like this if she or he were to awake after thirty years of hibernation. Whether browsing the number of Italian films screened in multiplexes today or simply looking at box-office figures, our reaction is bound to be negative. And let's not even mention the decline in research and stylistic and expressive experimentation, nor the invisibility of Italian films in Italy despite many titles' success in festivals abroad.

Over the past three decades or so, nearly all of the gains of the 1960s have been irrevocably undone.[18] At the same time, even in the roughest and most difficult years, when both the market and creativity have been at their lowest, there have still been efforts, attempts, and results that justify a small dose of hope.

Thanks to directors like Bertolucci, Fellini, Antonioni, the Taviani Brothers, Scola, Olmi, Rosi, Ferreri, Salvatores, Tornatore, Amelio, and Benigni, and thanks to other cinema professionals like Danilo Donati, Nicola Piovani, Milena Canonero, Dante Ferretti, Vittorio Storaro, Dante Spinotti, and Carlo Rambaldi, Italian cinema continues to receive top international honors, winning Oscars and prizes at Cannes, Venice, and Berlin. Italian cinema's prestige comes from its history but also from the quality of the films and its ability to speak to international audiences.

Arguably, Bertolucci represents the last great Italian director who will play a leading role in international cinema. He envisioned a cinema capable of marrying the classic lessons of the great masters with modernity. It was thanks to him—but thanks also to Dino de Laurentiis—that cinema professionals like Storaro, Rambaldi, Ferretti, Spinotti, and Pesucci began to work regularly on American and international films.

Thanks to the legacy of neorealism and the films of the 1960s, the love for Italian cinema abroad has never diminished, especially among erudite moviegoers. To a certain extent, foreigners have more appreciation for postwar Italian cinema (and even for directors who have debuted over the past three decades) than Italians themselves—a fact that has emerged from the excellent research conducted by Monica Repetto and Carlo Tagliabue.[19]

Italian directors have progressively lost their ability to tell stories that go beyond their own personal experiences. Today, a collection of restored silent-era Italian films has a better chance of successfully touring the United States than do current Italian films of even being screened outside of Italy, let alone across the Atlantic.

The closer we get to the present era, our work as historians becomes increasingly difficult. Our assessments can only be partial and the many individual elements of current Italian cinema are nearly impossible to categorize or compare. In a certain sense, the simplification of the elements and our discourse has been imposed by the situation itself.

From 1975 to 1985, the number of moviegoers decreased by almost 400 million. In the 1990s, that number dropped below 100 million tickets sold annually. By 1985, the number of working screens dropped from 6,500 to 3,400 and by the year 2000, that number fell to 2,400. While 230 films were produced in 1975, only 80 were made in 1985.[20]

Of course, the decade 1975–85 also saw a generational changing of the guard. But the personalities who emerged did not ignite the same contrasting passions as did the fathers of early decades (just think of the media interest—domestic and international—created by Fellini). What we do see is periodic overdoses of enthusiasm from a critic or group of critics, but such support does not suffice to sway public opinion. Despite the abundance of independent spirit, Italian directors have never been and have never felt so alone and rudderless.

In my previous guide to Italian cinema (published in 1991), I used the mathematical figure of "Cantor's dust" to describe a situation where points in space are multiplied but lack a common plane.[21]

The revolt against the fathers did not happen in the early 1960s, nor did it take place in 1968, when many directors heeded a call to (symbolic) arms by making westerns. Instead, it happened suddenly and unexpectedly in 1976, when a single director, Nanni Moretti, debuted with a Super 8 film entitled *Io sono un autarchico* (*I Am Self Sufficient*). Although he had not planned to kill anyone off, the fallout on Italian cinema was such that Moretti seemed to have abruptly cast off the ballast passed down by Italian cinema's previous masters. The young Moretti did not ferociously attack the "cinema of the fathers" the way the future directors of the Nouvelle Vague had done from the pages of *Cahiers du cinéma* in the late 1950s. The new director did possess, however, a strong sense of self and a will to make movies that would redefine filmmaking. He was driven by a quasi-religious fervor and he pushed himself to surpass the confines of the ego in his attempt to discover and stimulate his talents.

However appropriate it is to place Moretti in the greater context of new trends, it is also important to note that Italian cinema since 1976 has been marked by his charisma and his ability to interpret the humors and spirit of a generation of Italian filmmakers who do not identify with the furor of 1968. His contemporaries were dissatisfied with Italian cinema and they sought out an identity that could differentiate them from those who had preceded them.[22] Moretti's impact on Italian cinema since 1976 cannot be disputed, even if Michele Apicella, the successful director played by Moretti in *Sogni d'oro* (*Sweet Dreams*, 1981), who is acutely aware of the burden of such responsibility, is quick to say: "I don't represent young people. I'm barely able to represent myself."

It would be wrong to concentrate our attention solely on Moretti. But many consider him an indispensable role model who asserted—even under difficult conditions—his own poetics and authorship in the face of hostile forces. Many have been inspired by his strong sense of individualism, his innovation, his nonviolent killing off of the "fathers," his meticulousness and self-discipline, his intolerance of any idea passed down by his precursors, and his multifaceted methods of working. His proud loner attitude was born out of narcissism and self-esteem. It won him consensus and followers in the short term. and in the long term it activated other forces and conferred new faith in cinema.

As we have noted previously, the landscape of Italian cinema has been marked by a sense of loss but not by the disappearance of a "will to make movies." In fact, that will has grown together with increasing access to video cameras—the inevitable substitute for the movie camera. Thanks to its manageability and image quality, the video camera seems to have fulfilled Alexander Astruc and Zavattini's dream of *caméra stylo*. Today, as they imagined, people use video cameras as easily as they do a pen or typewriter.

In his 1985 "Open Letter to Young Filmmakers" (originally published in *Rinascita*), Goffredo Fofi addressed his ideal director with the following words: "Today, with relatively low costs, it is not difficult to make cinema (or video, which is also 'cinema'). The current generation enjoys possibilities that previous generations of *cinéphiles* did not even dare to dream of. It is a privilege, and as with all privileges, it is important to know how to use it properly and to recognize the responsibilities that come with it."[23]

Hundreds of new directors have appeared on the scene since then and many have traveled through space with the speed of a shooting star. While many have remained invisible, others have not received the attention that they deserve.[24]

Two Bridges: Fellini and Bertolucci

Now it is time for us to turn our attention to two directors who continued to serve as the cornerstones of Italian cinema over the past decades and who have bridged the gap between Italian cinema of the past and audiences across the globe: Fellini and Bertolucci.

In Fellini's later films, the director forced his characters to accept their emptiness and sense of dispersion and to fill the void with a false joy and false relationship to others. In the early 1970s, Fellini's gaze began to expand but so did the figures that moved in his frame. A form of gigantism marked his work, as if he were staging an enormous living museum of exaggerated, monstrous figures. With every film, his hypertrophic amusement part grew and his camera forced the characters to ride a roller coaster of heightened sensation and sudden emptiness. Some have interpreted his later films—*Prova d'orchestra* (*Orchestra Rehearsal*, 1979), *La città delle donne* (*City of Women*, 1979), *E la nave va* (*And the Ship Sails On*, 1983), *Ginger e Fred* (*Ginger and Fred*, 1985), and *La voce della luna* (*The Voice of the Moon*, 1990)—as metaphorical variations on Italy's political situation and the sense of imminent collapse, on the lack of communication and the triumph of noise pollution. The funereal veil that Fellini progressively draped over his work was born out a synchronic tendency—from one catastrophe to the next—toward apocalyptic dimensions. *E la nave va*, for example, envisaged a nuclear nightmare and it evoked—

using the only two elements to survive, man and the rhinoceros—a miniature version of Noah's ark. The end of the world, wrote Italo Calvino, was "a recurring them in Fellini . . . *E la nave va* is perhaps the most explicit in this regard. But this film does not impose such pathos on us as other Fellini films have. [It makes us feel] as if we all understood that the end of the world is our natural habitat, as if we could not imagine any other way of living."[25]

Even if he wore the robes of a mass-media Cassandra for more than a decade, Fellini never lost his hope in the future of cinema and he always found his vanishing point and salvation—an island on which he could land and let the phantoms of his imagination run free.

Beginning in the early 1970s, Fellini's films were marked increasingly by a sense that death was near and a perception of mortality. During this same period, Bertolucci, instead, embraced his role as the northern star of modernity.[26]

As he began work on the colossal *Novecento* (*1900*, 1976), Bertolucci finally found his true voice as epic narrator. With this film, he mastered all narrative registers and dramatic models as he orchestrated multiple stories and merged microhistory and history. The Po River Valley became the central character, its beauty violated at different moments in the story. Bertolucci draws the viewer closer to the landscape and the changing seasons through an emotional involvement that will be transformed over the course of the film, all the while maintaining the viewer's enchantment with never-before-seen worlds and places. Especially in the first part, the film brings the viewer in contact with the ways and shapes of farming life, just as Bertolucci had done splendidly in *Strategia del ragno* (*The Spider's Stratagem*). But the director also managed—as if through synesthesia—to make the viewer smell its aromas and hear its sounds. He plunged into that world in search of deeper meanings and in an attempt to evoke the iconographic tradition of nineteenth- and twentieth-century and contemporary painting.[27]

With *La luna* (*Luna*, 1979), Bertolucci turned his attention to private rather than choral motifs and he revived the theme of incest, which he had tackled previously in *Prima della rivoluzione* (*Before the Revolution*). Like *La tragedia di un uomo ridicolo* (*Tragedy of a Ridiculous Man*, 1981), *La luna* is a film about cultural repatriation. In both films, he was aided in his experimentation by Storaro's cinematography and Kim Arcalli and Gabriella Cristiani's editing. In the second film, he addressed not only terrorism but also the economic and industrial transformation of the farmer's world.

During this period, Bertolucci was one of the few Italian directors who made internationally competitive films. By the early 1980s, only a handful of Italian directors were capable of telling stories beyond the provincial.

Following *La luna* and *La tragedia di un uomo ridicolo*, Bertolucci cast his gaze onto uncharted waters and decided to go head to head with epic history. With *L'ultimo imperatore* (*The Last Emperor*, 1987), he tackled Chinese history, recounting the different phases of the last emperor's life and telling the story using the main character's point of view. The first contact between little Pu Yi, who had been anointed emperor at three years of age, and his seeming endless army lined up before him showed that an Italian director could create a new world on the screen and it returned a sense of magic to Italian cinema. For *L'ultimo imperatore*, Bertolucci won an Oscar and established himself definitely as one of the masters of international cinema.

Il tè nel deserto (*The Sheltering Sky*, 1990), based on a Paul Bowles novel, was yet another story of a search for self in which the characters flee the present and erase their true identities. Although the film is not perfectly balanced in all its parts, cinematographer Vittorio Storaro delivered some of the best work in his career and some of the best photography of the past three decades.

In *Piccolo Buddha* (*Little Buddha*, 1993), Bertolucci once again told a story of initiation. But in this case, the tale is filled with reflection on the need for religion, an element lacking in the previous film, and on the meeting of two worlds and two civilizations. Bertolucci seemed more and more interested in bridging worlds and different cultures, including European and American filmmaking. His was a view from on high and it was accompanied by narrative and visual experimentation of the greatest caliber for the depths of its echoes and the cultural and iconographic resonance wrapped by his imagery.

In *Io ballo da sola* (*Stealing Beauty* or *Dancing by Myself*, 1996), he returned to a story told against the Italian landscape, even though the Tuscan hills of this film are inhabited by a community of Americans. In both this and the previous film, Bertolucci's gaze was less detached and contemplative—and less reminiscent of Ford. His gaze seemed much closer than before: the camera's eye acts like a vampire who lusts after the body and the soul of the main character, after the miracle of her youth and innocence.

Based on a James Lasdun story and made for television, *L'assedio* (*Besieged* or *The Siege*, 1998) can be considered a "bedroom film" in which the director, nearly thirty years later and with much richer cultural and anthropological implications, once again portrays an encounter between and man and woman. But this time, they each come from different worlds. In the film, Mr. Kinsky utters only a few worlds to the young Shanduray: "I love you . . . I am hopelessly in love with you." At the end of the film and the end of the siege, the girl writes him a note after they have slept together: "I love you." Through Kinsky, Bertolucci seemed intent on reviving the spirit of the troubadours and the literature of courtly love. As he gives away all of his possessions without asking for anything in return, including the finale sacrifice of his Steinway piano, there are echoes of Boccaccio's Federigo degli Alberighi, who sacrifices his most prized possession and companion, a falcon, to win a woman's heart.

The Loss of the Center
(for Cinematic Experimentation)

In the mid-1970s, a series of untimely deaths left generations of Italian directors fatherless when De Sica, Visconti, Rossellini, Germi, Pasolini, Petri, and Petrangeli, among others, all died.[28] These deaths, perhaps, were not the principal cause of the system's weakening. Italian cinema was already going through a process of natural selection that would restrict the realm of possibilities. But the loss of these directors did represent a watershed and the beginning of a new phase in Italian cinema. While time would diminish the influence of most of these filmmakers, the memory of Pasolini has taken on monumental proportions and his work continues to have prolific effects on international cinema.

In the confluence of negative forces that reshaped Italian cinema, it is clear today that Rossellini's management of the Centro Sperimentale di Cinematografia played an important role. His concept of authoriality was born out of a mysterious combination of astral and divine influences. In the years of his presidency, Rossellini repelled the movement of 1968 as he asserted his own agenda and destroyed some of the strongest elements that had made the Roman school a benchmark of international cinema. Rossellini did not believe in the need for handing down knowledge or teaching the grammar of cinema.[29] Aspiring directors and film professionals accepted in the program had to find within themselves the light and a sense of their future in cinema. As an institution, the Centro had always believed in the importance of teaching all aspects of the form. Rossellini's indifference toward learning was one of the primary causes for the void that would be created in Italian cinema and for the modest results of Italian filmmakers. It is true that talent can bloom in moments and in places where you least expect it. But the overall strength of filmmaking is shaped by the level of skill offered by educational institutions and by filmmakers' ability to rise to new artistic and technologic challenges.

When we consider some of the 1970s graduates—like Rosalia Polizzi, Gianni Zanasi, Vito Zagarrio, Francesco Bruni, Roberto Petrocchi, Massimo Martella, Laura Belli, Isabella Sandri, Gianfranco Isernia, and Gianfranco Pannone, among others—we realize that only a few of them have been able to avoid anonymity and achieve a level of continuity in their filmmaking (Francesca Archibugi, for example, and more recently Gabriele Muccino). Others chose to study abroad, like Edoardo Winspeare, who received his degree in Munich. Others took courses in Los Angeles or New York, like Silvio Soldini, Giovanni Robbiano, and Emanuele Crialese. Fabio Segatori studied in Germany, Anna Negri in England. To understand the true potential of future Italian filmmakers, we must first know where they have studied, what has fed their curiosity, and their genetic code.

As we seek to interpret the successes and failures in Italian cinema over the past decades, sooner or later we will have to reflect seriously on what was taught and how it was taught at the Centro Sperimentale from the time of Rossellini's tenure there up to the present. We must try to understand the directorial and professional models the Centro created, the level of technical expertise available to the students, the Centro's professional standards, government investment, and the Centro's ability to keep in step with technologic advances. At a certain point, it became necessary to relieve Rome of its status as the capital of Italian cinema, to decentralize, and to inject the increasingly inert Italian film industry with new blood. It is now clear that you can make great films without having studied filmmaking. In this respect, Moretti has served as a model for many as he opened a new chapter in Italian film.

Perhaps because he felt he needed to atone for the sins of his father or perhaps because like his father he was confident that he could create a breeding ground for new talent using unconventional methods, Renzo Rossellini, then director of Gaumont Italia, opened a school with Gaumont itself. Although its doors remained open only for a short time, the school allowed directors like Daniele Luchetti, Giuseppe Piccioni, and Carlo Carlei to develop their talent and fulfill their aspirations.

In the early 1980s, RAI president Paolo Valmarana and Ermanno Olmi opened Ipotesi Cinema in Bassano, a school intended to revive Rossellini's unconventional spirit. Rather than technical know-how, the school's program focused on ethics and integrity in filmmaking and an approach to filmmaking that championed freedom of expression.[30] Olmi's school showed how modes and forms of cinematic storytelling were changing and how authoriality needed to find new forms of expression, recognition, and legitimization. In the arc of ten years, Francesca Archibugi, Augusto Tretti, and Mario Brenta (who, together with Toni Gregorio, played an important role as teacher and organizer at the school) would all pass through Bassano. Many directors made their first films there, like Maurizio Zaccaro, Giacomo Campiotti, Marcello Siena, Piergiorgio Gay, Stefano Masi, and Francesco Alberti. Ipotesi proved to be more of a laboratory for ideas and experimentation than a breeding ground for new talent. Together with Moretti, Ipotesi offered a new ethical model for aspiring directors in the 1980s. Like Moretti, Ipostesi helped to create faith in Italian cinema even in the difficult years of the next decade.

Many believed that the events of 1968 would lead to Italian cinema's palingenesis and an affirmation of new creative freedom. In fact, the year 1968 was marked paradoxically by the creation of a boundary that stifled experimentation. In the decade that followed, directors no longer sought to expand their horizons, nor did they take risks in their linguistic and expressive choices. There was no more contamination of forms and styles, nor was there any polysemy in their images, scripts, or soundtracks. Few directors attempted to affirm their autonomy through the transgression of existing codes. But a small number of experimental filmmakers were able to achieve financial success without compromising their integrity: Luigi Faccini, Mario Brenta, Gian Vittorio Baldi (who was also an important producer of films by Jean-Marie Straub, Mingozzi, Pasolini, Nelo Risi, and Robert Bresson), Silvano Agosti (who produced Piavoli's first film), Giuseppe Bertolucci, Fabio Carpi, Sergio Citti, Emidio Greco, Gabriele Salvatores, Gianni Amelio, Franco Piovoli, Tonino de Bernardi, Silvio Soldini, Ciprí and Maresco, Yervant Gianikian and Angela Ricci Lucchi, Corso Salani, and Alberto Rondalli, among others.

At the same time, the 1970s saw the birth of new and alternative channels for distribution. During this period, directors gravitated toward "poorer" forms of storytelling that they could control, and there were new places and occasions in which they could screen their products when they chose not to obey the laws of the market. Many chased the dream of absolute freedom but few were able to remain faithful to their own poetic world.

In Northern Italy, independent cooperative production houses began to appear, like I Cammelli and Studio Azzurro. In the early 1980s, they helped to launch the careers of Soldini, Salvatores, Giancarlo Soldi, Segre, Chiesa, Gabriella Rosaleva, Paolo Rosa, and Bruno Bigoni.[31] The birth of festivals like Cinema Giovanni di Torino in 1982 and then Anteprima the following year would also help a new generation of independent Italian filmmakers screen their work.

From the "Years of Lead" to the Years of Flight

During the elections of 1975, only a few months before his death, Pasolini published his "Abiura della Triologia della vita," an "abjuration" of the "Trilogy of Life," his three films Il Decameron (The Decameron), I racconti di Canterbury (The Canterbury Tales), and Il fiore delle Mille e una notte (A Thousand and

One Nights, *Arabian Nights*, or *Flower of the Arabian Nights*). The essay affirmed that the leftist victory in the elections marked Italy's depoliticization. Italians, he wrote, would live from that point on in a "process of adaptation to their own degradation."

This process reached its climax in the 1980s, when Italian cinema became the ultimate expression of Italy's loss of a sense of state and the triumph of the private over the public. In Italian comedies as well as other genres, film depicted a celebration of consumerism and derision of any form of participation in the political process. The Vanzina brothers' commercially successful films, for example, portrayed an expanding homogenization of behaviors based on exasperated individualism and the declining value of belonging to a civil society.

By the second half of the 1970s, political discourse in Italy no longer mattered to directors who had previously invested their creative energy in political films. The escalation of terrorism seemed unstoppable and could be interpreted with traditional ideological tools. The "years of lead" were a watershed for socially engaged and intellectual Italians. From then on, Italian directors seemed to exclude all political and civil discourse from the screen and many filmmakers found themselves rudderless.

Since the 1970s, directors have found it difficult to address the issue of terrorism and they have been forced to treat the subject with circumspection. Gianfranco Mingozzi was the first to tackle the theme of terrorism in *La vita in gioco* (*Playing for Your Life*, 1972). He was followed by Marco Tullio Giordana with *Maledetti vi amerò* (*To Love the Damned*, 1980), Bernardo Bertolucci with *La tragedia di un uomo ridicolo* (*Tragedy of a Ridiculous Man*, 1981), Gianni Amelio with *Colpire al cuore* (*Blow to the Heart*, 1983), and Giuseppe Bertolucci with *Segreti segreti* (*Secrets Secrets*, 1984). These directors sought to explore the relationships between the disappearing political "I" and the individual "I" who was no longer able to find a balance in society. It became more and more difficult for screenwriters—especially young screenwriters—to create a political and social ambience in their films. Unlike German director Margarethe von Trotta, who made *Die bleierne Zeit* (*Marianne and Juliane* or *The German Sisters*, entitled *Anni di Piombo* or *Years of Lead* in Italy) in 1981, young filmmakers were unable to tell stories from the terrorists' point of view, nor were they capable of penetrating the terrorist's psychology. The terrorist's motives and forces behind terrorism proved too difficult to decipher.

In Italian westerns, directors adeptly evoked a revolution that never occurred. But they never seemed to truly capture the ideals, characters, and dark forces behind terrorism. Even in Amelio's film, one of the most significant, terrorism plays only a supporting role since the focal point of the screenplay (by Amelia and Vincenzo Cerami) is the theme of generational differences. The story centers on the rift between a politically engaged father, who to some extent is an accomplice to terrorism, and a son who is entirely unaware of what is happening around him but does not hesitate to report his father.

The horizon of idealism began to disappear from sight as most Italian directors, old and new, turned their attention to the past and to the private. For most of them, the greater problem was how to escape the "years of lead" and many did so by shedding the weight of political and social involvement. It would take roughly a decade before a group of young Italian screenwriters revived socially engaged cinema using themes drawn from the past and the present, even though their interests were more social than political.

Moretti's Films as the Diary of a Generation

The ebb in social engagement affected the new generation of filmmakers by erasing the memory of the mythical and historical "fathers" of Italian cinema. The post-1968, post-revolutionary generation found its eponymous hero in Michele Apicella, director Moretti's alter ego beginning with *Io sono un autarchico* (*I Am Self Sufficient*) through *La messa è finita* (*The Mass Is Ended*). Apicella found himself in a state of growing confusion as he watched the old value systems crumble and discovered that he was unable to communicate with the texts of the past, nor was he able to find a substitute ("I don't understand anything," he says. "Maybe I picked the wrong ideology"). Apicella was an emblem for a generation of petit bourgeois who had come of age in 1968 and he was a medium through which Moretti portrayed the mythologies, code words, frustrations, symbols of prestige, clichés, dissociations, and common ground of those who had chosen radical protest as their form of expression. With extraordinary timeliness, Moretti aptly depicted their life journey, transformation, and irreversible failure to create an alternative culture. "Many years ago," says one character in *La messa è finita* (1985), "we had a plan and a shared dream. But we were wrong!" In *Palombella rossa* (*Red Wood Pigeon*, 1989), before the water polo match, the main character suffers an attack of amnesia. He knows that he is a Communist, but he only has a partial memory of his past. Today, his subsequent confusion and his attempt to discover his identity during the match evokes the transformation of Italian Communist Party secretary Achille Occhetto, who decided to turn a new page when he unapologetically turned his back on the Soviet Union and the Soviet bloc and changed the party's symbols and code words. Occhetto looked instead to the social democracies of continental Europe for the party's new model.

Thanks to his innate talent, Moretti was able to create a sort of autobiographical pact with his audience. He became the singer of their lives and beliefs. He was a representative of his generation's attempt to restore order to their otherwise confused and contradictory behavior.[32]

The screening of Moretti's first film in Rome in 1976 (at Adriano Aprà's legendary Filmstudio) was to become one of the decade's defining events. Moretti's approach to filmmaking was crude because he was self-taught, "self-sufficient," and so narcissistic that he seemed to suffer from autism. His early films gave no indication of his affiliation or familiarity with either Italian or foreign filmmakers. He never pushed himself beyond observations of the workaday, nor did he venture beyond the familiar spaces and symbols of petit-bourgeois life. He liked to portray the orators of the middle class living rooms and public schools with their overcrowded classrooms. But his filmmaking style was meticulous and organic, with a keen sense of irony and an ability to distort. In particular, he had an ability to simplify the most complicated elements, and his talent set him apart from all the other directors of that period.

The strength and guiding principle of Moretti's films was that he accepted his own petit-bourgeois origins. Not only was he able to tell his own story but he managed to transform his story into myth and give it cult status. From Nutella and sachertortes, to his checkered shirts and Vespa, his perfectly balanced irony and likeability made his character into a hero and symbol of his generation's hopes, passions, catch phrases, and idiosyncrasies. Members of his generation had lived through the "years of lead" without feeling the revolutionary fire that had inflamed the expectations of their older brothers. Moretti documented his generation's end-of-the-line. "Moretti," wrote Vito Zagarrio, "is the person we would like to be . . . He is our unhappy conscience. *La messa è finita* and *Palombella rossa* are political and cultural manifestos of a generation who has waited in vain for its new messiahs."[33]

As we search Moretti's films for an affinity or kinship with the past, we can turn to Roberto de Gaetano, who perhaps put it best when he wrote that "Moretti's films belong to the grotesque tradition of Italian comedy . . . [His work comes] close to a grotesque [form of] restitution to a society that has been stretched, frayed, and pervaded by pain and death."[34] Moretti calls for respect for the rules and for civil comportment—both public and private. His radicalism must not be confused with that of the preachers of permanent revolution. He does not want to destroy the society around him: he wants to reform and improve it.

But it was not until the 1990s that his gaze seemed to acquire a new depth and a new and more mature awareness as he began to turn his attention to Italian politics and the country's dysfunctional healthcare system, for example.

Caro diario (Dear Diary) was marked by a different way of looking at and relating to people, a different perception of space, of appropriating the signs of things, of sharing them or documenting their transformation. *Caro diario* (1993), *Aprile (April,* 1998), and *La stanza del figlio (The Son's Room,* 2001) marked three moments in Moretti's break from his auto-referential self and his inability to grow. Illness, a son, and secular reflection on destiny and chance delivered a new and different man and director who had finally learned to see others without giving up his place in the middle of the frame.

As if to contradict his own admission of narcissism, Moretti appointed himself as the director of a Warholian factory intended to help launch new Italian directors. The "autarchic" Moretti is one of the few figures in the Italian film industry who have worked openly to nurture new directors. Whenever possible, he has looked for opportunities to give young artists the self-confidence to make short films that reveal their directorial "spark."

As he matured, Moretti became more and more capable of stripping away every superfluous element from his films. His cinematography became more deliberate and more carefully constructed. In his later films, profound nuclei of meaning are delivered directly, in key moments as the director penetrates the heart of things by depicting events that could happen to anyone at any moment. His style became defined by the simplicity with which he tackled and resolved increasingly complex and dramatic situations. In his most recent film, he uses the main character's daily jog to introduce the viewer to the serene life rhythm of a normal person who is healthy and happy, professionally successful, balanced, thoughtful of others, active, and curious. His life is devoted to listening to others and deciphering the signs and symptoms of the persons around him only to experience childish astonishment and wonderment, for example, when he watches a group of Hare Krishna followers do a dance. He owes his life's fullness and fulfillment to the pleasure of living with his wife and children: a still vibrant physical relationship with his wife; the daily ritual of breakfast; his observations of the children's adolescent angst and their early sentimental skirmishes. He watches over his children with the personal satisfaction of knowing that they are truly independent individuals and that they are already entirely free to do as they wish.

There is a tangible sense of freedom and respect for the rules in Giovanni's family. The parents are fully committed to their work and their profession is the most evident manifestation of their civic and political life.

While there is no reference to their ideology, politics are evident in their daily life in terms of their sense of ethics and their need for complete loyalty and transparency. The son is troubled by the trick played on the professor and the lie he tells his father: he knows that he has betrayed principles that govern their family life, but he does not know how to free himself of this burden. As a result, the father is stricken with guilt, having chosen one path instead of another. Inside himself, he feels that he was one of the causes of his son's death. Giovanni can no longer find any meaning in his life or work. The son's friend is named Arianna. She plays a role drawn from mythology: she helps Giovanni and his family escape the infernal tunnel and leads them to the threshold of rebirth. From the moment she leaves them, everything depends on their strength and will to begin to live again.

The 1970s

However different from Moretti, the directors who debuted during the same period were part of a generation of filmmakers defined by separation and isolation rather than a belonging to an identical topological space. As we will see, a handful of screenwriters managed to create connections between different cinematic subjects. Theirs was a generation of erudite directors. They came of age during one of the most vibrant periods of Italian culture in the twentieth century, and they successfully digested forms and models drawn from literature, the figurative arts, and—obviously—cinema.

One of the most interesting figures from this period was Roberto Faenza, whose personality seemed split in two.

On one hand, there was Faenza, the recent graduate of the Centro Sperimentale, who debuted at the end of the 1960s with a film on the turmoil of 1968 (*Escalation*, 1968) and another in the same year on society's rudderless consumerism (*H2S*). He then drew from the era's repertoire to recount the pomp and ominous circumstances of Italian government in the postwar era in *Forza Italia!* (*Go Italy!*, 1977). Later, he tried his hand—with modest success—at genre films.

On the other hand, there was a Faenza, who after a nearly ten-year hiatus, took hold of his ability and identity as a narrator and began to make films about some of the most significant cultural and political themes in Italian twentieth-century history, all the while maintaining dutiful respect for the art of storytelling. This Faenza was a new director who, for all intents and purposes, debuted at the end of the 1980s. In the 1990s and in the first years of the new millennium, he made excellent films that showed stylistic, ideological, and cultural maturity, each based on an important literary work: *Mio caro dottor Gräsler* (*The Bachelor*, 1989), based on the Arthur Schnitzler novel, *Dr. Gräsler, Badearzt*; *Jona che visse nella balena* (*Jonah Who Lived in the Whale* or *Look to the Sky*, 1993), based on Jona Oberski's *Childhood*; *Sostiene Pereira*

(*According to Pereira* or *Pereira Declares*, 1995), based on Antonio Tabucchi's novel by the same title; *Mariana Ucria* (1997), based on *La lunga vita di Marianna Ucria* (*The Long Life of Marianna Ucria*) by Dacia Maraini; and *L'amante perduto* (*The Lost Lover*, 1999), based on Abraham Yehoshua's *The Lover*. With a more recent film, *Prendimi l'anima* (*The Soul Keeper*, 2002), based on the life of Sabina Spielrein, a Russian Jew and patient of Freud and Jung, he managed again to deliver an autonomous work created through rewriting and reinterpreting another.

Unlike Moretti, Pupi Avati was a director who still belonged to a generation nursed on American cinema and jazz. Even though he debuted at the end of the 1960s, his personality did not fully emerge until the second half of the 1970s, beginning with the film *Jazz Band* (1978). Among all the directors in recent generations, Avati—together with Bertolucci—was the most interested in memory and reconstructing (as if in a gigantic puzzle) a fresco of Italy's collective history by portraying everyday human interaction, rituals, farming life, and the nineteenth-century proletarian and middle-class experience, together with its micro-transformations over time. Most of his characters follow dreams by throwing their hearts across the Atlantic to the land of jazz and cinema, an ideal habitat where they hope to spend as much time as possible. Although there are a few exceptions in his filmography—like *Noi tre* (*The Three of Us* or *We Three*, 1984), based on Mozart's life, and *Bix* (1991), based on Bix Beiderbecke, both of which were filmed in the United States— Avati's films from the 1960s to the present represent an uninterrupted oral history composed of sad, happy, tragic, and melodramatic stories: *Le stelle nel fosso* (*Stars in the Ditch*, 1978), *Aiutami a sognare* (*Help Me Dream*, 1981), *Dancing Paradise* (1982, made for television), *Una gita scolastica* (*A School Outing*, 1983), *Festa di laurea* (*Graduation Party*, 1985), *Regalo di Natale* (*The Christmas Present*, 1986), *Sposi* (1987), *Storia di ragazzi e di ragazze* (*The Story of Boys and Girls*, 1989), *Fratelli e sorelle* (*Brothers and Sisters*, 1992), and *Festival* (1996). These films star everyday people whose futures are altered by an arbitrary or unforeseen event, an encounter, a family meal, a soccer match, or a round of poker. Avati did not care for stories in the round, but in his work as a whole he carefully mined and documented twentieth-century cultural material, including the transformation of daily life, collective behaviors, and social rituals. His visual style drew from the oral tradition of storytelling. He used memory and his characters' point of view to filter his realism ,and his films always had a magical, fantastical dimension. His talent as a narrator of epic tales emerged in the summation of smaller, different stories. It was only natural that he would try his hand at telling a chivalric tale. With *I cavalieri che fecero l'impresa* (*The Knights Who Made the Enterprise* or *The Knights of the Quest*,

2001), he took his uncommon storytelling ability to a new level in terms of narration, rhythm, cinematography, and the reconstruction of a faraway culture and a distant world.

In 1975, after completing his degree in film directing at the Centro Sperimentale, Peter del Monte made his debut with *Irene, Irene*. The film piqued the curiosity of critics, who recognized the influence of Bergman. Del Monte had a clear talent for lightness. He used meaningful glances, silences, and tense moods as tools of communication. He was a director capable of telling a story with a simple caress. Throughout his career, he developed and carefully articulated his poetics with film like *Piso pisello* (*Sweet Pea*, 1981), *Invitation au voyage* (*Invito al viaggio* [in Italian] or *Invitation to Travel*, 1982), *Giulia e Giulia* (*Julia and Julia*, 1987, his most difficult film, in which he explored the theme of personality disorder), *Tracce di vita amorosa* (*Traces of an Amorous Life*, 1990), *Compagna di viaggio* (*Traveling Companion*, 1996), *La ballata del lavavetri* ("The Ballad of the Window Washers," 1998), and *Controvento* (*Against the Wind*, 2000).

Ten-year gestation: it took Mario Brenta a decade to make each of his films. Brenta is arguably the most Franciscan director of the most recent generations. Perhaps better than any other, he metabolized the lessons of Olmi, Rossellini, and Bresson. After working as an assistant director in the early 1960s for Eriprando Visconti and 22 Dicembre Cinematografia (December 22 Cinematrophy), Olmi and Kezich's production house, he directed *Vermisàt* (*The Worm Catcher*, 1974), *Maicol* (*Michael*, 1980), and *Barnabo delle montagne* (*Barnabo of the Mountains*, 1994). In 1985, he made *Robinson in laguna* (*Robinson on the Lagoon*, a mid-length feature produced by Ipotesi Cinema for French television but never aired), a film of intensity, truth, and "excruciating" beauty, if you will. It is the love story of two handicapped youths and it culminates in their marriage. In Brenta, the viewer will find an exasperated search for essentiality and rigor. Brenta's cinema is a form of high artisanship in which every image and every sign is an absolute necessity. *Barnabo delle montagne*, based on Buzzati's novel by the same title, is a grand journey back in time set against the culture of farming and mountain life in the region of the Veneto.

After a long career directing documentaries and investigative reports for RAI television, Emidio Greco took nearly thirty years to make six films, which reveal lofty influences, perfect mastery of mise-en-scène, and masterful pacing of his actors. Throughout his career, Greco sought to render original translations of literary works.[35] He seemed to feel a stronger connection to Eastern Europe than to Italy. He told stories of characters who ran from reality and from themselves, and he managed to create images seemingly suspended between the real and unreal—something few Italian directors had achieved before him. His debut film, *L'invenzione di Morel* (*Morel's Invention*, 1974), was based on the novel *La invención de Morel* by Adolfo Bioy Casares, and his *Ehrengard* (1983) was adapted from the novel by the same title by Karen Blixen. *Un caso d'incoscienza* (*An Unconscionable Affair*, 1984) was shot for television. *Una storia semplice* (*A Simple Story*, 1991) and *Il consiglio d'Egitto* (*The Council of Egypt*, 2001) were adapted from works by Leonardo Sciascia. Outwardly, *Milonga* (1999), a work in which he played with the mechanisms of film noir, appears to be an artistic vacation for Greco. But from a narrative and directorial point of view, the film is a demanding study in genre, a self-imposed challenge to go head to head with the detective story. In this work, he unravels the plot using rhythms entirely new to him.

In 1972 (at nearly fifty years of age), Fabrio Carpi made his debut with *Corpo d'amore* (*Body of Love*). From a thematic and stylistic point of view, Carpi's films are among the most cohesive and coherent. His filmography includes *L'età della pace* (*The Peaceful Age*, 1974), *Quartetto Basileus* (*Basileus Quartet*, 1983), *Barbablù Barbablù* (*Bluebeard, Bluebeard*, 1989), *L'amore necessario* (*Necessary Love*, 1991), *La prossima volta il fuoco* (*Next Time the Fire*, 1993), *Nel profondo paese straniero* (*Homer: Portrait of the Artist as an Old Man*, 1997), and *Nobel* (2000). Carpi is perhaps the Italian director most similar to Eric Rohmer: his cinema grows with time and becomes lighter, cleaner, and more profound in its vision. Over the course of his career, Carpi delved into the themes of conflict between art and life, the Dionysiac moment of youth, and meditation on old age in relation to youth and beauty. But he also dealt with the theme of old age as a key moment in one's existence, a moment in which the fires of desire can still burn and in which the reasons for living can be found not only in memory.

In the mid-1970s, following a 1971 debut in television, Luigi Faccini's distinct personality as a director began to emerge. At one point, he seemed poised to inherit Pasolini's legacy in exploring alternative, different realities. He developed one of the most informed and coherent bodies of work of the past three decades of the century by refusing to compromise and his careful choice of objectives.[36] In 1976, he directed a skillful adaptation of Vittorini's *Garofano rosso* (*The Red Carnation*). In 1985, with *Inganni* (*Deceptions*), he became the first to make a movie about the life of Dino Campana and the poet's psychiatric hospitalization. He then made three important films, each with profound moral and social themes. In these works, he dealt with the realities of disenfranchisement and emotion: *Donna d'ombra* (*Woman of Shadows*, 1988), an intense film about life in Italy in recent years, a work that transmits love for life and for relationships by talking about death; *Notte di stelle* (*Starry Night*, 1995); and *Giamaica* (*Jamaica*, 1997).

Carlo di Carlo got his start as a film critic (and was even the editor-in-chief of the journal *Film selezione*). He worked as an assistant director for Pasolini and Antonioni (in recent years, Di Carlo has admirably devoted himself to the preservation of Antonioni's work). After he made six feature-length documentaries for German television, he directed his only Italian film in 1978, *Per questa notte* (*For This Night*), based on Juan Carlos Onetti's *Para esta noche*. As director, he liked to mix realism with imaginary and dreamlike elements, as if he were blending together Kafka, Borges, and Calvino.

Maurizio Ponzi got his start with the journal *Filmcritica*, the same publication that helped to launch Faccini's career. A devoted professional, Ponzi was full of hope and ambition and his early works were ascetic and Bressonian. He then suddenly converted to comedy and had the good fortune to discover Francesco Nuti, whose career he helped to launch with *Io, Chiara e lo scuro* (*The Pool Hustlers*, 1982), *Madonna che silenzio c'è stasera* (*Boy, Is It Quiet Tonight*, 1982), and *Son contento* (*I'm Happy*, 1983). He also made *Volevo i pantaloni* (literally *I Wanted to Wear Pants*, 1989), based on Lara Cardella's bestseller, translated into English as *Good Girls Don't Wear Trousers*, and *Italiani* (*Italians*, 1996).

Salvatore Piscicelli also emerged from the world of film criticism. After a short career as a documentary filmmaker, he began making feature-length films with *Immacolata e Concetta* (*Immacolata and Concetta: The Other Jealousy*, 1979), and then *Le occasioni di Rosa* (*Rosa's Chance*, 1981), *Blues metropolitano* (*Metropolitan Blues*, 1985), *Regina* (1987), *Baby Gang* (1992), and *Il corpo dell'anima* (*The Soul's Body*, 1998). Piscicelli was a leader of the new generation of young Neapolitan directors that emerged during this period. His cinema is at once physical, sensual, and detached. He moves his camera with his head and his heart and never hides his passion for Neapolitan culture. He took his models from 1950s American dramas and genre films. His rudderless characters struggle to defend their love. In *Il corpo dell'anima*, he managed to find a balance between desire, passion, and the serene acceptance that the passage of time is inevitable.

Giacomo Battiato is one of the most erudite and flexible directors of his generation. A cultural organizer, he has also written novels interesting for both their caliber and writing style. He got his start as an excellent television director, an experience that allowed him to develop his talent though his varied experiences before he made his debut as a film director with *I paladini* (*Hearts and Armour*, 1982), an fantasy-epic along the lines of John Boorman's *Excalibur* (1981). Battiato was skilled at genre films and ably exploiting the technical aspects of filmmaking. Magic, visual wonderment, and mythology are important elements in his films. His characters' psychological profiles were convincing even within the context of his epic and action films. He also made two episodes (the eighth and ninth) of the popular *Piovra* (*The Octopus*) television mini-series. His is not the richest of filmographies but his *Stradavari* (*Stradavarius*, 1988) and *Cronaca di un amore violato* (*Diary of a Rapist*, 1995) are among his more important works.

Marco Tullio Giordana started out as an artist. As a director, he was clearly influenced by Italian cinema and in particular by the works of Visconti, Rosi, and Pasolini. With his docudrama, *Pasolini, un delitto italiano* (*Pasolini, an Italian Crime* or *Who Killed Pasolini?*, 1995), he tried to re-create the last hours of Pasolini's life and to give weight to the theory—still unconvincing—that Pasolini's death was the result of a conspiracy. He made his debut as a director with *Maledetti vi amerò* (*To Love the Damned*, 1980), which won an award at Locarno. It was perhaps the first film to deal in a heartfelt manner with the theme of terrorism after Aldo Moro was murdered. Again, with his second film, *La caduta degli angeli ribelli* (*Fall of the Rebel Angels*, 1981), he returned to the theme of terrorism. Giordana loved visual excess and he favored a subjective, mobile use of the camera. With passion and intensity, he explored the dark zones in the myths of his generation, a difficult road to travel to find and affirm one's identity. *Appuntamento a Liverpool* (*Appointment in Liverpool*, 1988) was based on the Heysel Stadium tragedy when tens of Italian soccer fans died during a Juventus versus Liverpool match. In the film, the daughter of one of the deceased decides to travel to England for revenge.

From Trash to Cult

Toward the end of the twentieth century, when Italian Communist Party member Massimo d'Alema was Italy's prime minister, Oliviero Diliberto (a member of the Communist Refoundation Party) remarked that Lino Banfi was superior to Michelangelo Antonioni. In doing so, he joined the ranks of young film critics who were re-evaluating low-budget 1970s films. In the pages of specialized magazines like *Amarcord* and *Nocturno*, many writers conferred cult status to films once considered trash and compared them to the works of master filmmakers.

Before they sank and disappeared like the *Titanic*, saving themselves here and there on the rafts of television, Italian cinematic genres seemed to meld and mix together, their directors, actors, and writers blending together with one another.

As we have seen for all genres, the final frontier was always their conversion to eroticism and pornography, more or less soft. Many popular genres turned to erotic comedy and the continued success of these films seemed to slow erotic comedy's demise. First and foremost, erotic comedy became a receptacle for Italian vaudeville-era comics who, beginning in the late nineteenth century, had performed their routines prior to screenings in the great temples of cinema, like the Ambra Jovinelli in Rome and the Salone Margherita in Naples. Erotic comedy gave them a few years of life and greater visibility before they disappeared. Their jokes could be heavy-handed and their one-liners spared no politician or figure of power. In the five years that followed Pasolini's *Decameron*, it seemed that Italian cinema wanted to make the most of universal erotic literature: from *Decameron proibitissimo* and *Boccaccio mio statti zitto*, both by Franco Martinelli (literally *Very Forbidden Boccaccio* and *Shut Up, My Boccaccio*, also released as *Sexy Sinners*, 1972) to *Le calde notti del Decameron* by Gian Paolo Callegari (*The Warm Nights of the Decameron*, 1972), from *Canterbury proibito* by Italo Alfaro (*The Forbidden Canterbury* [*Tales*], 1972) to *Quel gran pezzo dell'Ubalda tutta nuda e tutta calda* by Mariano Laurenti (*Ubalda, All Naked and Warm*, 1972). During this period, many filmmakers decided to tell unbridled stories of vice in the home. For the most part, they did so sympathetically and they generally seemed to identify with their subject matter. In a unique cauldron of filmmaking, we see a mix of actors like Al Bano and Romina Power, Alvaro Vitali and Edwige Fenech, Lino Banfi, Renzo Montagnani, and Gianni Nazzaro, Nino d'Angelo and Alberto Lupo, Silvia Dionisio and Gloria Guida. The titles, too, were unusual: Carlo Vanzina's *Amarsi un po'* (*Love Yourself a Little*, 1984), Franco Amurri's *Il ragazzo del Pony Express* (*The Pony Express Boy*, 1986), Laurenti's *Uno scugnizzo a New York* (*Neapolitan Boy in New York*, 1984), Corbucci's *Rimini Rimini* (1987), Michele Tarantini's *La professoressa di scienza naturali* (*School Days*, 1976), Nello Rossati's *L'infermiera* (*I Will If You Will, The Nurse, The Secrets of a Sensuous Nurse*, or *The Sensuous Nurse*, 1978), Tarantini's *La poliziotta fa carriera* (*Confessions of a Lady Cop*, 1976), Laurenti's *Il sommergibile più pazzo del mondo* (*The Craziest Submarine in the World*, 1983), Umberto Lenzi's *Pierino la peste alla riscossa* (*Little Piero the Plague to the Rescue*, 1982), Laurenti's *Pierino torna a scuola* (*Little Piero Goes Back to School*, 1990), Giuliano Carnimeo's *Mia moglie torna a scuola* (*My Wife Goes Back to School*, 1981), and Laurenti's *Si ringrazia la regione Puglia per averci fornito i milanesi* (*We Thank the Region of Apulia for Having Provided Us with the Milanese*, 1982), among others.

With one swift blow, these comedies erased all of Italian cinema's efforts to achieve critical and cultural legitimization. But their success also acted as clotting agent that helped to stop the hemorrhage of the general movie-going public. Audiences enjoyed seeing the bodies of beautiful girls on the screen and hearing jokes worthy of army barracks, humor that had all but disappeared a few years earlier with the demise of vaudeville comedy.

Is there any good reason to study these films today? Their screenplays are nothing but a mix of prankish jokes, one-liners, and double entendres. In *La poliziotta fa carriera* (1976), Edwige Fenech manages to catch a little parrot that has escaped from its cage. "Here I am, helping some poor guy who lost his bird . . . Should I be the one to grab his bird?"[37] These films were made hurriedly but by no means did they lack in craftsmanship. Directors like Nando Cicero, Mariano Laurenti, and Sergio Martino regressed eroticism to the level of teenage voyeurism. They created grandiose monuments to the missing act, all the while generously exhibiting the scantily clad bodies of beautiful young women. With regard to homosexuality, racism, religion, and politics, their characters acted in the most politically incorrect manner but in a way that resonated with their audience's vision of the world. This is a world where priests do not hesitate to run their hands up the skirts of their young parishioners or where more virtuous priests are continuously tempted by young women who ask them to fasten their bras. In these films, the faithful pray to saints with unusually specific roles, like Don Ciccio da Lambrate (Don Fatman from Lambrate, a neighborhood in the outskirts of Milan), protector against caning, or San Popocchio (Pop-Eye), protector against the evil eye.

Did these films really have the power to unmask the emptiness of pseudo-intellectual cinema? Did they, as the defenders of these films claimed, reveal the inconsistencies of supercilious critics who "dined" with Antonioni and "laid" with Bergman? Did these films reflect the cultural and social divide in a country whose economic growth did not correspond to its ideological, social, cultural, sexual, and religious evolution? These films were the children of indifference and the legacy of Italy's vaudeville. Italian trash cinema portrayed politicians of both the right and the left as corrupt, inept thieves. It made fun of Italy's institutions and laws and it helped to reinforce indistinction among values and the conviction that "the stupid and ignorant are beautiful."

Although no one has said it yet, future scholars may see in these films the reasons behind the growth and political affirmation of the Lombard and Venetian separatist *leghista* movement of the 1990s. The provincial caricatures found in 1970s Italian trash films represent an important "family photo." They document a way of life and thinking that significantly reshaped politics in the decades to follow. Many of the first-generation "honorable" separatists who found their way into the Parliament seemed to have been catapulted there from the trash films of the 1970s and 1980s. They were the flesh-and-blood spokesmen and political interpreters of a ridiculous reality.

Young critics did not identify with the cinema of previous generations. They refused to consider cinema a "privileged aesthetic experience," just as they shunned any form of culture difficult to comprehend. These films continuously poke fun at abstract art, whether dodecaphonic music or hermetic poetry. Great works of literature are fair game as well, like Leopardi's celebrated poems "A Silvia" ("To Silvia") and "Il sabato del villaggio" ("Saturday in the Village), parodied with the addition of sexual references in *L'allenatore nel pallone* (*Coach in the Balls*, 1984). There is also continuous derision of Italy's public institutions, with the school system paying the highest price. These films feature a parade of frustrated, incompetent, and ignorant professors with wandering hands and lustful glances, vampires who often follow schoolgirls into locker rooms and showers.

Dusty old jokes make reappearances in these films in the form of double entendres, misunderstandings, and ignorance of things like food, beverages, and customs from other countries.

"That's your wife?" asks a character in Lenzi's *Pierino la peste alla riscossa* (*Little Piero, the Plague to the Rescue*, 1982).

"Yes, she is my wife from Japan, Urina Sumuri [Urinates on Walls]."

"She urinates on walls? And they haven't given her a summons?"

"Bring me some caviar," says a character in *Kakkientruppen* (*Troop Poop*, 1977), "two slices."

"But caviar is eggs."

"Well, then, bring me two caviar eggs."

On the subject of caviar, in Italo Zingarelli's *Io sto con gli ippopotami* (*I'm for the Hippopotamus*, 1979), one character says to another: "You know what it looks like? Like dwarf sheep poop."

Beginning with Pasolini's *Decameron* and even before the boom of red light films, female nudes dominated the screens of commercial movie theaters. From *Quel gran pezzo dell'Ubalda tutta nuda e tutta calda* (*Ubalda, All Naked and Warm*, 1972) to *Infermiera di notte* (*Night Nurse*, 1979), audiences contemplated women who used their bodies with increasing generosity (in *Pierino la peste alla riscossa*, the female lead cannot determine whether she has become pregnant by the town soccer team or orchestra). These female characters are objects of desire confined to male hunting grounds, as if in defense of early-twentieth-century anthropological convictions. "A woman thinks with her uterus," says actor Renato Pozzetto in Bruno Corbucci's *La casa stregata* (*The Haunted House*, 1982). They are the prey of men's worst instincts and they proudly flaunt their "loose ways": when a character in Giuliano Carnimeo's *Pierino medico della S.A.U.B.* (*Little Piero, Doctor at the Local Health Authority*, 1981) is called a "whore," she responds proudly, "Of course!"

Like a mail order catalog, Italian trash cinema offers every dysfunctional and negative element of Italian society in the post–Economic Miracle era. "North, South, East, West," says a character in Steno's *L'Italia s'è rotta* (*Italy Is Broken*, 1976), "wherever you turn, it's all a big mess." In a country where nothing functioned properly, the differences between Italy's regions seemed to increase their distance and to glorify their stereotypes. Corruption overflowed; illegality seemed to be inscribed in the genetic code of all Italians; tax evaders were applauded while honest tax payers were harassed. But at the same time, according to the logic of Giovanni Guareschi's *Il mondo piccolo* (*Small World* in Enrico Oldoini's *Miracolo italiano* [*An Italian Miracle*], 1994), the communist deputy makes love on a train with an "honorable" neo-fascist *missina* (member of the MSI [Italian Social Movement]).

These films did not disappear entirely. As if by the principle of communicating vessels, by the 1980s they had found their way to the television screen, with the same old one-liners and double meanings.

The Return to Writing and Storytelling

During the second half of the 1980s, faith in writing and storytelling was unexpectedly renewed.[38] For at least a decade, film producers had believed that for a film to be successful, directorial talent was merely an option. For years, producers thumbed their noses at the professional legacy that had conjoined various levels of Italian cinema. Now, suddenly, a new generation of writers appeared on the scene. In just a short period of time, the system took a clear change in direction. Italian films began to win awards abroad and filmmakers, increasingly more confident in their narrative ability, began to take more pleasure in storytelling. The principle "to make cinema one must know cinema" played an important role in reviving a system that had become fragmented and an industry that lacked leadership and shared goals. The birth of the Solinas prize also helped new storytellers and unknown filmmakers to blossom.

The new generation of screenwriters loved cinema and wanted to revive storytelling. These artists believed in well-constructed stories and cinema as a medium for measuring reality. They revived the concept of cinema as a mythopoeic machine and they were able to re-establish the broken link to the tradition created by Zavattini, Amidei, Flaiano, Pinelli, and Guerra. But they also studied classic American cinema and they absorbed the narrative potential of "road movies" and the cinema of Wenders, Rohmer, and Fassbinder.

Even though they seemed forced to the sidelines, Age and Scarpelli, Maccari, Geurra, Bernardino Zapponi, Ugo Pirro, Benvenuti and De Bernardi, Rodolfo Sonego, Ennio de Concini, and Suso Cecchi d'Amico were at the top of their game. Their tutelage played a fundamental role in the formation of the new generation of artists.[39] Filmmakers who debuted in the 1980s had begun to think about stories and to view the history of cinema as a public treasure and a renewed source for inspiration. These artists saw themselves as part of a tradition. They wanted to develop their plotlines within a narrative web that had unfolded and set in motion its shapes and forms over the course of decades. For many of these filmmakers, the study of cinema became a powerful source of inspiration and a vaccine against the influenza of television.

Suddenly, screenwriting became once again a central and necessary element of the trade. Perhaps more than any other craft, it proudly reaffirmed its ties to Italy's filmmaking tradition and it helped to mend the holes in a fabric that had come apart at the seams. Among others, the following writers made significant contributions to the rebirth of screenwriting in Italian cinema: Stefano Rulli and Sandro Petraglia, Vincenzo Cerami, Carlo Mazzacurati, Enzo Monteleone, Graziano Diana, Franco Bernini, Angelo Pasquini, Davide Ferrario, Umberto Marino, Umberto Contarello, Aurelio Grimaldi, Francesca Marciano, Roberta Mazzoni, Simona Izzo, and Francesca Archibugi. Many of them tried their hand at directing (since that was their common goal from the beginning). Others, like their masters, resisted the temptation to direct and asserted their independence and the centrality of the professional role. During this period, as writing once again began to be considered the backbone of Italian cinema, it became paradoxically easier to debut as a director than to be recognized for one's talents as a screenwriter.

The writers of the 1980s became the inheritors of the screenwriting legacy that had brought international acclaim to Italian cinema during the postwar era. They also embraced their predecessors' ethical sense of seeing and narrating and their love for craftsmanship (Cerami, for example, has often pointed out the similarities between his working method and that of a carpenter; thirty years earlier, Amidei compared himself to Renaissance master painters). They seemed to share the postwar ability to observe the world with the eyes of the mind but also to see it with the eyes of others. As of yet, no one has studied how it happened from a quantitative or qualitative point of view. But it is clear that the rules of the Renaissance atelier can be applied here: like their postwar counterparts, these artisans became masters.

At the very moment when Italian cinema seemed to be sinking to the bottom of the sea, well-constructed stories began to plug up the holes where the ship was taking on water. Over the course of just a few short years, despite the negative elements that had dragged it down for so long, Italian cinema once again began to enjoy international recognition.

These writers no longer worked on mediocre productions and they no longer wrote for star-driven films and films that were destined to be seen only by television audiences.

The sources of inspiration were varied: from pure fiction to stories ripped from the headlines; from the adaptation and reworking of literary texts and the works of contemporary, young Italian authors to historical reconstruction; from the postmodern revisitation of the narrative heritage of Italian cinema to minimalist observation of life in an apartment building or in a school; from the need to incorporate social and civil engagement into storytelling to a progressive openness toward stories with topological dimensions that push beyond Italy's borders.[40] Once again the weight of neorealism and following decades was strong. As filmmakers tried to give their stories a less localistic feel, they renewed their desire to construct films with a "message," political films, films endowed with a strong sense of polis, and films that dealt with values shared within a community.

While Suso Cecchi d'Amico was the only truly significant woman writer in the postwar period, recent decades have been marked by a platoon of women screenwriters, including Francesca Marciano (who worked for Pupi Avati, Salvatores, and Verdone), Silvia Napolitano (who wrote scripts for Peter del Monte), Roberta Mazzoni, Francesca Archibugi, Roberta Colombo, Maura Nuccetelli, Lidia Ravera, Silvia Scola, Doriana Leondeff, and Heidrum Schleef, among others. In recent years, Leondeff and Schleef have helped to write some of the best stories for directors Calopresti, Placido Soldini, and Moretti. Thanks to these two screenwriters, greater attention has been given to the "other half of the sky" and emotions began to assert themselves again. The father-son relationship reappeared in their writing and they dealt delicately with the world of children. But there are also social and political elements in their writing and questions about a waning sense of responsibility. They wrote on feminine memory and they wrote on the breakup of families.

Another datum turns out to be shared by screenwriters who debuted in the 1980s: a taste for narration and storytelling that borrows from cinema, reality, and the imagination; an ability to put oneself at the service of the story; the absence of narcissistic desire to tell autobiographical stories and uninteresting stories; exploration of dark dimensions, beginning with the discovery of night as a frontier (for example, in Davide Ferrario, Carlo Mazzacurati, and Luciano Mannuzzi); attention to landscape and its social and anthropological decay; an ability to make the story feel like it is an integral part of the landscape; and the new problems that unleash encounters with others like immigrants of color, illegal aliens, and characters who bring with them other stories. The taste for storytelling was strong in Mazzacurati. With *Il prete bello* (*The Handsomest Priest*), he tried to create the Veneto that he dreamed of. But in order to find strong emotions and values (something that we are losing), he was forced to go to the East and make *Il toro* (*The Bull*). And the taste for storytelling is just as strong in directors like Amelio, Moretti, Salvatores, Tornatore, Mario Brenta, Giacomoo Campiotti, Maurizio Zaccaro, Davide Ferrario, Marco Risi, and Marco Tullio.

Aside from a few exceptions, the screenplays of recent years have tended to focus more on characters, dialogue, and dramaturgical elements. Landscapes, now a neutral or indifferent backdrop, no longer play a dramatic role.

Screenwriters have shown remarkable ability in giving life to well-constructed characters, often heroic in their capability to defend their own sense of morality on a daily basis, selfless characters who place the collective good over the interests of the individual (as was the case of the director of the co-op board in Farina's *Condominio* [*Co-Op*]). In certain cases, these characters were based on real-life figures, like the magistrates in *Il giudice ragazzino* ("The Boy Judge"), a film about Rosario Livatino, a young Sicilian judge; or the lawyer Giorgio Ambrosoli in *Un eroe borghese* (*Ordinary Hero*), a film inspired by the book by Corrado Stajano; or Enzo Tortora in *Un uomo perbene* (*A Respectable Man*); or Peppino Impastato in *I cento passi* (*One Hundred Steps*); or the bio-pic *Placido Rizzotto*; or journalist Tina Merlin in *Vajont* (*Vayont Dam*). In other films, real-life and fictional characters were skillfully "blended" together: the teacher in *Mery per sempre* (*Forever Mary* or *Mary Forever*) and *Io speriamo che me la cavo* (*Ciao Professore!* or *Me Let's Hope I Make It*); the lawyer in *Notte italiana* (*Italian Night*); the journalist in *Muro di gomma* (*The Invisible Wall*); the doctor in *Grande cocomero* (*The Great Pumpkin*); or the policeman in *Ladro di bambini* (*The Stolen Children*). There were also memorable negative characters like minister Botero played by Nanni Moretti in *Portaborse* (*The Yes Man*) and Diego in *Domani accadrà* (*It's Happening Tomorrow*). On a less emblematic but equally representative level, there were also drifters, losers, persons affected by nostalgia for the past and all sorts of mental illnesses, fools, and outcasts. Many of them were fleeing not from society but from themselves in films like *Puerto Escondido*, *Marrakech Express*, *L'aria serena dell'Ovest* (*The Peaceful Air of the West*), *Piccoli equivoci* (*Little Misunderstandings*), and *Italia-Germania 4 a 3* (*Italy vs. Germany 4–3*).

Documentaries devoted to recent history have been impressive. But filmmakers did not seem content to make films about tragic heroes, scapegoats, everyday heroes, or average persons who defend simple civil and moral values. Nor did they favor the facile answers offered by sketches of everyday Italians. Instead, they asked new questions and leafed through mountains of documents as they took on the role of vicarious magistrate examiners. Thanks to cinema and to the happy marriage of good screenwriting and renewed social passion, directors discovered a new use for public information and historical documents. From the Republic of Salò to the present, these filmmakers reopened the case files of many unresolved investigations of Italian history. And in doing so, they renewed a tradition of postwar Italian cinema.

The link between documentary filmmaking and the postwar era was very clear. When it came to storytelling, however, directors favored stories about young people. The geographic and thematic affinities of these works and their shared references helped to group them within contemporary international cinema.

The 1980s Generation

The crisis of the early 1980s became more evident each year. With every new season, the Italian film industry seemed to expect a messiah. It was a ritual of over-the-top enthusiasm for any success alternating with periodic epicedia whenever it came time to review the balance sheets for the year.

Carlo Emilio Gadda called it the "damned Italian scabies of self-denigration": self-punishment and the inability to recognize qualities in other people are elements of the Italian character. But coupled with recent generations' widespread and growing disinterest in Italian cinema, Italians' self-denigrating spirit only made the damage worse. At a certain point, Italian cinema seemed to mean Italian television and American films were the only cinematic products available in Italy.

The ever-sensorially gifted Fellini recognized the transformation that was taking place and he could feel the widespread malaise. At the beginning of the 1980s, the cinematic landscape was on the verge of catastrophe, but Fellini envisioned a different possibility for the future: "When I started out, there was an air of disaster and carnage. But at the same time, there was a great desire to work and to rebuild the future from scratch. Now, there are times when there seems to be carnage as far as the eye can see and the wounds seem to run deeper. But that fever to create, that avidity and eagerness to begin anew, is gone."[41]

Far from being a bona census, this work is intended to be an overview of Italian cinema and an invitation to further study. In the pages that follow, we will examine some positive elements that have emerged in recent years, the variety of voices, and the performance of Italian cinema and its master filmmakers.

Even if we were to use shorthand, we could never analyze or attempt to focus on the more than three hundred filmmakers who have debuted over the past twenty-five years. Over the decades, many praiseworthy studies have systematized the many different figures operating in the industry (the systematic surveys conducted by organizers of the Pesaro Film Festival are among the most noteworthy). Unfortunately, no one has translated *Les années Moretti*, a work that I wholeheartedly recommend. This dictionary of Italian cineastes was written by Alain Bichon for the Annecy Film Festival. It includes portraits of eighty of the most important filmmakers from 1975 to 1999.[42] Let it suffice that we cite the names of and a few titles by directors who have show interesting and distinct personality in their work. We can consider ten-year periods as useful moments in the periodization of Italian cinema.

First of all, it is important to remember that the 1980s began with Cesare Zavattini's directorial debut, *La veritàaaa* (*The Truuuuth*, produced by Marina Piperno, one of the most intelligent and courageous producers of the past thirty years). In the context of his career, this work did not represent the fulfillment of a thirty-year-old dream but rather a starting point for a new cycle of creativity. Shot with the spirit and emotions of a newcomer, this surprising film was a melting pot in which Zavattini mixed a little bit of everything and told it all with a touch of joy. Zavattini emerges in this work like a Little Nemo—like an elf who distills drops of wise truth. At times, those drops seem apparently devoid of meaning. But as those drops travel through space and time, they reveal the exponentially growing difficulties of communication and the continuous shocks and interruptions in interpersonal communication in the world today.

After Moretti, the artist who revealed a clearly defined poetics and style was Gianni Amelio.[43] Amelio was not yet two years old when his father decided to leave the five hundred-person town of San Pietro Magisano in Calabria to search for his father, Amelio's grandfather, who had immigrated to Argentina and lost touch with the family. Amelio's father would return fifteen years later but by then he was a stranger to Amelio, who had been raised by his grandmother and mother. The heart of his poetic world lies in this separation, in the deep groove of relationships between fathers and sons, between adults and children, between siblings, and in the different ways that this separation can be recomposed.[44] Tullio Zurlini was the first to note the echoes of his films in Amelio's work. Amelio started out as an assistant director and the, for roughly ten years, he directed for television. At the end of the 1970s, he made *Il piccolo Archimede* (*The Little Archimedes*), based on a story by Aldous Huxley. This work had the structure of a bona fide film and was received enthusiastically by critics of the era for its directorial rigor, the admirable direction of the child, and Amelio's ability to delve deeply into adult-child relationships. His first film destined for theaters was *Colpire al cuore* (*Blow to the Heart*, 1983), written together with Cerami. As we have noted previously, this film was among the first to deal with the theme of terrorism. But it also focused on interpersonal communication—in this case between father and son—during a time when other directors were skimming over these values and issues. Amelio also directed a made-for-television drama on Enrico Fermi and his team of physicists, *I ragazzi di via Panisperna* (*The Panisperna Street Boys*, 1988). But he truly matured with the release of a series of four works that won him international recognition and played a fundamental role in bolstering Italian cinema: *Porte aperte* (*Open Doors*, 1989, based on the novel by Leonardo Sciascia), *Il ladro di bambini* (*The Stolen Children*, 1992), *Lamerica* (1994), and *Così ridevano* (*The Way We Laughed*, 1998).

Porte aperte marked yet another work on the difficulty of communication. Even though it used fascist Italy as its backdrop, this film represents a timeless reflection on political corruption in Italy during the late 1980s and the difficult choices faced by the Italian judiciary.

Lamerica is a dark story, an infernal voyage, in which pain, blood, speculation, death, and even hope are mixed together. In this film, Amelio blends the story of his family's immigrant experience together with direct accounts of the first landings of clandestine Albanians on the shore of Apulia in the early 1990s.

But it was with *Il ladro di bambini* that Amelio reached the peak of his creativity in this ten-year span: this was the moment when his style emerged controlled and dry, the emotional and dramatic semitones struck with precision, and his gaze moved in closely on the characters, capturing every micro-mutation. In this film, the young policeman—a *carabiniere*—must accompany two children—a brother and sister—to an orphanage in Southern Italy. With remarkable ability, Amelio has the character play a vicarious role as father and older brother as the three of them embark on a long and bitter journey through a deteriorated Italy, a country emptied of strength and hope and a landscape destroyed by speculation and a lack of civic duty.

Così ridevano explicitly drew from the Viscontian theme of Southern Italians' immigration to the north, love, and family. This film leads the viewer to the threshold of tragedy: it is the story of six long days in the life of two brothers, in six different years. The film's love story is so intense that it immediately borders on the pathological. The older brother is forced to assume excessive responsibility, while the younger is sacrificed in the name of love and blood and must pay the price for a crime he has not committed. This film is not perfect: every scene is brimming with excessive emotion. But it is the director's film most charged with "imploded" emotions: Amelio recounts the laws of "amoral familism" practiced in his homeland, the difficulties of integration. His participation in the film is strong, but he attempts at the same time to main an equidistant rapport with his characters.

Even though he did not obtain the resounding results and recognition that Amelio did, Giuseppe Bertolucci—screenwriter, documentary filmmaker, and theatrical director —continued to believe in Italian cinema in the difficult period of its recent history. He played an important role in the search for a new identity and new roads of expression. Bertolucci and Amelio explored new roads, they had faith in intellectual means over financial means, they stayed true to their course and worked in complete independence, and they both tackled the subject of terrorism when doing so was still taboo.

Written with Cerami, *Segreti segreti* (*Secrets Secrets*, 1984) explored irregular communicative and emotional flows in a bourgeois family as possible causes of terrorism. Bertolucci's style changed from story to story and he adapted it to his characters: from pseudo-documentary to an full-court exhibition of refined cinematic influences, from German expressionist film to the Minnelli's musicals. Bertolucci clearly loved directing and his extraordinary humility combined with the sheer fun he had using the camera. He was like a midwife who helped to birth a genius actor like Benigni. With his gaze, he knew how to capture and glorify the talents of actors of different generations, from Alida Valli to Mariangela Melato, from Lea Massari to Lina Sastri, Sabina Guzzanti, Francesca Neri, and Rosalinda Celentano. No other director in recent memory has shown herself or himself so capable in drawing out an actress's skills. In certain cases, he was able to impart a little aura of stardom upon the women working in his films—an element clumsily trampled over by the new generation of filmmakers.

He made his first film with Benigni, *Berlinguer ti voglio bene* (*Berlinguer: I Love You*, 1977). He would later write stories and screenplays for other Benigni films and directed *Tuttobenigni dal vivo* (*All Benigni Live*).

Other noteworthy Bertolucci films include *I cammelli* (*The Camels*, 1988); *Amori in corso* (*Love in Progress*, 1989); *Il dolce rumore della vita* (*The Sweet Noise of Life*, 1999); and *L'amore probabilmente* (*Probably Love*, 2001), a film in which he used digital technology for the first time.

Critics did not immediately notice Giuseppe Tornatore's debut, nor did they approve when they did pay attention. Perhaps more than any other, his was a cinema never entirely loved by the Italian or foreign critics. The story of this Sicilian director represents the most emblematic case of summary judgment and sentencing at the outset of a career—a judgment that was never again reviewed. Just as had happened to others (to Fellini more than any other), Tornatore's trials and tribulations were never-ending. And yet, in an industry where sloppiness, incompetence, and the absence of professional experience are increasingly rewarded, Tornatore proudly showed his skills as cinematographer, camera operator, and editor. He also demonstrated an ability to give his actors direction and to re-create ambiance in period films. Tornatore never hid his rich visual writing style nor did he shy from stories grand in scale (he was clearly influenced by Visconti, Leone, and Rosi).[45]

For his first film, *Il camorrista* (*The Professor*, 1986), he already enjoyed an impressive budget of 5,500,000,000 lire. He showed his ability to maneuver confidently through his choral tale and to open a window onto the world of organized crime by revisiting the stereotypes of the gangster film.

Before achieving international success, his next film, *Nuovo cinema Paradiso* (*Cinema Paradiso*), went through some ups and downs, receiving modest approval from critics and audiences. Like Mingozzi's *La vela incantata* (*The Magic Screen*, 1982), Scola's *Splendor* (1989), and Luciano Odorisio's *Via Paradiso* (*Paradise Street*, 1988), Tornatore's *Nuovo cinema Paradiso* told the story of a small Sicilian movie theater as the idealized center of a working-class world, a cathedral of desire, and a factory of dreams and imagination. Thanks to the producer, who cut nearly the entire second part, the film was granted a second life. It won an Oscar for Best Foreign Film and from Salt Lake City to Kyoto, it was a phenomenon: it had been some time since audiences identified with a film on a large-scale basis like they did with *Nuovo cinema Paradiso*.

After Bertolucci, Tornatore seemed to be the director who could tell stories capable of traveling beyond the Italian small town. With his *Stanno tutti bene* (*Everybody's Fine*, 1989), Tornatore completed a journey traveling north from Sicily to Turin, a route through Italy very similar to that in Germi's *Il cammino della speranza* (*Path of Hope* or *The Road to Hope*, 1950). The difference was that Matteo Scuro (the Sicilian father who goes to visit his children who live in five different places across Italy) visited places depicted in the grand cinema of the postwar era by Visconti, Rossellini, De Sica, and Fellini. But at each stop, the state of things has deteriorated and the light, magic, and energy have been removed. Tonino Guerra wrote the screenplay for this film. Even as he continuously runs into emotional and environmental debris, the lead character is steadfast in his desire to look to the future with optimism.

Una pura formalità (*A Pure Formality*, 1993) was perhaps the film in which Tornatore sought to stage his personal drama of having been continuously attacked and never having the chance to defend himself. In my opinion, this film represents one of the greatest directorial efforts and one of the best moments in Italian cinema in recent memory. Beyond Tornatore's ability to cast the shadow of Pirandello over contemporary cinema, this film's meticulous direction, the dramatic tension, the mastery of lighting, and the complexity and skill of the actors (Gérard Depardieu and Roman Polanski) make it one of the great examples of Italian cinema in the past decades. Tornatore masters every element in every scene. From the camera moves to the actors, he possesses a rhythmic sense of editing matched by few others: his greatest limitation perhaps is the fact that every so often he seems overwhelmed by the narrative material and by overly complex screenplays.

With *L'uomo delle stelle* (*Starmaker, The Star Maker,* or *The Star Man*), Tornatore returned to the theme of cinema as dream-machine. In his films, he follows the deambulations of a small-time conman during the early 1950s as he sells the dream of becoming an movie actor to the poor people in small Sicilian towns. Just as with *Nuovo cinema paradiso,* the first part of this film is told magnificently. But the second part gets bogged down and imprisons the director in his narrative materials. *La leggenda del pianista sull'Oceano* (*The Legend of 1900* or *The Legend of the Pianist on the Ocean*), based on *Novecento* (*1900s*), a theatrical monologue by Alessandro Baricco, and *Malèna* were instead two narrative displays of virtuosismo and directorial mastery. In both of these works, he proves to be a nearly complete master of both parts. It is thanks in part to Tornatore that Italian cinema is still able to reach a wide audience and that the industry can still think in terms of an international audience.

Of all the 1980s newcomers, Francesca Archibugi was the one who received the most attention from critics and the public for her first film, *Mignon è partita* (*Mignon Has Come to Stay,* 1988), which was released at the same time as *Nuovo cinema Paradiso* and *Mery per sempre*.[46] Her confidence in giving her actors direction was impressive, and she showed a remarkable ability to erase her presence in the film and to put herself completely in the service of her characters. A perfect student of cinematic culture and the films of Truffaut, Olmi, Scola, and Comencini, Archibugi mixed sweetness with irony and showed a delicate approach to the young stars of her films. Hers was a chronicle of families, their emotional education and the transformation of daily life and the problems of living with one's family. Her camera followed her characters without ever revealing her presence. With *Verso sera* (*Towards Evening,* 1990), Archibugi pushed herself even further: she told the story of strained affection between different generations as if it were a voyage into entirely uncharted waters. Even with *Il grande cocomero* (*The Great Pumpkin,* 1993), the story of a courageous child psychiatrist (based possibly on the life of Marco Lombardo Radice), she sought to explore the depths of the world of children and the different forms of violence that adults subject them to on a daily basis.

Con gli occhi chiusi (*With Closed Eyes*, 1994) is a story of impossible love in which—perhaps for the first time—the director decided to return to storytelling through images and a first-person narrative, an approach she seemed to have abandoned in previous films (Archibugi's very liberal adaptation of the Federico Tozzi novel—translated into English as *Eyes Shut*—inspired a ferocious response from critic and Italian literature scholar Luigi Baldacci in the Italian daily *Il corriere della sera*).

In *L'albero delle pere* (*Shooting the Moon* or *The Pear Tree*), she created one of her most complex and complete characters, but she tried to say too many things with this film. Here, the adults, increasingly imprisoned by a Peter Pan syndrome, are unable to take on the roles of fathers and mothers and the sharp reversal in the relationship between adults and adolescents does not flow convincingly.

Archibugi effortlessly makes the viewer feel how hard it is for her young characters to find their way in a world of increasingly irresponsible adults. Her stylistic signature is her ability to see that world from their point of view, a world in which their identity and roles are increasingly uncertain.

Gabriele Salvatores debuted in 1983 with a promising film, an adaptation of Shakespeare's *A Midsummer Night's Dream* (*Sogno di una notte d'estate*), which he had directed for the stage in Milan with the Teatro dell'Elfo. Little by little, he began to master the art of filmmaking and thanks to his partnership with Enzo Monteleone, he then made two films—*Marrakech Express* (1989) and *Turné* (*Tour*, 1990)—which gained him recognition and associated him with the group of thirty-something directors who had already begun to take stock of their own generation.[47] In his films *Kamikazen—Ultima notte a Milano* (*Kamikazen—Last Night in Milan*, 1987), *Marrakech Express*, and *Turné*, Salvatores depicts that zone of existence in which illusions begin to fall away and harsh reality suddenly cancels out dreams and hopes. Comparable to Moretti, he showed ability in telling group stories and depicting the bonds and disappointments of friendship. But his talent as a director also lies in his camera movement and a rhythm that varied according to dramaturgic necessity.

Based on stories by Renzo Biasion, Ugo Pirro, Renzo Renzi, and Mario Rigoni Stern, Salvatores's *Mediterraneo* (*Mediterranean*, 1991) won an Oscar for his ability to maintain continuity with the tradition of early postwar Italian cinema and its use of stereotypes, a liberal mix of epic elements, myths, and emotionally charged comedy. Using the world war as a backdrop, he managed to tell the story of a journey of conscience and a need to find a personal vanishing point, an Arcadia and refuge for eight Italian soldiers who did not feel like they were by any means participants in the war.

After *Puerto Escondido* and *Sud* (*South*), Salvatores's career seemed to enter into a new phase. With *Nirvana*, *Denti* (*Teeth*), and *Amnèsia*, his linguistic, narratologic, and stylistic interests shifted toward American cinema, taking him into stories that seemed to have been overseen by Tarantino. In his most recent films, his visual writing became more syncopated, the number of frames in a sequence multiplied, and so did the points of view. The construction of the image and the positioning of elements in space became much more precise. Salvatores is the most restless director of his generation and the most open to change, curiosity, and experimentation.

Daniele Luchetti debuted as a director in 1988 (thanks to Moretti) with *Domani accadrà* (*It's Happening Tomorrow*), a story set in Tuscany in 1848 on the eve of the first Italian War of Independence. The main characters are two horse thieves who are being chased by the Austrians for a theft gone awry. Even though set in the past, the film is a meditation on the present, on reality and different possible worlds, on responsibilities and on the role that everyone must play in fulfilling them. In *La settimana della sfinge* (*The Week of the Sphinx*, 1989), Luchetti replaced the chase with nighttime escapes, gunshots, and a young woman's dream to winning over a Don Juan antenna repairman who couldn't care less about her. Together with directors like Piccioni and Mazzacurati, Luchetti depicted the problems faced by his generation in a new and original way. In particular, he showed a knack for portraying young people's difficulties in achieving the true fulfillment of their identity. His style lent itself to his stories and characters, but he was not always rewarded by his methods. His most complex film and the one most closely linked to the political events of that era was *Il portaborse* (*The Yes Man*, 1990). Again here, as in Mazzacurati's first film, a young, innocent, and unknowing provincial character is unknowingly swept away by a mechanism of political corruption. The situation could crush him, but he manages to escape when moral indignation prevails. *Il portaborse* is a quasi manifesto, probably inspired by the enlightened Milanese judges who launched the first political corruption investigations in 1993.

The same year, Luchetti released his grotesque, surreal *Arriva la bufera* (*The Storm Is Coming*). The main character is a honest magistrate who is sent to a village in the south to resolve a dispute between two sisters quarreling over ownership of a local garbage incinerator. The metaphor was perhaps imperfect, but this film's timeliness and prophetic foresight of the collapse of Italy's public institutions were right on.

Again in *La scuola* (*School*, 1995), based on novels by Domenico Starnone, Luchetti employed his signature grotesque style to depict the decay of the Italian educational system. Neither critics nor audiences particularly liked

I piccoli maestri (*Little Teachers*, 1998), based on the novel by Luigi Meneghello, even though it was inspired by a call for unity and by forces equal yet contrary to those of his previous films. Luchetti was unable to convey his reading of history and the historical Resistance experience as a mere developmental phase for young people. The history of the Resistance is still so monumental that it does not tolerate such an excess of understatement and irony.

A loner and an anomaly, director Franco Piavoli developed a poetics and an ability to tell stories with images unlike any others in recent cinematic experience—Italian or foreign. At nearly fifty years of age, he made his first feature-length documentary, *Il pianeta azzurro* (*The Blue Planet*, 1982), and was immediately hailed as a master. Twenty years earlier, he had made quasi anthropological documentaries in which he observed the behaviors of groups of immigrants as they arrived at the train station in Milan, or football fans at the stadium, or young people at the end of their weekend. Piavoli is Italy's most legitimate heir to the documentary tradition of Robert Flaherty, Joris Ivens, Henri Stork, and Olmi. The small town of Pozzolengo is the center of Piavoli's universe: like few others, he had an ability to make extraordinary journeys through space and time without leaving the place where he lived. With just a few images, he could condense the landscape and life's metamorphoses in the different eras of the earth's surface. His was a metonymic cinema with epic and lyrical breadth. As he filmed the cosmogonies of a pond or even a drop of water, Piavoli managed to create temporal ellipses, conceptual syntheses, and lightning-fast transitions from the part to the whole. But he also delivered metaphors as he let nature's language fully unfold on its own. His cinema is charged with resonance and echoes from the great epic and natural poems, from Lucretius to Homer. In each of his films—from *Nostos* (*Nostos, the Homecoming*) to *Voci nel tempo* (*Voices in Time*), and the more recent *Al primo soffio di vento* (*At the First Breath of the Wind*, 2002)—the viewer can feel the epic and lyrical breath that traverses and guides his work. He knows how to make the wind, water, sky, and clouds become the stars. He knows how to capture the symptoms and the signs emitted by nature. Like a shaman, he knows how to organize them into a symphonic story in which noises and sounds are no less important than images.

Silvio Soldini was also one of those directors who managed to maintain his independence and control over his films. He debuted in the 1980s and was immediately recognized as a serious artist by critics. The plots of his first films were sparse and minimalist and were clearly influenced by Wenders. But his search for a stylistic signature and his own subject matter was also evident early on. The first films—*Paesaggio con figure* (*Landscape with Figures*, 1983) and *Giulia in ottobre* (*Giulia in October*, 1985)—revealed his visual meticulousness and his search for narrative essentiality. With the films that followed over the next ten years—*Un'anima divisa in due* (*A Soul Split in Two* or *A Split Soul*, 1993), *Le acrobate* (*The Acrobat*, 1997), *Pane e tulipani* (1999, his first success with audiences), and *Brucio nel vento* (2002)—his narration became more complex and his stories, while still minimalist in character, touched central themes of contemporary life, inter-individual relationships, and the search for authenticity. Soldini possessed a remarkable ability to define his characters and their relationship to the scene using a bare minimum of elements. His characters were credible and familiar in their disputes, tangled in the difficulties of fulfilling their dreams and their relationships, as they tried to take steps to change their destinies. His cinema is realistic but immersed in a fantastic, unreal atmosphere. Every encounter between his characters, every object, every line can be unforeseeable, implausible, and charged with symbolic intentions. At the same time, each encounter can help to magically resolve the problem, just like in a fable or in a story that has been condemned by reality to extinguish itself in the routine. With *Pane e tulipani*, Soldini achieved his greatest success in conveying his storytelling style to a vast audience and the film also represents one of his best directorial and narrative efforts.

Nino Bizzarri's films were made in the name of cinematic culture, cinephilia, and the search for excellence in visual writing. Alain Bichon called him the most French director of the Italian filmmakers. Among other films worth remembering from his brief filmography, *La seconda notte* (*The Second Night*, 1985) and *Segno di fuoco* (*Sign of Fire*, 1991) both seemed variations on the same dream of love but each was marked by different delusions and overwhelming passions.

The director of four films, Paolo Benvenuti was one of the directors who sought to continue the tradition of Rossellini's later films. He carried out his visual research in complete freedom but with absolute rigor within the tradition of Italian painting. In his films, he absorbed Italian mannerism and Caravaggio's luminism with a tendency toward abstraction. His was a cinema that never accounted for the laws of the market. After roughly fifteen years making documentaries, he debuted in 1988 with *Il bacio di Giuda* (*The Kiss of Judas*), followed by *Confortorio* (*Comfortation*, 1992), *Tiburzi* (1996), and *Gostanza di Libbiano* (*Gostanza from Libbiano*, 2000). In these works, beyond Benvenuti's attention to the story, he strived for visual quality in his attempt to re-create the atmosphere of an epoch borrowing from his full immersion in the iconosphere of Italian painting.

While Benvenuti fed his inspiration with Italian painting, Carlo Mazzacurati remained isolated against the landscape. Mazzacurati wanted to make movies because he had assimilated the lessons of the masters and he was part of a group of directors who shared his motivations and poetics. He was part of a small Paduan colony that included Enzo Monteleone (who later began directing in the 1990s) and Umberto Contarello, who immigrated to Rome in the early 1980s to study screenwriting and learn the trade of writing for cinema with some of the old greats. He understood early on—in part thanks to his self-produced road movie, *Vagabondi* (*Vagabonds*, 1983)—that his true calling was telling stories with a movie camera. In his films, he sought to unite the knowledge and cinematic images he had absorbed with his deep love for his home, preserving his memories and connecting them to the present. As a storyteller, Mazzacurati is at his best when he makes the viewer feel the connection between his characters and their environment and when he reveals unexpected, new connections. His characters' voyage is always a journey of initiation and self-discovery, in which the characters come in contact with previously unimagined and new dimensions of reality. His films shed light on otherwise dark zones and reveal their characters' strong emotions. As the human and natural environment irreversibly declines in his films, Mazzacurati continuously reaffirms those emotions. He is a director who looks at the present reality in terms of a loss of values. He always searches for the vanishing point in the negative chain of events, the moment when lost values are reappropriated. Love and friendship, for example, are two values constantly reaffirmed in his work.

His debut film, *Notte italiana* (*Italian Night*, 1987), was produced by Nanni Moretti. The second film, *Prete bello* (*The Handsome Priest*, 1989), was an adaptation of Goffredo Parise's novel (translated in English as *The Priest Among the Pigeons*), a film intended as a rediscovery of the mythologies of childhood. In 1992, he made *Un'altra vita* (*Another Life*), a remake of *Sorpasso* (*The Easy Life*), a film made thirty years earlier. This is the first film to deal with the subject of illegal aliens in an uncomfortable Italy, and it showed the fine line of demarcation between the dark side of society and the daily routine of normal life. In 1994, with *Il toro* (*The Bull*), he took his characters to Central Europe for the involuntary rediscovery of lost values. In 1996, he directed *Vesna va veloce* (*Vesna Goes Fast*), a work about the fragile nature of young persons' dreams to escape Central Europe and find paradise in Italy or other wealthier countries. In 1998, it was his turn to make a "coming-of-age" movie for television, *L'estate di Davide* (*Davide's Summer*). In 2000 he made *La lingua del santo* (*Holy Tongue*), a film in which for the first time he chose the lighter tones of comedy to navigate the region of the Veneto, in this case, a region blessed with riches and practically unrecognizable for the absence of any sense of the sacred. In more recent years, he and Marco Paolini created three splendid portraits of great Veneto writers, Mario Rigoni Stern, Luigi Meneghello, and Andrea Zanzotto. Each is depicted as a soon-to-be lost depository of knowledge and experience, bridges between the local reality of the Veneto and history, culture, and European and international literature. In his *A cavalla della tigre* (*Jailbreak* or *Riding the Tiger*, 2002, a liberal remake of Comencini's 1963 movie of the same name), he retold the story of the 1960s in a contemporary key. More so than for any other of his other films, you get the impression that the relationship to the landscape and its beauty gradually fades away and you have the perception that environmental decline is hopelessly unstoppable. Here again, Mazzacurati sought to reveal strong emotions that bring his characters together beyond the difficulties of life and the situations in which they are involved. This film felt like a transitional phase for Mazzacurati: he refined his abilities as a visual narrator and began to retrace the stories and anterior emotions of his characters by exploring them in close-up. With this work, he showed his ability to create different rhythms in the action. But what continued to interest him was the emergence of strong emotions, the desire to challenge adverse fate and to make a play to reverse destiny. At the same time, he did not quite find the perfect balance of comedy and drama in this work.

To extent that he, too, began as a film critic, Davide Ferrario's career can be compared to that of Faccini, Ponzi, and Di Carlo. Still under the influence of Wenders, his debut film, *La fine della notte* (*The End of the Night*, 1989), tells the story of the rough, long night of two boys and the homicide that follows. His second feature-length film was an excellent documentary on the Resistance, *Materiale resistente* (*Resistant Material*, 1995), co-directed with Guido Chiesa. He then made three films very different in nature from one another: *Tutti giù per terra* (*We All Fall Down*, 1997, based on Giuseppe Culicchia's novel), *I figli di Annibale* (*Children of Hannibal*, 1998), and *Guardami* (*Look at Me*, 1999). These works confirmed his strong ability to move in the margins of genre and to tell the story of the malaise of youth in a new and original manner. *Guardami* is a film in which he decided to move along the fine line (a line even more invisible today) that separates cinema and hardcore pornography. In this film, he tells the story of Nina, a character openly inspired by Moana Pozzi, arguably the most famous star—international and Italian—of the Italian porn industry. The film is not convincing because it is built around a life story clearly intended to be an *exemplum*, a character capable of reaching a high level of self-awareness and of releasing herself from the degradation of her profession only through pain and death. More recently, he has made films in Asia, Europe, and the United States in which he explores the world of pornography, its heroes and the frontiers of extreme sex.

Some of the directors who debuted in the 1980s can be grouped together for their thematic, stylistic, and narratologic affinities. Partly because their resources were limited, certain filmmakers chose to tell little stories, cast against tight spaces and with fewer characters. For many of them, the road movie was a rite of passage.

Giuseppe Piccioni debuted with a feature-length film in 1987 (after attending the Scuola di Cinema Gaumont), *Il grande Blek* (*The Great Blek*); an openly autobiographical work, it is the story of a group of young people growing up together in the province of Ascoli. His next film, *Chiedi la luna* (*Ask for the Moon*, 1991), was produced for television but made it to the theater. With this film, he showed his ability to tip-toe around his characters and observe them during an event or a casual encounter. He liked to break the rhythm of their daily routine by provoking a catastrophe, a profound crisis in their way of life and their relationships. This little film is admirable for the nearly imperceptible camera movements and how it manages to tell the story of the two main characters, who grow closer and closer until that inevitable moment when they find themselves in each other's arms. *Condannato a nozze* (*Condemned to Wed*, 1993) was a grotesque comedy and the two subsequent films—*Fuori dal mondo* (*Not of This World*, 1999) and *Luce dei miei occhi* (*Light of My Eyes*, 2001)—also went down this path. With these films, Piccioni reaffirmed his talent in plucking different strings of the story, making use of the unsaid, and making the viewer feel his characters' internal evolution.

Children of art, Carlo and Luca Verdone, the Vanzina brothers, the Comencini sisters, the Risi brothers, Manuel and Christian de Sica, and Giovanni Soldati sought to affirm their abilities as directors and actors as early as possible and to define their world beyond that of their parents.

After receiving his diploma from the Centro Sperimentale, Carlo Verdone became the spiritual leader of a group of comedians who got their start on television (Benigni, Pozzetto, Troisi, and Nuti)—in part because of his early success and in part because of his talent as a director. Together, they helped to renew the landscape of Italian comedy by giving greater depth to the stories and restoring the spectrum of comedic tones and notes that trash cinema had definitively abandoned.

As an actor, Verdone proved himself capable of reviving *fregolismo*, an Italian theatrical tradition named after nineteenth-century actor Leopoldo Fregoli, who possessed a legendary chameleon-like ability to "transform" himself into different characters. He found inspiration in the comedy of Alberto Sordi, and his Roman roughneck characters were modeled after Sordi's Nando Mericone. Verdone told the evolutionary story of the Roman *coatto*, a young man or boy who lived on the outskirts of Rome and was required to register with the police under "compulsory residence" (*domicilio coatto*) laws starting in the 1960s.

With his diptych of the early 1980s—*Un sacco bello* (*Fun Is Beautiful*, 1980) and *Bianco, rosso e Verdone* (*Red, White, and Verdone Green*, 1981)—he created some of the most significant personas of his rich gallery of characters. He then began to write stories that allowed him to showcase his directorial talent and to incorporate increasingly dramatic notes into his work. With every film, beginning in the mid-1980s, his style became lighter and lighter and his comedy more and more melancholic. He seemingly defined the term *melancomico* (melancomic—a play on the Italian *melanconico*, variant of *melancolico* [melancholic]), an expression that would be extended to other Italian directors as well). At his best, he had a Chaplinesque touch.

Over the course of twenty years, he made almost twenty titles and his films should also be analyzed in terms of his directorial evolution. *Compagni di scuola* (*Schoolmates*, 1988), *Maledetto il giorno che t'ho incontrato* (*Damned the Day I Met You*, 1992), *Al lupo, al lupo* (*Wolf! Wolf!*, 1992), *Viaggi di nozze* (*Honeymoon*, 1995), and *Sono pazzo di Iris Blond* (*I'm Crazy about Iris Blond* or *Iris Blond*, 1996) were among his most memorable films.

While Verdone was the direct descendant of the sovereigns of Italian comedy, Maurizio Nichetti was the son of Mack Sennett's slapstick. He was the child of the magic, wonder, and makeup of early silent film. Influenced by the great comics, he was also a student of Jacques Tati, Calvino, and Georges Perec. He liked to play on multiple possibilities in the development of the story and the fine line between dreams and reality. His comedy was perhaps the most rich with cultural echoes and in the best moments of his films, he reveals his ability to make the most of lessons learned from Zavattini.

He debuted in 1979 with *Ratataplan* and in the films that followed— *Ho fatto splash* (*Made a Splash*, 1980), *Domani si balla* (*Tomorrow We Dance*, 1982), *Il Bi e il Ba* (*The B and the Baa*, 1985), *Ladri di saponette* (*The Icicle Thief*, 1989), *Volere volare* (*To Want to Fly*, 1991), *Stefano Quantestorie* (*Stefano Somanystories*, 1993), *Luna e l'altra* (1996), and *Honolulu Baby* (2000)—he showed that he had an original approach to contaminating codes and to mixing animation with reality (thanks to his partnership with Guido Manuli, the hybridization of animation and reality in *Volere volare* effortlessly holds its own when compared to Robert Zemeckis's 1988 *Who Framed Roger Rabbit*). But above all, he showed that he knew how to make the most of his skills as actor and narrator and his ability to deconstruct and recompose the various parts of the storytelling mechanism.

When Massimo Troisi died, just after filming for *Il postino* (*The Postman*) had been completed, he was in a state of grace "more virtuous than ever" in terms of his ability to blend mime and words into a "sort of elixir," as Italian film critic Tullio Kezich observed in the pages of *Il corriere della sera* (June 5, 1994). With the same discretion and education with which he had appeared on television nearly fifteen years earlier, Troisi tip-toed out of the frame with a lightness entirely anomalous with respect to the vulgarity and heavy-handedness that typified Italian cinema in the 1980s.

With ingenious intuition, Ettore Scola offered Troisi the part of a lifetime when he asked him to play Pulcinella in *Il viaggio di Capitan Fracassa* (*The Voyage of Captain Fracassa* or *Captain Fracassa's Journey*). Even though Troisi was a full-fledged descendant of the Neapolitan theatrical tradition, his interpretation seemed more a product of a happy marriage between Pulcinella and the moonstruck Pierrot who dominated the international artistic scene throughout the eighteenth century. Even if his friendship with Scola did not have an immediate effect on his final directorial effort—*Pensavo fosse amore invece era un calesse* (*I Thought It Was Love*, 1991)—it did help him to refine his acting skills. Their friendship also taught him how to make the viewer feel his characters' pain and suffering—amorous and otherwise—through his gaze and it gave him a new understanding of contemporary cinema.

Massimo Troisi made his directorial debut in 1981 with *Ricomincio da tre* (*I'm Starting from Three*), a cinematic version of a theater piece that had already enjoyed success on television and on the stage. Troisi will probably not be remembered especially for his directorial talent—*Scusate il ritardo* (*Sorry I'm Late*, 1982), *Non ci resta che piangere* (*Nothing Left to Do but Cry*, 1984), and *Le vie del signore sono finite* (*The Ways of the Lord Are Finite*, 1987)—as much as for the evolution and maturation of his acting skills in the final years of his career, in the films directed by Scola, and in his final role in Michael Radford's 1994 *Il Postino*. In the final film he directed, the main character experiences the pangs of love and ultimately declares that "it's clear to me that a man and a woman are the persons least suited for marriage"—a temporary credo but more closed off from hope than in the characters' past. Then, thankfully, there was Troisi's performance in *Il postino*, a film in which Troisi's Pierrot gave the world his career's most heartbreaking hymn to life and to love.

For years, Roberto Benigni the director seemed proud of the fact—a badge of honor —that he had *not* studied at the Centro Sperimentale. In *Tu mi turbi* (*You Disturb Me* or *You Upset Me*, 1983), his debut film, the camera was there solely to serve his performance as an actor. In the films that followed—*Non ci resta che piangere* (co-directed with Troisi), *Il piccolo diavolo* (*The Little Devil*, 1988), *Johnny Stecchino* (*Johnny Toothpick*, 1991), and *Il mostro* (*The Monster*, 1994, a film that he conceived and co-wrote with Cerami at his side)—the direction never overshadows the story or the acting. This conscious, rational choice united rigor and simplicity and highlighted the story's mechanisms and Benigni's exceptional skills as an actor and mimic. When compared with other comics, Benigni seems to belong to another species. Part elf and part gnome, he makes his appearance like a sprite from the tales told by Tuscan farmers and he fills the scene with the physical and verbal impetuosity of an overflowing river. Like Petrolini and Totò, Benigni is first and foremost a gift to the Italian entertainment industry, an asset to Italian cultural heritage. While Petrolini's and Totò's fame never crossed national borders, Benigni—thanks to *La vita è bella* (*Life Is Beautiful*) and *Pinocchio* (*Roberto Benigni's Pinocchio*)— became an international cultural treasure. For the first time in his career, Benigni observed the world through the eyes of love and in doing so, he showed the world his power and established his credibility. The comparison between Benigni and Chaplin's *The Kid* is both legitimate and pertinent. Benigni managed to give his characters direction in a tragedy like the Holocaust in part by making the viewer bear all of the weight. But he also did so by credibly embodying the mythic figure of the individual capable of solving every enigma and delivering his child and companions to safety.[48] In *La vita è bella*, not only do Benigni's characters live in a perfect world untouched by the surrounding reality, but he also manages to make the father and son become a single entity. As a result, the father's death does not upset the son's victory and love of life. There is nothing heroic in Benigni's final gesture when little Giosué watches him march before the SS soldiers who will shoot him shortly thereafter. There is only the knowledge that he has managed to save his son and deliver to him love for life, a spiritual testament, and a high moral awareness.

Like Verdone, Ricky Tognazzi received his diploma from the Centro Sperimentale. Together with Marco Risi and Francesca Comencini, Tognazzi was one of Italian cinema's most attentive and competent personalities. His mission as a director was to depict history (the creative presence of screenwriter Simona Izzo was important in this regard). He took on difficult, highly controversial subjects like violence among sports fans (*Ultrà* [*Hooligans* or *Ultras*, 1991], winner of the Golden Bear in Berlin), racism, the life of Italian judges and their bodyguards, and the power of the Mafia (*La scorta* [*The Bodyguards* or *The Escort*, 1993] and *Excellent Cadavers* [released as *I giudici* in Italy, 2000], an American production). In the first phase of his career, he charted and explored these themes energetically. He inaugurated the second phase with *Canone inverso* (*Inverse Canon—Making Love*, 2000), arguably his most stylistically innovative film. A complex, meaningful work dense with internal resonance, this film takes the viewer on a journey through time, memory, emotion, history, and personal drama. It bestowed directorial maturity upon Tognazzi and it rightly positioned him as a world-class filmmaker.

The younger of the Comencini sisters, Francesca, chose the impracticable path of drama, making films like *Pianoforte* (*Grand Piano*) and *La luce del lago* (*La lumière du lac* or *The Light of the Lake*).

Cristina Comenicini, on the other hand, seemed the most capable of learning from her father, showing promise even with her debut film, *Zoo* (1988). She found success when she directed a dignified adaptation of Susanna Tamaro's bestseller *Va' dove ti porta il cuore* (*Follow Your Heart*, 1994). She then made comedies in which she told the story of changes in family relation-ships and an epochal change in the way families manage their emotions and educate their children: *Matrimoni* (*Marriages*, 1998), *Liberate i pesci* (*Free the Fish*, 2001), and *Il più bel giorno della mia vita* (*The Best Day of My Life*, 2002).

During the late 1970s and early 1980s, Marco Risi honed his skills as his uncle Nelo's assistant, working on middle-of-the-road comedies that enjoyed moderate success at the box office. But critics only began to pay attention when Marco made an Italian version of Robert Altman's 1983 *Streamers*: *Sol-dati—365 all'alba* (*Soldiers 365 Till Dawn* or *Soldiers—375 Until Dawn*). He then made *Mery per sempre* (*Forever Mary* or *Mary Forever*, 1989), *Ragazzi fuori* (*Boys on the Outside*, 1989, based on a story by Aurelio Grimaldi), *Il muro di gomma* (*The Invisible Wall*, 1991, based on the Ustica air disaster, with a screen-play by Andrea Purgatori), and *Il branco* (*The Pack*, 1994). And with *L'ultimo capodanno* (*Humanity's Last New Year's Eve*, 1998), based on a short story by Nicolò Ammaniti, Maro Risi brought splatter and a post-Tarantino sensibility to the Italian screen, drawing from writers who belonged to the *Gioventù can-nibale* (Cannibal Youth) movement, writers called "cannibals" by critics for their raw, disaffected style. Like the title of Soldini's excellent film *Un'anima divisa in due* (*A Soul Split in Two* or *A Split Soul*), Risi has a cinematic soul "split in two": on one hand, he's a bona fide natural (biologists would attribute this to regressive genes handed down by his father) and has a gift for comedy; on the other hand, there is a strong tendency toward social commentary in his films. This disassociation is the basis for some of his less than perfect results, but they also reflect his richness as an artist. Marco Risi made an important contribution to the renewal of Italian cinema over the past decades and to its connection to the tradition of Italian film. It is no surprise that his filmmaking has been called neo-neorealism. Like Moretti, Marco Risi produced films by newcomers in the second half of the 1990s.

In the "From Trash to Cult" section, we gathered observations and ele-ments that allowed us to analyze trash cinema. Now we must take stock of a group of directors and actors who were able to bring reluctant Italian cinema fans back to theaters over and over again during the 1980s and 1990s. Their audiences were made up of moviegoers who liked to laugh at comedy modeled after Italian and American films from the 1930s through 1960s and even the silent era and periodically, they managed to plug a leak in the constant hemorrhage of Italian audiences. Producers invested blindly in directors like Carlo and Enrico Vanzina, Neri Parenti, and Enrico Oldoini, and they delivered repeated success at the box office. These directors knew how to blend sure-fire ingredients and they had good—if not great—young actors and comedians at their disposal (from Massimo Boldi to Teo Teocoli, from Jerry Calà to Diego Abatantuono, from Christian de Sica, to Renato Pozzetto and Paolo Villaggio). Their comedic models worked because they were linked to a historical moment or because they had already been widely tested—from slapstick to sophisticated comedy. Their films were often remakes or parodies of important comedies from the past and the winning formula was that of grafting "low" comedy on to the body of sophisticated comedy.

Beginning in the 1980s, the Vanzina brothers made a series of films that—when seen today—help us to understand the transformation of an Italy that wanted to forget the "years of lead" and to live in an entirely new economic euphoria (at least for ten years or so). During that time, Italians experienced a complete renewal of consumerism and ways to get rich. Their successes included *Una vacanza bestiale* (*A Beastly Vacation*, 1980); *I fichissimi* (*Street Corner Kids*, 1981); *Eccezzziunale . . . veramente* (*Really Exceptional* or *Really Incredible*) and *Viuuulentemente . . . mia* (*Violently . . . Mine*, 1982); *Sapore di mare* (*Scent of the Sea, A Time for Loving*, or *A Taste of Sea*, 1982); *Vacanze di Natale* (*Christmas Holidays*, 1983), *Vacanze in America* (*Vacation in America* or *American Holidays*, 1984); *Yuppies* (1985); *Via Montenapoleone* (*Montenapoleone*, 1986); *Le finte bionde* (*The Fake Blonds*, 1988); *Miliardi* (*Millions* or *Billions*, 1990); *Sognando la California* (*California Dreaming*, 1992); and *A spasso nel tempo* (*Adrift in Time*, 1997).

Another director who deserves mention side by side with the Vanzinas is Neri Parenti, who picked up the baton from Luciano Salce in the Fantozzi saga with *Fantozzi contro tutti* (*Fantozzi Against the Wind*, 1980). His Fantozzi films contributed significantly to actor Paolo Villaggio's success during the 1980s. He then turned to films modeled after silent-era comedies: *Le comiche* (*The Comics, Funny Comedy, The Comedians*, or *The Comedies*, 1990), *Le nuove comiche* (*The New Comics*, 1994), and *Vacanze di Natale '95* (*Christmas Holidays '95* or *Christmas Vacation '95*, 1995).

Enrico Oldoini is another director who deserves mention: *Yuppies 2* (1986), *Vacanze di Natale '90* (*Christmas Holidays '90* or *Christmas Vacation '90*, 1990), *Anni '90* (1993), and *Miracolo italiano* (*Italian Miracle*, 1994).

These films were conceived using fast-food logic and they would run for just a few weeks (but they were viewed by millions of moviegoers during the holiday season). Thanks to their perfect timing and their late pop, hyperrealist style, they captured the superficial, artificial Italy that had been created by television: an Italy stylized by "made in Italy" ready-to-wear designers; a high-flying vulgar Italy, easily corruptible and lacking any sense of political or social duty; an Italy impervious to law and to even the most elementary moral and civic principles. But it was also an Italy that loved to show off its ephemeral status symbols with price tags and designer labels left in plain sight. However paradoxical it seemed, the troops led by Fantozzi and Abatantuono and directed by Vanzina and Co. were one of Italy's few lines of defense against the American invasion of the 1980s. They were worthy representatives not only of the self-indulgent spirit behind the famous Ramazzotti liqueur television advertisement "Milano da bere" ("Milan, Drink It Up") but also the spirit of "Italia da bere": the happily corrupt Italy of the 1990s, the Italy of "Tangentopoli" ("bribesville"), the Italy that suddenly found itself inundated with indictments, subpoenas, and arrests that ended the vacations of many.

The 1990s: Crisis between the Continuity of Tradition and Renewal

The 1990s began and ended with a series of prestigious international awards: in 1990, Gianni Amelio received an Oscar nomination for *Porte aperte* (*Open Doors*); the previous year, Tornatore won an Oscar for *Nuovo cinema Paradiso* (*Cinema Paradiso*); in 1992, Salvatores won it again with *Mediterraneo* (*Mediterranean*) while Fellini received an Oscar for Lifetime Achievement; and in 1999, *La vita è bella* (*Life Is Beautiful*) was honored with no less than three Oscars. In Cannes, *Ladro di bambini* (*The Stolen Children*), *La vita è bella*, *Caro diario* (*Dear Diary*), and *La stanza del figlio* (*The Son's Room*) each won Jury Prizes. In Venice in 1998, *Così ridevano* (*The Way We Laughed*) took a Golden Lion. Italian cinema was still represented on an international level by Bertolucci, and he was flanked by Tornatore, Benigni, and Salvatores—each one a director capable of thinking in terms of international audiences.

Callisto Cosulich has noted that—except for Fellini—professional life remained unhindered for the veterans and maestros of Italian cinema during the 1990s. In fact, for many it proceeded with Tayloristic speed. Like Roger Corman, Pupi Avati knew the system well and produced niche products that guaranteed profits and the reinvestment of revenue. He made an average of one title per year in the 1980s and 1990s, producing the films himself, and his pace has not slowed.[49] Monicelli made six films in the 1990s, as did Tinto Brass, who, in 2001, made a new version of *Senso* (*Black Angel*). Even Antonioni, who suffered a stroke, co-directed *Al di là delle nuvole* (*Beyond the Clouds*, 1994) with Wenders. Olmi was forced by illness to stop working in the 1980s but resumed in 1987 with *Lunga vita alla Signora!* (*Long Live the Lady!*) and then *La leggenda del santo bevitore* (*The Legend of the Holy Drinker*, 1998). Besides the splendid documentaries he made in the 1990s, he also released *Il segreto del bosco vecchio* (*The Secret of the Old Woods*, 1993) and *Genesi. La creazione e il diluvio* (*Genesis: The Creation and the Flood*, 1994), the first chapter of a television version of the Bible, and a work—as we will see—that seemed to mark a new milestone in his career and in Italian cinema, *Il mestiere delle armi* (*The Profession of Arms*).

We can just as well gloss over the great comedy filmmakers during this period (like Dino Risi, Bolognini, and Sordi). But certain directors did release important works in the 1990s, even though these films often were not as good as their earlier titles. Among these, the following deserve mention: Rosi's *La tregua* (*The Truce*, 1997, based on Primo Levi's book); and *Ferdinando e Carolina* (*Ferdinando and Carolina*, 1999) directed by Lina Wertmüller, who had directed Sophia Loren in *Sabato, Domenica e Lunedì* (*Saturday, Sunday and Monday*, 1990) at the beginning of the decade.

Even though the continuity with the tradition of postwar Italian cinema was never broken, the generational ties to that era began to loosen in the late 1980s. After their debut film, many new-generation directors proved unable to deliver another project in the medium or long term. Nobody threw in the towel but at the same time, no one seemed able to make a second film. The 1990s marked a phase in which the baton was definitively passed to the new generation. The directors who became the new models—and whose mastery was recognized by the new generation—were Moretti, Tornatore, Salvatores, Archibugi, and Mazzacurati.

The phenomenon of the new generation was due in part to the fact that Rome had gradually lost its hegemonic role as the capital of Italian filmmaking. From 1980 to 1990, new production houses and studios opened across Italy—from Turin to Milan, from the Veneto to Bologna, from Tuscany to Naples, from Apulia to Sicily.

The decade was marked by a striking new will to express oneself using cinema—even when the resources available were modest. But the downside to this was the lack of imagination and well-written dialogue.

When we consult the first census made by Mario Sesti in 1994,[50] or Vito Zagarrio's concise profile of the decade,[51] we see that each year there was at least one debut worthy of note. The most notable directors who debuted during this period (together with some of their titles) were as follows: Antonio Albanese with *Uomo d'acqua dolce* (*Fresh Water Man*, 1997); Sandro Baldoni; Andrea Barzini; Giulio Base with *Crack* (1991); Marco Bechis; Alessandro Benvenuti; Paolo Benvenuti; Bruno Bigoni; Claudio Caligari with *L'odore della notte* (*The Scent of the Night*, 1998); Mimmo Calopresti, Eugenio Cappuccio, Massimo Guadioso, and Fabio Nunziata with *Il caricatore* (*The Reel*, 1997); Giacomo Campiotti; Antonio Capuano; Carlo Carlei with *La corsa dell'innocente* (*The Flight of the Innocent*, 1992); Guido Chiesa with *Il caso Martello* (*The Martello Case*, 1992) and *Il partigiano Johnny* (*Johnny the Partisan*, 2000); Ugo Chiti with *Albergo Roma* (*Hotel Roma*, 1996) and *La seconda moglie* (*The Second Wife*, 1998); Ciprí and Maresco; Pappi Coriscato; Alessandro d'Alatri; Enzo d'Alò; Daniele Gaglianone with *I nostri anni* (*Our Years*, 2000); Matteo Garrone; Giuseppe Gaudino; Lucio Gaudino; Aurelio Grimaldi with *La discesa di Aclà a Floristella* (*Aclà* or *Aclà's Descent into Floristella*, 1992), *Le buttane* (*The Whores*, 1994), and *Nerolio* (*Black Oil*, 1998); Stefano Incerti with *Il verificatore* (*The Meter Reader* or *The Surveyor*, 1995); Simona Izzo; Wilma Labate with *La mia generazione* (*My Generation*, 1996); Luciano Ligabue with *Radiofreccia* (*Radio Arrow*, 1998) and *Da zero a dieci* (*From Zero to Ten*, 2001); Armando Manni; Luciano Mannuzzi; Massimo Martella with *Il tuffo* (*The Dive*, 1992) and *La prima volta* (*The First Time*, 1997); Mario Martone; Enzo Monteleone with *La vera vita di Antonio H* (*The True Life of Antonio H.*, 1994), *Ormai è fatta* (*Outlaw*, 2000), and *El Alamein* (*El Alamein: the Line of Fire*, 2002); Ferzan Ozpetek; Vanna Paoli with *La casa rossa* (*The Pink House*, 1992) and *The Accidental Detective* (2000); Leonardo Pieraccioni; Leone Pompucci with *Le mille bolle blu* (*A Thousand Blue Bubbles*, 1993) and *Camerieri* (*Waiters*, 1995); Pasquale Pozzessere with *Verso Sud* (*Going South*, 1992), *Padre e figlio* (*Father and Son*, 1994), and *Testimone a rischio* (*Risking Witness* or *Witness in Danger*, 1997); Pino Quartullo with *Quando eravamo repressi* (*When We Were Repressed*, 1992) and *Le donne non ci vogliono più* (*Women Don't Want To*, 1993); Sergio Rubini; Pasquale Scimeca; Daniele Segre; Michele Sordillo with *La cattedra* (*The Professorship*, 1991) and *Acquario* (*Aquarium*, 1997); Gianluca Tavarelli with *Portami via* (*Take Me Away*, 1995), *Un amore* (*A Love*, 1999), and *Qui non è il Paradiso* (*Here Is Not Paradise*, 2000); Ferdinando Vicentini Orgnani with *Mare largo* (*Open Sea*, 1998); Paolo Virzí; Fulvio Wetzl with *Mr. Rorret, ad altezza d'uomo* (*Rorret*, 1998), *Quattro figli unici* (*Four Only Children*, 1992), and *Prima la musica poi le parole* (*First the Music, Then the Words*, 2000); Edoardo Winspeare with *Pizzicata* (1996) and *Sangue vivo* (*Living Blood* or *Life Blood*, 1999); Maurizio Zaccaro; Vito Zagarrio with *La donna della luna* (*Woman in the Moon, The Night of the Full Moon*, or *Night of the Full Moon*, 1998) and

Bonus malus (*Good Bad,* 1993); and Gianni Zanasi with *Nella mischia* (*In the Thick of It,* 1995).

Some of the directors, like Zaccaro and Campiotti, got their start at Olmi's Bassano school, where the elder Olmi—if not anything else—imparted a distinct directorial code of ethics unto a wide variety of personalities.

After directing the medium-length feature *Tre donne* for Ipotesci Cinema (a film that already revealed some of his stylistic and thematic genius), Giacomo Campiotti directed *Corsa di primavera* (*Spring Race* or *Springtime Race,* 1989), *Come due coccodrilli* (*Like Two Crocodiles,* 1993), and *Il tempo dell'amore* (*A Time to Love,* 1999). From a thematic point of view, Campiotti is one of the most interesting and fierce defenders of the ecology of emotions. His characters live in world like that of the past few decades, a world that wants to free itself of the toxic residue of the past. From a stylistic point of view, he is a director with a subtle gaze that follows his characters without revealing its presence but never lacking in emotional involvement. His first film was clearly influenced by Olmi: an affectionate chronicle of life in the province of Milan, family dramas, the need for freedom, and the discovery of the world through the eyes of three eight-year-old classmates. The second film is based on a sophisticated series of flashbacks that cause the main character to remember an unhappy childhood full of pain and humiliation: memories of an absent father, family strife, and the devastating effect of domestic violence.

Maurizio Zaccaro received his director's degree from the Scuola di Cinema in Milan, and he worked as an assistant director on Olmi's *L'albero degli zoccoli* (*The Tree with the Wooden Clogs* or *The Tree of Wooden Clogs*) before he joined the Bassano school. But it was Pupi Avati who gave him the chance to make his directorial debut with a thriller, *Dove comincia la notte* (*Where the Night Starts, Where Night Begins,* or *Where the Night Begins,* 1981), filmed entirely in America during the same period that Avati was making *Bix,* his first English-language film. Together, Olmi and Zaccaro wrote the extraordinary *La valle di pietra* (*The Valley of Stone,* 1992), an adaptation of "Kalkstein," a 1848 story by Austrian Adalbert Stifter.

He then directed a series of films that did not seem to have much in common: *L'articolo 2* (1992), *Cervellini fritti impanati* (*Acting Out* or *Fried Crumbed Brains,* 1996), and *Il carniere* (*The Game Bag,* 1997), and some films for television, including a modern-day adaptation of De Amicis's novel *Cuore* (translated in English as *The Heart of the Boy*), and his most challenging film, *Un uomo per bene* (*A Respectable Man,* 1999). In fact, Zaccaro's stories were always about frontiers: he showed his audience the absurdity of laws, the monstrosities of war, and insanity. *Un uomo perbene* was what the Americans call it a "legal thriller" and it is a remarkable film on a number of levels: its strong moral motivation, Enzo Tortona's daughter's passionate quest for posthumous justice in the name of her father, and its careful translation of history into high cinematic, dramatic, and powerfully moralistic terms.

Sergio Rubini made his first film after having spent five years as one of the most popular actors among young Italian cineastes and after having worked with Valentino Orsini, Giuseppe Ferrara, and Federico Fellini. For his first film, he chose a play by Umberto Marino, *La stazione* (*The Station*, 1990), which had already been brought successfully to the stage. In this work, as in all the films that have followed, he tells the story of men whose lives are turned upside down by the sudden irruption of a woman. In the earlier films, the story was shaped by the theatrical text. But with *Il viaggio della sposa* (*The Bride's Journey*, 1997), he chose to tell a story set in the seventeenth century and he sought to give the story cultural and visual depth by filling it with sophisticated literary and artistic references. *Il viaggio della sposa* was arguably his most ambitious film as a director but it was also his film least appreciated by critics.

Michele Placido decided to take up directing after a twenty-year career as a theatrical and cinematic actor. In recent years, success has seemed to smile only upon comic actors. Placido made comic films, but he also tackled stories with high dramatic content and he took advantage of everything he had learned from the directors he had worked with, from Rosi to Damiani, from Lizzani to Bellocchio. His cinema was closer to the narrative and directorial modes of the maestros than to the directors of the 1990s. But—beyond any of his noble intentions—this was also perhaps his limitation. He told powerful stories in each of his films and real events, like that of Giorgio Ambrosoli, based on the book by Corrado Stajano, in *Un eroe borghese* (*Ordinary Hero*, 1995). In his first film, *Pummarò* (*Tomato*), he tells the story of young man from Ghana who is searching for his brother, a tomato picker. This was probably the first Italian film to deal with the exploitation of illegal immigrants in Italy. In *Le amiche del cuore* (*Close Friends*), he told a story of incest, domestic violence, and loneliness. In *Del perduto amore* (*Of Lost Love*), he chose to tell the brief story of a young militant, a member of the Communist Party in Calabria in the 1950s, who decided to use his own money to create a school for underprivileged girls. As with his other works, this film could have been made in the 1960s or 1970s but in many instances, it has a narrative breath reminiscent of Kurosawa or John Ford. In his recent *Un viaggio chiamato amore* (*A Journey Called Love*), he told the story of an *amour fou* between the already mature poet Sibilla Aleramo and the young Dino Campana.

Director of *Strane storie* (*Weird Tales*, 1994) and *Consigli per gli acquisti* (*Commercial Break*, 1997), Sandro Baldoni was a willing inheritor of Zavattini's spirit and Magritte's surrealism, both of which he dissolved into small, everyday stories. He developed his first film from a short, as did the following directors: Corso Salani, the most extraordinary exponent of a group of filmmakers capable of making bare-bone movies with nearly no financial backing whatsoever and director of *Voci d'Europa* (*The Voice of Europe*, 1989), *Gli ultimi giorni* (*The Last Days*, 1992), *Gli occhi stanchi* (*Tired Eyes*, 1995), and *Occidente* (*West*, 2000); Antonietta de Lillo, who made *Matilda* (1989, a prize-winner at Annecy); Gianni Zanasi, who made *Nella mischia* (*In the Thick of It*, 1995); and Matteo Garrone, one of the most interesting figures to emerge in recent memory and director of *Terra di mezzo* (*Land in Between*, 1996).

After he worked for nearly a decade at the Archivio nazionale della resistenza (National Archive of the Resistance) in Turin, directing a series of important documentaries, Mimmo Calopresto debuted as a director of feature-length films with *La seconda volta* (*The Second Time*, 1994), produced by and starring Nanni Moretti. This work not only marked the birth of an important new director but it also reinvigorated the movie-going public's faith in cinema as a medium for social commentary. The film told the story of an attempt to understand the motivation behind a terrorist attack by creating a dialogue between the terrorist and the professor she has shot. The attempt fails. But the viewer is forced to come to terms with Italy's "season" of terrorism and the impossibility of forgiveness. His second film, *La parola amore non esiste* (*Notes of Love*, 1998), took a close look at emotion and neurotic pathologies. The third, *Prefersico il rumore del mare* (*I Prefer the Sound of the Sea*, 2000), combined the difficulty of creating cinematic emotion and passion with a wider view of the setting and the different ways that characters act with others. The viewer can feel the morality and rigor that lie behind every one of Calopresti's choices, behind every camera movement, every sound, and every line. The essentiality of his style and the power of his frame make him one of the most important filmmakers of his generation and a director to watch.

Thanks to comedy writer Umberto Marino, Andrea Barzini was able to make at least two films that revived the spirit of the 1970s, two works that represent cinematic equivalents of coming-of-age novels for a generation seemingly untouched by the "years of lead": *Italia-Germania 4 a 3* (*Italy vs. Germany 4–3*, 1990) and *Volevamo essere gli U2* (*We Wanted to Be U2*, 1992).

Inspired by similar motivations, *L'estate di Bobby Charlton* (*Bobby Charlton's Summer*, 1995) was the re-creation of a moment in Italian history from the 1960s. It was the third film by Massimo Guglielmi, who had debuted in 1988 with *Rebus*, a work based on a story by Antonio Tabucchi.

Mario Martone got his start in avant-garde theater (he was the founder of the Neapolitan experimental theater group Falso Movimento [False Movement]) and made his debut as a director in 1992 with *Morte di un matematico napoletano* (*Death of a Neapolitan Mathematician*), in which he re-created the final moments of the great mathematician Renato Cacioppoli, who committed suicide in 1959. The film won the Jury Prize at the Venice Film Festival, probably for the performance delivered by theatrical actor Carlo Cecchi, who made his screen debut with this film. But Martone played an important role in bringing together what would later be called the "Neapolitan School of the 1990s."[52] Following *Morte di un matematico napoletano*, he made the excessively Pasolinian *I vesuviani* (*The Vesuvians*) and *Teatro di guerra* (*Rehearsal for War* or *Rehearsals for War*), an adaptation of one of his plays. But his most convincing effort was *L'amore molesto* (*Nasty Love*). In a Naples suddenly missing its visual stereotypes, the female lead embarks on a painful journey into her subconscious. She subsequently discovers a painful truth and is reconnected with her deceased mother. *Teatro di guerra* is more of a "work in progress" than a bona fide film. A "behind-the-scenes" backstage look at a play in production, it reveals the hopes and misery of a theatrical group surviving at the margins of mainstream theater.

Pappi Corsicato is perhaps the most unpredictable Neapolitan director in recent memory. Director of just a handful of titles, he was clearly influenced by Almodóvar (for whom he worked as an assistant director) but also by Pasolini, who was a model for other Neapolitan directors as well. Besides his segment in *I vesuviani*, he made three films between 1993 and 2000: *Libera* (*The Neapolitans*, 1993), *I buchi neri* (*Black Holes*, 1995), and *Chimera* (2000). His work is remarkable for its visual and narrative brilliance and Mediterranean symbology. In his films, Corsicato sought to communicate sensuality and vitality despite the unfolding of events and the deterioration of his characters' world.

More than any other member of the Neapolitan School, Antonio Capuano was the director who worked at the fringes of Italian cinema. He was the most free and was not afraid to use vulgarity and shocking imagery in his films. At the same time, he did not hesitate to show his appreciation of Bertolt Brecht. He chose difficult subject matter and did not shy away from the "politically incorrect": juvenile delinquency in *Vito e gli altri* (*Vito and the Others*, 1990); the pedophilia of a priest who dares to defy the Camorra (the Neapolitan Mafia) in *Pianese Nunzio, 14 anni a maggio* (*Pianese Nunzio, Fourteen in May* or *Sacred Silence*, 1996); and eroticism unleashed in an Argentine soap opera actor when he and his companion view the pornographic frescos of the villas in Pompeii in *Polvere di Napoli* (*The Dust of Naples*, 1998).

Even with her first film, *Tano da morire* (*To Die for Tano*, 1998), Roberta Torre showed impressive skills as a narrator, a mastery of rhythm, true talent with the use of music (thanks in part to her collaboration with Nino d'Angelo), and clear ability in developing her story. One of the most original directors of the 1990s, Torre ably navigated the narrative and visual stereotypes of the Mafia and Southern Italy, even though she was not always able to keep her directorial talent in check. Those stereotypes exploded on the screen thanks to her sarcastic spirit, which seemed to strike at the very core of the Mafia's power. *Sud Side Story* (*South Side Story*) was perhaps her weakest film: it is her least innovative, but it still reveals her promise as one of Italian cinema's best directors in the new millennium. In 2002, she finished her full-length feature *Angela*. In this film, she employed the detached curiosity of an anthropologist as she portrayed the normalcy of a young woman living beyond the reach of the law, the wife of a Sicilian Mafia boss and drug trafficker.

The cinema of Ciprí and Maresco was more extreme and even less mainstream. They made their directorial debut with *Lo zio di Brooklyn* (*The Uncle from Brooklyn*, 1995), a film that dripped with the same desperate, revolting sub-humanity that had animated their shorts for Enrico Ghezzi's *Cinico TV* (*Cinic TV*). It is as if Pasolini's sub-proletariat world survived a nuclear war and then began to emit anguished signs of life—desperate and despairing signs of life—to which no religion or any social organization could respond. Their second film, *Totò che visse due volte* (*Totò Who Lived Twice*, 1998), was even more extreme and desperate. The violence of certain scenes led to its being sequestered on grounds of religious defamation.

Alessandro d'Alatri made his debut with *L'americano rosso* (*Red American*, 1991) following a long career directing television ads. The film was striking for its sense of rhythm and its accurate depiction of life in Italy in the 1930s. But it was with his second film, *Senza pelle* (*No Skin*, 1994), that D'Alatri truly showed his ability to tackle challenging, ambitious stories. This film tells the story of a mentally disturbed young man who falls in love with a postal employee. In his third film, *I giardini dell'Eden* (*The Garden of Eden*, 1998), D'Alatri offered a non-hagiographic version of the life of Christ in the years not covered by the Gospels. *Casomai* (*If By Chance*, 2002) told the story of a young couple who wanted at all costs to stay together but was destroyed by the excessive attention of their friends and relatives. The syncopated, highly realistic dialogue was surprisingly good, and D'Alatri showed true narrative creativity and good sense of rhythm in this film.

Alain Bichon observed rightly that director Renzo Martinelli risked being a victim of the same ostracism that affected Tornatore. Over the past few decades, critics' whims—their likes and dislikes—have been affected by a new series of factors. For directors who come from the world of advertising, reception by critics is almost always negative. As far as Martinelli is concerned, it is worth remembering that after a children's film he made—*Sarahsarà* (*The Waterbaby*, 1994)—he made a courageous film about an event similar to a story told by Ken Loach in *Land and Freedom* (1995), a film in which a group of anarchists are killed by Communists during the war in Spain: in *Porzûs* Martinelli recounts an episode of fratricide among communist soldiers stationed along the Yugoslav border during the final days of the Resistance (the same circumstances in which Pier Paolo Pasolini met his death). After this film, with the help of Furio Scarpelli, Marintelli unsuccessfully tried to make a film based on book by Carlo Mazzantini and set—like Pasolini's *Salò* —in the fascist Republic of Salò. Instead, he made a rigorous and on many levels exemplary re-creation of the tragedy of the Vajont dam (*Vajont*, 2000), a film in which he re-created the event using highly accurate documentation while using new technologies to achieve a realistic depiction of the collapse of Mount Toc and the subsequent flood that destroyed the towns of Erto, Casso, and Longarone, killing more than two hundred thousand persons.

A Turkish national, Ferzan Ozpetek worked as a assistant director for a number of directors (including Ponzi, Veronesi, Nuti, Ricky Tognazzi, and Marco Risi) before he landed his first film *Il bagno turco* (*Steam: The Turkish Bath* or *Hamam: The Turkish Bath*, 1997). As with later films by Özpetek, like *Harem Suare* (*Harem Soirée*, 1999) and *Le fate ignoranti* (*His Secret Life* or *The Ignorant Fairies*, 2001), *Il bagno turco* dealt with the theme of sexual identity and the loss of certainty. Ozpetek was interested in openness, comprehension, and acceptance of alternative realities—cultural, religious, and sexual. In his composition of the frame and the strong sense of viewer participation he created, Ozpetek brought back to life the lessons of Visconti, Bolognini, and Pasolini, successfully applying them to contemporary situations.

Of the small colony of Tuscan actors and directors who played a central role in Italian cinema during the second half of the 1990s, Paolo Virzí was the first to debut after he had written scripts for Salvatores, Montaldo, and Felice Farina, among others. With *La bella vita* (*Living It Up*, 1994), he told a love story set in the working-class world of Piombino, a steelworks town that was going through an identity crisis and seemed aware of its inevitable extinction, a story distantly reminiscent of Truffaut's *Jules et Jim*. Virzí loves to work within the constraints of minimalist stories, alternating and mixing realistic tones with light ironic distortion ripe with sympathy and affection for his characters. *Ferie d'agosto* (*Summer Vacation*, 1996), *Ovosodo* (*Hardboiled Egg*, 1997), and *Baci e abbracci* (*Kisses and Hugs*, 1999) brilliantly touched strings of comedy as well as those of production design.

Fuochi d'artificio (*Fireworks*, 1997) was Leonardo Pieraccioni's third film. It did not match the outstanding results of *Il ciclone* (*The Cyclone*, 1996, one of the biggest-earning films of all time), but it did well nonetheless at the box office. As if by merely picking up the pieces and leftovers of *Il ciclone*, it brought in roughly 50 million lire thanks to a early run of six hundred prints. Pieraccioni did not set out for success at any cost but *Il ciclone* was blessed by a series of elements that came together brilliantly if unexpectedly. While Virzi's storytelling veered toward the sociological and political (as if a reincarnation of Emmer), Pieraccioni cast off the ballast of any such intentions and rewrote Cinderella with a male lead. He mixed and blended together ingredients seemingly borrowed from cartoons (creating a Tuscan version of Donald Duck), from silent-era comic films, from the early talkies by Camerini, and from the "rosy" neorealism of the 1950s. For *Il ciclone*, Pieraccioni chose an absolutely average character, a story-less character who does not have many great expectations for the future. An entirely arbitrary event—the arrival of a troop of beautiful Spanish ballerinas at the doorstep of a house in the middle of the Tuscan countryside—upends all of his rhythms, expectations, and life plans. In this film, chance and chaos guide Pieraccioni's time-tested plot up until a happy ending that allows him to coronate his dreams of love with a beautiful princess who arrives out of nowhere. Compared to the army of comedians who preceded him, Pieraccioni possessed a comedic sensibility born out of his affectionate observations of daily life, the repetition of life's provincial rituals, and a tolerance for a variety of ways of life. Pieraccioni the actor identified perfectly with his character. Rather than distorting the character, he continuously submitted him to stressful situations that were new to him. Such experiences revealed his character's inadequacies (in a sympathetic light) but they also brought out his curiosity and his will to accept any challenge. The hero of all of Pieraccioni's films is an individual who lives one day at a time, a decent person but a nincompoop when it comes to any type of sentimental situation. Basically, he's a late-romantic hero and destiny rewards him with the love of his life. *Il cyclone* was a truly family-friendly film: with this film actor/director Pieraccioni became the first Italian filmmaker in decades to bring different generations of Italian moviegoers together again.

Thanks to the success of Pieraccioni and others who came before him, like Benigni and Nuti, as well as that of Paolo Virzí and Giorgio Panariello, "Tuscan humor" became a new albeit short-lived genre of Italian cinema and was intensely exploited by filmmakers. The triumphant success of *Il cyclone* helped to bolster the careers of many Tuscan comedians. Directors like Giorgio Panariello with *Bagnomaria* (the title is a play on "bain-marie" and *Maria's Swimming Pool*, 1999) and *Al momento giusto* (*At the Right Moment*, 2000) and Massimo Checcherini with *Lucignolo* (*Wick*, 2000) and *Faccia da Picasso* (*Picasso Face*, 2001) managed to bring their odd-ball characters from theater and television to the big screen. They were happy to ride on the coattails of their colleagues, although their comedic style was rougher around the edges from a cinematic point of view and their stories were more loosely woven together and clearly tended toward a lower common denominator.

At the height of Pieraccioni's success and just as audience numbers began to dip critically, the comic team of Aldo, Giovanni, and Giacomo was officially sanctioned by moviegoers. The three actors had achieved notoriety thanks to their appearances on the television show *Mai dire gol* (*Never Say Goal*). In their debut film, *Tre uomini e una gamba* (*Three Men and a Leg*, 1997), they did nothing else but rehash previously tested material from their repertoire, but their exceptional performances evoked the spirit of the great clowns of American silent film.

With each film, their artistic ability grew, as did their narrative and dramatic ambition. With *Così è la vita* (*That's Life*, 1998) and *Chiedimi se sono felice* (*Ask Me if I'm Happy*, 2000), they began to pay more attention to the storytelling mechanism. The second of these two films is complex in its structure and is based on sophisticated reflections on fiction and acting. In certain moments, you can see the long shadow of Pirandello in this film.

Thanks to its success with audiences, Gabriele Muccino's *L'ultimo bacio* (*One Last Kiss* or *The Last Kiss*, 2001) was immediately recognized and consecrated as the emblem of a generation that did not want to grow up. It brought the spotlight (as well as interest from foreign film producers) to a director who had made two other films—*Ecco fatto* (*That's It*, 1998) and *Come te nessuno mai* (*But Forever in My Mind*, 1999)—in which he had already shown his ability to direct nonprofessional actors and to portray all the small and large traumas of adolescent life. A skilled filmmaker with an excellent sense of timing and rhythm, Muccino deserves praise for his knowledge and talent as a director, even though the stories he has told up until now are for the most part fragile. Paradoxically, his most mature script was *Soap story* (1998), a Tarantino-influenced screenplay never produced. Muccino attended the Centro Sperimentale and he put his studies to good use. In some ways, his thirty-something characters are the distant relatives of Fellini's *Vitelloni* (*The Young and the Passionate*). Like their 1950s counterparts, they shirked responsibility, they dreamed of escaping, and they reveled in their fraternity.

One of the defining characteristics of the generation of 1980s filmmakers was the acknowledgment of ties to the history of previous generations. Today, with few exceptions, cinematic allusions are more sporadic and less important than in the past. Cinema is no longer viewed as a dominant cultural realm that can be home to and define one's life. Filmmakers still use cinematic allusions but today they are more often explicit references instead of nearly invisible, self-appropriated, and metabolized cultural references.

Nearly thirty years after his death, Pasolini is one of the few tutelary deities left. His films continue to serve as models for moving within the new realities of underground culture, social disenfranchisement, misery, prostitution, and the contradictions of consumerist society and its members' struggle to survive. Besides Zavattini and Fellini, Pasolini's corpus of works has proved the only postwar collection of films capable of reviving itself and offering a constant, over-arching communion with multiple generations of filmmakers.

The connection between Italian audiences and Italian cinema seems to have broken in recent years. Italian cinema is no longer appreciated by its natural public and there has been no sign of this trend changing. In fact, in 2002, Italian movie theaters experienced a bona fide stock-market crash. As early as 2001, Salvatores spoke of the crisis at Cannes: "We tell miniscule stories that are barely recognizable to foreigners." But beyond the problem of facing foreign audiences, Italian cinema has become increasingly and dramatically more foreign, invisible, and unrecognizable at home. Recent data confirm this trend. In 2001 alone, box-office numbers dropped by 50 percent. In many ways, the Italian cinema crisis is analogous to that of an industry much more stable during the twentieth century, the auto industry. When you compare the respective trends side by side, it is clear that Italians turned away from Italian cinema just as they did from Italian automobiles because they found products elsewhere, products that mirrored new desires and expectations.

The detachment was gradual but was accelerated beginning in 1999: for example, while Stefano Incerti's *Prima del tramonto* (*Before Sunset*) took in 86 million lire at the box office, Ranieri Martinotti's *Branchie* (*Gills*)—based on an Ammaniti novel—earned only 33 million and Maurizio Ponzi's *Besame mucho* just 15 million. Fewer than twenty films earned 1 billion lire or more. In recent years, Italian audiences—and in particular, young persons—seem to have decided that television is the appropriate place to watch Italian movies. As a result, many directors have chosen not to spend years living in limbo and instead have made sometimes dignified and important films. More than ever, we need to devote systematic study to made-for-television cinema.

The box-office champion of 2001 was Neri Parenti's *Merry Christmas* and other films were successful as well: Antonio Albanese's *Il nostro matrimonio è in crisi* (*Our Marriage is on the Rocks*); Luciano Ligabue's *Da zero a dieci* (*From Zero to Ten*); Soldini's *Brucio nel vento* (*Burning in the Wind*); Salvatores's *Amnèsia*; and perhaps more than any other, even though it conceded nothing to the moviegoer, Bellocchio's *Ora della religione* (*The Religion Hour* or *The Religion Hour: My Mother's Smile* or *Hour of Religion*). The biggest disappointment was *Il principe e il pirata* (*The Prince and the Pirate*) by Pieraccioni, who proved incapable of pumping new blood into a well-squeezed formula.

But there are some elements—however few—that give us reason to have a small dose of optimism. After years of darkness and desperation, two films released at the beginning of the new millennium validated those who believed in Italian cinema and its potential to reassume its competitive status within the context of European and international cinema in a relatively short period: Nanni Moretti's *La stanza del figlio* (*The Son's Room*) and Ermanno Olmi's *Il mestiere delle armi* (*The Profession of Arms*). Using entirely different approaches, these filmmakers hedged their bets on visual storytelling, pushing the viewer to watch the image and to learn and to reflect upon every element of the image itself. A one-man band and director capable of dominating every element on the set, Olmi played the role of pontiff in the church of past masters, including directors distant from his world, from Eisenstein to Welles, from Kurosawa to Bergman, from Bresson to Fellini. As never before, he revealed his ability to create a world not only in the story of the final six days in the life of a sixteenth-century *condottiere* but in nearly every sequence and frame. Of all his films, this was the richest in terms of its references to other works and it was the work least weighed down by pedagogical and moralistic intentions.

However different their paths, Olmi and Moretti give us reason to continue to believe that cinema is a form of knowledge and experience and that it offers an alternative means of approaching and seeing (with our eyes and minds) new realities and realities that surround us. For both of these directors, however different their working methods, sophisticated visual is part of their poetics and it reveals that part of their lives and their deepest convictions have been blended into their films.

From May 2001 through the spring of 2002, roughly forty Italian directors made their debut, including the following noteworthy filmmakers: Vincenzo Marra's with his surprisingly good *Tornando a casa* (*Sailing Home*); Paolo Sorrentino with *L'uomo in più* (*One Man Up*); Fabio Rosi with *L'ultima lezione* (*The Final Lesson*), a film that re-created the circumstances of Federico Caffè's disappearance in the 1980s; Daniele Vicari with *Velocità massima* (*Vmax* or *Maximum Velocity*); and Claver Salizzato with *I giorni dell'amore e dell'odio* (*Days of Grace*), a film about the massacre of fifty thousand Italian soldiers on the Greek island of Cefalonia in the final years of World War II. Even though they were not entirely new to the scene, other young directors also made notable films during this period, like *L'imbalsamatore* (*The Embalmer* or *The*

Taxidermist) by Matteo Garrone and *Respiro* (*Respiro: Grazia's Island*) by Emanuele Crialese, a filmmaker who showed confident mastery of story, directing, and photography and who was one of the only Italian cineastes capable of giving his work a mythical dimension.

As never before, Southern Italian filmmakers—from Naples to Sicily—have emerged recently as a powerful force. More than ever, they are making stories that reach beyond the world of the Mafia and the Camorra. They have given the south a privileged position in historical memory that helps to understand Italy's transformation over the past fifty years. In their films, the south denotes an attempt to unearth forgotten stories of the struggle for the most elementary rights of women and men. But it also laboratory for linguistic and expressive experimentation, a confluence of historical and mythological themes, and a crossroads of influences arriving from the entire landscape of the arts. For these filmmakers, the south represents an attempt to revisit narrative, thematic, and visual stereotypes: filmmakers like Roberta Torre and the directorial team Ciprí and Maresco have created extreme works by irreverently and corrosively playing on Mafia stereotypes. Although their working methods are antithetical, they both employ visual writing, color, sound, noise, and the rhythms of editing to tell their stories.

As the central role of Cinecittà has been diminished (even though Rome is still a favorite location for filming) and centers for film production have sprung up in every region of Italy, many directors from many different generations—from Olmi to newcomer Valeria Bruni Tedeschi—have traveled to different continents and different European countries to make their films. Olmi chose Montenegro as the set for his last film (the film's main character is a nineteenth-century Chinese woman pirate). Directorial team Aldo, Giovanni, and Giacomo chose New York as for their *La leggenda di Al, John, e Jack* (*The Legend of Al, John, and Jack*). Bernardo Bertolucci returned to Paris to make a film set in 1968. Valeria Bruni Tedeschi also went to Paris to make her first film as director. Daniele Luchetti shot his last film in Greece. Enzo Monteleone went to Africa to re-create the battle of El Alamein and to pay homage—with the best Italian war movie since Monicelli's *La grande guerra* (*The Great War*)—to the heroic Italian soldiers sent to their slaughter without sufficient rations and ammunition and outgunned and outnumbered by Montgomery's troops. Monteleone's film was a homage to the great American war movies but also to writer Mario Rigoni Stern, who delivered an antiheroic, up-close account of the painful, tragic epic of Italian soldiers on the various fronts of World War II.

I like to think that Italian cinema can move and breathe beyond the atmosphere here at home and I hope that it can go out into space and come in contact with other worlds. I believe that its curiosity and respect for other cultures will allow it to obtain a new cinematographic citizenship. "I am a citizen of the cinematograph," said Jean Renoir. Today, my hope is that young Italian filmmakers aspire to cinematographic citizenship by going back to the movies, immersing themselves in epic history (past and present), digesting it, assimilating genetic information from as many continents as they can, conceiving their works in terms of cinema, even though many of them will be forced to create their works for television.

At present, there are many roads open to Italian filmmakers and they can intersect in as many ways.

On one hand, there are films like Gionata Zarantonello's *Medley*, produced for just 20 million lire, conceived for Internet viewing. Or Matteo Garrone's early films, *Terra di mezzo* (*Land in Between*, 1996) and *Ospiti* (*Guests*, 1998), films produced with the smallest of casts. Or all of the films directed by Carso Salani, a true miracle-worker in terms of producing and directing with means previously unheard of.

On the other hand, there is Benigni with his undying faith in Italian cinema and his love for its past, his creativity and ability to discover wonderment—among other things—through his imagery.

In 2002, the centenary of Zavattini's birth, Benigni made *Pinocchio*. He was so exited and so full of love for Zavattini that he wanted to project it onto the clouds, just as Zavattini had proposed as he sought to find optimism in the ruins and destruction of war.

Pinocchio is first and foremost the most sincere homage ever made to Fellini: the butterfly that lands on the Blue Fairy's fingers at the beginning of the film might as well be a reincarnation of the director himself. He's come back to life to guide us, with his light touch, to a perfect, fantastic world, more true than truth and created out of pure imagination. But all of Benigni's collaborators embraced the spirit of Fellini in telling the story of the puppet's peripeteia and his rites of passage and initiation. In doing so, they sought to reveal the characters core, his *nocciolo* (pit) in Italian (from the Latin *nucleus*), the word believed to be the etymon for the Tuscan dialectal term *pinocchio* (possibly *pino* [pine + *nocciolo*, or pit]). With extraordinary faithfulness to the original story by Collodi, Benigni tells the story from the Blue Fairy's point of view, with the puppet as the subject of the action, obviously. Love plays a privileged role as the fulcrum and motor of the story and the universe. In revisiting the text, Benigni and his production designer Danilo Donati also revived the many great illustrations of Pinocchio that have been created over the years, from Attilio Mussino on. But Benigni also made Pinocchio his own through his sense of freedom, desire for adventure, value of friendship, faith in others, and need to preserve his curiosity and predisposition toward wonder forever.

Benigni's *Pinocchio* cost more than 40 million Euros: a record sum for Italian cinema and for an art-house film that was marketed using blockbuster strategies. Reasons of the heart seemed to prevail over financial concerns in the making of this film. Benigni's love for the puppet and for his profound sense of hunger and thirst for freedom emanate from the puppet's frenetic motions and its mechanical tick-tock voice.

The outlook for Italian cinema is much more encouraging and promising than it was just a few years ago, even though the prognosis remains—it cannot be avoided—unclear. On one hand, it has become more and more difficult for a newcomer to find his or her way into theaters. On the other hand, filmmakers have begun to accept the fact that the theater is no longer the only "sacred" place for screening their films. Today, "small" films travel many different routes and consistently reach audiences at the end of their journey, be it through festivals, art-house circuits, public and private television broadcasts, satellite television, videocassettes, DVDs, and the Internet. If we begin again to conceive films within the framework of European production and intended for international audiences, we realize that the life of even a small film may not be so rewarding at the box office in the short term but in the end, they may ultimately pay for themselves and create new opportunities for producers and directors. On the other hand, beyond all the ifs, ands, and buts, filmmakers need to start thinking on a larger scale, even if they are small. And they need to do so without turning their backs on the heritage of artisanal knowledge that precedes them in all aspects of filmmaking. They need to invest their energies in experimentation with images, sound, and narrative, and they need to cross over into new technological frontiers and the new possibilities these frontiers open up for an endless number of new stories.

If Italian cinema is to become competitive again, filmmakers have to once again begin believe that they can fly. They need to move within the world of international cinema with the lightness of a butterfly and the proud self-awareness of their own identity and history. Even if Italian cinema is not in the best of health today, Italian filmmakers must not ignore or avoid the challenges of the global market any longer.

EPILOGUE 2007

Black clouds have formed on the horizon of Italian cinema in recent years. Even though 2006 brought satisfaction and remarkable success with critics and audiences at Cannes, in 2007 no Italian film competed at the festival: only Olmi's *Centochiodi* (*One Hundred Nails*) was screened "out of competition" and Daniele Luchetti's *Mio fratello è figlio unico* (*My Brother Is an Only Child*) was screened in the "Quinzaine des Réalisateurs" section. I have always loved Italian cinema and I continue to consider it—without reservation—the Art of the Twentieth Century, able more than any other to renew other art forms. But, given the current situation, I find it more and more difficult to see signs or reasons for hope in its immediate future. In retrospect, certain recent films—when seen as a whole—reveal renewed metabolic processes: with his *Il caimano* (*The Caiman* or *The Crocodile*), Moretti seems to have looked to the lessons of Fellini for guidance; with *Il regista di matrimoni* (*The Wedding Director*), Bellocchio showed himself a student of Visconti; Kim Rossi Stuart's debut film *Anche libero va bene* (*Along the Ridge*) was clearly inspired by the work of De Sica; and Paolo Sorrentino drew from the tradition of comedy Italian-style for his *L'amico di famiglia* (*The Family Friend* or *Friend of the Family*). These films do not bring to mind an umbilical cord that continues to resist being severed from postwar Italian cinema but rather transplanted stem cells that guarantee a sick body the possibility of returning to full vitality. Moretti's and Bellocchio's films represent an important and original reflection on the state of Italian cinema and they show that the two directors have chosen to react to the limits of today's scaled-down Italian cinema. Moretti and Bellocchio know that it is impossible, today, for a young director to imagine making cinema comparable to that of Fellini and Visconti. But they have also declared their faith, as the new generation of Italian filmmakers, in the narrative possibilities of a technological and iconographic landscape that would have been unimaginable just a few short years ago. In this regard, we should also note Saverio Costanzo's recent film, *In memoria di me* (*In Memory of Me* or *In Memory of Myself*) and Emanuele Crialese's *Nuovomondo* (*Golden Door, The Golden Door,* or *Ellis Island*).

Released in the spring of 2007, *Centochiodi* will be Olmi's final film, at least according to the director himself. Like Moretti's *Il caimano*, it is a prevalently ideological work, noteworthy for its strength, its authorial will, and the fallout that it will have on directors of future generations. For all intents and purposes, with this film Olmi has managed to tie together all the threads of his previous work with the many cinematic masters to whom he pays tribute in it: from Bresson to Bergman, Rossellini, Pasolini, Zavattini, and Piavoli, and, looking beyond Western Europe, even with directors like Zanussi, Mikhalkov, and Kiarostami. Once again, Olmi has asked himself the question, how does one live a true life? How does one avoid the conditioning of religious and secular power and the mirages and flashing lights of consumerist civilization? He does so with an overture of rare power in which the dramatic discovery of the destruction of the books (combined with a light touch worthy of Mozart) allows him to move from a tragic to an ironic and playful style. This film is a modern inflection of the *alter Christus* and his stateless condition. Olmi sets out with an elementary reclamation of acts and forms of solidarity, colloquial modes of a "simple life" that can still be found in many areas of Italy and the world, merely grazed by industrialization and prosperity. He then rediscovers a world of strong values and sentiments that come before culture and can do without it. He gradually has his main character enunciate his personal convictions and truths and they cause him to appear as the materialization of Christ to his small group of followers.

But let us return to the overview.

A number of factors have contributed to the current chaotic state of Italian film production and the many unforeseeable developments that have taken shape: Cinecittà has lost its role as the capital of Italian cinema and film production has become decentralized; methods of production have changed dramatically and there are growing opportunities to make homemade films at extremely low costs (these works are like prostheses of the filmmaker's gaze and they live and breathe the same air as the directors, who invariably release them outside the normal channels of distribution); and there has been a gradual passage of many narrative forms from cinema to television. Beyond the metamorphosis and perceptible transformation of the defining traits of Italian cinema, these elements have also shown the mid- and long-term vitality of Italian cinema's DNA. Italian cinema's genetic profile was first established at the end of World War II by Rossellini, De Sica, and Zavattini and it was linked to their faith in cinema as a new form of communication and narration open to all.

One important factor is economic and political in nature and is related to the drastic cuts made by Berlusconi's government in the Fondo Unico per lo Spettacolo (Single Fund for Performing Arts) in 2005. Over the course of one year, the fund was reduced by 40 percent, dropping from 464 million Euros to 300 million. Despite an amendment to the legislation, which limited the decrease to 15 percent, the Italian government's decision to reduce its investments in culture ran counter to the policy of other European countries. The subsequent coalition formed by Prodi did not do much to help things and as of the writing of this epilogue, we are still waiting for new legislation for the film industry. In Spain, for example, the 9.6 percent growth of investment in culture was more than three times the rate of inflation. In France, there was a 3.5 percent increase, while in England growth was capped at 2 percent. The diminishment of support and investment in added value, which had helped to bolster Italy's identity in the twentieth century, accelerated the unraveling of a fabric composed of heterogeneous elements that already lacked any common denominators. Italy's professional resources are second to none when it comes to cinema, but it has fallen into a deep coma and the funds necessary for its organs' survival began to evaporate the moment the government decided that cinema was an unproductive expenditure and that it did not represent a cultural investment.

The second important factor is the Italian movie theater's long and nearly irreversible agony. Perhaps one of the reasons that new generations of Italians do not care for Italian cinema is the ideological and pedagogical nature of Italian film. When they do watch Italian films, they seem to prefer alternative media. Alex Infascelli's recent film H 2 odio (Hate 2 0) was released directly on DVD and was sold at newsstands as a supplement to a daily paper and a weekly magazine. With very few exceptions in the early months of 2007, young Italian moviegoers chose not to go to a movie theater when an Italian film was playing. In this case, Italian cinema's identity is not a favorable element. But to a moviegoer who looks to the horizons of global communication, it can represent a sort of ballast or chain that limits the potential for fun, thus shortening those horizons.

The third important element is Italian filmmakers' attempts to change the nature of co-production partnerships in order to ensure that Italian films become de-provincialized. Italy has always been at the forefront of such partnerships, beginning with its co-production accords with France at the end of the 1940s. It has always managed to develop its co-productions with other countries that were willing to assume varying levels of risk and it has done so intelligently and with an eye to the future. The expansion of production horizons did not mean that Italian filmmakers would turn their backs on Italian identity and stories rooted in Italian culture. Beginning in the 1970s, an increasing number of made-for-television films helped to create a new European production network that favored works capable of touching upon European history, historical figures, and shared mythologies. In this era of inevitable and accelerated globalization, even the Japanese have showed an interest in Italian film production. On May 2, 2006, the Rome-based Italian national daily *Il messagero* published the following article in its arts section: "Tokyo Seeks Emotion: The Japanese Want to Co-Produce Our Cinema." Currently, Italian cinema accounts for an important slice of the Japanese market, with 34 percent of total box-office sales. The Japanese love Italian cinema for what has made it great throughout its history: its realism and magic, its sophisticated artisanal character, and the commanding presence of its directors.

If we examine production data from 2000–2005, we discover that of the 591 films made, 142 were co-productions and of those, 75 were co-produced with a major studio. Production companies from a number of countries have partnered with Italian companies and besides the obvious partner, France, they include Great Britain, Spain, Germany, Switzerland, Hungary, Portugal, Turkey, Romania, Belgium, Greece, Austria, and Albania. Maybe only one title has been co-produced with each of these latter countries over the past five years but something has begun to happen. European co-production is sure to grow in the future, for both cinema and television.

Beginning in the 1980s, with the rising power of producers of the major Italian public and television networks, Cinecittà lost its position at the center of national film production in Italy. The gradual decentralization of Italian film production has slowly led some directors to move beyond Italy's borders, especially for the production of historical films that require large casts of extras. Increasingly, Eastern Europe has become a destination for Italian film production, even though in many cases the entire film is not shot there. The same is true for other Western European countries, like France, whose filmmakers began to look eastward as early as the early 1990s.

In recent years, together with the decentralization of film production in every Italian region, the industry has also seen directors from different generations go to other European countries and even other continents to make their films, from Fabio Carpi and Ermanno Olmi to newcomers like Valeria Bruni Tedeschi and Saverio Costanzo. They have been driven away not by the logic of necessity or to cut costs. Nor have they gone abroad to find locations and faces that have all but disappeared in Western Europe or because they have lost touch with their national identity. The reason behind this trend is a new perception of the Italian national identity, the new problems that Italian directors wish to investigate, and an urge that has matured over the course of time: Bernardo Bertolucci returned to Paris to make *The Dreamers*, set in 1968; as early as the early 1990s, Marco Bechis had set his debut film in Patagonia and his more recent films have been shot in Argentina; even more recently, Francesca Comencini, told a turbid story of domestic violence in her *La bestia del cuore* (*Don't Tell* or *The Beast in the Heart*, 2004), set in the United States. And Emanuele Crilese dedicated his most recent film, *Nuovomondo* (*Golden Door*, *The Golden Door*, or *Ellis Island*, 2006), to the dreams of millions of Italian immigrants who came to America in the early twentieth century. David Ballerini set his debut film, *Il silenzio dell'allodola* (*The Silence of the Lark*, 2005), in early 1980s Ireland. With highly sophisticated experimental imagery, he told the story of Bobby Sands, an IRA member who died after more than sixty days of torture and hunger strikes—a universal, emblematic, and perennial story of torture and violence. Following a nearly thirty-year hiatus, Vittorio de Seta, despite endless setbacks, made a film on the odyssey of illegal immigrants who travel on makeshift rafts from the shores of Africa to those of Sicily. For her *Lezioni di volo* (*Flying Lessons*, 2007), Francesca Archibugi attempted to weave the story of her characters with the realities of India and Gianni Amelio went to Cina to make his *La stella che non c'è* (*The Missing Star*, 2006).

Two souls coexist and inhabit recent Italian cinema. One is provincial, the other wishes to feel like its part of the new Europe and even wants to push itself further and come in contact with far-away images and realities. This soul will continue to expand the borders of the New Europe.

In an interview that he gave to the weekly magazine *Reset*, Bernardo Bertolucci said that "more than ever before, I find it difficult to explain to young people how I make a film or how one makes a film . . . Cinema used to be part of a shared heritage. Now it is as if it didn't exist anymore and needs to be reinvented." Bertolucci revealed to the interviewer that not only did he feel that Italian cinema had lost touch with its roots but that Italian cinema has definitively become a child of television. The language of cinema is no longer recognized as a point of reference by new generations, he said.

Luckily, even during moments of crisis, things continuously change. Many transformations are taking shape in Italian cinema, some clearly visible and others behind the scene, and many filmmakers are taking stock of the situation and taking the necessary steps to revive the industry.

For years, Italian cinema seemed incapable of renewing itself from a dramaturgical and expressive point of view. More recently, Italian filmmakers have looked to vaster frontiers and their mentality has been that of the European who recognizes his roots and is seeking, despite the limited economic means at his disposal, to expand and change his ways of looking at the world. And Italian directors are embracing the new challenges of globalization and are revisiting increasingly necessary basics of do-it-yourself production, story-telling, and stylization.

Over the past few years, we see—here and there—directors with a forward-thinking gaze. Beyond the filmmakers we have mentioned above, a few others should be noted, like Giordana, whose *Quando sei nato non puoi più nasconderti* (*Once You've Been Born You Can No Longer Hide*) was a triumphant success at Cannes in 2005, and Amelio, whose *Meglio gioventù* (*The Best of Youth*) was called an "epic" work by *Time*'s film critic. Thanks to the same stylistic and moral tension that had guided his previous works, Giordana managed to tell an Italian story with implications, consequences, and characteristics that interest the entire international community. Giordana dramatically put a large number of problems on the table and he interpreted them from the point of view of a fourteen-year-old boy who (over the course of just a few hours) is given the chance to discover a reality that millions of Italians and European prefer to ignore. In fact, these problems are shared by all and can no longer be avoided. In films made in the past, all you had to do was leave Italy and go to Eastern Europe to find authentic values and memory now lost in Italy. In Giordana's film, the immigrants' situation appears as an image in Italy's subconscious, an image from a history and a past not so remote and not yet repressed or forgotten. There is no loss of identity in this film. Instead, there is a search for solidarity in taking on the problems of other people who would otherwise be lost.

Many filmmakers in recent years have sought to expand their gaze and deal with themes that interest the new European community. You get the impression that Italian filmmakers are attending an uninterrupted banquet with the mystical body and blood of Rossellini (and that of Zavattini, Olmi, and Pasolini as well).

The history of cinema and in particular the history of the cinematographic market over the past decades paints a picture of Europe increasingly crushed by the hegemony of American cinema. Fewer and fewer filmmakers are capable of entering into partnerships that are not purely financial in nature. But this has not precluded the possibility—even in the short term—of creating stories and cultural forms that will coagulate into new codes. Filmmakers have begun to think in terms of a post-national collective identity and they are beginning to conceive of cinema as more than just a "memory bank" of the horrors and tragedies of the "short [twentieth] century." Increasingly, filmmakers see cinema as a representation and projection of a collective desire and as a creative energy that can transcend the confines of the European community.

During this crucial transformational phase, cinema can be an added value, a cultural resource destined to play an essential strategic role in Europeans' anything-but-simple processes of integration and adaptation of centuries-old dream that has suddenly become a reality.

Despite a drastic drop in production, the year 2005 did see the release of films capable of competing on an international stage, like Francesco Munzi's *Saimir*. Munzi seems to look to the Dardenne brothers for inspiration: in this intense and morally engaged film, he explores the world of the Albanian Mafia and how a young boy, Saimir, the son of an illegal immigrant trafficker, dreams of a normal life. Even Saverio's *Private* (2005), filmed entirely in the Palestinian territory with a bare-bones cast, was nominated for an Oscar. This film is a great example of a film industry that is renewing itself and has everything it needs to face the challenges of international cinema.

Even though the health of Italian cinema does not give us much cause for optimism, I am hopeful that the future evolution of the Italian cinema species will give rise to new generation of poets on the multimedia scene: may they tell new stories in all possible forms and with all possible means! I hope they will preserve their roots and their memory of the past as they tell those stories with characters who know that they live in a global village and are aware that they are capable of adapting to its size and its models.

. ᴗ NOTES ᴗ .

PREFACE

1. For any film released in English-speaking countries, the film's commercial English-release title and its variants (if any) have been used. In certain instances, when a film has not been released in an English-speaking country, the title has been translated *ex novo*.—Trans.

INTRODUCTION
THE EPIC HISTORY OF ITALIAN CINEMA

1. Marc Bloch, Marc Léopold Benjamin Bloch, Peter Putnam, and Peter Burke, *The Historian's Craft*, trans. Peter Putnam (Manchester: Manchester University Press, 1992), 54.

CHAPTER 1
THE SILENT ERA

1. G. Fabri, *Al cinematografo* (1907), ed. Sergio Raffaelli (Rome: Associazione Italiana per le ricerche di storia del cinema, 1993), 18.

2. A. Bernardini was the first to report a great deal of this information in his indispensable essay "La presa di Rome, prototipo del cinema italiano" (in *La meccanica del visibile*, ed. A. Costa [Florence: La casa Usher, 1983]).

3. According to recently discovered documents, the national debut of the film seems to have taken place on September 16 at the Cinematografo Artistico di Livorno. See R. Bovani and R. del Porro, *La presa di Rome. XX settembre 1870: contributi alla storia di un film* (Livorno, 1998).

4. See F. de Lucis (ed.), *La Fiera delle meraviglie. Lo spettacolo popolare a Reggio Emilia nell'Ottocento* (Comune di Reggio Emilia, 1981), 25.

5. G. Cincotti, "Il Risorgimento del cinema," in D. Meccoli, G. Cincotti, and G. Calendoli, *Il Risorgimento italiano nel teatro e nel cinema* (Rome: Editalia, 1961), 129.

6. G. P. Brunetta, *Il viaggio dell'Icononauta* (Venice: Marsilio, 1997).

7. A. Bernarndini, *Cinema italiano delle origini. Gli ambulanti* (Gemona: Cineteca del Friuli, 2001).

8. R. Musil, "Eindrücke eines Naiven," *Die Muskete* 36 (1923).

9. L. Fantina, *Tempo e passatempo. Pubblico e spettacolo a Treviso tra Otto e Novecento* (Padua: Poligrafo, 1988), 188.

10. A. Guadreault, "Mais oú est le bonimenteur italien," in *A nouva luce. Cinema muto italiano*, vol. 1, ed. M. Consa (Bologna: Clueb, 2001).

11. S. Raffaelli, "Quando il cinema era mobile," *La ricerca Folclorica* 10, no. 19 (1988): 103–12. See also *La lingua filmata* (Florence: Le Lettere, 1991), 27.

12. Bernardini, *Cinema italiano delle origini*, 53.

13. O. Fasolo, "Il cinematografo svelato," *Natura e arte* (February 1907): 331.

14. "Il giudizio del pubblico," *La vita cinematografica* (February 28, 1913).

15. In particular, see A. Bernardini, *Cinema muto italiano*, 3 vols. (Bari: Laterzo, 1980–81). This work was among the first to recognize the important importance of the two decades spanning 1895–1914.

16. "Il cinematografo," *La perseveranza* 14 (March 30, 1896).

17. In *Il Sole* (November 18, 1906), someone complained about the "loud and annoying yelling reminiscent—in the middle of Milan—of the primitive system used by barkers at country fairs" (reprinted in *L'Aurora* 16 [1906]: 6).

18. The bibliography on early screenings now covers nearly all of Italy. The following texts, published in recent years, not cited in any order of importance, include a monograph on cinema in Tyrol: G. Rondolino, *Torino come Hollywood*, Quaderni piemontesi (Turin: Cappelli, 1980); V. Angelini and F. Pucci (eds.), *Materiali per una storia del cinema delle origini* (Turin: Studio Forme, 1981); A Bernardini (ed.), *Cinema e storiografia in Europa* (Comune di Reggio Emilia, 1984) (in particular, see the third section); F. de Lucis, *C'era il cinema, Reggio Emilia, 1896–1915* (Modena: Panini, 1985); S. Salvagnini et al., *La scena e la memoria: Teatri a Este 1521–1778* (Este: Biblioteca Comunale, 1985); Fantina, *Tempo e passatempo*; M. Quargnolo, *Quando i friulani andavano al cinema* (Gemona: La Cineteca del Friuli, 1989); G. Calzolari, *I cinematografi di Parma* (Parma, 1989); D. Kozanovich, *Trieste al cinema* (Gemona: La Cineteca del Friuli, 1995); R. de Berti, *Un secolo di cinema a Milan* (Milan: Il Castoro, 1996); P. Caneppele, *Il Tirolo in pellicola* (Provincia Autonoma di Bolzano, 1996); L. Jacob and C. Gaberscek, *Il Friuli e il cinema* (Gemona: La Cineteca del Friuli, 1996); L. Cuccu (ed.), *Il cinema nelle città, Livorno e Pisa nei 100 anni del Cinematografo* (Livorno: ETS, 1996); L. Morbiato, *Cinema ordinario* (Padua: Il Poligrafo, 1998); S. Scandolara, *Nostro cine quotidiano. Le Gorizie al cinema* (Gorizia: Kinoatelje, 2001); M. Bonetto and P. Caneppele, *Inizi lo spettacolo! Storia del cinematografo a Trento (1896–1918)* (Trento: Museo storico di Trento, 2001); R. Bovani and R. del Porro, *La fotografia animata a Lucca* (Pisa: Edizioni ETS, 2001).

19. A. Bernardini, "Il cinema muto italiano. 1905–1909. I film dei primi anni," *Bianco e Nero* (1996).

20. For more on Stefano Pittaluga, see Tatti Sanguineti's work-in-progress, of which some early results have been published in "L'anonimo Pittaluga," *Cinegrafie* (special edition, 1998).

21. V. Castronovo, "Una borghesia illuminata," in *Le fabbriche della fantasticheria* (Turin: Testo & Immagine, 1997), 13.

22. See A. Bernardini, "Neapolitan Cinema. The First Years," and V. Martinelli "The Evolution of Neapolitan Cinema to 1930," in *Napoletana. Images of a city*, ed. A. Aprà (Milan: Fabbri, 1993). See also G. Bruno, *Rovine con vista* (Milan: La Tartaruga, 1995).

23. See Rondolino's pioneering work *Torino come Hollywood*. See also the more recent D. Bracco, S. della Casa, P. Manera, and F. Prono (eds.), *Torino città del cinema* (Milan: Il Castoro, 2001).

24. R. Redi, *La Cines. Storia di una casa di produzione italiana* (Rome: Di Giacomo, 1991).

25. For brevity's sake, I will cite only a handful of the many theses that have been defended at Italian universities since cinema became a field of study in the 1970s: A. Trinchi, *Il contributo di ambrosio alla nascita e allo sviluppo del cinema italiano* (Università di Turin, 1972); A. Gesualdi, *Le origini del cinema nel Veneto* (Università di Padova, 1984); A. Trevisan, *L'altro teatro a Venice* (Università di Bologna, 1985); C. Zilio, *Dalla Fiera al Cinematografo: lo spettacolo viaggiante in Italia (1889–1911)* (Università di Padova, 1989); P. T. Poncino, *Turin e il cinema: 1900–1930. Le società del muto nei documenti d'archivio* (Università di Turin, 1995); M. Liberti, *La nascita del cinema a Turin e il suo contesto culturale* (Università di Turin, 1996); and P. Bragaglio, *Il cinema a Brescia dalle origini all'avvento del sonoro* (Università di Brescia, 1998).

26. See A. Navantieri's useful profile of this production house, "Film d'Arte, ma Italiana," *Cinegrafie* 15 (2002): 205, 217.

27. These memoirs can be found at the Museo del cinema (Cinema Museum) in Turin. They are cited here from A. Friedemann, *Appunti per la storia dell'industria cinematografica a Turin. Stabilimenti e teatri di posa* (Turin: Associazione Fert, 1999), 45.

28. See G. Bertellini, "Epica spettacolare e splendore del vero. L'influenza del cinema storico italiano in America (1908–15)," in *Storia del cinema mondiale*, vol. 2, part 1, *Gli Stati Uniti* (Turin: Einaudi, 2000), 127–266. See also *Cinema italiano nel mondo* (Pescara: Associazione Flaiano, 2002).

29. V. Martinelli (ed.), *Cinema italiano in Europa* (Rome: Associazione italiana per le ricerche di storia del cinema, 1992).

30. Friedemann, *Appunti per la storia dell'industria cinematografica a Turin*.

31. The Library of Congress in Washington, D.C., archive of all of Kleine's films and files is a true gold mine for scholars of silent film-era Italian film. I used the collection for the first volume of *Storia del cinema italiano*, 3 vols. (Rome: Riuniti, 1979). See R. Horwitz and H. Harrison (eds.), *The George Kleine Collection, a Catalog* (Washington, D.C.: Library of Congress, 1980).

32. F. Colombo, *La cultura sottile* (Milan: Bompiani, 1998).

33. See G. P. Brunetta, "No Place Like Rome," *Artforum* 28 (Summer 1990): 122–25; G. de Vincenti, "Il kolossal storico-romano nell'immaginario del primo Novecento," *Bianco e Nero* 9, no. 1 (1988): 7–26; and M. Wyke's book *Projecting the Past* (London: Routledge, 1997).

34. See G. P. Brunetta, "La conquista dell'impero dei sogni," in *Pirandello e D'Annunzio nel cinema*, ed. C. Catania (Centro di ricerca per la narrativa e il cinema, 1988),

9–30. The most recent contribution to the vast bibliography on this subject is I. Ciani's *Fotogrammi dannunziani* (Pescara: Ediars, 1999), which draws from a great deal of first-hand material.

35. M. Verdone, *Spettacolo romano* (Rome: Golem, 1970), 141–47.

36. Giuseppe Prezzolini, "Paradossi educativi," *La Voce*, August 22, 1914.

37. See P. Cherchi Usai, *Pastrone* (Florence: La Nuova Italia, 1985); and Cherchi Usai (ed.), *Giovanni Pastrone. Gli anni d'oro del cinema a Turin* (Turin: UTET, 1986).

38. A. Costa, "Il mondo rigirato: Saturnino versus Phileas Fogg," in P. Bertetto and G. Rondolino, *Cabiria e il suo tempo* (Turin and Milan: Museo Nazionale del Cinema, 1998), 295–310 (republished in A. Costa, *I leoni di Schneider* [Rome: Bulzoni, 2002]).

39. The most recent attempt to study the international star system resulted in a rich retrospective entitled *Star al femminile* ("The Feminine Side of 'Star'"), a co-production by the Cineteca di Bologna and the Centre Pompidou. The retrospective was also accompanied by a catalog, with slight variations in the Italian and French editions, edited by Gian Luca Farinelli (Bologna, 1999) and Jean-Loup Passek (Paris, 2000), respectively.

40. See A. Costa's essay, "Malombra sullo schermo," in *I leoni di Schneider*, 71–100.

41. In 1916, French critic Paul Féval wrote of Francesca Bertini: "She is strange and she is unique. You could say without a doubt that even if someone were to rival her someday, it would still be impossible to surpass the plurality of her metamorphoses."

42. The Puccini syndrome was adeptly defined by D. Martino, in *Castastrofi sentimentali* (Turin: Edt, 1993), as "that perfectly perverse marriage of emotions, conflicts, suffering, and catharses that predated Puccini's operas. It survived Puccini and poured over into cinema. It is an extraordinary propulsive element."

43. U. Barbaro, "Neorealismo (1943)," in *Neorealismo e realismo* (Rome: Editori Riuniti, 1975).

44. Curzio Malaparte, "Verità sul cinema," *Prospettive* 2 (1937): 8.

45. See U. Barbaro's "Un film italiano di un quarto di secolo fa," *Scenario* 10 (October 1936), reprinted in *Servitù e grandezza del cinema* (Rome: Editori Riuniti, 1961).

46. See S. Zappulla Muscarà and E. Zappulla, *Martoglio cineaste* (Rome: Editalia, 1995), as well as their superbly documented chapter "Martoglio e il cinema," in *Nino Martoglio* (Caltanissetta: Sciascia, 1985), 347–93.

47. A great deal has been written about the relationship between futurism and cinema. The following are among the most important: M. Verdone's *Cinema e letteratura del futurismo* (Rome: Edizioni di Bianco e Nero, 1968) (republished, Trento: Manfrini, 1990); *Poemi e scenari cinematografici d'avanguardia* (Rome: Officina, 1975); "Futurismo e cinema," in *La città del cinema* (Rome: Skira, 1985). These also include a series of contributions by G. Lista: *I futuristi e la fotografia* (Modena: Museo Civico d'Arte Contemporanea, 1985); *La scène futuriste* (Paris, 1989); "La ricerca cinematografica futurista," in *La città che sale*, ed. G. P. Brunetta and A. Costa (Trento: Manfrini, 1990), 30–37; *La Scène Futuriste* (Paris: Cnrs, 1989); "Un inedito marinettiano: 'Velocità,' film futurista," *Fotogenia* 2 (1995): 6–25; and his most important and comprehensive work on the subject, *Cinema e fotografia futurista* (Milan: Skira, 2001).

48. G. Lista, "Futurisme et cinema," in *Peinture, Cinéma, peinture*, ed. G. Viatte (Hazan, 1989), 59.

49. F. T. Marinetti et al., "Cinematografia futurista," *L'Italia futurista* 1 (November 15, 1916): 10, reprinted in F. T. Marinetti, *Teoria e invenzione futurista*, ed. Luciano de Maria (Milan: Mondadori, 1968), 104.

50. F. T. Marinetti, "La cinematografia astratta è un'invenzione italiana," *L'Impero*, December 1, 1926.

51. E. Settimelli, "La prima nel mondo della Cinematografia Futurista," *L'Italia futurista* 2, no. 1 (February 10, 1916).

52. This important text by Corra was published together with the *Manifesto del futurismo* and the article "La cinematografia astratta è un'invenzione italiana" in G. Rondolino, *Il cinema astratto. Testi e documenti* (Turin: Tirrenia Stampatori, 1977), 131–44.

53. Following their clandestine publication in 1911, the essay "Fotodinamismo futurista" and the photographs appeared in a second edition in 1913. They were republished, together with three (however dimly informative) essays on the works' relationship to cinema by Maurizio Calvesi, Maurizio Fagiolo, and Filiberto Menna in 1970 (Turin: Einaudi).

54. P. Virilio, *Guerre et cinéma: logistique de la perception* (Paris: L'Etoile, 1984).

55. A. G. Bragaglia, "L'arcoscenico del mio cinematografo," *In Penombra* 2 (January 1919): 24.

56. R. Redi, "L'Italia: l'Uci e la grande depressione," in *Cinema & Film. La meravigliosa storia dell'arte cinematografica*, ed. G. P. Brunetta and D. Turconi (Rome: Curcio, 1987), 345–53. See also Red's accurate survey of film production during the 1920s in *Ti parlerò . . . d'amor. Cinema italiano fra muto e sonoro* (Rome: Nuova Eri, 1986).

57. V. Martinelli, *Il cinema muto italiano. I film del dopoguerra*, 4 vols. (Rome: Edizioni del Bianco e Nero, 1980–81).

58. For a more complete analysis, see A. Farassino and T. Sanguineti (eds.), *Gli uomini forti* (Milan: Mazzotta, 1983); and M. dall'Asta, *Un cinéma muscle* (Crisnée: Yellow Now, 1992).

59. See my *Storia del cinema italiano*, 4 vols. (Rome: Editori Riuniti, 1993), vol. 1, 245.

60. G. Kleine, "Memorandum for Dr. Pedrazzini" (November 12, 1923), in the Kleine Papers, Motion Picture Division, Library of Congress, Washington, D.C.

61. A. Bernardini and V. Martinelli, *Leda Gys, attrice* (Milan: Coliseum, 1987).

62. In *L'eterna invasione. Il cinema italiano degli anni venti e la critica italiana* (Sacile: La Cineteca del Friuli, 2002), V. Martinelli identifies and lists all of the American films that were screened in Italy during the 1920s. His filmographic study is augmented by an impressive collection of texts taken from film reviews from the same era.

63. See E. G. Laura's recent and well-documented work on Luce, *Le stagioni dell'aquila* (Rome: Ente dello Spettacolo, 1999).

64. Thanks to N. Genovese's *Febo Mari* (Palermo: Papageno, 1998), Mari's leading role in silent film-era films has been rightly restored.

65. The first important critical essay on D'Ambra was G. Calendoli's "Il grottesco roseo di Lucio d'Ambra," in *Materiali per una storia del cinema italiano* (Parma: Maccari, 1967), 125–33.

66. L. d'Ambra, *Trent'anni di vita italiana*, 3 vols. (Milan: Mondadori, 1928–29). In particular, see vol. 2, chapter 12.

67. See A. Aprà and L. Mazzei (eds.), "Lucio d'Ambra. Il cinema," *Bianco e Nero* 5 (2002).

68. S. G. Germani and V. Martinelli, *Il cinema di Augusto Genina* (Pordenone: Biblioteca dell'Immagine, 1989).

69. See the filmographies in Farassino and Sanguineti (eds.), *Gli uomini forti*; and Dall'Asta, *Un cinéma musclé*.

70. See A. Costa's analysis of this film: "Maciste aux enfers," in *Cinémémoire* (Paris, 1993), 76–80.

71. A. Blasetti, *Sole*, ed. Adriano Aprà and Riccardo Redi (Rome: Di Giacomo, 1985).

CHAPTER 2
FROM SOUND TO SALÒ

1. See C. Taillebert, *L'Institut international deu cinématographe éducatif* (Paris: L'Harmattan, 1999).

2. J. A. Gili, *Stato fascista e cinematografia* (Rome: Bulzoni, 1981); Gili, *L'Italie de Mussolini et son cinema* (Paris: Veyrier, 1985); and Gili, *Le cinéma italien à l'ombre des faisceux* (Perpignan: Institut Jean Vigo, 1990).

3. Sanguineti, *L'anonimo Pittaluga*.

4. I have developed this thesis over the years, beginning with *Umberto Barbaro e l'idea del neorealismo* (Padua: Liviana, 1979) and *Intellettuali cinema e propaganda tra le due guerre* (Bologna: Patron, 1972). For an overarching panorama of 1930s Italian cinema, see the new edition of my *Storia del cinema italiano*, vol. 2.

5. Two interesting works on this period were published in America during the 1980s: E. Mancini, *Struggles of the Italian Film Industry during Fascism, 1930–1935* (Ann Arbor: University of Michigan Press, 1985); and M. Landy, *Fascism in Film: The Italian Commercial Cinema* (Princeton: Princeton University Press, 1986).

6. F. Savio's works remain fundamental to the study of this period: *Ma l'amore no. Formalismo, propaganda e telefoni bianchi nel cinema italiano di regime. 1930–1943* (Milan: Sonzogno, 1975) and his interviews in *Cinecittà anni trenta*, 3 vols. (Rome: Bulzoni, 1979).

7. Beside the rich bibliography in G. P. Brunetta, "Divismo, misticismo e spettacolo della politca," in *Storia del cinema mondiale*, vol. 1 (Turin: Einaudi, 1999), see also Laura's recent work *Le stagioni dell'acquila*.

8. G. Bottai, "Dichiarazioni a favore della legge," *Lo spettatcolo italiano* 2 (July–August 1931): 7.

9. See P. Iaccio's excellent documentation in "Sotto l'elmo di Scipio. La storia del cinema fascista," *Rivista calabrese di storia contemporanea* 1, no. 2 (December 1998): 63–87.

10. M. Isenghi, "La marcia su Roma," in Isenghi (ed.), *I luoghi della memoria* (Rome and Bari: Laterza, 1997), 313–29. For an analysis of the portrayal of "fascists in action," see also G. Miro Gori, *Patria diva* (Florence: La casa Usher, 1988), 73–77.

11. G. P. Brunetta, "Autoritratto rurale del fascismo," in *Incontri di Orbetello* (Orbetello: Agrifilmfestival, 1985), 19–23.

12. See Blasetti, *Sole*.

13. See V. Zagarrio, "Ideology Elsewhere: Contradictory Models of Italian Fascist Cinema," in *Resisting Images, Essays on Cinema and History*, ed. R. Sklar and C. Musser (Philadelphia: Temple University Press, 1990), 149–72.

14. G. P. Brunetta, "Il sogno a stelle e striscie di Mussolini," in *L'estetica della politica. L'Europa e l'America negli anni trenta*, ed. M. Vaudagna (Bari: Laterza, 1989).

15. Ibid.

16. The most comprehensive study of this problem remains L. Quaglietti's *Ecco i nostri!* (Turin: Eri, 1991). See also M. Beyet's excellent doctoral thesis, *L'image de l'Amérique dans la culture italienne de l'entre deux guerres*, 3 vols. (Université d'Aix en Provence, 1990). See also the important chapter on American cinema in J. Hay's *Popular Film Culture in Fascist Italy* (Bloomington: Indiana University Press, 1987).

17. Toplitz's memoir remains a useful resource: *Ciak a chi tocca* (Milan: Edizioni Milan Nuova, 1964).

18. See P. Minghetti's "Mussolini e/o Forzano nel segno delle sconfitte 'momentanee' di Napoleone e Cavour," in *Il cinema dei dittatori*, ed. R. Renzi (Bologna: Cappelli, 1992), 53–59.

19. S. della Croce, "Tirrenia, la prima città del cinema," in *Il cinema nelle città*, 161–223.

20. A. Farassino and T. Sanguineti, *Lux Film. Esthètique et système d'un studio italien* (Editions du Festival du film de Locarno, 1984).

21. One year after his appointment, Freddi's budget was already in the black. See his "Per il cinema italiano," *Intercine* (special issue, August 1935): 26–29.

22. For a history of the Centro, see in particular F. M. de Sanctis's contribution to the proceedings of the conference held on the occasion of the Centro's fiftieth anniversary, *Vivere il cinema. Cinquant'anni del Centro Sperimentale di Cinematografia* (Rome: Presidenza del Consiglio dei Ministri—Dipartimento per l'Informazione e l'Editoria, 1985), 18–27. See also E. G. Laura's contribution to the sixtieth-anniversary conference, *Vivere il cinema. Cinquant'anni del Centro Sperimentale di Cinematografia* (Rome: Presidenza del Consiglio dei Ministri—Dipartimento per l'Informazione e l'Editoria, 1995), 26–37.

23. L. Codelli and F. Liffran, "Cinecittà ou l'utopie fasciste," in "Rome, 1920–1945," ed. F. Liffran, *Autrement* (1991): 195–210.

24. For an accurate filmography and the best documentation of Luce's history, see Laura's *Le stagioni dell'acquila*.

25. Redi, *Ti parlerò . . . d'amor*, 11–15.

26. See A. Aprà's introduction to *Scritti sul cinema* by A. Blasetti (Venice: Marsilio, 1982).

27. S. Masi (ed.), *A. Blasetti* (Rome: Comitato Blasetti per il centenario della nascita, 2001).

28. See R. Ben-Ghiat, *La cultura fascista* (Bologna: Il Mulino, 2000), and in particular, 121–55, where the author analyzes the complexity of the relationship between cinema and fascist culture.

29. See S. Hill, "The Art of History: Picturing the Risorgimento in Blasetti's 1860," in *Pagina pellicola pratica*, ed. R. West (Ravenna: Longo, 2000), 69–83.

30. L. Freddi, *Il cinema*, 2 vols. (Rome: L'Arnia, 1949), vol. 1, 156–57.

31. See V. Zagarrio and C. Salizzato (eds.), *La corona di ferro* (Rome: Di Giacomo, 1985).

32. A. Farassino (ed.), *Mario Camerini* (Locarno: Yellow Now, 1992).

33. L. Miccichè (ed.), *De Sica. Autore, regista, attore* (Venice: Marsilio, 1992).

34. Among the many studies on Zavattini, see in particular A. Bernardini and J. A. Gili (eds.), *Cesare Zavattini* (Paris: Pompidou, 1990); and the essay "Il paradosso dell'autore," in O. Caldiron, *Il paradosso dell'autore* (Rome: Bulzoni, 1999).

35. See G. Gubitosi's *Amedeo Nazzari* (Bologna: Il Mulino, 1998), a good historical-biographical profile that ties Nazzari to this period in Italian history.

36. See S. Masi and E. Lancia (eds.), *Stelle d'Italia: piccole e grandi dive del cinema italiano dal 1930 al 1945* (Rome: Gremese, 1994).

37. Freddi, *Il cinema*, vol. 1, 157.

38. Ibid.

39. Freddi, *Il cinema*, vol. 2, 127.

40. For an analysis of this relationship, see G. P. Brunetta and J. A. Gili, *L'ora d'Africa del cinema italiano. 1911–1989* (Trento: Materiali di lavoro, 1990).

41. See the chapter "L'Afrique de l'autre," in *Génériques des année*, ed. M. Lagny, M.-C. Ropars, and P. Sorlin (Paris: Presses Universitaires de Vincennes, 1986).

42. See M. Argentieri (ed.), *Schermi di guerra* (Rome: Bulzoni, 1995); and Argentieri, *Cinema in Guerra* (Rome: Editori Riuniti, 1998).

43. The only collection of essays on De Robertis was gathered by F. Prencipe (ed.), *In fondo al mare . . . Il cinema di Francesco de Robertis* (Bari: Edizioni del Sud, 1996).

44. While a great deal has been written about Rossellini, the literature devoted to his early works is for the most part evasive and vague. One book that does not avoid discussing Rossellini's propaganda films is T. Gallagher's meticulously documented *The Adventures of Roberto Rossellini. His Life and Films* (New York: Da Capo Press, 1998). The most recent work that examines his participation in propaganda filmmaking is E. Seknadje-Askenazi's "Il realismo di Rossellini. La prima trilogia," *Il nuovo spettatore* 1 (special issue, 1997): 11–116. See also *Roberto Rossellini et la Second Guerre mondiale* (Paris: L'Harmattan, 2000), in which the author further develops the essay.

45. Hay, *Popular Film Culture in Fascist Italy*, 37–63.

46. Roland Barthes, A *Lover's Discourse: Fragments*, trans. Richard Howard (New York: Hill and Wang, 1978), 127–28.

47. See P. M. de Santi, "e l'Italia sogna. Architettura e design nel cinema déco del fascismo," in *Storia del cinema mondiale*, vol. 1, 429–83; A. Farassino, "Cosmopolitismo ed esotismo nel cinema europeo fra le due guerre," in ibid., 485–508; and V. Ruffin, "L'Europa nel cinema italiano degli anni trenta," in ibid., 619–59.

48. See V. Ruffin and P. d'Agostino's research in *Dialoghi di regime* (Rome: Bulzoni, 1997).

49. A Martini (ed.), *La bella forma* (Venice: Marsilio, 1992).

50. R. Campari, *Il fatasma dell bello. Iconologia del cinema italiano* (Venice: Marsilio, 1994); see in particular chapter 2.

51. R. Monti, *Les Macchiaioli et le cinema* (Paris: Editions Vilo, 1979).

52. G. Barberi Squarotti, P. Bertetto, and M. Guglielminetti (eds.), *Mario Soldati. La scrittura e lo sguardo* (Turin: Lindau, 1991).

53. L. Longanesi, "L'occhio di vetro," *L'Italiano* 8, nos. 17–18 (January–February 1933): 35.

54. See the most recent and well-documented study of the journal, L. Scotto d'Ardino's *La revue Cinema et le néorealisme italien* (Paris: Presses Universitaires de Vincennes, 1999).

55. C. Camerini (ed.), *Acciaio* (Turin: Nuova Eri, 1990).

56. Of the vast literature on *Ossessione*, G. Aristarco's commemorative essay, "Il neorealismo cinematografico," which appeared as an insert in *L'Europeo* (June 4, 1976), is worth revisiting.

57. U. Barbaro, "Realismo e moralità," *Film* 6 (July 31, 1943): 31.

58. Federico Zeri, *La percezione visiva dell'Italia e degli italiani* (Torino: Einaudi, 1976), 63.

59. See in particular C. Pavone, *Una guerra civile* (Turin: Bollati Boringhieri, 1991).

60. I was able to study these documents thanks to the kindness of Monica Venturini, Giorgio Venturini's daughter, and ANICA, which allowed me to examine Giorgio Venturini's archive conserved at ANICA's main office in Rome.

61. This speech was transcribed in an account of the inaugural ceremony in *Film* 7, no. 6 (March 1944): 1.

62. "Dissolvenze," *Film* 8, no. 8 (March 18, 1944).

63. "Promemoria per Mussolini" (today found in the Archivio di Stato), reprinted by Laura in *L'immagine bugiarda* (Rome: Annci, 1986), 347–55.

64. "Pursuant to the interested party's request, the Technical Office . . . has ascertained, with regard to Dr. Giorgio Venturini . . ., that Dr. Venturini acted to obtain the return of film materials that had been transferred to Germany . . . In the course of his tenure, propaganda films were not produced. The only film with propagandistic leanings was *Aeroporto* ('Airport'), which was authorized by the Germans. Our office has also ascertained that Dr. Venturini worked to ensure that cinematic materials were not subsequently transported from Venice to Germany . . . After contact had been made between Venturini and the Liberation Committee, Venturini indirectly passed

on information and let it be known that he would guarantee their requests." The report can be found in Freddi, *Il cinema*, vol. 2, 475–76. This report helped Venturini to avoid punitive action against him following the war and the subsequent purges of fascist collaborators.

CHAPTER 3

FROM NEOREALISM TO *LA DOLCE VITA*

1. "Cinema italiano. Manca tutto ma si lavora lo stesso," *Mondo Nuovo* 1, no. 1 (March 19, 1945): 24.

2. The most detailed account of the making of *Rome città aperta* can be found in G. Rondolino's *Rossellini* (Turin: UTET, 1989).

3. See B. Corsi, *Con qualche dollaro in meno* (Rome: Editori Riuniti, 2001).

4. See E. di Nolfo, "La diplomazia del cinema americano," in *Hollywood in Europa*, ed. D. W. Elwood and G. P. Brunetta (Florence: La casa Usher, 1991), 29–40; and G. P. Brunetta, "La lunga marcia del cinema americano in Italia tra fascismo e guerra fredda," in ibid., 75–87. See also E. di Nolfo, "Documenti del cinema americano in Italia nell'immediato dopoguerra," in *Gli intellettuali in trincea*, ed. S. Chemotti (Padua: Cleup, 1977), 133–44.

5. B. Vigezzi, "De Gasperi, Sforza, la diplomazia italiana e la politica di potenza dal trattato di pace al patto atlantico," in E. di Nolfo, R. H. Rainero, and B. Vigezzi, *L'Italia e la politica di potenza in Europa (1945–1950)* (Milan: Marzorati, 1988), 3.

6. G. L. Rondi, "*Paisà* di Roberto Rossellini," *Tempo*, March 9, 1947.

7. C. Lizzani, "L'Italia deve avere il suo cinema," *Il politecnico* 1 (October 13, 1945): 3.

8. For the earliest attempts to give a historical economic profile of Italian cinema, see L. Quaglietti, *Storia economico-politca del cinema italiano 1945–1980* (Rome: Editori Riuniti, 1980); and *La città del cinema* (Rome: Napoleone, 1979). More recent studies can be found in *Con qualche dollaro in meno*; B. Corsi, "Le coproduzioni europee del primo dopoguerra: l'utopia del fronte unico di cinematografia," in *Hollywood in Europa*; Corsi, "Eutanasia di un'unione," in *Identità italiana e identità europea nel cinema italiano dal 1945 al miracolo economico*, ed. G. P. Brunetta (Turin: Fondazione Agnelli, 1996); and Brunetta, "L'utopia dell'unione cinematografica europea," in *Storia del cinema mondiale*, vol. 1.

9. See M. Livolsi (ed.), *Schermi ed ombre. Gli italiani e il cinema del dopoguerra* (Florence: La Nuova Italia, 1988).

10. See J. Gili and A. Tassone (eds.), *Parigi-Rome le coproduzioni italo-francesi (1945–1995)* (Milan, 1995).

11. See A. Grasso's landmark work, *Storia della televisione Italiana* (Milan: Garzanti, 1992).

12. See T. Sanguineti (ed.), *Italia taglia* (Bologna: Transeuropa, 1999).

13. See T. Sanguineti (ed.), *Totò e Carolina* (Bologna: Transeuropa, 1999).

14. For a detailed history of Galatea Films, see S. Venturini, *Galatea S.p.A.* (*1952–1965*). *Storia di una casa di produzione cinematografica* (Rome: Associazione per le ricerche di storia del cinema, 2001).

15. For a complete and highly detailed census, see A. Bernardini, *Cinema italiano 1930–1995. Le imprese di produzione* (Rome: ANICA, 2000).

16. H. Kaufman and G. Lerner, *Hollywood sul Tevere* (Milan: Sperling and Kupfer, 1982).

17. V. Zagarrio (ed.), *Dietro lo schermo* (Venice: Marsilio, 1988). See also A. Bernardini and V. Martinelli, *Titanus* (Milan: Coliseum, 1986).

18. J. G. Auriol, "Entretiens romains," *La revue du cinéma* 3, no. 13 (May 1948): 54.

19. J. L. Godard, "L'Afrique vous parle de la fin et des moyens," *Cahiers du cinéma* 94 (April 1959): 22.

20. F. Zeri, *La percezione visiva dell'Italia e degli italiani* (Turin: Einaudi, 1976), 63–64.

21. For a detailed account of the Quirino Film Festival, see C. Cosulich (ed.), *Rome '45 il risveglio delle arti* (catalog) (Rome: Editalia, 1995).

22. See the facsimile edition of *Sud*, ed. Giuseppe di Costanzo (Bari: Palomar, 1994).

23. "Finally, an Italian film! . . . a film that tells our stories, our country's experiences, and events that affect us," wrote C. Lizzani. "*Rome città aperta*," *Film d'Oggi* 1 (November 3, 1945): 20. "Finally, our own film that belongs to us, heartfelt and sincere, made of introspection and suffering. This film's roots run deep in our recent past, which it depicts with a painful simplicity that is immune from any layering of rhetoric," wrote M. Gromo. "*Rome città aperta*," *La Nuova Stampa*, November 18, 1945. N. Ivaldi edited a rich and important anthology of reviews in *La Resistenza e il cinema del dopoguerra. Quello che scrissero allora* (Venice: La Biennale, 1970).

24. For international reviews of Rossellini, see A. Aprà (ed.), *Rosselliana* (Rome: Di Giacomo, 1987).

25. J. Desternes, "*Rome ville ouverte* et *Paisà*," *La revue du cinéma*, special edition 1, no. 3 (December 1, 1946): 64.

26. S. Tery, "La revoilà l'Italie de Garibaldi," *L'Humanité*, November 30, 1946.

27. Bazin's most important articles on neorealism have been gathered in *Qu'est ce que le cinéma. Une esthétique de la réalité: le néorealisme*, 4 vols. (Paris: Editions du Cerf, 1962). These include "Le réalisme cinématogrpahique et l'école italienne de la Libération" and "Difesa di Rossellini," originally published in *Cinema Nuovo*.

28. *Esprit*, April 24, 1947.

29. See A. Costa, "Aimons l'Amérique . . . aimons l'Italie! Il cinema italiano e una 'certa tendenza' della critica francese 1945–1965," in *Identità italiana e identità europea*, 408–39.

30. See G. C. Castello, *Il cinema neorealistico italiano* (Turin: Eri, 1962), 59–61.

31. See my essay "Il cinema legge la società italiana," in *Storia dell'Italia repubblicana*, vol. 2 (Turin: Einaudi, 1995), 781–844. See also my "La ricerca dell'identità nel cinema italiano del dopoguerra," in *Identità italiana e identità europea nel cinema italiano*, 11–67.

32. Cocteau, *Le passé défini* (Paris: Gallimard, 1983), 351.

33. A. Asor Rosa, *L'alba di un mondo nuovo* (Turin: Einaudi, 2002).

34. I. Calvino, "Presentazione," in *Il sentiero dei nidi di ragno* (Turin: Einaudi, 1964), 7 (trans. in *The Path to the Nest of Spiders*, translated from the Italian by Archibald Colquhoun, with a preface by the author translated by William Weaver [Hopewell: Ecco Press, 1976], v–vi).

35. J. Cocteau, *Le passé defini* (Paris: Gallimard, 1983), 351 (trans. in *Past Tense*, translated by Richard Howard [San Diego: Harcourt Brace Jovanovich, 1987], 300).

36. P. Sansot, *Les gens de peu* (Paris: Puf, 1991).

37. M. Sesti, "La vita quotidiana nell'età neorealista," in *Neorealismo. Cinema italiano 1945–1949*, ed. A. Farassino (Turin: Edt, 1989), 115–20.

38. One early and important study of European documentaries is R. Odin (ed.), *L'âge d'or du documentaire* (Paris: L'Harmattan, 1998).

39. See D. Carpitella, "Film etnografico e mondo contadino in Italia," in *Cinema e mondo contadino*, ed. P. Sparti (Venice: Marsilio, 1982).

40. P. Scremin (ed.), *Carpaccio, vita di un documentario d'arte* (Turin: Allemandi, 1991); *Cinema e arte. Documentari d'arte dal 1940 al 1960* (Bologna: Cineteca di Bologna, 1962); A. Costa (ed.), *Carlo Ludovico Ragghianti. I critofilm d'arte* (Udine: Campanotto, 1995); A. Costa, *Il cinema e le arti visive* (Turin: Einaudi, 2002) (this work examines a number of Italian documentaries on art); P. Scremin, "Viatico sui documentari sull'arte," in *Carlo Ludovico Ragghianti e il carattere cinematografico della visione* (Milan: Charta, 2000), 150–61.

41. I am referring in particular to the earliest study by G. Bernagozzi, *Il cinema corto. Il documentario nella vita italiana, 1945–1980* (Florence: La casa Usher, 1980).

42. See L. Micciché (ed.), *Studi su dodici sguardi d'autore* (Turin: Lindau, 1995).

43. See M. A. Frambotta, *Il governo filma l'Italia* (Rome: Bulzoni, 2002).

44. See *La macchina e il cinema* (Brescia: Fondazione Micheletti, 1995); and A Medici, *Filmare il lavoro* (Rome: Archivio audiovisivo del movimento operaio, 2000).

45. See I. Caputi, *Il cinema di Folco Quilici* (Rome: Edizioni di Bianco e Nero, 2000).

46. G. Rondolino, *Storia del cinema d'animazione* (Turin: Einaudi, 1974).

47. G. Bendazzi, *Cartoons. Cent'anni di cinema d'animazione* (Venice: Marsilio, 1992).

48. See, for example, P. Zanotto and F. Zangrando, *L'Italia di cartone* (Padua, 1973).

49. So much has been written about Carosell that for sake of space, I will cite only M. Giusti, *Il grande libro di Carosello* (Milan: Sperling and Kupfer, 1995).

50. See M. Zane, *Scatola e sorpresa* (Milan: Jaca Book, 1998).

51. M. Corti, *Il viaggio testuale* (Turin: Einaudi, 1978), 66.

52. P. P. Pasolini in F. Fellini, *Le notti di Cabiria* (Bologna: Cappelli, 1965), 231. The definition "vital crisis" inspired the title of one of the most recent and original re-readings of Italian cinema: P. A. Stiney, *Vital Crises in Italian Cinema* (Austin: Texas University Press, 1995).

53. F. Bolzoni, "Il paesaggio nel cinema e nella narrativa italiana del Novecento," *Bianco e Nero* 17 (February 1956): 2.

54. See A. Farassino, "Neorealismo storia e geografia," in *Neorealismo*, 21–36.

55. C. Zavattini, *Neorealismo ecc.*, ed. Mino Argentieri (Milan: Bompiani, 1979), 323.

56. P. Iaccio, "Cinema e Mezzogiorno," in *Storia del Mezzogiorno*, vol. 14 (Naples: Edizione del Sole, 1995), 324–55.

57. S. Martelli, "Letteratura, cinema e mondo contadino," in *Il crepuscolo dell'identità* (Salerno, 1998), 137–76.

58. See T. Meder, *Vom Sichtbarmachen der Geschichte Der Italienische "neorealismus."* *Rossellinis Paisà und Klaus Mann* (Munich: Trikster, 1993); and *The Adventures of Roberto Rossellini*, 180–84.

59. See A. dalle Vacche, *The Body in the Mirror* (Princeton: Princeton University Press, 1992), 180–90.

60. Bernardini and Gili (eds.), *Cesare Zavattini*.

61. Philip Morris, in partnership with the Associazione Amici di Vittorio de Sica, restored *Sciuscià* (with a catalog edited by Lino Micciché, Rome, 1994) and all of De Sica's postwar masterpieces. Recently, a growing number of Italian films have been restored and a number of philological and textual analyses have been published.

62. For the most comprehensive biography, see G. Rondolino, *Luchino Visconti* (Turin: UTET, 1982). So much has been written about Visconti's work and in so many languages that for sake of space, I will cite only Y. Ishaghpour, *Visconti. Le sens et l'image* (Paris: La différance, 1984).

63. See L. Micciché, *Visconti e il neorealismo* (Venice: Marsilio, 1990); and L. Micciché (ed.), *La terra trema. Analisi di un capolavoro* (Turin: Lindau, 1993).

64. G. Aristarco, "Senso," *Cinema Nuovo* 4 (February 10, 1955): 52.

65. For sake of space, I will cite only M. Lagny, *Senso, Luchino Visconti, Synopsis* (Paris: Editions Nathan, 1992).

66. S. Toffetti (ed.), *Rosso fuoco. Il cinema di Giuseppe de Santis* (Turin: Lindau, 1996).

67. C. Lizzani, *Riso amaro* (Rome: Officina, 1978).

68. G. Grignaffini, "Racconti di nascita," in *La scena madre* (Bologna: Bononia University Press, 2002), 275–76.

69. See Toffetti (ed.), *Rosso fuoco*.

70. See A. Farassino, *Giuseppe de Santis* (Milan: Moizzi, 1978).

71. R. Renzi, *La bella stagione. Scontri e incontri negli anni d'oro del cinema italiano* (Rome: Bulzoni, 2001). This volume gathers essays on 1940s and 1950s Italian cinema spanning a long period. It helps us understand the meaning behind the fractious battles between critics and the ideological flags they flew. Later generations of film critics did not enjoy such ideological privilege.

72. On Rossellini's ideology, see M. Oms's polemical article "Du fascisme à la démocratie chretienne," *Positif* 28 (April 1958): 9–18.

73. L. Micciché (ed.), *Il cappotto* (Turin: Ass. Philip Morris, 1992), 35.

74. T. Sanguineti (ed.), *La spiaggia* (Genova: Le Mani, 2001).

75. Barberi Squarotti, Bertetto, and Guglielminetti, *Mario Soldati. La scrittura e lo sguardo.*

76. The most recent overview of Germi is M. Sesti's *Tutto il cinema di Pietro Germi* (Milan: Baldini & Castoldi, 1997).

77. For an excellent account of the Italian star phenomenon in postwar Europe, see S. Gundle "Il divismo nel cinema europeo, 1945–60," in *Storia del cinema mondiale*, vol. 1, 759–86.

78. Goffredo Fofi and Franca Faldini, *L'avventurosa storia del cinema italiano raccontata dai suoi protagonisti, 1935–1959* (Milan: Feltrinelli, 1979), 390.

79. See S. della Casa, "Cinema popolare italiano del dopoguerra," in *Storia del cinema mondiale*, vol. 3 (Turin: Einaudi, 2000), 779–823.

80. The following are among the most important works on cinematic operas during the postwar period: P. Pistagnesi, A. Aprà, and G. Menon (eds.), *Il melodramma nel cinema italiano* (Incontri cinematografici di Monticelli Terme, 1977); D. Turconi and A. Sacchi, *Un bel dí vedemmo* (Pavia: Amministrazione provinciale di Pavia, 1984); C. Bragaglia and F. di Giammatteo, *Italia 1900–1990. L'opera al cinema* (Florence: La Nuova Italia, 1990); G. Casadio, *Opera e cinema* (Ravenna: Longo, 1995); M. Marchelli and R. Venturelli, *Se quello schermo io fossi. Verdi e il cinema* (Genova: Le Mani, 2002).

81. V. Caprara (ed.), *Spettabile pubblico. Carosello napoletano di Ettore Giannini* (Naples: Guida, 1998).

82. G. Debenedetti, "Il cinema e gli intellettuali," *Intercine* 8 (August 1935): 59.

83. R. Renzi, "Omero ha cominciato così," *Cinema Nuovo* 3, no. 34 (May 1, 1954): 239.

84. The most authoritative, reliable, and best-documented biography of Fellini is T. Kezich, *Fellini* (Milan: Camunia, 1987). The most original work on Fellini is P. Bondanella's *The Cinema of Federico Fellini* (Princeton: Princeton University Press, 1992).

85. M. Antonioni, preface to *Sei film* (Turin: Einaudi, 1964), xvi. Beyond the many critical essays by and on Antonioni and his films and the interviews, see the monumental six-volume homage to his life's work: C. di Carlo (ed.), *L'oeuvre de Michelangelo Antonioni* (Rome: Cinecittà International—Ente autonomo gestione cinema, 1987–92).

86. Of the vast bibliography on Antonioni, see also L. Cuccu, *La visione come problema* (Rome: Bulzoni, 1973); G. Tinazzi, *Antonioni* (Florence: La Nuova Italia, 1975); S. Chatman, *Antonioni or the Surface of the World* (Berkeley and Los Angeles: University of California Press, 1985); J. Mayet Giaume, *Michelangelo Antonioni, le fil interieur* (Crisnée: Yellow Now, 1990).

87. See M. Marcus, *Italian Film in the Light of Neorealism* (Princeton: Princeton University Press, 1986).

88. The Centro Cinema Città di Cesena has published a number of Pietrangeli's writings, edited by Antonio Maraldi: A. Pietrangeli, *Verso il realismo*, with a preface by Fernaldo di Giammatteo (Cesena: Il Ponte Vecchio, 1994); A. Pietrangeli, *Sala di*

proiezione, with a preface by Gian Piero Brunetta (Cesena: Il Ponte Vecchio, 1994); Pietrangeli, *Neorealismo e dintorni*, with a preface by Antonio Costa (Cesena: Il Ponte Vecchio, 1995); *Panoramica sul cinema italiano*, with a preface by Carlo Lizzani (Cesena: Il Ponte Vecchio, 1995); U. Barbaro and A. Pietrangeli, *Appunti sulla regia cinematografica*, with a preface by Giorgio Cremonini (Cesena: Il Ponte Vecchio, 1995); S. Cecchi d'Amico and A. Petrangeli, *Soggetti inediti*, with a preface by Suso Cecchi d'Amico (Cesena: Il Ponte Vecchio, 1997); A. Pietrangeli, *Lampi d'estate e altri soggett*, with a preface by Ugo Pirro (Cesena: Il Ponte Vecchio, 1997); and A. Pietrangeli, D. Fo, P. P. Pasolini, and T. Pinelli, *Serajevo. Trattamento per un film*, with a preface by Dario Fo (Cesena: Il Ponte Vecchio, 1998).

89. See G. P. Brunetta (ed.), *Bolognini* (Rome: Ministero degli Affari Esteri, 1978).

90. *Totò*, ed. Goffredo Fofi (Rome: Samonà e Savelli, 1972), 61.

91. R. Escobar, *Totò* (Bologna: Il Mulino, 1998), 110.

92. F. Rossi, *La lingua in gioco* (Rome: Bulzoni, 2002).

93. V. Spinazzola, *Cinema e pubblico* (Milan: Bompiani, 1974), 120.

94. D. Paolella, "La psichanalyse du pauvre," *Midi-Minuit Fantastique* 12 (May 1965).

95. L. Moullet, "La victoire d'Ercole," *Cahiers du cinéma* 131 (May 1962): 40.

96. See Fernaldo di Giammatteo, "Prélude à Cottafavi," *Bianco e Nero* 10–11 (October–November 1960).

97. Goffredo Fofi and Franca Faldini, *L'avventurosa storia del cinema italiano raccontata dai suoi protagonisti, 1935–1959* (Milan: Feltrinelli, 1979), 389.

98. The original line in Italian is "li credevo più di fegato," or literally, "I thought they had more liver"; in Italian, the expression *di fegato* is synonymous with "courageous"; and calf's liver with onions is a classic dish of Venice.—Trans.

CHAPTER 4
FROM THE BOOM YEARS TO THE YEARS OF TERROR

1. For an in-depth analysis, see the most recent edition of my *Storia del cinema italiano*, vol. 4, and *Cent'anni di cinema italiano*, 2nd ed. (Rome: Laterza, 1998).

2. E. Monaco, *Cinema italiano 1960* (Rome: Anica, 1960).

3. Quaglietti, *Storia economico-politica del cinema italiano*, 222. See also C. Biarese, "Les structures économiques du cinéma italien 1959–1974," *Cinéma '74* 190–91 (September–October 1974): 75–90.

4. S. Zambetti, "Cinema e pubblico in Italia negli anni sessanta. Gli indirizzi produttivi, i generi, il film popolare," in *Storia del cinema*, vol. 3, ed. A Ferrero (Venice: Marsilio, 1980), 56–78.

5. M. Salotti, "1957–1064: L'industria cinematografica italiana gonfia i muscoli," in *Sull'industria cinematografica italiana*, ed. E. Magrekku (Venice: Marsilio, 1986).

6. L. Solaroli, "72 milioni di spettatori perduti nel cinema in Italia in quattro anni," *Filmcritica* 9, no. 101 (September 1960): 616–19.

7. See the essays on the problems of postwar film financing in *Storia del cinema mondiale*, vol. 1; and Livolsi (ed.), *Schermi ed ombre*.

8. *See also* A. Bernardini, *"Le collaborazioni internazionali nel cinema europeo,"* in *Storia del cinema mondiale*, vol. 1.

9. A. Fago and A. Piro (eds.), *La carica dei 28. Storie italiane di leggi, di soldi e di film invisibili* (Rome: Procom, 1986).

10. See C. Zanchi, "La lenta eutanasia di un articolo," in M. Sesti, *La scuola italiana* (Venice: Marsilio, 1996), 219–37, which lists the films that were subsidized between 1967 and 1996.

11. Grasso, *Storia della televisione italiana;* F. Anania, *Davanti allo schermo. Storia del pubblico televisivo* (Florence: La Nuova Italia, 1997).

12. *Modi di produzione del cinema italiano. La Titanus* (Rome: Di Giacomo, 1986).

13. F. Colombo, *La cultura sottile* (Milan: Bompiani, 1998), 241–60.

14. See my "Il giardino delle delizie e il deserto," in *Schermi ed ombre*, 60–91.

15. See A. Aprà's meticulously documented essay, "Carmelo Bene oltre lo schermo," in *Per Carmelo Bene* (Milan: Linea d'ombra, 1995).

16. See the interviews transcribed in A. Tassone (ed.), *Parla il cinema italiano*, 2 vols. (Milan: Il formichiere, 1979–80).

17. L. Micciché, *Cinema italiano degli anni sessanta* (Venice: Marsilio, 1965) (there have been numerous reprints and updated editions). See also "I 'meravigliosi' anni Sessanta del cinema italiano, in *Cinema & Film*, ed. L. Micciché (Rome: Curcio, 1998) vol. 5, 1376–1418; "Il sogno interrotto del cinema italiano," in *Cinema & Film*, ed. L. Micciché (Rome: Curcio, 1998) vol. 6, 1703–28; A. Aprà and S. Parigi, *Viaggio in Italia. Gli anni 60 al cinema* (Rome: Carte Segrete, 1991).

18. G. Benedetti, "Commemorazione provvisoria del personaggio uomo," *Cinema Nuovo* 14, no. 177 (September–October 1965): 326–44.

19. For an overview of the new European cinema, see A. Aprà, "Les nouvelles vagues," in *Storia del cinema mondiale*.

20. See *La cinepresa e la storia* (Milan: Mondadori, 1985); and *Cinema storia resistenza* (Milan: Franco Angeli, 1987).

21. The screenplay has been reprinted in G. de Bosio and L. Squarzina, *Il terrorista* (Vicenza: Neri Pozza, 1963), with an introduction by Ferruccio Parri and an anthology of reviews.

22. P. d'Agostini, *Romanzo popolare: il cinema di Age e Scarpelli* (Naples, 1991).

23. G. Grignaffini, "Gli indifferenti. Cinema e industria Italiana," in *Cento anni di industria*, ed. V. Castronovo and N. Tranfaglia (Milan: Electa, 1988), 278–85.

24. P. Bertetto, "Turin nel cinema: l'identità imperfetta," in *Architettura e urbanistica a Turin (1945–1990)*, ed. L. Mazza and C. Olmo (Turin: Allemandi, 1991), 170.

25. G. P. Brunetta, "Lo schermo grigionero," in *Un'avventura internazionale. Turin e le arti, 1950–1970*, ed. I. Gianelli (Turin: Charta, 1993), 100–112.

26. For all of these films, see *Cinema italiano servi e padroni* (Milan: Feltrinelli, 1977); and P. Bertetto, *Il più brutto del mondo* (Milan: Bompiani, 1982).

27. For a more general overview, see P. Ortoleva, *Il movimento del '68 in Europa e in America* (Rome: Editori Riuniti, 1998); and Ortoleva, "Naturalmente cinefili. Il '68 del cinema," in *Storia del cinema mondiale*, vol. 1, 935–52.

28. J. A. Gili, *Francesco Rosi. Cinéma et pouvoir* (Paris: Editions du Cerf, 1976); and S. Gesù (ed.), *Francesco Rosi* (Acicatena: Incontri con il cinema, 1991).

29. T. Kezich and S. Gesù, *Salvatore Giuliano* (Acicatena: Incontri con il cinema, 1991).

30. J. A. Gili, *Arrivano i mostri* (Bologna: Cappelli, 1980); M. d'Amico, *La commedia all'italiana* (Milan: Mondadori, 1985); M. Monicelli, *L'arte della commedia*, ed. Lorenzo Codelli (Bari: Dedalo, 1986).

31. See A. Accardo, *Age e Scarpelli. La storia si fa commedia* (Rome: Ancci, 2001).

32. See S. Bernardi (ed.), *Si fa per ridere . . . ma è una cosa seria* (Florence: La casa Usher, 1985).

33. See S. Raffaelli, "Il dialetto nel cinema," in *La lingua filmata* (Florence: Le Lettere, 1981).

34. T. Sanguineti (ed.), *Il cinema secondo Sonego* (Bologna: Cineteca di Bologna, 2000).

35. Monicelli, *L'arte della commedia*.

36. J. A. Gili, *Luigi Comencini* (Paris: Edilig, 1981).

37. V. Caprara, *Dino Risi* (Rome: Gremese, 1993).

38. There are a number of interesting essays on and studies of Scola. The best were collected in a tribute published by the Pesaro Film for the director's seventieth birthday: V. Zagarrio (ed.), *Trevico-Cinecittà. L'avventuroso viaggio di Ettore Scola* (Venice: Marsilio, 2002).

39. See M. Hockhofler, *Marcello Mastroianni* (Rome: Gremese, 1993); C. Costantini, *Marcello Mastroianni* (Rome: Riuniti, 1996); and E. Biagi's interview with the actor, *La bella vita* (Milan: Eri-Rizzoli, 1996).

40. F. Deriu (ed.), *Vittorio Gassman* (Venice: Marsilio, 1999).

41. A. Bernardini and C. G. Fava, *Ugo Tognazzi* (Rome: Gremese, 1978).

42. See her biography in P. Carraro's *Le Dive* (Bari: Laterza, 1985), 167–95.

43. Whereby people were asked to donate their last banknotes to a cancer research group before Italy switched over to the euro.—Trans.

44. F. Deriu, *Gian Maria Volonté. Il lavoro dell'attore* (Rome: Bulzoni, 1997).

45. G. M. Contro, *Il mercato del terrore. Mostri e maestri dell'Horror* (Milan: Feltrinelli, 1998).

46. In S. Marocchi and R. Piselli, *Bisarre Sinema! Horror all'italiana* (Florence: Glittering Images, 1996), 5.

47. R. Freda, *Divoratori di celluloide* (Milan: Il Formichiere, 1981).

48. S. Della Casa, *Riccardo Freda, un homme seul* (Crisnée: Yellow Now, 1993).

49. E. Martini and S. Della Casa, *Riccardo Freda* (Bergamo: Bergamo Film Meeting, 1993).

50. L. Palmerini and G. Mistretta, *Spaghetti Nightmares. Il cinema italiano della paura e del fantastico visto attraverso gli occhi dei suoi protagonisti* (Rome: M&P Edizioni, 1996), 5.

51. A. Pezzotta, *Mario Bava* (Florence: Il Castoro, 1987).

52. R. Pugliese, *Dario Argento* (Florence: Il Castoro, 1987).

53. The storylines from Argento's early films have been collected in *Profondo Thrilling* (Milan: Sonzogno, 1975).

54. L. Codelli, "Il West in Europa l'Europa nel West," in *Storia del cinema mondiale*, vol. 1, 921–33.

55. Vincenzo Leone's artistic name was Roberto Roberti.—Trans.

56. See O. De Fornari, *Tutti i film di Sergio Leone* (Milan: Ubulibri, 1984); and C. Frayling's *Sergio Leone: Something to Do with Death* (London: Faber and Faber, 2000).

57. De Fornari, *Tutti i film di Sergio Leone*.

58. E. Natta, "Dalla colt alla mitra," *La Rivista del Cinematografo* (December 1968).

59. At the time, T. Ranieri astutely observed that "there is no true distinction between the Italian western and the violence portrayed in other 'made-in-Italy' genres." "Il western casalingo," *Teatro e Cinema*, no. 1 (January–March 1967).

60. S. Micheli, *Morricone. La musica e il cinema* (Modena: Ricordi, 1994).

61. The first to analyze the cop thriller film genre in Italy was G. Buttfava in his article "Procedure sveltite," *Patalogo 2. Annuario del 1980*. The essay was reprinted in *Gli occhi del sogno*, ed. L. Pellizzari (Rome: Biblioteca di Bianco e Nero, 2000).

62. Visconti is one of the most written-about directors of Italian cinema. See D. Bruni and V. Pravadelli, *Studi viscontiani* (Venice: Marsilio, 1997); and V. Pravadelli (ed.), *Il cinema di Luchino Visconti* (Rome: Biblioteca di Bianco e Nero, 2000). These two volumes are collections of papers presented at a conference and retrospective devoted to the director.

63. A. Costa, "Visconti. Il Gattopardo e la scena storica," in *Immagine di un'immagine* (Turin: UTET, 1993), 109–27.

64. V. Pravadelli (ed.), *Visconti a Volterra. La genesi di Vaghe stelle dell'Orsa* (Turin: Lindau, 2000).

65. See A. Frintino and P. M. de Santi (eds.), *Mauro Bolognini. Cinema tra letteratura, pittura e musica* (Pistoia: Brigata del Leoncino, 1997).

66. F. Camon, *La donna dei fili* (Milan: Garzanti, 1986).

67. O. Caldiron, "Il gioco del doppio," in *De Sica*.

68. Micciché, *Cinema italiano degli anni sessanta*, 65.

69. The novel was translated in 1965 with this title.—Trans.

70. Perhaps the best profile of Germi was written by M. Sesti, *Tutto il cinema di Pietro Germi* (Milan: Baldini & Castoldi, 1997). Others worth mentioning include V. Attolini, *Il cinema di Pietro Germi* (Lecce: Elle Edizioni, 1986); and A. Aprà, M. Armenzoni, and P. Pistagnesi (eds.), *Pietro Germi. Ritratto di un regista all'antica* (Parma: Pratiche, 1989).

71. G. Morelli, G. Martini, and G. Zappoli, *Un'invisibile presenza. Il cinema di Antonio Pietrangeli* (Milan: CSC-Il Castoro, 1998). See also chapter 3, note 87, on the publication of Pietrangeli's archives.

72. A. Zanellato's landmark profile of Lattuada, *L'uomo (cattiva sorte): il cinema di Lattuada* (Padua: Liviana, 1972), has yet to be surpassed. *Il cappotto* (Turin: Lindau, 1995), a companion to the restoration of the film by the same title, edited by Lino Micciché, offers updated and significant information as well.

73. See *Il cinema di Vittorio de Seta* (Catania: Maimone, 1995).

74. The "stone in the mouth" is a traditional, symbolic gesture used in Mafia circles, whereby a stone is placed in the mouths of murdered turncoats after they are "silenced."—Trans.

75. The most passionate and well-documented work on Cavani is G. Marrone's *The Gaze and the Labyrinth* (Princeton: Princeton University Press, 2000).

76. M. Gieri, *Contemporary Italian Filmmaking* (Toronto: Toronto University Press, 1996).

77. See the essays gathered in the important collection edited by P. Bondanella, *Federico Fellini. Essays in Criticism* (Oxford: Oxford University Press, 1988).

78. "Eight minus," the equivalent of a "B-" in the American scholastic grading system.—Trans.

79. This quote is taken from a conversation with Georges Simenon on the occasion of the release of *Casanova* in France (*Carissimo Simenon. Mon Cher Fellini* [Milan: Adelphi, 1997], 126.)

80. G. Tinazzi (ed.), *Michelangelo Antonioni. Identificazione di un autore* (Parma: Pratiche, 1985).

81. S. Chatman and G. Fink, *L'avventura* (New Brunswick: Rutgers University Press, 1989).

82. L. Cuccu, *Antonioni. Il discorso dello sguardo* (Pisa: ETS, 1990).

83. C. di Carlo, "Il colore dei sentimenti," in M. Antonioni, *Deserto rosso* (Bologna: Capelli, 1964), 17.

84. Jean A. Gili, "Elio Petri et le cinéma italien," *Rencontres d'Annecy* (1996): 8 (see also the revised version in *Elio Petri* [Rome: Cinecittà Holding, 2001]).

85. See Pirro's impassioned chronicle of his experience as a screenwriter, *Soltanto un nome nei titoli di testa* (Turin: Einaudi, 1998) and his *Il cinema della nostra vita* (Turin: Lindau, 2001).

86. See his essay published together with the script on the occasion of the film's restoration in P. Iaccio (ed.), *Bronte* (Naples: Liguori, 2002).

87. C. Landricina (ed.), *Gianfranco Mingozzi. I documentary* (Rome, 1988); M. Graffeo (ed.), *Gianfranco Mingozzi. I film* (Bologna: Fusconi, 1994).

88. *Taranta* refers to the tarantula and the exorcism practiced to cure the spider's bite, that is, the *tarantella*.—Trans.

89. A. Achilli and G. Casadio, *Elogio della malinconia. Il cinema di Valerio Zurlini* (Ravenna: Edizioni del girasole, 2001).

90. Jean Gili, *Le cinéma italien* (Paris: UGE, 1978), n.p.

91. See the essays gathered after two decades of research in G. Zigaina, *Hostia. Trilogia della morte di Pier Paolo Pasolini* (Venice: Marsilio, 1995). See also G. Zigaina and C. Steinle, *Pier Paolo Pasolini. Organizzare il trasumanar* (Venice: Marsilio, 1995). So much has been written about Pasolini. Perhaps the best biographies are found in B. D. Schwartz, *Requiem* (New York: Pantheon, 1992); and H. Joubert-Laurencin, *Pasolini, portrait du poète en cineaste* (Paris: Editions Cahiers du Cinéma, 1995).

92. G. P. Brunetta, "Longhi e l'officina cinematografica," in *L'arte di scrivere sull'arte*, ed. Giovanni Previtali (Rome: Editori Riuniti, 1982), 47–56.

93. M. Fusillo, *La Grecia secondo Pasolini* (Florence: La Nuova Italia, 1996).

94. See my "Itinerario di Pier Paolo Pasolini verso il mito di Edipo," in *Edipo. Il teatro greco e la cultura moderna*, ed. B. Gentili and R. Pretagistini (Rome: Edizioni dell'Ateneo, 1982), 388–93; and "Il viaggio di Pasolini dentro i classici," in the special issue of *Galleria* 25, nos. 1–4 (January–August 1985): 67–75 (edited by Rosita Tordi).

95. S. Toffetti (ed.), *La terra vista dalla luna. Il cinema di Sergio Citti* (Turin: Lindau, 1993).

96. See R. Campari and T. Schiaretti, *In viaggio con Bernardo* (Venice: Marsilio, 1994).

97. S. Bernardi, *Marco Bellocchio* (Milan: Il Castoro, 1998).

CHAPTER 5
FROM THE 1970s TO THE PRESENT

1. See Corsi, "La sala brucia," in *Con qualche dollaro in meno*, 102–3.

2. B. Torri, "Italia: la crisi dell'industria e l'industria della crisi," in *Film '81*, ed. L. Micciché (Milan: Feltrinelli, 1981), 85–98.

3. These figures are reported in A. Bernardini, *Il cinema sonoro, 1970–1990* (Rome: Anica, 1993).

4. U. Rossi, "Il pubblico del cinema," in *Il cinema del riflusso*, ed. L. Micciché (Venice: Marsilio, 1997), 26–44.

5. See M. Bagella, "L'economia latitante. Il cinema italiano e la globalizzazione," in *Il cinema della transizione*, ed. V. Zagarrio (Venice: Marsilio, 2000), 249–63.

6. C. Wagstaff, "Il nuovo mercato del cinema," in *Storia del cinema mondiale*, vol. 1, 847–903.

7. F. Contaldo and F. Fanelli, *L'affare cinema* (Milan: Feltrinelli, 1979).

8. See M. Bagella, L. Becchetti, and A. Simoncini, "La performance in sala dei film prodotti in Italia nel periodo 1985–96," *L'industria* 3 (1999).

9. See *Le botteghe dell'immaginario* (Rome: Anica, 1986).

10. E. Marini, "Il futuro nascosto in una selva di sigle produttive," *Cineforum* 262 (1987): 22–23.

11. F. Petrocchi, *Il cinema della televisione italiana. La produzione cinematografica di Rai e Finivest (1976/1994)* (Turin: RAI-ERI, 1996).

12. Laura, *Le stagioni dell'aquila*.

13. Fago and Piro (eds.), *La carica dei 28*.

14. M. Conforti, "Un bilancio degli ultimi anni dell'art. 28," *Gulliver* 7–8 (1992): 9–13.

15. M. Repetto and C. Tagliabue (eds.), *La vita è bella?* (Milan: Castoro, 2000).

16. See T. Paris (ed.), "Quelle diversité face à Hollywood," *CinémAction* (special edition, 2002), in which European production and distribution issues are examined and new scenarios are hypothesized.

17. See "La svolta del cinema Italiano. Fu vera gloria?" *Cinecittà* 5 (July–September 2001), edited by Paolo d'Agostini. This special edition includes seventy interviews with Italian directors, actors, and producers.

18. See L. Micciché's overview of the 1960s and 1970s in "Linee e tendenze del cinema italiano," in *Film '81*, 5–84.

19. Repetto and Tagliabue (eds.), *La vita è bella?*; and Repetto and Tagliabue, *Vecchio Cinema Paradiso* (Milan: Il Castoro, 2001).

20. M. d'Arcangelo and G. M. Rossi, *Gli anni maledetti del cinema italiano (1975/1985)* (Florence: Mediateca regionale, 1986).

21. G. P. Brunetta, *Cent'anni di cinema italiano* (Bari: Laterza, 1991).

22. See U. Paola and A. Floris, *Facciamoci del male. Il cinema di Nanni Moretti* (Cagliari: Cuec, 1990).

23. G. Fofi, *Dieci anni difficili. Capire con il cinema, 1975–1985* (Florence: La casa Usher, 1985), 262–64.

24. In recent years, we have seen the publication of a number of surveys that document the many filmmakers who have emerged over the past twenty years. Among others, see Micciché (ed.), *Il cinema del riflussoi*; L. Micciché, *Schermi opachi. Il cinema italiano degli anni ottanta* (Venice: Marsilio, 1988); F. Montini, *I novissimi. Gli esordienti del cinema italiano degli anni ottanta* (Turin: Eri, 1988); Montini (ed.), *Una generazione in cinema. Esordi ed esordienti italiani (1975–1988)* (Venice: Marsilio, 1988); M. Sesti (ed.), *Strutture e immaginario di un altro cinema (1988–1996)* (Venice: Marsilio, 1996).

25. I. Calvino, "Processo a Fellini. La parola alla difesa," *La Repubblica*, November 24, 1983, 16.

26. R. Campari and M. Schiaretti (eds.), *In viaggio con Bernardo* (Venice: Marsilio, 1994).

27. Campari, *Il fantasma del bello*.

28. For a succinct overview of the relationships between Italian directors over the past three decades, see P. d'Agostini, "Il cinema da Moretti a oggi," in *Storia del cinema mondiale*, vol. 3, 1076–1112.

29. F. di Giammatteo, "Gli anni della contestazione," in *Vivere il cinema. Sessant'anni del Centro Sperimentale di Cinematografia*, 1995.

30. E. Allegretti and G. Giraud (eds.), *Ermanno Olmi. L'esperienza di Ipotesi Cinema* (Genova: Le Mani, 2002).

31. For a more complete survey of the cooperative production house phenomenon, see G. Capizzi, A. Fornuto, and G. Volpi (eds.), *Isole—Cinema indipendente italiano* (Turin: Aiace, 1992).

32. J. A. Gili, *Nanni Moretti* (Paris: Gremese, 2001).

33. V. Zagarrio, "Il gioco dello stivale," *Vivilcinema* 37 (December 1991): 8.

34. R. de Gaetano, *La sincope dell'identità* (Turin: Lindau, 2002), 88.

35. A. Sicchitano, "Emidio Greco. Lo splendore nel nulla," in *Garage* (special edition, 1997).

36. M. Morandini and L. Faccini, *Uno scorridore ligure di Levante* (Florence: L'Atelier, 1999).

37. *Uccello*, or bird, is slang for the male sex.—Trans.

38. G. Muscio, "Un cinema di storie. Sceneggiatori e nuovo cinema italiano," *Script* 1 (May 1992): 23–27; and Muscio, "Sceneggiatori e nuovo cinema italiano," in "New Landscapes in Contemporary Cinema," ed. G. Marrone-Puglia, *Annali d'Italianistica*17 (1999): 185–94.

39. See *Scrittori per il cinema* (Pescara: Ediars, 1998).

40. A. Meneghelli, "Il cinema italiano e le nuove leve letterarie," in *New Landscapes in Contemporary Italian Cinema*, 203–16.

41. F. Fellini, "La parola all'imputato," *La Repubblica*, November 23, 1983, 17.

42. A. Bichon, *Les années Moretti. Dictionnaire des cineastes italiens, 1975–1999* (Annecy: Annecy Cinema italien, 1999).

43. See: E. Martini (ed.), *Gianni Amelio: le regole del gioco* (Turin: Lindau, 1999); and R. de Gaetano (ed.), *Gianni Amelio* (Rubettino: Saveria Mannelli, 1997).

44. Of the many essays on Amelio, one of the most memorable is M. Vorauer and M. Aichmayr's *Gianni Amelio. Festschrift* (Wels: Kinova, 1999).

45. S. Toffetti (ed.), *Giuseppe Tornatore* (Turin: Lindau, 1995).

46. C. Proto (ed.), *Francesca Archibugi* (Rome: Audino, 1994).

47. R. Grassi, *Territori di fuga. Il cinema di Gabriele Salvatores* (Alessandria: Falsopiano, 1997).

48. See U. Curi's brilliant analysis in *Lo schermo del pensiero* (Milan: Raffaello Corina, 2000).

49. See L. Codelli's "La Factory di Pupi Avati," in *New Landscapes in Contemporary Italian Cinema*, 253–57.

50. M. Sesti, *Nuovo cinema italiano. Gli autori, i film e le idée* (Naples: Theoria, 1994).

51. Zagarrio (ed.), *Il cinema della transizione*, 1–31.

52. *Loro di Naples: il nuovo cinema napoletano 1986–1997* (Palermo: Edizioni della battaglia, 1997).

INDEX OF NAMES.

⌣ INDEX OF FILMS ⌣